I0191686

DISSENTING FORCES

Dissenting Forces

A History of Abolition and
Black Thought in Higher Learning

Michael E. Jirik

NEW YORK UNIVERSITY PRESS
New York

NEW YORK UNIVERSITY PRESS
New York
www.nyupress.org

© 2025 by New York University
All rights reserved

Please contact the Library of Congress for Cataloging-in-Publication data.
ISBN: 9781479836611 (hardback)
ISBN: 9781479836697 (library ebook)
ISBN: 9781479836642 (consumer ebook)

This book is printed on acid-free paper, and its binding materials are chosen for strength
and durability. We strive to use environmentally responsible suppliers and materials to the
greatest extent possible in publishing our books.

The manufacturer's authorized representative in the EU for product safety is Mare
Nostrum Group B.V., Mauritskade 21D, 1091 GC Amsterdam, The Netherlands.
Email: gpsr@mare-nostrum.co.uk.

Manufactured in the United States of America

10 9 8 7 6 5 4 3 2 1

Also available as an ebook

To past, present, and future students of Africana Studies

To all the Knubians

To Candace

CONTENTS

Introduction

On the night of August 20, 2018, a group of student protesters at the University of North Carolina–Chapel Hill surrounded Silent Sam, a Confederate statue on campus, and tore it down. The statue had long been controversial, dating back to its erection in 1913 when a speaker lauded the Confederacy and bragged about violently assaulting an unnamed African American woman. The statue was a marker of white supremacy on campus, its history rooted in the university's historical connections to slavery. In toppling the statue, however, students protested anti-Black racism on campus. The event marked an evolution in student activism for racial justice. In April 2019, students at Georgetown University voted to implement a student fee dedicated to supporting health care and educational programs in communities of descendants of enslaved people sold by university officials in 1838. Coming from students was an institutional reparations program for a descendant community. More recently, college students have been among the foremost protesters and organizers in the Movement for Black Lives in the wake of the deaths of George Floyd, Breonna Taylor, Merci Mack, and so many others.[1] As these cases demonstrate, students have played pivotal roles in social movements, demanding remedies to racism and other inequalities in society today. These examples are among many in recent years illustrating the tensions on college campuses between the legacies of slavery and the pervasiveness of white supremacy on the one hand and social movements seeking to deconstruct oppressive systems exploiting historically marginalized peoples on the other. They also reveal a renewed student movement for Black freedom at universities and in society more generally. While contemporary forms of racism and injustice at universities are rooted in academia's historical ties to slavery and racism, the student activists imagining new ways of living and seeking to build a different world today also have a history, and it is rooted in the abolition movement.

Dissenting Forces is a study of Black resistance and thought and abolitionist dissent at colleges, theological seminaries, and universities in the United States. It examines the ways people within and on the boundaries of institutions transformed them into contested spaces in which they challenged the political economy of Atlantic slaving and participated in a movement for Black freedom. Over the course of the early nineteenth century, academia was part of the terrain upon which the fight for abolition unfolded. Its promoters were enslaved and free Black people and some whites. Black abolitionists outside of these institutions also crafted original ideas about higher learning and its utility for advancing the freedom struggle. The argument for Black higher learning was twofold: Black people believed that education at the highest levels would demonstrate their humanity and equality, which necessarily demanded abolition, for it struck at the very foundation of ideas that underpinned enslavement and racism, the idea of racial inferiority. Black higher learning would thus be a tool of resistance that would refute racist and proslavery ideas in higher learning and society. But Black higher learning was more than that. Black abolitionists argued that studying and learning for all Black people would improve their collective lived experiences. Central to this history is the role of Black students and some white students whose agitation represents a new history of student activism and illuminates the importance of protests for Black freedom in higher learning before the US Civil War. Collectively, the actions of enslaved people, Black and white students, and other agitators in the movement reveal the origins of the fight for Black liberation in higher learning.[2]

Student abolitionists heretofore have been neglected in histories of abolition and studies of higher education. *Dissenting Forces* redefines who was an abolitionist and centers college students. During the movement's transformation in the antebellum period, college students were among abolition's most important grassroots agitators. Black and white students contributed to the development of abolitionist thought in campus debates, essays, orations, and pamphlets, where they made arguments for emancipation, Black rights, and human equality. Student abolitionists went on to become important movement workers as organizers, lecturers, and teachers. They established local antislavery societies in colleges and surrounding communities where there were none. They helped spread the movement and its ideology. Using a variety of tactics, student abolitionists developed a politics of resistance to slavery, colonization, and racism, all of which were tethered to colleges. Black students specifically fueled the movement in significant ways, as they were representatives for racial and women's equality and became agitators on a transnational scale. They also developed arguments for Black freedom based on African history, the Haitian Revolution, women's rights, and by refuting scientific racism. The arguments of Black students mark significant contributions to Black intellectual history and represent a nascent form of Black Studies. Historically, their protests marked the formulation of a novel concept: student activism for Black freedom.[3]

This study defines "student abolitionist" in two ways. The term is used throughout the book to describe Black people studying in higher learning who made arguments for a new humanity based on their freedom and equality.[4] The meaning of student abolitionism in the antebellum period embraced immediate emancipation and Black rights.[5] The social and economic backgrounds of students who supported abolition were multivalent. Black students who studied informally at colleges were student abolitionists, as were the first Black men who were admitted into the colleges as official students. Black women students were among the most important agitators as they were original theoreticians on the meaning of higher learning, redefining it as a tool for Black women's liberation. Some early Black students came from modest backgrounds while others had been enslaved. Some were fugitive slaves, like James W. C. Pennington, and studied on the boundaries of universities because officials refused to admit them. In this way, they acquired knowledge on their terms and used the university subversively, challenging its intellectual and social exclusivity. Black students were radical insurgents in slavery's colleges. They critiqued the racist assumptions of American society and refuted knowledge that was foundational to the university. They produced a new understanding of the utility of higher learning. No longer would it serve the so-called common good, which in effect perpetuated white supremacy. Instead, Black students made arguments for Black freedom and for building a different world. In their protests and writings, Black student abolitionists produced knowledge and ideas that propelled the freedom struggle, which, in turn, produced new ways of thinking in colleges, revealing the liberatory potential of Black Studies and its connection to social movements. Thus the term "student abolitionist" describes both students' participation in the abolition movement and the social and intellectual challenge it posed to colleges alongside how students thought critically about racism, exploitation, and inequality, while also imagining the terms of Black liberation, using critical knowledge to inform their agitation. In socially and intellectually hostile spaces of the campus, Black students crafted an alternative epistemology of Black humanity, which was a radical challenge to the American college.

Many of the student abolitionists in this project were also white men, which is indicative of the racist and sexist exclusionary nature of higher learning in US history. In the early nineteenth century, most white college students, and indeed most faculty, presidents, and trustees, who were also white men, adamantly opposed abolition and instead supported the American Colonization Society (ACS), an organization whose northern members objected to slavery but were also against racial equality and Black citizenship. The racist project of the ACS was popular on college campuses in the late 1810s and 1820s and, as this book demonstrates, the organization was created and sustained largely by white students and faculty. The ACS on campus came under attack, however, by Black and white student abolitionists. A stark divide emerged on campus between student abolitionists and college colonizationists over slavery, colonization, and abolition. Contingents of white students struggled to organize abolition societies, but supporting a movement for Black freedom was intolerable for college officials. Conflicts unfolded on several campuses over the efficacy of promoting a movement to build an exclusively white polity versus a vision for Black freedom and interracial democracy, the latter of which was antithetical to the dominant culture and society that the colleges underpinned. Some student abolitionists recognized the limitations of organizing on campus and became immersed as workers in the broader movement, which helps explain the expansion of the abolitionist constituency in the 1830s.

Along with student abolitionists, another significant population opposed to slavery in higher learning was enslaved people themselves. This book conceptualizes slave resistance at colleges as central to abolitionist dissent and the development of Black thought on the boundaries of higher learning. The exploitation of enslaved people and their labor was inextricably intertwined with colleges since their inception. Colleges as institutions often owned enslaved Africans, as did presidents, faculty, and students. Scholars have shown how white students and faculty inflicted violence on enslaved people on campus, highlighting the brutalities of college slavery. Where slavery existed, so too did slave resistance, and the history of slavery and universities is no different. Enslaved people resisted college slavery; they absconded from campuses or college-owned plantations. Through their actions, they made arguments against enslavement and for Black life on their terms. Significantly, slave culture also manifested on campuses and is evidence of enslaved people's spirituality and cultural practices, revealing the presence of African cosmology and intellectual histories. Slave culture on campus thus represented a subversive, alternative epistemology that was at once adverse to the intellectual foundations of the West and its colleges as well as reveals African-influenced worldviews and ways of knowing. Slave culture as the intellectual product of enslaved people is central to the history of slave resistance to college slavery.[6] The history of Black thought as a dissenting force in higher learning is rooted in the culture and resistance of enslaved Africans on campus. Indeed, slave culture helps to explain the impetus behind other forms of resistance like fugitivity. Slave resistance in higher learning was a manifestation of Black thought and was a form of abolitionist dissent; when enslaved people resisted college slavery by running away, they were agents of abolition. As noted above, some fugitive slaves like Pennington also used the university for study for their own education. Thus slave resistance assumed multiple functions in the history of abolition and higher learning. Enslaved people resisted the brutalities of college slavery while others appropriated the university space for study and cultivated knowledge for themselves and their communities in pursuit of liberation. Fugitive slaves studying on the boundaries of colleges were also student abolitionists, revealing the direct influence of slave resistance on the development of student abolitionism. While education was crucial to enslaved people's conceptions of freedom, this study demonstrates that some sought college learning and acquired it. A study of slave resistance to college slavery reveals that enslaved people's thoughts and actions profoundly shaped the dissenting forces of Black thought and abolition at colleges.

This book also refines the meaning of abolition in the antebellum period. Abolition meant immediate emancipation, political, economic, and civic equality, women's rights, and Black self-determination. This study shows that the abolitionist fight against racism in northern states included racism at colleges. Along with enslaved people, Black abolitionists exposed and critiqued slavery's connections to colleges. They challenged their opponents who cited white southern patronage as reason to quell student abolitionism or reject Black admission demands. As a counter to slavery's colleges, Black abolitionists crafted novel ideas about the utility of higher learning as advancing the cause of Black freedom and as a tool for transforming the world. Beginning in the 1820s, Black abolitionists conceptualized the significance of, and produced explicit demands for, Black higher learning. Over the course of the antebellum period, debates unfolded over integrating existing colleges or creating a separate Black college. It was a question of reforming existing institutions or exercising self-determination in promoting Black institutions. For the latter, Black abolitionists crafted proposals to institutionalize an expansive version of learning in which Black students from all backgrounds would receive an education in classical learning, manual labor, and the mechanical arts, which would lead to the development of critical knowledge and consciousness among Black people. Black education, by and for Black people, would facilitate unity and strengthen the movement. While some Black abolitionists disagreed on the means of Black higher learning, they all agreed on its significance for the advancement of Black communities. Their ideas and proposals reveal not only the rich, original ideas Black abolitionists produced to critique the slavocracy and its colleges; they were profound examples of Black self-determination. And the experiences of Black student abolitionists significantly shaped this debate. The struggle for Black freedom included the fight for abolition in higher learning.

Dissenting Forces is also conceptualized as a contribution to a long history of Black Studies and its historical encounter with the university in the United States. The history of Black Studies transcends any affiliation with Western institutions and is rooted in Africana ways of knowing and being in the world, the study of which Greg Carr describes as a "long view of genealogies of African intellectual work."[7] While the history of Black Studies at US universities is usually told as part of the Black student movements of the Black Power era in the mid-twentieth century, there is a longer historical trajectory of Black Studies that remains understudied.[8] The world of Black writing, learning, oral traditions, and other forms of knowledge of the early nineteenth century constitutes one such understudied area. This project focuses on an early encounter of Black thought with the university, specifically through the actions, ideas, and writings of enslaved people, Black students, and other Black abolitionists of the period, which necessarily makes this project narrower in focus than the capaciousness of Black study in autonomous Black spaces and organizations of early Black history in the United States. This work is one facet of a larger, multifaceted history of Black study.[9]

This early encounter represented a clashing of intellectual traditions in the space of the academy, where Black perspectives encountered Western traditions of knowledge. As with the Black Studies movement of the 1960s and '70s, the challenge Black students and Black thought posed to the academy came *from outside institutions*. In this period, it came from Black thinkers, ministers, students, and other agitators, as well as from enslaved people. It came from a social movement for Black freedom. But the challenge in the antebellum period was not to create Black Studies departments in the university; rather, the struggle was over Black people using higher learning as a tool for liberation, combining their learning with their lived experiences, history, and traditions to expose the myths of the American project and create something new. Before the emergence of the modern university and the advent of academic disciplines, Black people understood and critiqued the American college and conceptualized alternatives. Significantly, Black students and other Black abolitionists created knowledge derived from struggle and developed an understanding of Black history and humanity both to challenge racist notions that were embedded in the academy and to understand themselves on their own terms. In other words, through organizing and participating in a social movement, Black students and other Black abolitionists created knowledge about, and critiques of, their oppression and formulated a vision of the world they sought to create for Black freedom, all of which flew in the face of the intellectual orientation and function of the university. The idea of Black higher learning thus came from Black people as a means to study, learn, and transform. They proposed nascent ideas of what would become Black Studies, connecting the development of knowledge and learning to creating a new humanity. This book illuminates a historical genealogy of a radical tradition of Black protest in and outside of Western institutions of higher learning. Black students and intellectuals of the early twentieth century, and later during the Black Power era who established Black Studies in the university, and Black students and other Black abolitionists of the antebellum struggle for Black humanity in higher learning, are connected through a shared vision in their demands for learning as central to Black life and living. This history demonstrates that such demands, and their substance, transcend time and space.[10]

Some may object to the connection drawn through time between nascent Black Studies in the antebellum period and the advent of academic Black Studies in the twentieth century. While the context of each period was indeed distinct, the content and meaning of Black Studies in both periods are analogous. In both periods, Black students, intellectuals, and other agitators created knowledge derived from Black experiences and struggles to fuel a social movement for Black liberation. In both contexts, Black people critiqued racism and racist academic thought within universities and appropriated the campus to make demands for Black liberation. In both contexts, Black people used study and learning to free themselves. In both contexts, the substance and purpose of Black Studies encountered the university. The specificities of historical context in each period show how each generation contributed to the long arc of the Black freedom struggle. While acknowledging distinct historical contexts, this book seeks to contribute to a genealogy of continuity of Black resistance through time, of African-descended people engaging in clashes over ideas and meanings of humanity in higher learning as parts of social movements to remake the world. As racism in higher learning evolved over time, so did the struggle for Black freedom on and beyond campuses. This interpretative framework, of acknowledging historical specificity and context as much as continuity over time, provides a more holistic understanding of the problems of colleges and universities since their formation, which continue in the present, as well as the consistency of Black resistance to those problems. It raises fundamental questions about the nature and function of universities. It also shows how Black freedom movements have produced critical knowledge and alternative concepts for transforming the world.[11] Such struggles for Black freedom have proven to be anathema to the political project of universities.

* * *

Universities are products of the social and cultural order in which they exist. The intellectual and social composition of universities often reflects their political orientation. From their inception, American colleges have been inherently politicized entities for numerous reasons, including the constituencies they served and excluded, their facilitation of settler colonialism, their dispossession of Indigenous peoples, and the fact that they benefited from Atlantic slaving. Colleges and universities were not passively involved in these systems of oppression; they were institutions where whites crafted ideas to justify the violent processes of enslavement, dispossession, and exploitation.[12] From the seventeenth century to 1860, institutions of higher learning predominantly—although not exclusively—served the interests of and benefited propertied white men at the exclusion of women, Black and Indigenous peoples, and poor whites, and prepared students for careers as ministers or teachers, or in the professions of medicine, law, and politics. With few exceptions, colleges at the institutional level supported neither abolition nor racial equality, as those ideas necessarily challenged the financial and ideological systems of the academy and those who controlled them.[13] College leaders and faculty largely practiced racial exclusion, manufactured ideas of human hierarchies and inferiority, supported slaveholding patronage for revenue, and by extension slavery itself, or simply supported slavery outright. The legacies of these logics extend into the present, as universities continue to rely on and perpetuate economic and ideological systems of exploitation and the rationales for them. But beyond those who controlled institutions, other social groups not in official positions of power within and outside of institutions supported ideologies at odds with those in power. Enslaved people, Black students, and other abolitionists fit this latter description. In some cases, abolitionist insurgencies in colleges produced moments of possibility for institutional change, revealing the political power of students and of protest, and the impact of social movements on institutions. It is imperative to distinguish between colleges and universities as institutions and the varied constituencies who have occupied or have sought to occupy them.

The history of Black thought and abolitionist dissent in colleges illuminates how the dynamics of power and resistance between slavery and abolition unfolded in higher learning. Resistance to slavery in the history of colleges also reveals the tensions between agitation and structural power. As institutions remained financially and ideologically tied to the slaving economy, Black and white abolitionists fought to use colleges as spaces to study and debate slavery, cultivate an education in abolitionist ideals, procure new activists for the movement, and affirm the humanity of Black people. They harnessed the function of colleges, both as sites of study and as spaces of knowledge production and intellectual development, towards subversive ends. Advocating Black freedom in slavery's colleges was radical and political. The fact that some students used the college for abolitionist study provides historical antecedents for a recent argument made by Robin D. G. Kelley regarding the Black freedom struggle's relationship to academia in the present and future. His argument echoes W. E. B. Du Bois's reflection on his time at Harvard, that Black people and their allies dedicated to transformative change are in the university but not of it.[14] In other words, Black people and allies dedicated to human flourishing and creating new ways of living must use the university subversively for study and to gain critical knowledge but cannot be of the university, as it is an arbiter of exploitation and because of its embeddedness in, and sustaining of, racial capitalism as a world system and its epistemological privileging of Western civilization. This framing describes how abolitionist ideology existed at most colleges among students—in but not of them—and it especially cogently frames the experiences of Black students. Fred Moten and Stefano Harney refer to this as "fugitive study" and "the undercommons," subversive practices and spaces used for study to challenge the epistemic orientation and function of the university. This book offers a long history of that concept. Abolitionists struggled to change colleges to reflect their ideals, an ultimately fraught endeavor then and now. The enduring question about the role of the university in society that was as applicable then as it is today is: What is the nature of universities in the West, as well as who controls them, who benefits from and participates in them, what type of knowledge and ideas are taught and learned, what is the nature of the financial systems that sustain them, and what is the purpose of college education? Throughout the history of the university in the West, its main function can be described as "the subordination and perversion of knowledge by its suturing to the interests of power and privilege."[15]

For abolitionists, the role of the college in society was clear: it was used as a site in which to challenge the intellectual underpinnings of slavery and racism. As abolitionists in higher learning refuted racist ideas from within, they created new knowledge about the role of students in society as promoters of Black freedom. They developed analyses to understand how power and oppression functioned in the slaveholding republic. In short, abolitionists used higher learning to develop critical analyses of systemic problems and to promote Black liberation. On an analytical level, abolition represented an insurgent refutation to the terms of knowledge and order on which the existence of the American college was based. By affirming Black history, life, and culture, Black higher learning was the antithesis of the US university. Importantly, as the book's title connotes, *Dissenting Forces* frames abolition and Black thought as subversive forces, and it must be emphasized that they both were forces external to, and represented an insurgency in, the academy.

In the flourishing and relatively new field of universities and slavery studies, historians have documented the pervasive connections of the Atlantic slaving economy to the founding and development of colleges and universities throughout the United States, the Caribbean, and Britain.[16] Over the last two decades students, faculty, archivists, and descendants of enslaved people have produced numerous studies, reports, and digital archives detailing histories of slaving and universities. These studies began in the early 2000s in the wake of public debate regarding reparations for slavery. In many cases students have been at the forefront of these studies, conducting research and demanding that university officials confront their institutions' histories and their legacies.[17]

Scholarly monographs on universities and slavery are also numerous. Craig Wilder's study has defined the field, illustrating how the oldest universities in the United States had financial ties to the Atlantic slaving economy and the forced removal of Indigenous people. Wilder also explains how scholars from these institutions created pseudoscientific notions of race. More than simply benefiting from the profits generated by slaving, universities fostered the promotion of theories that were used to justify the enslavement of Africans and the dispossession of Indigenous peoples. Other scholars have traced the development and proliferation of proslavery academic thought at southern universities, how institutions owned enslaved people and boards of trustees and administrative officials oversaw their labor, and how medical schools participated in a cadaver trade where professors stole the bodies of deceased Black people for study, which contributed to the rise of racist scientific ideas. Much of this scholarly work rightly has focused on the complicity of universities with slaving and collectively has been essential in demonstrating how universities have been facilitators of exclusion and oppression, arbiters of the processes of settler colonialism, the evolution of slavery, and the creation of racist thought.[18] These works coincide with important studies on "land-grab" universities in the Midwest and western parts of the United States as well as scholarship in critical university studies.[19]

A systematic examination of the evolution of Black resistance and abolition within and outside of colleges is absent from most works on slavery and universities.[20] Some scholars have studied antislavery at colleges in broader works on academic freedom and civil liberties but have dismissed its importance or presented anachronistic critiques of abolitionists.[21] Other scholars have examined the rise of antislavery at individual institutions to explain student involvement in the movement.[22] This focus implies that students active in abolition at one institution were atypical or the sole precedents for student activism in the movement.[23] While important, these works perpetuate narratives about students in abolition as unique or isolated to individual institutions. Building on this work, this book shows that abolition at colleges has a longer history. It evolved and proliferated at multiple institutions over time. It also shifts perspective to enslaved people and Black abolitionists on the boundaries of higher learning to demonstrate the insurgence of Black thought and resistance in higher learning.

Historians of abolition have often examined the social composition of the movement and provided various answers to the question: Who were the abolitionists?[24] This study inserts Black and white college students as integral historical actors in the movement's history. Many, however, were not middle-class misfits.[25] Most student abolitionists denounced slavery and colonization and advocated Black rights on moral and religious grounds. Other historians have focused on evangelical Christianity as a catalyst to abolitionism in the 1830s. Evangelical social reform led to the abolitionist conversion of many white students in the 1830s, as they understood the work of abolition as their "sacred vocation."[26] Evangelical revivalism and the turn to immediatism provided the opening for many northern whites, including students, to join an existing movement.[27]

Adding to histories that center Black women in the movement, this book highlights Black women abolitionists' advocacy for higher learning and its political implications.[28] Black women abolitionists such as Phillis Wheatley and Maria Stewart and Black women students Lucy Stanton and Sarah Parker Remond were among the most vocal critics of academia. They refashioned the meaning of higher learning as a tool for Black women to make claims for emancipation and women's rights. Unlike many of their men colleagues who opposed women's rights, Black women abolitionists made higher learning a contested space for their liberation.[29]

Dissenting Forces situates the rise of Black thought and abolition in higher learning and student abolition in the broader context of abolition as a radical social movement.[30] It also recovers the radical nature of Black thought in, and Black abolitionist formulations of, higher learning as a tool for liberation in the age of slavery. If universities, colleges, and seminaries were a third arm of American civilization built on slavery and settler colonialism and were incubators of racist ideas, then abolition and Black thought were dissenting forces therein.[31] This book offers a new chapter in the history of the movement through the lens of abolition's intellectual and social implications for slavery's colleges.[32]

Tracing the history of fugitive slave resistance, and Black abolitionist agitation within and on the boundaries of institutions of higher learning, *Dissenting Forces* shows how Black people fought for a new humanity at colleges. They gave new meaning to higher learning and its function.[33] Alongside electoral politics, transportation, churches, schools, and law, colleges were among the various terrains and institutions in which the struggle for Black freedom unfolded in early US history.[34] This book demonstrates that African Americans conceptualized original ideas about the meaning of higher learning and that Black struggles for freedom have always included a form of higher learning.

Before the US Civil War, Black learning at every level had radical potential for a society based on the enslavement and oppression of Black people. At a time when Black education was outlawed in southern states and tremendously restricted in the North, Black people produced knowledge that refuted ideas that underpinned proslavery thought and northern prejudice, especially in academia. Black abolitionist thought on higher learning was critical and generative. It subverted the very logic and meaning of higher learning as an intellectual appendage of the slavocracy and was a reimagination of the meaning and function of colleges.[35] Building on scholarship on early Black education, *Dissenting Forces* presents a history of the significance of higher learning in early Black history.[36] Additionally, the controversies over slavery, abolition, and racism at colleges and universities more broadly demonstrate that they were at the cutting edge of social, intellectual, and political trends on those issues, and this work takes seriously the role of student abolitionists therein.[37] The best works on colleges, students, and struggles for Black freedom have focused on twentieth-century student movements.[38] This book seeks to recover the genealogy of that struggle in the abolition movement.

Using a thematic framework, the book constructs a narrative arc to demonstrate how the dissenting forces of abolition and Black thought evolved over time in higher learning. Drawing on primary sources from US and British archives, including newspapers, rare student essays, pamphlets, and orations, faculty lectures, Black abolitionist writings, and records of antislavery societies and student organizations, the book reveals a rich, multifaceted history of abolitionist protest at colleges. It examines a multitude of agitators at institutions across time and space, including colleges, universities, and seminaries in New England, the mid-Atlantic, the Old Northwest, and the upper South. Rather than focus on one specific college, it explores a history of people and ideas that confronted multiple institutions, demonstrating the wide-scale nature of abolitionist dissent at colleges.

* * *

The book is divided into two parts. Part 1 traces the development of student abolition as a concept and Black students who embodied it in contrast to the ACS on campus. Chapter 1 recounts a history of people of African descent who studied informally and formally at colleges, including the earliest Black men to garner admission in American colleges. The first study to assess the lives of the earliest Black college students in the United States together, the chapter reconstructs their experiences as students and how they shaped arguments for abolition and emigration. Chapter 2 shows how in the 1810s–1820s denominational colleges became bastions of the American Colonization Society, an organization opposed to the main tenets of abolition, namely, racial equality. College colonizationists were central to the founding of the ACS and underpinned its membership in New England. They promoted the racist idea that Black people could not be equal to whites in the United States and used the prospect of slave rebellions to make claims for removing free Black people from the polity. The ACS on campus was representative of a dominant culture of white supremacy in higher learning and, alongside slavery, posed a formidable obstacle to abolition.

Part 2 is organized thematically to demonstrate the continuity and evolution of resistance to slavery and racism in US higher learning over time. Chapter 3 transitions to enslaved people's thought and actions on campus. Before the Black student abolitionists described in chapter 1 emerged on campuses, enslaved people resisted college slaving. They practiced African cultural traditions, which subversively propelled their resistance and created knowledge that refuted racist academic thought. The chapter conceptualizes slave resistance as a form of abolitionist dissent at colleges, arguing that enslaved people's cultural practices and those who resisted college slavery by running away were original progenitors of Black thought in higher learning. Their resistance to college slavery constituted acts of protest. Chapter 4 focuses on the transformation of abolition in the 1830s and traces the proliferation of white men student abolitionists across northern campuses. They precipitated conflicts with colonizationist faculty and the broader public. The college became a site of radicalization for some white students who in turn moved beyond the campus and became active in the broader movement. Many white student abolitionists' positions foreshadowed the fissures in the movement as many became political and evangelical abolitionists, siding against women's rights, signifying the limitations of their activism. The book culminates in chapters 5 and 6, which examine the evolution of Black abolitionist thought about higher learning and the struggles for equality of Black student abolitionists at multiple northern institutions. Black students produced significant critiques of higher learning and scientific racism, and promoted Black women's rights, signaling a nascent formation of Black Studies and its connections to Black freedom movements. The epilogue sketches the legacy of Black higher learning among Black students and intellectuals who became part of a tradition of using Black Studies for self-determination and for the liberation of all Black people. A tradition of Black higher learning for imagining and building a different world continued into the twentieth century and beyond.

Dissenting Forces is a history of resistance to slavery and racism in American colleges. Not a celebratory narrative of colleges supporting liberal reform, the history of abolition and Black thought in higher learning is instead a history of dissent for Black freedom in historically unequal institutions that were the early colleges. The history of abolition and Black thought in higher learning reveals a nascent formation of Black Studies and its historical encounter with the university. It reveals a history of Black students and other Black abolitionists who connected study, knowledge, and agitation to Black liberation, a vision necessary for a new world centering Africana humanity and community, and by extension all humanity. It is a history of profound opposition to evolving structural inequities and reveals the historical centrality of student protest to social movements and freedom struggles. The student movements for Black freedom in the twentieth century and the current student movement on campuses today for the liberation of the Black World and Palestine are the heirs to the student abolitionist legacy. By centering Black resistance and Black and white students, this study provides new understandings of Black intellectual history, radicalism on campus, and Black historical visions for higher learning.

Finally, this work seeks to contribute to a Black history tradition that is critical of the West and its institutions. It attempts to include in that tradition an important episode in the history of Black thought on education for liberation, for Black life dedicated to community. The fact that some Black abolitionists understood the necessity of Black institutions grounded in community remains significant, for integration on the terms of whiteness was and remains inherently flawed. At a time when Black history is once again under attack, new histories are required to meet the challenges we face today as a global community. As Vincent Harding observed, Black history must expose the lies of America and its institutions at their core and provide groundings for creating a society that centers our common humanity—a Black history that can lead to realizing Sylvia Wynter's notion of a new definition of what it means to be human, a Black history Lawrence Reddick asserted is based on a faith, a Black history grounded in Du Bois's radical historiography and the notion of the Coming of the Lord; a Black history for life, living, and being and for community.[39]

PART I

Student Abolition as a Concept Versus Colonization

As some of the oldest colleges in the United States emerged, Black people made claims to study in them. Many studied informally with sympathetic presidents or professors, that is, not as official students in the regular college course. They were students with a passion for learning, study, and knowing the world. By the 1820s, selected Black student men gained admission into a handful of colleges. The presence of Black students and their intellectual production based on African history and Black resistance were subversive in the academy. College presidents and faculty, however, did not perceive individual Black students as threats to the social order. Instead, they believed that educating Black men for missionary careers would facilitate the colonizationist plan of removing free Black people from the polity and converting African people to Christianity on the African continent. The Black students of the 1820s confronted the dilemma facing Black communities: whether to emigrate or fight to transform the United States. Some occupied each position at different moments. That Black thought was a dissenting force in higher learning in the 1820s is put in stark relief given that the American Colonization Society dominated the social and intellectual culture of northern colleges on the question of Black people's place in society. As Black students introduced the concept of student abolition in US higher learning, it conflicted with the ideology of the colonizationists, providing fodder for a clashing of social movements and a struggle over the meaning of humanity on campus.

1

Black Students and the Academy

In 1793, the Black writer and abolitionist Lucy Terry Prince sought admission for her son, Festus, at the newly established Williams College. While the application was rejected, Prince proceeded to lecture a trustee for three hours, quoting scripture and legal texts demanding admission. The trustee became "not a little perplexed and discomfited" yet their decision remained unchanged.

The Prince family knew the founder of the college, Ephraim Williams, and his relatives. With these ties in place, Prince seized the opportunity to speak to the trustees, hoping the connections would aid her case. The racist decision went unchanged, and Williams College became an exclusionary space for white male students and faculty. But Prince's determination for her son to acquire a college education is an early example of Black people contesting the boundaries of colleges in the early United States. In their persons and arguments, Lucy and Festus Prince critiqued the white intellectual foundations of American colleges and exemplified a critical Black consciousness and a desire for learning. Through their protest for admission at Williams College, the Princes set a significant precedent on which many Black abolitionists would build in subsequent decades.[1]

Abolitionist dissent and Black thought at colleges manifested in the early decades of the nineteenth century as a result of the collective protests of free Black people. Building on Lucy Prince's efforts, free Black people began actively contesting the racial exclusivity of colleges and repurposed the learning space of the campus for their own ends, marking a subversive presence of Black learning. This development reveals how free Black people sought to harness the educational possibilities of the college and develop their own knowledge to propel abolition forward. Black people's learning, combined with their lived experiences, provided the tools to further expose the myths of a racist, hierarchical American society and culture. A product of the convergence of Black worldviews with European-based education systems was the appropriation of the ideologies of the dominant culture to make claims for Black freedom.[2]

Between 1823 and 1828, six men of African descent received college or seminary degrees in the United States. In descending order, they are Alexander Twilight, Middlebury College (1823), Edward Jones, Amherst College (1826), John Brown Russwurm, Bowdoin College (1826), Edward Mitchell, Dartmouth College (1828), John Newton Templeton, Ohio University (1828), and Theodore S. Wright, Princeton Theological Seminary (1828). Two of the students were born in the Caribbean— Mitchell in Martinque and Russwurm in Jamaica.[3] The students had disparate backgrounds; Jones and Mitchell were born into relatively materially wealthy families and Russwurm attended a private academy, while Wright and Twilight had more humble backgrounds. Templeton was unique among the group. Born to enslaved parents and manumitted as a child, Templeton received an education from the social structure early in life. Attending college in the United States during the 1820s was rare for anyone, making the early Black students' respective stories significant.[4] While they were few in number, the young Black scholars' achievements mark a watershed in the history of higher learning. They had the task of demonstrating Black humanity in the American college, institutions that were hostile to Black life and thought. Early Black students represented an insurgency of Black thought and abolitionist ideology on college campuses. The result was a clash of ideological forces of historical magnitude.

Early Black students manifested alternative knowledge within the college as formal students and made demands for a new humanity. Significantly, African history and Black radicalism were central to the arguments Black students made in their work. For example, the writings of Templeton evoked ancient African civilizations to rebuke racist notions prominent in the academy positing that Black people had no history and should be removed from the country. Instead, Templeton highlighted that the arts and sciences, and humanity itself, emerged from Africa in the ancient world. Likewise, Russwurm praised the Haitian Revolution in his writings. Using the example of a slave rebellion to promote abolition and Black self-determination, Russwurm made arguments for Black freedom that were the antithesis of the white-washed knowledge and ideologies of academia. Taken together, the writings of Templeton and

Russwurm marked an alternative epistemology that centered Black history, humanity, and resistance. In their persons and in their writings, these early Black students marked a new strand of Black thought as an insurgent force within academia.

As a result of Black protest on the boundaries of colleges and the work of the early Black students, a new meaning and function of college education was fashioned. Rather than perpetuating social-structure notions of the so-called common good, Black higher learning helped advance the struggle for Black liberation. The young Black intellectuals of the 1820s became part of a growing body of Black thinkers who imagined creating a world of Black freedom. After they completed their degrees, many of the early Black students became immersed in the abolition movement as teachers, writers, and ministers. Black students used their learning to aid the struggle for Black freedom, marking the emergence of a novel concept. In their actions Black students crafted a notion of Black higher learning, using their college education to work towards freedom.

The life trajectories of early Black students lay bare the dilemma Black people encountered throughout the antebellum period: whether to organize for political reform within the United States or seek Black liberation elsewhere in the world. Unlike college colonizationists, who advocated for the removal of African Americans for racist reasons, Black students centered Black liberation and humanity as their guiding principle for fostering change, and the question was where that could be accomplished. For early Black students encountering the problem, there were no easy solutions.

The history of Black students in the 1820s raises a number of questions, including the circumstances under which white officials admitted Black students. A significant factor was the pervasiveness of the American Colonization Society (ACS) on campuses, examined in chapter 2. Evangelical colonizationists believed in educating Black men for missionary careers in Liberia, the ACS-sponsored colony in West Africa. Colonizationists hoped that this would have a dual effect: free Black people would be removed from the polity and Christianity would spread across the African continent.[5] The fact that selected Black students were educated alongside whites yet they still could not live in the country on an equal basis further demonstrates the illogic of colonizationists' racist thinking.

Centering the earliest Black admissions at colleges reveals a counter-history to traditional studies of early American colleges. This chapter explores the lives and work of early Black men students and the social and intellectual implications for the academy.[6] It frames their presence and success at colleges as abolition in action. Their life trajectories manifested the mission of Black Studies, using education for the liberation struggle.[7] The history of abolition and Black thought as dissenting forces at colleges during the early nineteenth century reveals a robust yet nascent social movement confronting the slavocracy's colleges and fostering an alternative vision for the purpose of higher learning.

A series of political, social, economic, and geographic transformations occurred during the early national period. The success of the Haitian rebels in establishing the first independent Black nation in the Western hemisphere was of tremendous consequence. It helped inspire a plethora of slave rebellions in the United States and the Caribbean that typify this era, as slave resistance continued to fuel Black freedom struggles.[8] A new generation of Black women and men who became legally free in the United States because of northern states' gradual emancipation laws inherited the abolition movement, which had been long in the making. Together they built the first Black churches and schools in the United States. Black women and men established literary societies, where together they educated themselves in reading, writing, and oratory skills. They learned about the world and contemplated their place in it. Black institutions formed the foundation of Black communities, their protest tradition, and organizational networks of the movement.[9] Education was an important element of Black self-determination. As Lois and James Horton wrote, "For African Americans, as for Americans generally, education was both the foundation of freedom and one of its benefits." For Black people, education served specific purposes. It served as a rebuke to racism and had the potential to transform their lives and material circumstances. It was a source of knowing and empowerment. Black institutions provided space for collective learning, and Black people made education a pillar of the struggle. Beginning in the late eighteenth century and sometimes with the help of whites, Black communities built schools in cities like New York, Philadelphia, and Boston. Black women such as Eleanor Harris and Ann Williams taught in these schools for young Black boys and girls, who attended during the day while adults did in the evening. African Free Schools played an important role in early Black education, and they prepared a handful of students to pursue higher learning. While Black educational efforts faced economic and social hardships, Black people persisted in their efforts to learn.[10] Black education was first and foremost a product of Black community organizations and the knowledge and understandings of the world gained through their lived experiences and traditions.[11] This formed the basis of Black education, and the advent of selected Black men attending colleges was a product, and only one part, of that larger history. In short, Black students came from families and communities where institution building was central to sustaining Black life. Institutions were where Black people convened, discussed, debated, studied, and learned together about the world around them. As Sterling Stuckey observed, there were extensions of African culture in free Black northern communities, as evidenced in their institutions, where the ethic of collective learning, broadly conceived, unfolded. It was out of this context and armed with a Black consciousness that many Black students confronted white academia and cultivated a sense of learning for collective liberation.[12]

The early Black students gave new life to the idea of student abolition, a concept that developed in an earlier generation. The notion of student abolitionists, or students advocating the end of slavery and promoting a new humanity, has its origins during the mid-eighteenth century. In 1773, the young African poet Phillis Wheatley published *Poems on Various Subjects, Religious and Moral* in which she directed a poem to students at Harvard.[13] Wheatley originally drafted the poem in 1767 when she was about fifteen years old. The poem recognized the potential students had as agents of social change. Wheatley wrote that students were charged with examining the great questions of the age and had the potential to "mark the systems of revolving worlds." Wheatley evoked a religious argument of redemption. Citing the example of Jesus dying to save humanity from sin, she believed students should guard against sin. "Improve your privileges while they stay, ye pupils," Wheatley cautioned, "and each hour redeem ... or good or bad report of you to heav'n."[14] For Wheatley, guarding against sin was capacious, including the sin of enslaving Africans. If we take Wheatley's instruction to students to guard against sin to include slavery, it becomes clear that Wheatley called on

Harvard students to act against slavery.[15] "Suppress the sable monster in its growth," she instructed, perhaps a reference to ending slavery, as it was the students' "greatest foe" that caused "endless pain" and brought "ruin to the Soul."[16] As a young African girl, Wheatley instructed Harvard students to participate in antislavery as it had a redemptive quality that bore directly on the enslaved and the students' salvation. The poem marked the nascent conceptualization of the idea of student abolition, and as a work of Black thought, it represented an insurgent idea on the boundaries of academia.

Wheatley's call for student abolition was nothing short of transformative. The implications of the form she employed are equally as significant as her message. Writing from the position of "Ethiop," Wheatley invoked African history and intellectual traditions that were central to antiquity but ignored in the university. Writing under the pseudonym of an African author, Wheatley invoked African epistemology and history in her instruction of the students. Wheatley assumed the position of teacher, and using knowledge derived from African intellectual traditions instructed white students to participate in antislavery. Wheatley, at age fifteen, put forth a novel interpretation of the meaning of higher learning, one that would lead students to remedy sins like slavery and facilitate liberation. The African knowledge she represented was an epistemological challenge to the university. As a theorist and teacher, Wheatley centered Black humanity and history in the poem in formulating her argument that students should work to abolish slavery.

Published in London in 1773, Wheatley's poems had a significant impact on the development of student abolition in rural England. Her poems, along with the writings of the African abolitionists Ignatius Sancho and Olaudah Equiano, provided inspiration to an elder white scholar, Peter Peckard, of Magdalene College, Cambridge. In the 1780s, Peckard preached and published several sermons calling for the abolition of the slave trade and asserting racial equality. In his writings he drew on and cited the work of Sancho, Wheatley, and Equiano. These African writers, equipped with knowledge and cultural groundings from their respective African backgrounds, used the tools available to them in the English language to make appeals for abolition and Black humanity. Peckard studied their works and in turn instructed teachers at Magdalene to use his abolitionist sermons for the instruction of students. He famously set the thesis topic that Thomas Clarkson took up and upon which he wrote his influential work on slave trade abolition, propelling him to fame in the movement. A group of students and faculty subsequently became involved in the anti–slave trade movement. Peckard read Wheatley's poems and would have encountered the call to Harvard students, which likely inspired his thinking. Emerging from Wheatley's and Peckard's work is a nascent idea of student action against slavery and of studying arguments for abolition.[17] Black and white students in the United States would give the idea new life.

Some of the first people of African descent to study at early American colleges did so as unofficial students. Along with the Prince admission case, Black intellectuals such as Betsy Stockton, Caleb Watts, Bristol Yamma, and John Quamine pierced the boundaries, however briefly, of Dartmouth College and the College of New Jersey, respectively, setting significant precedents for Black people in the academy. The Black minister Lemuel Haynes also gave antislavery orations at Yale and was recognized as an important theologian with an honorary master of arts degree from Middlebury College. While they were not official students, these Black thinkers on the boundaries of the campus had implications for the intellectual project of the early colleges. As Black people studying and lecturing at colleges, their collective presence functioned as protests against the restrictive nature of the colleges as exclusive spaces for white men. They were indeed students, and the knowledge and learning they cultivated refuted academic notions of racial inferiority. They used their respective educational training as teachers and ministers to advance the cause of Black freedom. This early Black intellectual insurgency on the boundaries of higher learning laid the groundwork for the admissions of Black students at selected colleges in the 1820s.[18]

Among the earliest people of African descent to gain a college degree in the United States was Alexander Twilight. Born in 1795 in Corinth, Vermont, Twilight was clearly of mixed ancestry. His father, Ichabod, was of African or Afro-Indigenous descent. His mother was either white or mixed race.[19] Alexander was raised on the farm Ichabod purchased in Corinth, and while the family owned land, they were materially poor. From ages eight to twenty, Alexander was an indentured servant to William Bowen, a local farmer. Twilight eventually purchased the remainder of his contract a year before its expiration and decided to pursue formal education. He immediately enrolled in a grammar school and within six years completed all the requirements in secondary as well as college preparatory courses. In 1821, at age twenty-six, Twilight enrolled at Middlebury College with junior status.[20]

Two years later, Twilight graduated with a BA degree from Middlebury. From extant sources, it appears that his mixed-race ancestry did not preclude his pursuit of academic training because Twilight likely passed as white. He progressed through his college career, studying moral philosophy, theology, and logic, which were typically taught in the third and fourth year of the college course.[21] Twilight completed the necessary degree requirements and graduated in 1823. Not much is known of Twilight's experience at Middlebury, and extant sources from him that document his thoughts on his college days or later life are yet to be found.

Twilight went on to become a teacher and Congregational minister, first in Peru, New York, and subsequently in Vergennes, Vermont. But in Brownington, Vermont, he became an important leader in education and local politics. Twilight led efforts in constructing a four-story granite school building. During his time in New York, he was married to Mercy Ladd Merill, who was white, and their marriage lasted over thirty years. In 1836, he was elected to the state legislature and fought against the allocation of county taxes for multiple grammar schools. Instead, he believed that taxes should fund one central county school in Brownington. Twilight taught and ministered in Brownington for most of his life. In 1855 he suffered a stroke that left him paralyzed. He died in 1857 at age sixty-two.[22]

Since Twilight's ancestry was likely unknown to Middlebury officials and students, his experience was unique and distinct from that of subsequent Black students. It is likely that Twilight passed as white, not only at Middlebury but throughout his life. Early accounts remembering Twilight made no mention of his complexion or ethnicity. It was not until the twentieth century that researchers discovered Twilight's mixed ancestry.[23] Twilight's life represents the limitations of forcing people into rigid racial categories. But the precariousness of Twilight's racial identity does not preclude the historical significance of his life. What is clear is that Twilight was of African descent and completed a college degree, a rare occurrence for any person at the time. Indeed, he built on the legacy of Lemuel Haynes, who had received an honorary degree from Middlebury seventeen years earlier. Middlebury, however, remained a largely exclusive college for white men. By the 1830s, the college rejected the admission of Black students. Not until 1849 would Middlebury admit another Black student, Martin Freeman.[24]

In 1822, while Twilight was in his second year at Middlebury, Edward Jones enrolled at Amherst College. Jones was born circa 1808 in Charleston, South Carolina, to free parents, Jehu and Abigail Jones.[25] The Joneses were among a group of free Black people in Charleston who were relatively materially wealthy.[26] Jehu Jones grew up enslaved but was manumitted by his owner and apprenticed as a tailor. The elder Jones eventually became a skilled tailor, and he also owned a luxury hotel in Charleston, where Abigail worked as a cook. Jones was also a member of the Brown Fellowship Society, a benevolent organization of free Black members of the Protestant Episcopal Church that provided education for free Black people in the city. The minister of the church and a teacher in the society was Christopher E. Gadsden, who was also the local agent of the ACS. From an early age, Edward Jones attended the society's school, where Gadsden was his teacher, shaping him for a missionary career. As a member of the ACS, Gadsden was connected to Amherst faculty who were also colonizationists, which helps to explain why Jones was sent to Amherst, as the outlook of the ACS, in part, was to train Black missionaries to leave the United States.[27]

Jones entered college in 1822 at the age of fourteen or fifteen, which was not uncommon at the time.[28] Not much is known about Jones's personal experiences at Amherst, aside from his academic progression. He advanced through the regular college course, which included recitations in the Greek Testament and Hebrew as an upperclassman. As a senior Jones studied theology.[29] Jones excelled academically while being the only Black student at the college.

Jones's time at Amherst is mostly an enigma, as sources from Jones's perspective remain elusive as well.[30] Despite this limitation, the intellectual and social presence of Edward Jones at Amherst had subversive implications. While Jones came from a materially wealthy Black family and had received an elite education, his presence and intellectual accomplishments at Amherst College punctured the boundaries of white conceptualizations of colleges and who they served. In his achievements at an all-white institution that fostered anti-Black sentiments, evidenced by its members' embrace of ACS ideology, Jones made emphatic arguments for Black humanity.[31]

Jones graduated from Amherst on August 23, 1826, at the age of eighteen and began looking for meaningful work. After graduation, Jones relocated to New York City, where family members were residing. While at Amherst, he switched his residence from Charleston to New York because of the punitive state law that was codified in the wake of the Denmark Vesey case in 1822 barring free African Americans from reentering South Carolina. The law effectively prevented Jones from rejoining his family in Charleston.[32] While in New York, Jones joined another early Black college graduate, John B. Russwurm, as an assistant editor of Samuel Cornish's newspaper, *Freedom's Journal.* Jones worked there for a short time late in 1827, and, the following year, Jones entertained his options for a career in medicine. Meanwhile, Jones and Russwurm became close friends. Russwurm wrote on his behalf to Ralph Gurley, the ACS leader, inquiring whether the ACS would fund Jones's medical training if he emigrated to Liberia. The ACS ultimately rejected the proposal, and Jones's dream of medical training was for naught. But Africa increasingly occupied his mind. He pursued further learning in preparation for a missionary career.[33]

As an unofficial student, Jones attended Andover Theological Seminary (ATS), where he studied Arabic "without the assistance of a teacher" in preparation for missionary work in Africa. By 1828, the ACS was actively promoting the education of young Black men for African missions, which helps to explain why Jones was able to study at ATS. ACS officials believed that Black missionaries required formal training: "It is as a matter of the first importance, that all those who may at this early period become residents at the Colony, should not only be persons of moral worth and industrious habits, but also possessed of that Agricultural and Mechanical skill which will secure them access to all the neighboring nations," and "an attempt to instruct them [Native Africans] in the arts and Christianity" will prove successful for the colony. That ACS officials advocated "a practical knowledge of the arts of more enlightened nations" and instruction in "agriculture and the liberal arts" describes their educational vision for Liberia, and Black missionaries, they believed, would facilitate this endeavor, in all of its imperialist implications.[34] Preparation in the liberal arts and Christianity in the United States could be acquired formally at colleges and seminaries. The colleges as predominantly religious institutions could help answer this call. The founding of Liberia and the ACS's desire for formally trained Black missionaries, dating back to 1823, likely helps to explain why college officials admitted select Black students.

The Church Missionary Society (CMS), a British benevolent organization, also promoted the education of Black missionaries, aligning with the vision of the ACS. An indication of this shared interest was a letter Gurley published from the CMS in January 1827 specifically calling for Black missionaries. Their duties, the CMS secretary wrote, "would be religious instruction of liberated Africans congregated in Sierra Leone." A thorough knowledge of the English language and composition were requirements as well. Most importantly, they wrote, candidates had to be "intelligent, decided," and exhibit "mature piety, with sound judgment" and devotion to God, the Gospel, and the Church of England.[35] This outlook had an imperialist framing as well, as the ACS and the CMS sought to instill British-American knowledge systems as part of the colonial regime in West Africa. Edward Jones fit all these criteria. The turn to educating Black missionaries within the ACS and CMS, combined with the fact that ATS was an ACS stronghold, explains why Jones was able to study there.

While studying at Andover, Jones had been a student in the African School in Hartford, Connecticut, which was the product of the Protestant Episcopal Church. In 1828, American Episcopalians had taken up the call from the CMS, establishing the institution dedicated to preparing Black ministers for African missions. After completing a year of study, Jones was ordained an Episcopal priest in 1830. He also received an honorary master of arts degree from Trinity College in Hartford. Soon thereafter, Jones traveled to England and then to Sierra Leone.[36]

Why Jones chose the path he did is not clear. The young Black intellectual encountered the dilemma Black people would face throughout the antebellum period: the intransigence of American racism. In the late 1820s, and in his early twenties, Jones was one of the most formally educated Black persons in the United States. However, he soon realized that his intellectual training did not alter the racial hierarchy. Jones experienced this firsthand, as he was forced to give up his pursuit of medical training since no school would allow him to enter. Given his decision to leave the United States for Sierra Leone, he seemingly believed that the highest degree of Black freedom and autonomy could be achieved in West Africa. It was likely this dilemma, as well as the fact that he could not legally return to his family in South Carolina, that propelled Jones to leave the United States. Jones's close friendship with Russwurm also played an important role in his decision. After arriving in Liberia, Russwurm persuaded Jones to emigrate, writing, "I long to see young men, who are now wasting the best of their days in the United States, flocking to this land as the last asylum to the unfortunate. I long for the time when you, my dear friend, shall land on the shores of Africa, a messenger of that Gospel which proclaims liberty to the captive and light to those who sat in great darkness! Oh, my friend, you have a wide career of usefulness before you."[37] Russwurm's beckoning message resonated with Jones as he was finishing his studies in 1830 and convinced him to emigrate to West Africa. A question that remains unanswered is the nature of Jones's relationship with other Black people during his time after Amherst and before he left for Sierra Leone. Jones believed that working with Africans in Africa was his life's calling rather than staying in the United States.

Arriving in Sierra Leone in 1831, Jones became an important teacher and supporter of African rights over the British colonial regime. He initially became a schoolmaster in Kent and, in 1841, Jones officially joined the CMS and was appointed principal of the Fourah Bay Christian Institution, which became Fourah Bay College in 1848. He served as its president until 1856. In 1864, Jones traveled to England, where he died in 1865 at the age of fifty-seven. He never returned to the United States. Jones's work in Sierra Leone exemplifies a commitment to African freedom. He aided formerly enslaved Africans in searching for their families in the African interior. As Nemata Blyden writes, Jones opposed British colonial policies and provoked the ire of one official who called for Jones's resignation in Kent. The official described Jones's actions as exhibiting a "total disregard for all authority," setting an "indolent example," and instilling "democratic doctrines, . . . rendering it [his resignation] essential." Jones also sided with other Africans in opposition to the colonial governor in Sierra Leone. He was later dismissed from a newspaper editorship in 1862 for criticizing the governor. Jones's impact on his students at Fourah Bay is also a significant component of his legacy. Some of his students went on to become pioneering Pan-Africanists, including Samuel Ajayi Crowther, James Africanus Horton, and James Johnson.[38] Indeed, Jones as a teacher and agitator provided an example of Black freedom and autonomy that his students could emulate. Jones also became a naturalized citizen of Sierra Leone, and over the course of his life, he embraced his African heritage. In 1848, Jones provided testimony before the House of Commons on his work in Sierra Leone and was asked about the intellectual abilities of African students he taught. His reply is telling. "I see no difference," Jones stated, between his students and any other students. Jones added, "I am one of them myself." The questioner proceeded: "You observe no disqualification in the black race?" to which Jones replied, "None whatever."[39]

While Edward Jones's life is difficult to piece together, it is evident that he believed in, embodied, and championed Black freedom and African autonomy. While acquiring college education, Jones stood as a critique of racism in American colleges. He leveraged his formal learning in the interests of African people. He worked with Africans and freedpeople in Sierra Leone for autonomy and self-determination. His life's work represents a nascent Black nationalist sensibility. As an educator he mentored young Black students and challenged colonial authorities. In doing so, he helped prepare a generation of Pan-Africanists. In this light, Jones was a Black intellectual who dedicated his life to Black freedom, learning, and self-determination.

In 1824, while Jones was in his second year at Amherst and a year after Twilight graduated, three other young Black men entered three colleges—Edward Mitchell at Dartmouth, John Newton Templeton at Ohio University, and John Brown Russwurm at Bowdoin.[40]

Templeton was born circa 1807 to his parents, Pompey and Terak, and was one of nine children. Thomas and Anne Newton Williamson of Spartanburg district, South Carolina, owned Templeton and his family as slaves. Templeton's parents and siblings were nine of the twenty enslaved people the Williamsons owned. Thomas's will stipulated that upon his death, the people he owned would be manumitted and sent to live with his son, William Williamson, a Presbyterian minister, in Chillicothe, Ohio. Templeton was freed at age six and moved to Ohio with his entire family. While John was a child, Anne Williamson taught him to read and write, which facilitated his enrollment at Ripley Academy, where he excelled in his studies. Templeton's academic talents garnered the attention of Robert G. Wilson, a colleague of William Williamson and president of Ohio University. In 1824, Wilson offered Templeton the opportunity to matriculate at the university.[41] Wilson was also a colonizationist, which likely influenced his decision to admit Templeton and prepare him for missions in Liberia.

By the time Templeton entered Ohio University, the institution was twenty years old. Established in 1804, it was the first university in the Old Northwest. The original trustees and General Assembly of Ohio believed that "institutions for the liberal education of youth, are essential to the progress of arts and sciences, important to morality, virtue and religion; friendly to peace, order and prosperity of society, and honorable to the government that encourages and patronizes them." Such was the university's founding vision. Not mentioned was the settler-colonial foundation of the institution; its founding was a result of a military campaign against Shawnee, Miami, and Delaware tribes. The violent removal and murder of Indigenous people facilitated the emergence of the first university in Ohio.[42] Templeton was part of a small group of freshmen who entered the university in 1824.

As a student, Templeton worked on campus. He was "college servant" to President Wilson, living and working in the president's home in exchange for a small wage that deferred the costs of his education. The situation mirrored a manual labor arrangement that colleges adopted in the 1820s and 1830s for students to work and defer their college expenses. The college servant was a permanent position held by other students and was not a unique arrangement for Templeton's situation. However, being a Black student and formerly enslaved, Templeton brought a unique perspective to the job. Due to this arrangement, Templeton did not board among white students at the college. Not much is known about his college experience. In addition to his tasks in Wilson's home, Templeton progressed through the regular college course. He was a member of the Athenian Literary Society, where he participated in debate topics such as "The Present State of the Slave in the United States."[43] While his perspective on this question is not known, Templeton's response surely challenged white students' perspectives on "the Slave."

Templeton graduated from Ohio University on September 17, 1828. Along with the other graduates, Templeton gave a commencement oration. His speech was entitled "The Claims of Liberia." Reflecting Templeton's training at the university, Wilson prepared him to become an ACS missionary.[44] Reports of the 1828 commencement appeared in contemporary publications. According to an observer, the topic resonated deeply with Templeton. The observer explained, "Templeton delivered a very well composed speech on 'The Claims of Liberia' for his theme, but showed himself rather too deeply affected by his subject to do justice to himself or to excite the interest in the audience his production merited." A local newspaper listed him among the graduates "as a young man of color."[45]

Templeton's original commencement address has not survived, but he gave a speech with the same title the following July. The speech reveals a conflicted colonizationist position. The opening line is particularly revealing. "It is with great reluctance that I appear before you this day in behalf of the claims of Liberia," he remarked. He requested aid from his audience in placing "the sons of Africa" in "that land where they might enjoy the rights and privileges of a free people." He believed Africa could be a place for Black freedom. Templeton came to support the ACS's mission to provide the financial means to Black people who were willing to relocate to Africa. Nowhere in the speech does he explicitly advocate the removal of free Black people or perpetuate racist notions, staples in the colonizationist platform. To the contrary, he had an extended commentary demonstrating Black and African humanity. He began by examining African history and the prominence of "Egypt and Carthage" in ancient history, as they were a part of "the catalogue of great nations." The African continent from which humanity emanated was significant for Templeton. However, Templeton viewed African religious practices, particularly Islam, in a derogatory fashion and attributed the fall of African polities to their rejection of Christianity. But the greater evil for Africans, Templeton believed, was the rise of the transatlantic slave trade and bondage in the Americas.

Slavery was an "evil of unbounded extent, and inexpressible weight," Templeton remarked, and Africa's "children are cruelly dragged into hopeless slavery in the West Indies, and North and South America."

Templeton's words had special resonance, as he and his family experienced enslavement. Emphasizing antislavery sentiment, he singled out the hypocrisy of the American Revolution's legacy of slavery and freedom. This was a radical critique of the United States from a young Black scholar. Templeton explained that colonization was born out of antislavery sentiment. For some colonizationists, especially northern clergy, antislavery was indeed a motivating factor, but slaveholders as well as other white supporters of the ACS favored the removal of free Black people, not ending slavery. Since slavery had long existed in the United States, Templeton argued, it should be ended gradually; as he wrote, "Its demise must therefore be gradual, in order that its total overthrow be permanent." But Templeton separated himself from the ACS with his views on racial ideology, as they were more aligned with the views of Black abolitionists. Templeton asked his audience how God could have made Black people a separate race when they were capable of "intellectual improvement and eternal joy" just the same as other people. He asked, Were not "Asop and Terrence Africans," whose writings from antiquity remained influential? By evoking these African writers, Templeton marked a lineage of Africana thought, to which he was also contributing. Templeton continued, "And have not recent events brought into view, multitudes [of Black people] who are capable of the highest improvement in all arts and elegancies of life"? Here Templeton was living proof of human equality and Black learning. He continued, lauding African achievements: "The genius of Africa begins to shine forth in spite of every obstacle, and dispel that rubbish which has for ages concealed her beauty, and ere long will exhibit to the world, those productions which have been disputed to have existed in the African race. Yes, that time, spoken by the Prophet of old, is not far distant, when Ethiopia shall stretch forth her hands unto God." Templeton's arguments align more with Black emigrationism than with the language and racism other ACS members espoused. Templeton likely saw the ACS as a potential facilitator of this idea and procurer of funds for Black emigration. He also highlighted the ACS as a vehicle to suppress the transatlantic slave trade that continued illicitly.

Along with his arguments for racial equality, the main thrust of Templeton's speech was soliciting aid to fund the transportation of about "2,000 slaves who are to be set at liberty" in North Carolina and were ready to leave for Liberia. He entreated his audience "to consider the degraded state of the slave" rather than systematic removal of free African Americans. Templeton saw the ACS as a financial vehicle for freedom for enslaved people willing to participate. He ended with a passionate call for abolition as he wrote, "O, Justice, when will you arise to avenge the rights of injured Africa! But by your benevolent acts this day, she may yet become a happy land—slavery entirely abolished—and America gain that reputation, which would otherwise be impossible."[46] Templeton's speech reveals a nascent Black emigrationist sensibility. Manifest in his speech is the tension between his own subjectivity as a Black intellectual and the richness of African civilizations versus the racist logics of American society, which were fundamentally at odds. It is telling that Templeton highlighted only the antislavery nature of the ACS, alongside of which was his forceful case for Black humanity, racial equality, and the history of Africa. By evoking "Asop and Terrence," he situated himself within African intellectual traditions.

Upon graduation, Templeton moved to Chillicothe, likely reuniting with his family. Colonizationists praised Templeton as "a graduate of Athens College" for his speech.[47] Templeton, however, rejected the ACS. He remained in Ohio and began teaching in the A.M.E. Church School where, by the early 1830s, a vibrant community of Black people supported abolition. For example, on July 5, 1832, reverend of the African Union Baptist Church David Nickens gave an abolitionist sermon that critiqued the hypocrisy of July Fourth celebrations. He called on local Black people, men and women, to unite, refute racial stereotypes, and reform society through education and racial uplift. Templeton may have attended the lecture; it was held in his school.[48] The Black abolitionist context and focus on community in Chillicothe shaped Templeton's worldview and had a significant impact on his life trajectory.

In the early 1830s, Templeton began to eschew his tacit support for colonization and embraced abolition. In 1834 he was among the founders of the Chillicothe Colored Anti-Slavery Society. Its constitution categorically rejected the ACS as antithetical to efforts to "elevate the people of color to that station to which God and nature have entitled them." Templeton was elected corresponding secretary of the society.[49] He continued to teach in Ohio until 1836, when he moved to Pittsburgh and continued his work, becoming the first teacher and principal of the city's African School. Prior to his arrival in Pittsburgh, Templeton was reportedly arrested in western Virginia for teaching Black people to read and write.[50] Templeton's immersion in the Black community as a teacher and organizer transformed his ideology, and he became a local leader for Black freedom.

In 1837, Templeton was involved in local reform efforts and political protests, working with Black people to unite and build organizations for their liberation in Pittsburgh. In February, Templeton helped found the Young Men's Literary and Moral Reform Society and was elected corresponding secretary. The principal aim of the organization was the "literary, moral and intellectual improvement of the young and rising generation." Members planned to establish a library in which they would promote learning, morality, and "instruction in the mechanical arts."[51] Joining Templeton in helping found this organ was Martin Robison Delany. In September, Templeton reported that the members met regularly "for the improvement of our minds." Templeton emphasized the importance of a united effort among Black people "to stand the assaults and attacks of our enemies." He lauded Samuel Cornish's newspaper, *The Colored American*, as integral to that project.[52] After creating the Young Men's society, Templeton was involved in establishing a broader auxiliary to the American Moral Reform Society and was elected recording secretary. Templeton, John H. Butler, and Orange Lewis were among the founders of the Young Men's society and also held leadership positions in the broader organization. Along with other Black youth, Templeton helped lead uplift and broader abolitionist efforts in Pittsburgh during the late 1830s. Both Pittsburgh societies—the Young Men's Moral Reform Society and the Moral Reform Society—were auxiliaries to the American Moral Reform Society, which emerged out of the Black convention movement and aimed to bring together Black people of all backgrounds "to consult on the general welfare, and to digest the best plans for the moral improvement, and elevation of the whole." The means of improvement included a network of educational endeavors. The society supported institutions of learning and encouraged lectures on scientific and literary topics, as well as the establishment of newspapers, libraries, and reading rooms.[53] Templeton and other members believed that participation in this communal educational strategy by and for African Americans would foster community and facilitate a learned and engaged Black culture. Joining Templeton and other young Black men in leadership roles were John B. Vashon and Lewis Woodson. In June, Templeton wrote to *The Colored American* protesting the state of Pennsylvania's attempts to disfranchise Black men. He provided an account of a meeting where Black people resolved to petition the state legislature and document the churches and schools Black people funded, as well as the taxes they paid, to challenge the suppression of their voting rights. Templeton emphasized that such action was illegal and that white legislators had "no constitutional right to disfranchise colored men, any more than they have to disfranchise colored haired men."[54] The convention rejected the oppressive legislation, and Templeton helped lead the charge. The following year, Templeton was involved in efforts to organize a state convention to combat the disfranchisement laws the Pennsylvania legislature ultimately codified. In August of 1841, Templeton was an officer of the Black state convention of Pennsylvania, serving as a secretary of the proceedings.[55] By 1841, Templeton had become an important freedom worker in Pittsburgh's Black community.

Templeton remained active as an abolitionist and educator in Pittsburgh throughout the 1840s. Drawing on his affiliation in the Young Men's Literary and Moral Reform Society, Templeton helped Delany print the newspaper *The Mystery*. Delany was the editor, and Templeton was part of the publishing committee. In addition to running the African School in Pittsburgh, Templeton also taught night classes for adults, underscoring his commitment to Black learning and uplifting all Black people in the community. In the summer of 1850, Templeton joined in local efforts denouncing the new Fugitive Slave Law and continued his abolitionist work in the city. In 1851, Templeton suddenly died at the age of forty-four.[56] At the time of his death, he was married to Rebecca Louisa and had a five-year-old son, John. He was also mentoring Richard Fountain, a student who lived with the Templetons. Templeton's life trajectory was that of a Black intellectual and organizer. Refuting and transcending social-structure racist logics, he became a formally educated teacher and organizer. In his writing, he drew on the legacy of the ancient culture and intellectual traditions of Africa and subsequently fought for Black freedom in Chillicothe and Pittsburgh. His work as a teacher was intertwined with the vision of Black liberation. Templeton challenged the racist boundaries of colleges and used his education as an agitator and organizer for the collective advancement of his people. He helped to fashion a nascent notion of Black higher learning. His organizational work and contributions to Black life and learning constitute a significant example of a nascent Black Studies project in practice.

In 1825, while Edward Jones and John B. Russwurm were juniors, and Mitchell a sophomore, Theodore S. Wright entered Princeton Theological Seminary. Born in 1797 in New Jersey to free parents, Wright grew up in Providence, Rhode Island, and Schenectady, New York, all the while attending Methodist schools taught by white teachers. Later in life, Wright remembered his early educational experiences fondly. When Wright was nineteen years old, his father, R. P. G. Wright, who was originally from Madagascar, attended the Philadelphia convention of 1817 that condemned the ACS. His father's involvement in abolition played a formative role in Wright's early education. In the early 1820s, Wright also attended New York's Free African School, where he met Samuel Cornish, who became Wright's mentor.[57] After finishing at the African Free School, Wright applied to several colleges but was rejected at all but one. He attended Princeton's seminary and studied there for three years. Wright had been deeply enmeshed in Black community and institutions prior to pursuing higher learning. He brought a Black consciousness to his studies.

Wright's relationship with Princeton students and faculty in the mid-1820s was positive. Writing eight years after his graduation, Wright revealed that he had "profound respect and affection for my 'Alma Mater,' for the worthy professors and students." Wright proclaimed, "I always feel, while at Princeton, that I am in the midst of fathers and brethren" dedicated to holy work.[58] Wright attested to the respectful interactions he experienced while studying there. Wright, however, left out an important ideological division that existed between himself and the rest of the Princeton Seminary community. The faculty and students at Princeton were ardent colonizationists. Princeton men were well represented in local and state ACS organizations. Two of the most prominent Princeton colonizationists were professors Archibald Alexander and Samuel Miller.[59] When Wright entered the seminary, he challenged the colonizationist notion that Black people could not be equal with whites. In 1827, Wright's second year at the seminary, Cornish and Russwurm started *Freedom's Journal*, in which anticolonizationist essays appeared. Wright quickly became involved in his mentor's paper. From its first printing, he was listed as an agent for the newspaper, helping to disseminate *Freedom's Journal* at Princeton. Recalling the paper's impact, Wright wrote, "It came like a clap of thunder!"[60] Initially, Miller and other faculty subscribed to the newspaper, but by September 1827, just six months after the paper began, Princeton faculty became critical of *Freedom's Journal* for its opposition to colonization. Miller had seen enough, and he sent a letter to Cornish canceling his subscription. Accompanying the letter was a critical essay denouncing the paper's abolitionist position. The arguments of the editors, the author of the essay claimed, would do harm to the cause of Black rights, which were better represented in the ACS. Miller warned Cornish against attacking the ACS at the risk of losing white subscribers to his newspaper. In the same issue where the seminary professor attacked abolition, Wright's name remained listed among the paper's agents, defying the beliefs of faculty. The young Wright embodied abolitionist principles as he studied at a white institution and challenged the colonizationist ideology of the faculty and students. In the wake of Miller's rift with *Freedom's Journal*, Wright later wrote, "All the faculty and the students gave up the paper."[61] He remained an agent for the Black newspaper.

Wright graduated from the seminary in 1828 and became a minister in New York City, where he dedicated his life to the struggle and Black education. He was a founding member of the American Antislavery Society, and his orations attacked racism and slavery, one as concomitant to the other. Wright also brought a unique perspective to his critiques of racial prejudice. An episode of racist violence at Princeton Seminary helped catalyze his critiques of American racism for the rest of his life.

On September 20, 1836, Wright returned to Princeton for the seminary's annual commencement exercises. As Wright exited the seminary chapel after an event, he heard, "Out with the [n*****r]!—Out with the [n****r]!" Sophomore Thomas Ancrum was the perpetrator and came from behind Wright, grabbed him by the collar, and proceeded to physically and verbally assault him. As Ancrum attacked Wright he shouted, "What do you do here?" and "Don't let me see you here again." A member of the seminary subsequently intervened and stopped the attack. Ancrum was from a slaveholding family in South Carolina. The year prior to his assault of Wright, he had organized a mob against an abolitionist. The presence of Wright, a Black person at the seminary, posed a direct challenge to his worldview. Ancrum's unmitigated attack was representative of the broader anti-abolitionist violence of the mid-1830s and shows that anti-Black violence occurred on campus. In addition to Ancrum's flagrant racism, Wright was insulted that such an event occurred on the steps of the seminary chapel. Upon reflection, Wright eschewed any vindictive feelings. "Let me be assailed by the hand of ruthlessness," he proclaimed, "and even beardless violence—and I will smile and be happy, so long as I may stand forth to the view of infinite excellence . . . of moral worth, so long as I am enabled to maintain a conscience void of offence toward God and toward man." Wright occupied the moral high ground. But academic achievements and holy orders could not prevent racist violence at the seminary.

Several newspapers reported the incident, but Princeton leadership dismissed the accounts. President of the seminary James Carnahan maintained that the facts represented in the case "appear to have been manufactured." Making no reference to Wright, as an alumnus or as a minister, Carnahan claimed that only a derogatory comment was made to a "respectable man of color" and that no violent attacks occurred. Such was the story Princeton leadership decided to report, effectively washing their hands of any responsibility to respond to the racist violence of a white student. Ancrum eventually became a prominent slaveholder and staunch supporter of the Confederacy during the Civil War. Ancrum's attack, combined with Carnahan's pitiful response, exemplifies Princeton's embrace of white supremacy during the antebellum period.[62] The academy fostered racism, and the assault on Wright was a violent manifestation of that context.

A month after the assault, Wright addressed northern racism at the annual meeting of the New York State Anti-Slavery Society. He critiqued prejudice "in public houses, on board steamboats, in stages," and at "worshipping assemblies and schools." The source of these injustices was "the very spirit of slavery." While Black northerners were legally free, in practice, Wright maintained, "still we are slaves," signifying that northern racism and southern slavery were intertwined. It was in everyday actions, Wright believed, that prejudice must be confronted and eradicated.[63] Wright's speech joined the northern and southern struggles for Black freedom.[64] His critique of racism in northern institutions such as Princeton showed that Black abolitionists critiqued racism in higher learning.

Wright's life was dedicated to abolition. He worked to improve the lives of Black people, especially through education. He helped establish the Phoenix Literary Society in New York City, which was a learning and study space for Black men and women. Wright was also an advocate of higher learning for Black women. He condemned women's seminaries for excluding Black girls and women and colleges for shutting their doors to Black men. He also continued critiquing the church for appeasing slaveholders and proslavery ministers. While he remained an ordained Presbyterian minister, he was critical of the denomination's position on slavery. As a founding member of the New York Vigilance Committee, Wright also aided fugitive slaves. He believed in militant political action in ending slavery and racism. He was also a mentor to Henry Highland Garnet and Charles B. Ray. Wright was active in the Black convention movement and a supporter of Garnet's call for slave rebellions. Wright continued his work until his death in 1847.[65] Wright's life as a minister, teacher, and mentor was extremely valuable to the struggle. Working in Black organizations and institutions, he applied his learning to the advancement of Black people. Like Templeton, Wright connected the meaning of Black higher learning to the struggle for Black freedom.

While the intellectual production of some of the early Black students on campus is difficult to reconstruct, John Russwurm's writings survive and reveal a radical Black consciousness. Russwurm was born on October 1, 1799, in Port Antonio, Jamaica. His mother was Black, but her status remains disputed, as she is variously described as an enslaved woman, a free person of color, and a domestic servant. Very little is known about her life. Russwurm's father was a white merchant from the United States. Russwurm's mother died either at childbirth or when he was very young. In 1807, the elder Russwurm sent his son to Montreal for schooling. Five years later, John moved to Portland, Maine, where he came under the patronage of Calvin Stockbridge, who helped fund his education at Hebron Academy, an elite school in New England. He attended the academy for a short time, and by 1819 he was preparing for college. To make a living, Russwurm left Maine and taught for the African Free Schools in Philadelphia and New York and then in Boston, where he spent the most time teaching. In Boston he was immersed in a vibrant Black community. He became good friends with Prince Saunders, Thomas Paul Sr., Primus Hall, and David Walker. As a result of his association with Black abolitionists, Russwurm became deeply interested in the history of Haiti, the Haitian Revolution, and Black emigration to the island. Paul and Saunders both promoted emigration to Haiti and lauded the example of the first independent Black nation in the Western hemisphere. Saunders also published the *Haytian Papers* (1816). Teaching Black students in Boston and being in community with Black abolitionists was integral to shaping Russwurm's consciousness and understanding of the Black freedom struggle. Russwurm became closely acquainted with Paul and likely boarded at his home. In the early 1820s, Russwurm began to pursue college learning.[66]

Russwurm entered Bowdoin College in the fall of 1824, the same year Mitchell and Templeton started their respective college courses. Russwurm, however, passed the required examinations, qualifying for junior status. Russwurm's intellectual growth and achievement in his admission exam demonstrate how Black people mastered college curricula without entering colleges, a product of Black people's commitment to learning and participation in Black schools. Accounts attest to Russwurm's acceptance among white students at the college. Fifty-six years after Russwurm graduated, Alpheus Packard, a professor of classical literature who taught Russwurm, recounted Russwurm's experience at Bowdoin. "It should be remembered," Packard maintained, "to the credit of his fellow-students in Brunswick, that peculiar as his position was among them, they were careful to avoid everything that might tend to make that position unpleasant."[67] The presence of a Black student at Bowdoin was "peculiar" to whites at the college, a signal that Bowdoin was defined as a white institution socially and intellectually. Contemporary evidence in part corroborates this assertion of acceptance. Russwurm partook in some aspects of college life. In October 1824, Russwurm accepted an invitation to join the Athenaean Literary Society. "Gentlemen of the Athenaean Society," Russwurm wrote, "with alacrity I accept your kind invitation."[68] The records of this society were destroyed in a fire, leaving one only to speculate on the role Russwurm played in the organization. The other student literary society, the Peucinians, debated questions regarding slavery, colonization, and racial ideology while Russwurm was there, which reveals the intellectual climate and positions of Russwurm's white peers on these issues.

The Peucinian debate records reveal a student body that was informed on current social issues related to slavery and notions of race. After a heated debate in August 1824, the Peucinians decided that "the clandestine Slave Trader is the greater enemy to man" than "pirates." In October of 1825, the Peucinians voted favorably for colonization, as they believed the "aggregate of human misery will be ultimately diminished" by it. A month later, they voted in favor of official recognition of Haiti as an independent republic by the federal government, perhaps a signal of Russwurm's influence. A final noteworthy entry came in March of 1826 when the Peucinians concluded that "the mental inferiority of the African is owing to moral causes" and not physical ones.[69] A definitive connection cannot be drawn between Russwurm's presence and intellectual achievements in the formulation of these queries or in the outcomes of the debates. The nature of the latter question presupposed the notion that Africans were mentally inferior and raised the question as to the cause of this perceived reality. The question itself is evidence of racist positions, which were a logical product of the white orientation of the college and the knowledge it fostered. The resolution, however, demonstrated that students might have believed in the potential for racial uplift. These entries from the Peucinians help provide a window into some of Russwurm's colleagues' views on questions surrounding slave trading, colonization, and racial ideology. The majority of Peucinians supported colonization, condemned slave trading, and retained racist assumptions. Adding to the students' embrace of colonization, the board of trustees and overseers of the college were well represented in the ACS. Five of them held leadership positions in the Maine state auxiliary to the ACS.[70] In addition to the ACS presence, the legacies of slavery were also visible at Bowdoin.

President of Bowdoin William Allen had personal ties to slavery. At a young age Maria Malleville Allen, Allen's wife, was bequeathed Phebe Ann Jacobs, an enslaved woman, from her mother, who was the wife of John Wheelock, the president of Dartmouth College. Born in 1785, Jacobs moved to Brunswick with the Allens when William accepted the presidency of Bowdoin in 1820. She continued to live with the Allens at Bowdoin, overlapping with Russwurm's time there, until Maria Malleville died in 1828. Jacobs subsequently chose to live on her own and supported herself as a laundress for students. She died in 1850.[71] Russwurm would have been well aware of this context at Bowdoin, that students and college officials supported colonization and that the president of the college had owned an enslaved woman. Beyond this context, Russwurm's view of his experiences is unclear. He boarded away from the campus, and even though students invited him to socialize with them beyond the literary society, he never answered the invitations.[72] Russwurm seemingly never wrote about his time at Bowdoin, but it is safe to conclude that while he experienced some positive social experiences, he was the lone Black student at a white college where some students and officers believed that Black people should leave the country and questioned their intellectual capacities. In this environment, Russwurm sharpened his abolitionist convictions by studying the Haitian Revolution.

Russwurm's interest in Haiti grew during his time at Bowdoin. In a January 1826 letter to his cousin, Russwurm revealed his aspirations of becoming a physician and where he would practice. "After August brighter prospects will dawn upon efforts of many years," Russwurm wrote. "If not particularly invited by the Haytian Govt then, I shall study Medicine in Boston previous to an emigration to Hayti."[73] Russwurm's plans were clear. In preparation for emigration to Haiti, he studied the Haitian Revolution and grew fascinated with Toussaint Louverture. He wrote a twenty-two-page essay entitled "Toussaint L'Overture, the Principal Chief in the Revolution of St. Domingo," examining Louverture's life and role in the revolution. It depicts Louverture as a virtuous leader who led the revolution for Black freedom and subsequently to repel European colonialism. Russwurm wrote of Louverture's admirable leadership during the first phase of the revolution: "The fertility of his invention, the correctness of his judgement, the celebrity of his prosecution, the extent of his labours, in the combined and the multifarious business of war and government, astonished both friends and foes." After abolition was won and before Napoleon's invasion, Russwurm explained Louverture's reception among freed people. "The fame of his martial achievements and the excellence of his general character, ensured him a most enthusiastic reception every where among the blacks," he wrote.[74] While the essay is mostly a vindication of Louverture's leadership, Russwurm was critical of his policy of forcing freed people into contracts for wages with former slaveholders in the wake of emancipation. Russwurm observed, "Hence arose one of the greatest difficulties which Toussaint had to overcome." At the end of the essay, Russwurm qualified his depiction of Louverture and wrote, "Beyond all doubt, his character had its blemishes." Russwurm's critique aligned with the concerns of the Black masses. The essay reveals expertise on the history of the Haitian Revolution and highlights Louverture's dedication to repelling imperial powers. Russwurm's conclusion summarized the legacy of Louverture. He wrote, "The talents and virtues of Toussaint L'Ouverture, entitle him to the grateful recollections of his liberated countrymen—that his character exhibits many of those fine qualities which have distinguished the most illustrious governors and commanders." He condemned French leaders, for "his sufferings and death left a stain of treachery and cruelty on the government under whose merciless oppression he perished."

Russwurm's laudatory essay about a significant leader of the Haitian Revolution was a radical act as a Black student at a white college in 1825. Russwurm's essay explicitly refuted racist thought dominant in the academy. He placed Louverture on the same level as any leader who fought valiantly for freedom from oppressive colonial rule. Indeed, the essay mirrored the treatment of Louverture "prevalent in abolitionist writings of the early nineteenth century."[75] It is unclear whether Russwurm wrote the essay as part of the college course or as an oration delivered in the literary societies. He may have written it for himself. What is clear is that Russwurm's essay praised the example of Louverture and the success of the Haitian Revolution. It aptly reveals Russwurm's abolitionist convictions and erudition as a young intellectual. It also represented the advent of a Black radical epistemology in the white academy. The resistance and humanity of the slave rebels were centered in Russwurm's writing, and together they explained the success of the revolution for Black freedom. As a graduating senior, Russwurm composed a commencement address that built on his portrait of Louverture.

Russwurm delivered a commencement oration in 1826 entitled "The Condition and Prospects of Hayti," which was a more direct and forceful argument supporting slave resistance and Black freedom than his earlier essay. His opening paragraph proclaimed the freedom of all people. "A principle of liberty," Russwurm asserted, "is implanted in his breast, and all efforts to stifle it are fruitless as would be the attempt to extinguish the fires of Etna." He continued, explaining the human spirit's inevitable desire for freedom. Critiquing the Declaration of Independence, Russwurm revised its opening line with, "It is in the irresistible course of events that all men, who have been deprived of their liberty, shall recover this previous portion of their indefeasible inheritance." He asserted the impossibility of preventing Black people from pursuing freedom. "It is in vain to stem the current; degraded man will rise in his native majesty, and claim his rights," Russwurm assured his audience. While freedom and rights "may be withheld from him now," he wrote, referring to enslaved people in the United States, Russwurm observed, "the day will arrive, when they must be surrendered." The example of Haiti, Russwurm argued, held a prominent place in the history of people fighting for liberation. He followed the radical tradition of looking to the Haitian Revolution rather than the American one as the true example of people overcoming their oppressors for freedom and justice. "After years of sanguinary struggle for freedom and political existence," Russwurm continued, "the Haytiens on the auspicious day of January first 1804 declared themselves a free and independent nation." It was the unquenchable thirst for freedom and self-determination among the enslaved, Russwurm observed, that made this possible. There was no changing the outcome. "Nothing can ever induce them to recede from this declaration," Russwurm proclaimed. The example of the Haitian Revolution revealed that slavery could not "destroy our faculties," he wrote, which Haitians would demonstrate as free people. His use of the word "our" reveals Russwurm's ideological solidarity with people of African descent in the diaspora and in particular the slave rebels. He identified the struggle of enslaved people in Saint Domingue with his own as part of the larger Black struggle to remake the world.

Russwurm also challenged anti-Black perspectives of the revolution. He explained that the rebels' actions during the war were in self-defense and in response to French attempts to reenslave them. For who had a right to dictate how Black Haitians should defend themselves against their oppressors, he asked rhetorically. Now in freedom, Haitians had established an independent government and "a career of glory and happiness unfolds itself before them." In closing, Russwurm looked forward to a time when Haiti would "exhibit a picture of rapid and unprecedented advances in population, wealth, and intelligence."[76] Russwurm's address was as much calling for Black freedom as it was demonstrating that after freedom came, Black people could govern themselves. His oration called for abolition and Black self-determination. It was Russwurm's first public address and marked his entrance into a new realm of abolitionist protest. It was a manifestation of a critical consciousness that was shaped by being in community with Black people in Boston, teaching Black students, being mentored by Paul Sr. and Saunders, and studying Black resistance. Russwurm lauded the example of resistance, and violence if necessary, as a right of Black people in the fight for freedom. Russwurm was a radical intellectual and student abolitionist.

Russwurm's presence and his writings on the Haitian Revolution represent a subversive Black epistemology at Bowdoin. His oration and essay on Louverture were early studies of the Haitian Revolution by a Black scholar in an American college. It was a historic development. At a time when racist notions dominated the campus in the form of the ACS and justifications for slavery, Russwurm refuted such claims. Rather than offering a narrative of progress and European nation building in the West—narratives sustained by the American college—Russwurm focused on Black people who overthrew slavery and colonialism. It was that tradition that needed to inspire Black people in the United States and around the world that there was hope for creating a new, autonomous Black life in freedom. In his writings and in his person, Russwurm punctured the racialized intellectual and social foundations of the American college. His writings were a radical alternative understanding of the Western world centered on Black struggles for freedom and self-determination. Significantly, in the development of his consciousness and ideology, Russwurm came to an understanding of the Black Radical tradition. He understood the historic significance of the enslaved rebels' revolution.[77] His work marked a theoretical contribution to Black radicalism. During Russwurm's time at Bowdoin, he was a student abolitionist and a progenitor of Black thought critiquing the epistemological foundations of the West and its colleges. After graduating in September 1826, he traveled to Boston, where he stayed with Paul for a short time. He did not pursue a medical education nor did he travel to Haiti. He also rejected an offer to work in Liberia for the ACS. He then went on to New York City and was immersed in Black communities and the movement.[78]

Russwurm joined Cornish and in 1827 established *Freedom's Journal*, the earliest Black newspaper in the United States. Russwurm published several essays denouncing colonization and advocated Black rights. As an editor, Russwurm wielded his education for Black learning and advancing the liberation movement. In early 1829, Russwurm reversed his positions on colonization. He became an agent for the ACS, moved to Liberia, and served as a superintendent of schools. He also edited the *Liberian Herald* and became governor of Cape Palmas. Russwurm ultimately emigrated to Liberia under the auspices of the ACS, but his impulse was that of a Black emigrationist. Russwurm's governorship in Liberia had mixed results. Winston James argues that he established positive relations with Indigenous Africans in the surrounding area of the Maryland colony. However, he was a settler-colonial governor who sought to create civilization infused with Western political, economic, and cultural ideas in Liberia. His contradictory legacy is that of an early Pan-Africanist and emigrationist whose embrace of the Haitian Revolution as a young scholar was a decided assault on white supremacy in academia. That sensibility informed his work to improve the lived experiences of African people in Liberia.[79]

Russwurm's writings on Haiti are among the most significant documents in the history of Black student writings. They mark a precedent for Black radical thought at an American college. Recognizing the significance of slave resistance and Black self-determination, Russwurm challenged the position of college colonizationists who used the fear of slave rebellions and Black insurrection to call for the removal of Black people. Russwurm instead saw enslaved people's resistance as the inevitable result of the human desire for freedom. Russwurm's writings were part of Black people's wider intellectual assault on the contradictions of the American project. Such critiques were infiltrating the campus.

As new colleges were being built in the early nineteenth century, Black people made campuses sites of protest for Black knowledge, humanity, and freedom. The protest of the Princes at Williams inaugurated a wave of Black protest on the boundaries of the colleges, and the learning of informal students such as Betsy Stockton marked important precedents for Black education in the academy. The early formal Black students marked a turning point in the history of Black higher learning and gave new life to the concept of student abolitionists. Far from being examples of liberal inclusion, Black students studying on campus and their epistemologies represented a direct challenge to the white-washed intellectual and social edifice of the academy. Templeton's and Russwurm's writings were assertions of Black freedom knowledge. The former evoked classical African civilizations and history and the latter praised the Haitian Revolution. By drawing on African history and slave revolt, Russwurm and Templeton came to an understanding of Black radicalism, marking its insurgence, however temporary, in the academy. Their writings were a significant precedent on which subsequent Black students and critics of higher learning in the antebellum period would build. Jones, Templeton, and Wright each dedicated his life's work to organizing, teaching, and improving the lived experiences of Black people as part of the liberation struggle. In doing so, they changed the purpose and function of higher learning, equipping Black students to work in the struggle with and for their people. Through their work and writings, they introduced a nascent concept of Black higher learning. The writings and later work of these students reveal a manifestation of the function of Black Studies, an education for liberation, grounded in community. The life trajectories of the early Black students also reveal a nascent Black student abolitionist diaspora.

After 1830, Black student abolitionists like Jones and Russwurm believed that their work would best serve Africans outside of America's racist hierarchical society. For them, Sierra Leone and Liberia, respectively, became their homes, where they worked to build autonomous Black communities. While their exact underlying motivations for emigration are difficult to reconstruct, their experiences as the only Black students at their respective colleges likely played a role, having exposed them to the racially exclusive geography of higher learning. In these experiences they came face to face with an evolving racist culture, the stark limitations of the American project. The history of early Black graduates thus has important ties to the growth of Black emigrationist efforts in the 1820s and reveals that some early Black students participated in the project of self-determination. In these examples of Black emigrationism and abolitionist efforts to transform the United States, early Black graduates helped craft solutions to slavery and racism that Black people would increasingly debate over the course of the antebellum period. In this sense, the lives of early Black student abolitionists offer a window into the vibrancy of Black thought in the 1820s, as they were at the forefront of Black-led solutions to slavery and racism in the United States and abroad.

2

Colonization's Colleges

In June 1823, two white students from Andover Theological Seminary traveled to Washington, DC, to meet with leaders of the American Colonization Society (ACS) to discuss the organization's future. The ACS was in a dire state, lacking financial resources and organizational management. Ralph Gurley, the leader of the ACS, invited the students to discuss their report, which offered solutions to improve the organization. The students had recently established a committee on colonization in the Society of Inquiry, a student organization at the seminary. After studying the ACS's platform, Andover students resolved to spread its message. The two white students were Solomon Peck and Leonard Bacon. Bacon authored the report outlining arguments favoring the removal of free Black people from the United States and offered advice for reviving the organization. Gurley welcomed the students' initiative and embraced Bacon's plans, which facilitated the growth of the ACS in the 1820s, especially among white evangelicals in New England.[1]

The June meeting was a crucial moment in the history of the ACS, but it also represented the impact students had on the organization. While white students and faculty had supported the ACS from its founding in 1816, Bacon's report and the support of seminary students reveal that white students in higher learning were a significant demographic of the ACS constituency. They helped shape the organization's platform and operations. Indeed, as a result of his essay, Bacon became a prominent colonizationist, and the report fostered widespread acclaim for colonization among other white seminary and college students.

The founding and evolution of the ACS was deeply intertwined with American colleges and seminaries. The arguments college colonizationists made were premised on racist ideas that coincided with timid antislavery views. White students and faculty were among the ACS's earliest advocates. Throughout the 1820s, they fueled the movement, developing its ideological outlook and becoming leaders at the local and national levels. The role of Andover Theological Seminary (ATS) is central to this history, as students such as Samuel Mills helped instill the ACS with a focus on religious missions. Bacon came to endorse colonization because of its message of spreading Christianity to Africa, but white students also saw colonization as a means to alleviate the threat of slave rebellions in the United States by removing free African Americans from the polity. Believing that the presence of free Black people had detrimental effects on the enslaved population because they represented freedom and enticed enslaved people to rebel, student colonizationists used the threat of slave rebellions to make claims for removal. As a result, they appropriated the actions of enslaved people, not to end slavery but to advance a movement to create an exclusively white nation. College colonizationists also championed the ACS as an antislavery organization in principle, yet they constantly left the question of emancipation to the proclivities of slaveholders. This chapter argues that college colonizationists' commitment to antislavery was merely in the abstract and their deference to slaveholders on the matter resulted in complicity with upholding slavery, as the majority of slaveholders had no interest in manumitting enslaved people they owned and instead intended to expatriate free Black people. Inextricably foundational to college colonizationists' arguments for the removal of free African Americans from the country was a racist argument that Black people could never be equal citizens with whites. Indeed, they perceived free Black populations as threats to the political and social order. Black freedom in the United States was antithetical to their ideas of order and nation. It was no mistake that college colonizationists, and the ACS more generally, often reassured their audiences that they were not interested in targeting enslaved people for removal; that was left to slaveholders. Their object was convincing free Black people to leave the country. These arguments were at the core of the colonizationist message that emanated from American colleges in the 1820s.

After the publication of Bacon's report, college students from New England to the Old Northwest began establishing auxiliary colonization societies on campuses. They debated the merits of the ACS, which often resulted in students embracing its program. They penned essays and donated money to the ACS. Student colonizationists went on to become leaders in the national organization, while many others became local agents for state societies. As higher learning spread westward into the Ohio Valley, the ACS spread with it. Before 1830, presidents, faculty, and most students of Miami University, Ohio University, Western Reserve College, and Lane Seminary endorsed the ACS. The ACS firmly took root at New England colleges as well, such as Amherst. By 1830, colleges and the colonization movement were inseparable. With trustees, faculty, and students active in the movement, colleges and seminaries in effect lent institutional support to the ACS, which helps explain how the movement spread and gained popularity among whites in northern states. Colleges and seminaries were institutional pillars of the colonization program.[2] In other words, because of the strength of colonization and their financial connections to slavery, colleges and seminaries as institutions were anti-abolitionist, and indeed largely anti-Black, in their ideological and social contexts. The rise of the ACS on campus was fundamentally at odds with the Black struggle to create a new humanity. By the 1820s, Black and white abolitionists thus had to fight both proslavery and ACS forces in the academy.

American institutions of higher learning had been founded on racist and gendered notions of who could receive college- and seminary-level education. But the advent of the ACS and its inseparability from these institutions marked an evolution as institutions actively supported a movement that prescribed racist ideologies of exclusion regarding who could be equal citizens in the United States. The proliferation of the ACS on campuses was a logical manifestation of the racist ideology that was foundational to the intellectual and political project of the colleges. As Black people in northern states became legally free as a result of gradual emancipation, white students and faculty built on the settler-colonial ideas central to colleges. They embraced notions of inequality, that freedom and rights in the United States were exclusive to white people. In other words, the ideas about African inferiority that percolated in higher learning were not innocuous but instead gave rise to a social movement on campus to remove people of African descent from the polity. The growth of American higher learning was indeed wedded to the economy of Atlantic slaving, but by 1830 it also was firmly intertwined with the racist ideology of the ACS.

This chapter builds on important work that has explored colonization and colleges and reexamines the early history of the ACS as an organization. Colleges played a central role in the ACS's history. Campuses were intellectual and social spaces ripe for organizing around racist ideas, and white students and faculty were important actors in the movement.[3] The ACS was largely a reactionary movement responding to the growth of free Black communities in northern states, and to slave rebellions. Throughout the ACS's early history, however, Black people refuted its racist arguments and denounced it as a solution to slavery and racism.[4] Colonization received widespread acclaim among northern and southern whites, including Henry Clary, James Madison, James Monroe, and Bushrod Washington. While these figures were official leaders of the organization, professors and students led, and underpinned the membership of, ACS auxiliary societies.

As the slaveholding interest expanded geographically, so too did slavery's colleges. Conflicts over Missouri's status did not quell the tensions between antislavery and the slavocracy.[5] The spread of chattel slavery and the emergence of the internal slave trade facilitated the expansion of the nation, and with it, the continued dispossession of Indigenous peoples.[6] The expansion of slavery strengthened slave economies, which continued to sustain American colleges and financed the construction of new ones. In turn, colleges as institutions performed the work of social and cultural warfare and continued providing intellectual legitimacy for enslavement and Indigenous dispossession. White college students were part of the broader national conversation over slavery's extension. As the nation expanded, new theories of racial difference began to emerge from institutions of higher learning as well.[7] These theories coincided with the rise of the Second Great Awakening, which broadly sought to quell the economic excesses and by-products of capitalism and instill moral virtue in society through evangelical revivals. The Awakening gave rise to the so-called benevolent empire and various reform initiatives, including the ACS. Within this context of political and social transformation, a wave of new denominational colleges emerged.

The rise of denominational colleges was a result of the so-called democratization of American Christianity and a desire for an educated ministry in the new nation. Congregationalists and Presbyterians believed that ministers should receive formal instruction, as they competed with other denominations for religious control in the growing slaveholding republic.[8] Colleges such as Williams, Middlebury, Bowdoin, and Amherst were Congregationalist in orientation. Rooted in the New Divinity of Samuel Hopkins, Congregationalism in the early decades of the nineteenth century was intertwined with the burgeoning reform societies. Young men were drawn to the New Divinity because of its emphasis on social reform, as clergy believed in guarding against the social excesses of the revolutionary period. They believed the spread of Christianity would help usher in a millennial era. In some cases, this meant forcibly spreading Christianity among nonbelievers domestically and abroad. In other cases, however, it emphasized human equality and civil and religious liberty.[9]

Aspiring young white men of the New Divinity were typically materially poor, came from rural New England communities, and yearned for social mobility. Economic transformations and a dearth of available farmland forced them into new career paths. This demographic primarily comprised the new colleges, whereas Harvard and Yale increasingly attracted youth from elite families interested in legal, political, and medical careers, many of them slaveholding families.[10] The denominational colleges mainly sought to educate new ministers while theological seminaries provided advanced training for the ministry and became the preeminent institutions of advanced education in the country. In response to the Unitarian ascendance at Harvard, Congregationalists established Andover Theological Seminary, which was the first seminary in the country and quickly became associated with missionary endeavors.[11]

The establishment of the ACS in the 1810s was no accident. It coincided with the rise in anti-Black thought. As Black abolitionists contested racial exclusion in American society, an evolution in racial ideology emerged that posited the natural inferiority of Black people. Scholars of the eighteenth and early nineteenth centuries played a prominent role in developing a science of human hierarchies. Notions of human difference gained currency at a time when gradual emancipation was unfolding in northern states, which marked significant growth in free Black communities and Black institution building. In response, some white politicians and clergy began to fear racial mixing and imagined the future of the United States without Black or Indigenous peoples. This racial ideology underpinned anti-abolitionist arguments and favored the perpetuation and extension of slavery. It also coupled with the emergence of the benevolent empire that sought to spread Christianity. Arguments for racial inferiority merged with benevolent organizations, and the product was the ACS, which attracted a significant national following among northern and southern whites. The rise of the colonization movement coincided with the emergence of denominational colleges, and the social and intellectual inequalities that characterized the colleges provided important fodder for the growth of the ACS. As a result of the convergence of the benevolent empire and questions of race, ATS became an epicenter of the colonizationist scheme. The missionary outlook of the ACS was in large part due to Andover students and alumni. The advent of organized colonization and its connection to colleges and seminaries represented a new challenge to abolition.[12]

The ideological origins of colonization can be traced back to the late eighteenth century, most prominently in Thomas Jefferson's *Notes on the State of Virginia*. It was Jefferson's racist arguments claiming the necessity of removing African Americans from the polity that in February 1816 inspired Charles Fenton Mercer, a delegate in the Virginia House of Delegates, to convert Jefferson's idea of removal into federal policy. But the impetus for an organization based on Black removal came from Robert Finley, an official at Princeton Theological Seminary.[13] Finley was a graduate of the College of New Jersey (1787) and a Presbyterian minister in Basking Ridge, New Jersey.[14] The impetus for organized colonization was directly tied to Princeton, but the missionary outlook that came to epitomize ACS ideology emerged from Andover.

Established in 1808, ATS was dedicated to advanced training for Congregational ministers. Andover quickly gained a reputation for its role in missionary endeavors as faculty members Moses Stuart, Leonard Woods, and Ebenezer Porter held prominent positions in the American Bible Society, the American Education Society, and the American Board of Commissioners for Foreign Missions (ABCFM). Preparing pious youth for the ministry and missions was central to an ATS education. Seminary students helped lead the charge. In 1809, Samuel J. Mills and Adoniram Judson were among the founders of the ABCFM. In 1811, Mills helped establish the country's first Society of Inquiry on Missions, and Judson is considered America's first foreign missionary.[15] A central aim of the Society of Inquiry was to "inquire in the state of the heathen; the duty and importance of missionary labors; the best manner of conducting Missions, and the most eligible places for their establishment";

and also to incite interest in the importance of missions.[16] From the outset, the student missionaries saw non-Christians from a paternalistic, racist perspective and believed in the necessity of conversion as a prerequisite to salvation. Mills led two missionary endeavors into the western territories in 1812–1813 and 1814–1815. He encountered Indigenous people, enslaved people, and various white settlers in his travels. He distributed the Bible and preached to any who would indulge him. He published detailed reports of his journeys and urged clergy to establish benevolent organizations in the West.[17]

During his trip, Mills frequently wondered if a colony for African Americans could be established somewhere in the West. By the time of his travels, Mills had long been interested in the conditions of Africans. As a student at Williams College (class of 1809), Mills recorded in his diary in the midst of a religious revival, "I long to have the time arrive, when the Gospel shall be preached to the poor *Africans*, and likewise to all nations." During his missions in the 1810s, among the topics Mills kept in mind was "an Institution for the benefit of the Africans."[18] Mills attempted to establish a colony for Black people in Ohio, Indiana, and Illinois but failed due to local white opposition. He also sought advice from Black abolitionists Paul Cuffee and Jeremiah Gloucester regarding the establishment of an "African School," the purpose of which, Mills explained, "was to qualify young men of color for teachers of schools and preachers of the Gospel, in the hope of exerting an influence in correcting the morals and manners of their brethren . . . should an effort be made to settle them by themselves, either in this country or abroad."[19] Mills's missionary endeavors, coupled with his ideas of creating Black settlements, exemplified precisely what Finley hoped to channel in the ACS. Mills's missionary education at Andover and his racial ideology propelled him to the colonizationist cause. After his work in the West, he traveled to Washington, DC, where he helped establish the ACS in December 1816. That November, Finley had unveiled his plan for organizing the society to professors and students at Princeton, who soon became his followers.[20] The origins of organized colonization had significant ties to the seminaries at Princeton and Andover.

As Craig Wilder asserts, "The ACS was born on campus."[21] Indeed, Princeton was where organized colonization first took shape, and the missionary component of the organization came from Mills and his co-agent in the ACS, Ebenezer Burgess. Burgess was a classmate of Mills at ATS, where they both contemplated colonization. Burgess graduated in 1815 and became a professor of natural philosophy at Burlington College, Vermont. In 1817, he joined Mills as the inaugural agents of the ACS and journeyed to Africa. Their mission was to locate land where a colony could be established and submit a report of their findings to, and solicit aid from, the federal government. The first two agents of the ACS were graduates of ATS. The missionary outlook of Mills and Burgess, which they honed on campus, combined with the patronage of Princeton scholars, created the vision for the ACS. While attending the December meeting in Washington, DC, Mills met Finley and became an ACS leader. The organization was deemed the "American Society for Colonizing the Free People of Colour of the United States." Reflecting the organization's official title, another leader of the society, Henry Clay, a slaveholder, clearly revealed that the focus was on removing free Black people, not ending slavery. The society was not to "deliberate upon, or consider at all, any question of emancipation, or that was connected with the abolition of slavery." Clay represented the slaveholding wing of the new organization, which wielded significant influence and would clash with white northerners who subscribed to a gradualist approach to emancipation paired with removal.[22]

The ACS was a conservative organization dedicated to creating a white nation by removing free Black people, and colleges and seminaries were inextricably tied to it. The leadership of Mills and Burgess fostered the connection between colonization and academia. Writing from Washington, DC, to the Andover Society of Inquiry in March 1817, Mills encouraged students to form an auxiliary colonization society. He wrote, "I think it would be well to form a Colonization Society in the Seminary, auxiliary to the one formed here." He also informed students that he would send colonization pamphlets to them, establishing ties from the official organization to the campus.[23] The connection between ATS and colonization would strengthen in subsequent years. Additionally, Mills's idea for an African colonizationist school was realized in the 1820s; however, he did not see this plan come to fruition. He died in 1818 during the expedition to Africa. Burgess returned to the United States and remained active in the ACS until his death in 1871.[24] The colonizationist plan had an immediate impact at colleges.

College students in the 1810s frequently debated the issue of colonization in their literary societies. As a result of Finley's meeting at Princeton in November of 1816, students quickly joined the ACS camp. In February 1817, students in the American Whig Society of the College of New Jersey supported federal aid to the ACS. In the fall of 1818, Yale students in the Brothers in Unity had a heated debate over the legitimacy of colonization. Those in favor ultimately prevailed. Among the students involved was a young Leonard Bacon. While his vote is unknown, Bacon's recent biographer suggests that the 1818 debate was likely Bacon's first exposure to the colonization question. In 1820, the year Bacon graduated, the Brothers in Unity again held a debate, resulting in the affirmation of colonization. That same year the president of Yale, Jeremiah Day, became vice president of the New Haven Colonization Society. In 1823, Day was listed among the vice presidents of the national organization. Other college officials quickly came into the fold. The president of the University of North Carolina, Joseph Caldwell, was also the president of the auxiliary colonization society in Chapel Hill. In 1817, Finley took his colonizationist vision to the South and became president of the University of Georgia. Alumni and trustees of Columbia College provided leadership in the New York auxiliary society.[25] White college and seminary students, faculty, presidents, and alumni were all integral to the origins and development of the colonizationist program. They provided the intellectual scaffolding for missions and Black removal. For them, colonization was a benevolent project to spread Christianity in Africa, remove a supposedly inferior population, and construct a white society in the United States.

Their benevolence rang hollow, however, and Black people emphatically denounced the program as early as January 1817. The vast majority would continue to reject the ACS throughout the antebellum period, while some enslaved people used ACS funds to facilitate their freedom, paired with their leaving the country. Between 1817 and 1821, the ACS experienced a period of growth in northern and southern states. By 1822, however, the tides had changed. The organization was dumping funds into the struggling colony in Liberia. It also lacked institutional management, and sufficient federal aid remained elusive. These challenges, combined with divisions among ACS members over the Missouri Crisis and stringent Black opposition, rendered the ACS nearly defunct.[26]

The impetus to revive the organization emerged from Andover students in the Society of Inquiry, who reinvigorated the ACS in 1823. On February 18, the Society of Inquiry appointed a committee to investigate "whether the society ought at present to make any exertions in favor of the black population of our country." The committee developed recommendations that would guide the society's activities on the subject. The members of the committee included Leonard Bacon and Solomon Peck.[27] As the students began their investigation, they initiated a correspondence with Gurley, an agent of the ACS and a Yale graduate (1818). Gurley was a classmate of Bacon's and graduated two years before Bacon. The letter, which Bacon wrote, characterized free Black people as "more wretched than slaves can be," and argued that they "must always remain a separate cast[e]." They believed these reasons justified Black removal, which would rid the country of a supposedly degraded populace and spread Christianity to Africa. In turn, the students dedicated themselves to colonization and to awakening New England to the cause. The letter effectively alerted the fledging ACS that a group of seminary students shared the society's vision. They were committed to spreading its message, gaining new members, and collecting donations.[28] The ACS now had a group of young white students devoted to colonization, which represented a new demographic of organized colonizationists. While students had been involved in the ACS project, the Andover case in 1823 reveals students initiating a direct relationship with the national organization. Instead of the movement trickling down to the seminary, it began to emanate outwards from it. In April, Bacon presented his "Report on Colonization" to the Society of Inquiry, which marked a new chapter in the history of the ACS.

Bacon's "Report on Colonization" was a call to unite white northern and southern efforts on racist grounds to support the ACS. Bacon conspicuously focused his attack on "the blacks in the northern and middle states." Bacon believed that free African Americans were either paupers or imprisoned. Racial prejudice, Bacon claimed, "must always cut off, the negro from all that is valuable in citizenship." Bacon assured his readers that the general rule regarding free African Americans was that "the blacks are degraded, without any proper means of improvement, or any sufficient incentive to exertion." Bacon clearly posited racist arguments about Black people and their role in society.[29] Bacon also claimed that the condition of enslaved people in the US South were "generally . . . much superior to that of the slave in the West Indies" and that "slaves have no reason to complain and the friends of humanity have no reason to complain for them."[30] After asserting that enslavement was benign, Bacon extended an olive branch to slaveholders. He assured that a white North-South coalition "of course must not have the abolition of slavery for its immediate object." He merely saw colonization as a potential route, with federal aid, that would entice slaveholders to voluntarily manumit enslaved people and be awarded compensation. Bacon's plan lacked further specificity as to how emancipation would unfold. It rested on slaveholders to take up the task.[31] The chief reason for the failures of the ACS was first and foremost overwhelming Black opposition to it, but the reliance on slaveholders to implement emancipation hampered its efforts from the outset. Many slaveholders had little interest in ending slavery but were supportive of removing free Black people from the polity. Bacon was attempting to bring slaveholders into the fold along with northern white evangelicals. The crux of Bacon's conciliatory message that he hoped would foster sectional cooperation was white supremacy, as well as the fear of slave resistance and its implications for the country.

Bacon used the fear of slave rebellion to justify colonization.[32] Bacon believed many slaveholders concurred with Jefferson's admission that if enslaved people rebelled on a large scale, providence would side with the oppressed. He quoted Jefferson's warning, "The Almighty has no attribute which can take side with us in such a contest." After extrapolating the enslaved population, which he claimed would be twelve million by 1880, Bacon feared Black slaves would outnumber free whites. But before then Bacon lamented "how much terror and anxiety must be endured, how many plots detected, how many insurrections quelled."[33] He continued, "Plots! And insurrections! These are words of terror." Referring to enslaved people, he observed, "They are surrounded by memorials of freedom. The air which they breath is free." Enslaved people "are never slow in learning that they are fettered, and that freedom is the birthright of humanity." From this context Bacon feared that "a Toussaint or a Spartacus, or an African Tecumseh" would emerge and "his fellow slaves will flock around his standard." He worried that "a general insurrection in the southern states might, indeed, destroy their cities" and "might desolate their plantations." Bacon assured that such an insurrection would not ultimately succeed, as it had in Saint Domingue, until generations later when the enslaved population swelled to larger proportions. Slave resistance was a national problem, Bacon reasoned, and a rebellion would solicit a national response. He proclaimed, "There is hardly any enterprize [sic] to which the militia of Vermont or Connecticut would march with more zeal than to crush a servile rebellion."[34] After stoking fears of slave rebellions, Bacon posited that enslaved and free people were "dangerous to the community, and this danger ought to be removed." For Bacon, the problem was the threat of slave rebellion, but it was also the dearth of loyal Black people. "The danger is not so much that we have a million and half of slaves, as that we have within our borders nearly two millions of men who are necessarily any thing rather than loyal citizens."[35] Bacon believed that all Black people posed a threat to the stability of the republic and had to be removed. Again, Bacon's plan was for free Black people. There was no plan for emancipation beyond slaveholders' willingness to manumit their slaves, hardly a strategy worthy of the term "antislavery."

The only solution for Bacon was colonization. In order to gather widespread endorsements for the ACS, Bacon concluded, the organization needed restructuring. Bacon turned to the Bible Society, the Missionary Society, and their auxiliaries for examples to model. Employing agents to spread the movement and establishing auxiliaries would facilitate individual donations, which the ACS desperately needed. In Bacon's eyes, the ACS was practical, necessary, and promoted the national interests of the republic. The report ended with a common refrain that the ACS would spread Christianity throughout Africa.[36] The ACS had to take root in New England, Bacon reasoned, and soon more northern colleges became an important arm of the colonizationist constituency.

Bacon's report to the student-run Society of Inquiry at ATS was a blueprint for the ACS going forward. The argument that underpinned his colonizationist ideology was the threat of slave rebellions. Writing in the wake of the Denmark Vesey planned rebellion in South Carolina, Bacon was well aware of the impact slave rebellions had on the slavocracy. The radical legacy of the Haitian Revolution loomed large in his consciousness as well, as he feared the ascendance of a Toussaint Louverture who would lead a massive slave revolt in the United States. The actions of enslaved people shaped Bacon's reactionary colonizationist outlook as a seminary student. But unlike Russwurm and his radical history of Haiti, Bacon appropriated the slave rebellion to serve racist ends. While admitting that slavery was a political and moral evil, he targeted free Black people as a supposed source of degradation that had to be removed as a first step in whitening and saving the United States. Rather than attacking racism and the political, social, and economic structures that underpinned it, he emboldened it and cloaked it in benevolent rhetoric to make a renewed call for colonization.[37]

The Society of Inquiry immediately adopted Bacon's resolutions, which stipulated that Andover students would spread the ACS and established a colonization organization on campus. Committee members also became advocates of Bacon's plan for establishing an "African College." The young colonizationists contemplated the efficacy of such an institution, but considerable disagreement arose over its location. Some believed it should be built in Liberia, where, they believed, all remedies towards improving the conditions of African Americans should take place, not in the United States. Colonizationists envisioned Black education as a link to Black removal. Yet, believing in this plan was contradictory, as it was an acknowledgment of Black education, i.e., self-improvement, which flew in the face of colonizationist claims of the permanency of Black degradation and inequality. As the succeeding chapters will show, this colonizationist plan became increasingly contentious, as African Americans argued that education on their terms, especially higher learning, underpinned claims for abolition and Black rights.

By the time Bacon submitted his report to the Society of Inquiry, he had already entered into correspondence with Gurley. The ACS was so impressed with Bacon's outlook that it called a special meeting in June of 1823 to consider his "Report." Gurley and other leaders realized the potential a seminary could have in fostering new proponents for the movement. In their mind, Andover students would lend the movement intellectual legitimacy and set an example of participation in social reform for young white evangelical college students. Bacon and Peck met with ACS leaders Elias Caldwell and Francis Scott Key on their way to Washington, DC. Bacon recommended that the organization appoint traveling agents to spread colonization and form auxiliaries as well as publish a monthly periodical. As a student, Bacon had quickly ascended to leadership in the colonization movement. His "Report" was published in the annual report of the ACS as well as the *Christian Spectator*, and it became well known in New England. Upon graduation, Bacon took a position as minister of Center Church in New Haven, where he continued as a leader in colonization.[38] Bacon's report rejuvenated the ACS and helped establish ATS as a pillar of the movement. Students and alumni from ATS played prominent roles as leaders and members at critical stages of the founding and evolution of the ACS.

By 1824, the changes Bacon recommended were in full force. ACS agents solicited donations and encouraged the formation of auxiliaries throughout the country. It soon became apparent that colleges and seminaries would increasingly lead these efforts. A pair of agents visited ATS and found that students there demonstrated "a thorough knowledge of the affairs of our Society, and a unanimous and determined disposition" for colonization. "A kindred and we trust equal zeal exists at the Seminary at Princeton," they added. The importance of the seminaries to the movement was not lost on the agents. Their report continued, "The influence of these two distinguished schools cannot fail to be felt in every State of the Union." The agents' hope was soon realized. James Nourse, a graduate of Princeton Seminary (1825), became an ACS agent and helped establish auxiliary societies in North Carolina in the late 1820s. In 1825, Horace Sessions, a graduate of Andover (1824), toured Rhode Island, Connecticut, and Massachusetts, collecting over a thousand dollars in ACS memberships. Agents also reported in 1824 that "a strong desire is felt to recommend and promote our cause" among students in the theological department at Hampden-Sydney College in Virginia, and in July of 1825, students formed a college auxiliary society. In December, they donated thirty dollars to the ACS.[39] In 1827, Yale students in the Linonian Society believed that the federal government should patronize the ACS. Between 1828 and 1831, Andover students donated nearly seventy dollars to the ACS. In the late 1820s, the Andover students published annual reports summarizing developments in the ACS. They also were among the leading proponents of establishing the Massachusetts Colonization Society.[40]

As institutions of higher learning spread westward, the ACS followed in their wake. Indeed, new colleges in the West served as colonizationist outposts. In 1827, Robert H. Bishop, president of Miami University, and

Robert G. Wilson, president of Ohio University, were vice presidents of the Ohio Colonization Society. Charles B. Storrs, professor of theology and later president at Western Reserve College, was the secretary of the Portage County Auxiliary Society. Students and faculty at Miami created an auxiliary organ and wrote essays lauding colonization. One essay published in a student literary journal declared that the "United States appears in favor of freeing the country from the burden of the black population," who were "a distinct caste among us" and were "injurious and dangerous," especially in the southern states. The racist essay bears the stamp of Bacon's influence regarding the fear of slave resistance as an ACS argument. It closed with a reference to "the fate of St. Domingo" as justification for removal. Miami University students were well versed in appropriating slave resistance for colonizationist ends.[41] Miami professors and students also published a literary journal for the college and surrounding Oxford community in which essays touting colonization appeared. Students such as David Stewart and William McClain went on to become leaders in local and national ACS organizations.[42] In late 1831 or early 1832, Western Reserve students donated forty dollars to the ACS. In May of 1831, students at Lane Seminary established a colonization society and invited an ACS agent to address their organization. In 1829, Ohio University students of the Athenian Society pursued codifying racial exclusion in state law. They demanded the state of Ohio "pass a law prohibiting the free people of color from still being within its borders."[43] The student colonizationists thus sought to implement in state law the racist ideology of the ACS and bar Black people from Ohio. The early histories of Miami and Ohio Universities, Western Reserve College, and Lane Seminary are thus inextricably intertwined with the racist outlook of the colonization movement.[44] Racial exclusion and Black removal were fundamental components of the collegiate experience that was promoted in these new colleges. As slavery and settler colonialism spread westward, their concomitant was colonization's colleges.

New outposts for colonization emerged in New England colleges as well. Trustees of Middlebury College Chester Wright and Chauncey Langdon were active in the Vermont Colonization Society. At the 1826 commencement exercises, they welcomed Francis Scott Key, who gave a colonizationist address. It spurred a meeting that evening, led by Wright and Langdon, where attendees declared their unwavering approbation for the state auxiliary and called on Vermonters to donate to the ACS. The meeting aligned Middlebury publicly with colonization.[45] The president of Union College, Eliphalet Nott, was a leading colonizationist in New York. In 1829, he was the featured speaker at a meeting held in the New York Senate chamber that resulted in the formation of the New York State Colonization Society. His speech was antislavery in outlook, but he merged it with racist depictions of African Americans, and claimed that, "whether bond or free, their presence will be for ever a calamity." Nott drew explicitly on Bacon's "Report" and emphasized the fear of slave resistance to justify colonization. It was only a matter of time before "some second Toussaint Louverture" should arise, a derisive nod to the Haitian Revolution. He quoted Bacon's assertion that northern militias would help quell a slave rebellion. Like Bacon, Nott advocated white militarized violence against Black rebels fighting for freedom. After Nott's speech, he was elected vice president of the state society. Bacon's student report thus had a lasting influence on college leadership and continued to shape the movement.[46]

Perhaps the most thoroughly colonizationist college in New England during the 1820s was Amherst. The college had close ties with ATS. Amherst graduates often continued their training at the seminary, and two of Amherst's earliest professors came from ATS.[47] Solomon Peck, who was Bacon's partner in the Society of Inquiry and joined him at the ACS meeting in 1823, was appointed professor of Latin and Hebrew languages in 1825. Samuel M. Worcester, who was a classmate of Peck's and Bacon's, joined the faculty as librarian in 1824 and became a professor of rhetoric and oratory in 1825.[48] Having witnessed and participated in the colonizationist fervor at ATS, Worcester and Peck spread the ACS message in western Massachusetts, where colonization had not yet taken root.[49] In 1825, Worcester published a collection of essays on slavery and colonization that originally appeared in the *Boston Recorder*. The essays cover a range of topics regarding slavery and ancient history, religion, politics, and morality. The early essays are decidedly antislavery, as Worcester engaged proslavery religious arguments and asserted that slavery was antithetical to Christian principles. Worcester also condemned in the strongest of terms the sexual exploitation of enslaved women. The nation ought to be "unpardonably outraged, by the existence and toleration of ungodliness so *intolerable*—so execrable," Worcester wrote.[50] Worcester clearly articulated religious antislavery arguments, which represented the antislavery legacy of the New Divinity, and denounced sexual violence against Black women. Again the specter of slave resistance reared its head, signaling Bacon's influence. Worcester asked, "Would you pillow your head upon a sleeping lion?" Worcester reasoned that if the United States would go to war with a foreign adversary, a dual threat would manifest in the opposing forces combining with enslaved people in the South. Despite legal and vigilant efforts to quell the threat of slave rebellions, nearly every year "plots have been detected, which, had they ripened into execution," would have propelled enslaved rebels through a version of the Haitian Revolution. It is noteworthy that in this essay, Worcester did not explicitly call for colonization, but his solution was to "Feel and Act" for "humanity," "your country," "your religion," and "the external welfare of fellow immortals."[51]

In a subsequent essay, Worcester was more forthright about his support for enslaved people asserting their rights through rebellion and embraced the success of the Haitian revolutionaries. Worcester noted the hypocrisy and racism of supporting white revolutionary efforts and not Black ones. "Washington we almost worship," he observes, "but an African slave and a hero of freedom? Impossible." He quickly reversed course, however, and claimed that slaveholders had a right to murder enslaved rebels for political expediency. If Worcester's essays ended there, most of his arguments could have aligned with those of abolitionists. These conflicting views, however, ultimately underpin Worcester's advocacy for colonization. He went on to pacify slaveholders, arguing that they had good intentions.[52] In his final essay, he quickly turned to colonization, which he believed was "the most flattering and magnificent" project of benevolence. Indeed, it was no mistake that his series of essays culminated in a call for colonization. Emancipation, he wrote, "will be the work of years," perhaps unfolding over "fifty or hundred years."[53] While antislavery in spirit, Worcester embraced colonization in practice, paired with the utmost gradualist emancipation plans. Indeed, he claimed to support slave resistance, but that argument functioned as Bacon's did: to reinforce the call for removal, not to codify Black rights. As a professor at Amherst, Worcester spread colonizationist ideals through his published writings. Amherst faculty like Worcester helped mold colonizationist advocacy at the college.

Amherst students endorsed the ACS in college essays. In an 1827 senior composition, Ebenezer Bradford argued that the federal government should patronize the ACS, whose design was "one of the noblest that ever engaged the thoughts of man." According to Bradford, the principal aim of the ACS was to remove free Black people from the polity because of the "prejudices imbibed against them" and because "the color of their skin" formed "eternal walls of separation between them and the whites." As long as Black people were in the United States, Bradford continued, they "must always be treated as an inferior race of beings." As a result, Bradford believed that Black people necessarily had to be removed from the United States. He argued that it was in the interest of the whole country to patronize the ACS. His essay goes on to describe free Black people's relation to slavery. "Their influence on their brethren in slavery [is] extremely injurious for it renders them discontented" and they "stood in the way of their emancipation." Bradford's allusion to the connection between the free Black population and slave resistance became clearer as he wrote, "They contain the seed of future insurrections and massacres, and threaten in various ways our future tranquility and safety." Bradford, like other college colonizationists, saw the ACS as a progressive plan for white people that would benefit the country. But like other colonizationists, he proposed no coherent plan for emancipation aside from slaveholders' manumissions. Bradford was well versed in colonizationist ideology and deployed familiar arguments based on racist ideas and a fear of slave resistance. He explicitly condemned free Black people, however, because of their very presence and for fomenting rebellions. For Bradford, it was not necessarily slavery but free Black people that threatened the country. Bradford went on to ATS for a year and became a minister in various churches from Vermont to Wisconsin.[54]

Complementing Bradford's essay was that of Lucius F. Clark, simply titled "Africa." In his senior essay, Clark disparaged African people. "In short," Clark summarized, "the inhabitants of Africa, as a people, were and are to this day a proud, idle, thievish, vengeful, cruel, inconstant, suspicious, cowardly, race." Clark went on to laud British parliamentary efforts in sponsoring Sierra Leone. In turn, he praised the ACS for establishing the colony of Liberia and envisioned it as a conduit of civilization and liberty. In reality, it was an imperial project. Clark's essay depicted

Africa generally as degraded and only redeemable through the ACS and white-led efforts at Christianization and civilization. He graduated with Bradford and went on to become a professor of chemistry and natural history at East Tennessee College (later renamed University of Tennessee at Knoxville).[55]

George Washington Boggs also wrote an 1827 essay that lauded the ACS. Boggs had attended Hampden Syndey College from 1824 to 1825, when students founded an ACS auxiliary. According to Boggs, only Christian nations could enjoy civil liberty and therefore the diffusion of Christianity, he believed, would resolve the problems of "polytheism, polygamy, and slavery." He looked to New England as an exemplar where "Christianity exists in its purest form" and vices, including slavery, had been abolished. Boggs pondered how the United States could avoid the fates of failed republics in history. The colonization movement was central to his solution, as it would prevent "civil dissentions, tumults, and factions" and spread Christianity across the Atlantic. Boggs went on to Princeton's Theological Seminary and became a missionary in India in the 1830s.[56] The senior essays of Bradford, Clark, and Boggs reveal a thriving colonizationist ideology at Amherst College in the late 1820s. While the essay topics were distinct, colonizationist arguments tied them together, which demonstrates that students were well versed in ACS ideas, especially the fear of slave resistance and the notion that the removal of free Black people would secure the nation. For them, Black freedom was detrimental to the country. They also showcase a crystallization of eurocentric ideology in academia, where white students began to apply their education imbued with racist ideas to support a social movement to create a white country and entertained imperial ambitions of spreading Christianity in African societies. White college student endorsement of the ACS was the logical extension of the intellectual foundation of the university. College leaders helped foster this environment.

Adding to these efforts was the president of the college, Heman Humphrey. On July 4, 1828, Humphrey preached a sermon arguing that intemperance was worse than the slave trade. Humphrey made increasingly dubious and racist claims that elevated the value of white lives affected by alcohol over Black lives impacted by slavery and the slave trade. He also characterized the enslaved population as a "sleeping volcano," a reference to slave rebellions.[57] While Humphrey does not explicitly mention colonization in the speech, this type of remark had become common ACS parlance. At the end of the sermon, Humphrey collected thirty-one dollars in donations from students for the ACS.[58] In addition to writing colonizationist essays, students helped finance the movement. By 1831, members of the college had donated $147.70 to the ACS. The largest donations came in the wake of Fourth of July colonizationist sermons. Gurley encouraged clergy to preach the ACS message and collect donations annually during July Fourth celebrations. The tactic effectively merged white patriotic celebrations with Black removal, and it was successful on several campuses.[59] The Fourth of July colonizationist sermons used the legacy of the Revolution to foster an ideology of American freedom for white people only. The largest single donation from Amherst students came after the July Fourth sermon in 1831, as Worcester reported that fifty dollars had been collected from the students. Writing to Gurley, Worcester beamed, "It will be gratifying for you to know that the young gentlemen of College take much interest in your Society, and will probably do you much service when they come into public life." Worcester and Humphrey became colonizationist leaders at the local and state levels. Worcester collected donations from students and residents of the Amherst community. In 1831, Worcester, along with ATS students, helped establish the Massachusetts Colonization Society and became a manager of the organization. In 1832, Humphrey was elected president of the Hampshire County Colonization Society. That year, an ACS agent visited the college during commencement week and described Humphrey as "a warm friend of the cause."[60] Amherst College had become a bastion of the movement. Faculty fostered colonizationist sentiment on campus and spread it throughout the state while students financed the ACS and presented pro-ACS arguments in their writings.

* * *

The history of the ACS, its origins and its growth as a movement, is deeply intertwined with American colleges and seminaries. The movement's leaders came from colleges, and students and faculty created knowledge underpinning the organization and became a crucial constituency of the movement. Racist ideology was the core of their outlook. College colonizationists appropriated the actions of enslaved people and created a reactionary movement to remove free Black people from the United States with the aim of creating a white republic. A fear of slave resistance and students' portrayal of Black freedom as a threat to American institutions were at the heart of the arguments for expatriation. The missionary component of the ACS attracted them as well. It aligned with their evangelical worldview of spreading Christianity across the globe. Student and faculty participation in the ACS reveals that the educational values academia promoted were coded in whiteness. This was the context early Black students were up against and further demonstrates the significance of their radical writings. A white student speech provides a useful window into the question of colonization's impact on college education.

In an 1829 July Fourth oration, Giles B. Kellogg, a senior at Williams College, promoted college education fused with colonization. He described the ACS as "the best and the only successful plan which is likely to succeed" in ending slavery. He evoked the legacy of the American Revolution and claimed that the ACS was to finish the work left undone by the founding generation and create a white republic. But it was his pointed assertion regarding the role of students and colleges in the ACS that is significant. As Kellogg addressed "men of more compassion, of more liberal views," he explained that it was "sowing plentifully the seminal principles of a virtuous education" that would solve the country's problems with slavery. He continued, "It is by multiplying the intellect through the medium of the press; it is by cleansing the fountain-head of public opinion, by guiding the stream and opening new channels of pure, healthful waters to feed it; it is by teaching moral sentiments, imparting kindred truths to kindred minds; it is by forming intellectual conspiracies and storming the enemy's works that man's deliverance from slavery is to be accomplished."[61] Kellogg's grandiose statement is a reflection of the type of liberal education colleges in the 1820s promoted. Kellogg's education in Western thought fused neatly with colonizationist ideology and the goal of the movement to create a white republic. His outlook of spreading the benefits of education was embedded with his belief in who could receive that education and who would be excluded, reinforcing hierarchies of human beings. The effect, he surmised, would lead to the end of slavery, but it also meant that Black people would be removed from the country. For Kellogg and other college colonizationists, a college education for promoting a notion of the common good was inextricably intertwined with activism in a racist social movement. By promoting colonization, students and faculty actively infused the idea of liberal education with creating a white republic. Colleges as institutions lent credibility to a racist social movement. Academia was the handmaiden of the ACS.[62]

The dominant intellectual orientation of the colleges from the colonial period provided the scaffolding for a social movement like the ACS to flourish at colleges, and the social and political context of the early nineteenth century proved ripe for fusing racist ideas with the evangelical reform impulse of the Second Great Awakening. These ideological factors intersected with academia, which in turn underpinned and propelled a racist social movement. The ACS on campus marked a new ideology based on established academic norms. It was the logical extension of the intellectual and social foundations of the academy. By the late 1820s, the function and educational mission of many colleges became inseparable from the ACS. The ideology of the ACS also paired well with the pseudoscience of race that was developing in academia, a pairing of racism in social reform and in science. The history of the ACS would ultimately have a lasting impact on college campuses and helps to explain why many American colleges have been historically white spaces socially and intellectually. While colonization was a dominant intellectual and social force at colleges in the 1820s, it did not go uncontested in those spaces. It was what Black abolitionists and some whites were up against as they fought for Black freedom.

PART II

Black Thought and Black Higher Learning

The book now transitions to the beginnings of Black resistance to slavery and racism in American colleges. Part 2 begins with the actions and knowledge of enslaved people on campus. African cultural forms shaped enslaved people's consciousness, which informed their pursuit of life and living on their terms. It facilitated their resistance to and flight from college slaving. Enslaved people also used college learning for their own purposes and crafted critiques of racist academic thought based on their experiences and on African history as alternative sources of knowledge. They appropriated higher learning for Black liberation. Following in the footsteps of the Black students of the 1820s, a wave of Black and white student abolitionists of the 1830s became insurgent agitators for Black freedom on campus. Marking a departure from the 1820s, Black students and their allies represented an evolved abolition movement for immediate Black freedom and rights. Black and white student abolitionists were an important part of the abolitionist assault on the slavocracy. Student abolition evolved from a concept, from an intellectual and social demonstration of Black freedom among individual Black students in the 1820s, to assuming the guise of a social movement. In turn, Black abolitionists developed ideas about the utility of colleges for Black freedom. The question was whether to work within existing white colleges or create an independent Black college. The intellectual work and social activism of the abolitionists described in this book created knowledge based on Black history and experiences to make demands for Black liberation, which represents a nascent form of Black Studies and its encounter with slavery's colleges in antebellum America.

3

Black Culture, Black Resistance

From its inception in 1693, the College of William and Mary was bound to enslaving African people. Enslaved people built the campus and worked various jobs within the institution. William and Mary's ties to slavery, slaving economies, and Indigenous dispossession are representative of the oldest colleges and universities in the United States. As early as 1702, William and Mary as an institution owned enslaved Africans. Unlike having an individual owner, enslaved people belonged to the college, whose board of governors oversaw their labor. In 1718, the college purchased seventeen people for 467 pounds to work on a college-owned plantation along the Nottoway River. Enslaved labor sustained the college, and the profits made by slave-produced goods and the hiring out of college slaves endowed scholarships for students. In 1742, however, two enslaved people escaped from the plantation. Two members of the faculty, in turn, went to investigate the matter and "put things to rights." While the ultimate fate of the runaway slaves is unknown, their resistance to enslavement illuminates an alternative, subversive history of colleges and slavery. By fleeing the college-owned plantation, the escaped slaves resisted college slavery, and by implication they subverted the political, social, and economic power of colleges as beneficiaries of slaveholding.[1] In their struggles to live on their own terms, enslaved people's ideas about freedom were revealed.

Studies of early American colleges necessarily require understanding their connections to slaving and dispossession, but they also require an understanding of slavery's contested nature at colleges, beginning first and foremost with enslaved people themselves. Where slavery existed, so too did slave resistance, and the history of universities and slavery is no different. The origins of Black thought and abolitionist dissent at colleges began with enslaved Africans resisting bondage. Such resistance was informed by their knowledge, their consciousness. A focus on the actions of enslaved people in college slavery goes beyond histories of slavery and universities that mostly frame the lives of enslaved people through the lens of labor and reveals the challenges enslaved people leveled against college slaving. Slave resistance also provides fertile ground to study the significance of the epistemologies of enslaved people that informed such resistance and were subversive intellectual forces in the eurocentric American college.

The resistance, culture, and thought of enslaved people at colleges reveal not only the contested nature of slavery in higher learning but also the presence of a Black epistemology in the history of the academy. In addition to functioning as refutations in proximity to the racist customs and ideas that were crafted in the early colleges, the knowledge, culture, and resistance of enslaved people on campus marked struggles for living on their terms as African people. Enslaved people's resistance was the product of a cultural consciousness created among the enslaved on and beyond the campus. Slave resistance at colleges was one product of slave culture on campus, a culture comprised of African traditions and ways of knowing; they were practices of survival, preservation, and being. This tradition of Black consciousness and resistance was linked to the university but was antithetical to its intellectual foundation, orientation, and social function. It existed figuratively, and in some cases literally, on the boundaries of the institutions. In other words, the cultural practices of enslaved people at universities represented forms of knowledge that contradicted the intellectual and social composition of the American college. In intellectual and social environments hostile to autonomous Black life and thought, the resistance and culture of enslaved people connected to higher learning reveal an alternative tradition of knowledge of Black humanity and freedom.

For the leaders of American colleges, people of African descent were exploitable beings used to serve their interests and those of the institution. Over time, white scholars would make arguments justifying enslavement based on notions of African inferiority, the idea being that Black people were a separate species bereft of any knowledge, traditions, or culture that contributed to humanity. For these whites, enslaving Black people was natural and beneficial to society. These racist ideas formed the epistemic core of the American academy. This social and intellectual environment helps explain, in part, the terms of Black people's presence at the colleges. This was the context Black people were up against, a context that is more widely documented in the history of slavery and universities because of the historically constructed nature of university archives. An abundance of materials produced from white perspectives has been preserved therein—those of white faculty, presidents, board members, and students. Such processes of preservation have come at the expense of, and have done violence to, the history of Black people. It is a violence reflective of the university's past and a product of its racist epistemic foundation.[2] The history of slavery at universities, then, has been mostly based on white perspectives, relegating enslaved people's lives to account ledgers, bills of sale and rent, and other documented expenses related to their labor, whites inflicting violence on them, and arguments justifying enslavement. In many histories of universities and slavery, except with respect to their labor and as mediated through white lenses, the lives of enslaved people apart from their enslavement are rarely ever mentioned or conceptualized. To understand the lives and worldviews of enslaved people in college slavery necessarily requires other forms.[3] This chapter is an attempt to recover a history of the epistemology and actions of enslaved people in college slavery and to consider their implications for the history of the university.

This chapter traces the contours of slave culture and resistance at Georgetown College (Georgetown University), among enslaved people owned by students at King's College (Columbia University) and faculty at the University of North Carolina–Chapel Hill, and the cultural forms of enslaved people connected to the College of William and Mary, revealing that enslaved people both resisted college slavery and produced a culture that was antithetical to the knowledge of the academy. A key focus will be enslaved people who absconded from college slavery. In their escapes, enslaved people were agents of abolition; they rejected the terms of college enslavement and sought freedom. Enslaved people who ran away from college slavery manifested a knowledge about freedom in the world of higher learning. The consciousness of enslaved people who ran away was a product of the culture enslaved people created.[4] Slave culture in higher learning is illustrative of the subversive presence of Black thought on campus.

Enslaved people who ran away from bondage also pursued college learning. In doing so, they appropriated the university, using it in subversive ways as a means of learning and knowing. As historians have argued and as this chapter shows, enslaved people longed for freedom and education. As enslaved people studied and learned to read and write in English in clandestine formations, their desire for freedom often intensified.[5] Many worked to free themselves either by legal manumission or by running away and sought education at all levels. As former slaves and students, these Black student abolitionists experienced slavery firsthand and demonstrated that higher learning was included in enslaved people's definition of freedom. Not only did they challenge slavery through their resistance, but by appropriating university space, they strengthened Black freedom claims by attacking American racism and slavery in the intellectual sphere of the college. As formally educated Black intellectuals, they debunked the very foundations of proslavery and colonizationist arguments positing racial inequality and subordination as the natural terms of order. More specifically, they also refuted scientific racism, a burgeoning field among white scholars emanating from the academy, and critiqued the connections colleges had with slavery.[6] Formerly enslaved people thus crafted original arguments against slavery and racism in higher learning. Enslaved people's resistance and their knowledge production were central to the emergence of Black thought and abolitionist dissent in higher learning. The epistemology of enslaved people was a subversive force in the context of the college and should not be misconstrued as part of the college; it existed in the space of the college but was antithetical to its nature and function. Enslaved people's knowledge was a permutation of Black thought and contributes to a long-view history of African intellectual traditions encountering the university. The African epistemologies that informed slave culture and slave resistance represent a historical form of Black Studies encountering the university. Put differently, a history of Black Studies' proximity to the university can be found among enslaved Africans on campus.

Centering enslaved people's actions and knowledge within and on the boundaries of universities provides an alternative understanding of the early history of higher learning, one that frames colleges as spaces where Black freedom and humanity were contested, and centers the liberatory thought and actions of enslaved people who sought to create a new humanity.[7] In short, fugitive slaves escaping college slaving and slave culture contributed to the development of abolitionist dissent at colleges. Enslaved people also sought to harness the educational possibilities of institutions of higher learning. Thus slave resistance—running away from college slaving and former slaves studying at colleges—produced distinctive streams of abolitionist dissent at colleges.[8]

The knowledge of enslaved people in college slavery included knowing how to traverse the campus controlled by their oppressors as well as possessing the skills they had as laborers. On a daily basis, enslaved people were in the purview of multiple authoritative factions—faculty, students, and in some cases college stewards who oversaw their labor—which produced the possibility of numerous threats to their persons. The way enslaved people traversed this environment was crucial, and their age and gender shaped those experiences. For example, enslaved women and girls faced violence from white students, specifically rape and other forms of sexual violence. Enslaved men and boys faced violent punishments from students, faculty, and stewards. In order to combat this vicious environment, enslaved people on campus had strategies of resistance and survival that would have been similar to those of enslaved people in other contexts.[9] Enslaved people's knowledge also included the skills they honed as laborers on campus. Procuring wood and water, building and maintaining fires, cooking, cleaning, washing, sweeping, constructing and maintaining buildings, carpentry, digging, masonry, brick building and laying, and services provided to students and faculty all required various forms of knowledge. In short, the knowledge of enslaved people included strategies of survival for navigating the violent exploitative context of their lived experience on campus and the skills they had as laborers.[10]

Enslaved people, however, were not reducible to the labor they performed or the violence inflicted upon them. They were never unthinking subjects, chattel, or simply appendages of individuals who owned them. They were not socially dead as a result of the slave trade or slavery in the Americas. Enslaved people were not those things because they were human beings. As Cedric Robinson wrote of captive Africans in the transatlantic slave trade, "The cargoes of laborers also contained African cultures, critical mixes and admixtures of language and thought, of cosmology and metaphysics, of habits, beliefs, and morality. These were the actual terms of their humanity. These cargoes, then, did not consist of intellectual isolates, deculturated Blacks—men, women, and children separated from their previous universe. African labor brought the past with it, a past that had produced it and settled on it the first elements of consciousness and comprehension."[11] Enslaved Africans had knowledge and understandings of the world. They had memory of their pasts, of ancestors, and culture. When Africans resisted slavery, they were not only reacting to violent oppression and exploitation; a cultural consciousness rooted in the African background informed their acts of defiance.

Included in the worldviews they brought were ideas and experiences about learning. African peoples have had systems and protocols for learning and study since the beginnings of human history, dating back to ancient Kemet. For example, the Yoruba-, Igbo-, Sudanese-, and Bantu-speaking peoples all have ideas about educating the whole person, where young people learn the culture of their people, the ways of making a living and learning for life. In these societies, learning is integrated into the daily lives of every person in the community; everyone goes through a process of education that is ongoing. Significantly, African learning practices emphasize the cultivation of individual character as part of and contributor to the larger community. The interconnectedness of human relationships, the natural world, the spiritual world, and the interests of the community over the individual are paramount.[12] While under assault by slaving regimes, African learning traditions among enslaved people persisted in clandestine formations. Learning in and for community would prove to be an extension of African values in North America, as exemplified in institution building—churches, mutual aid societies, and schools—in northern Black communities. The value of community, first introduced in cultural practices among enslaved people, would evolve and impact ideas for Black higher learning. The African background shows that long before enslavement, Africans had learning traditions before encountering European educational forms in North America. As scholars have shown, the cultures enslaved Africans created in the Americas were rooted in African epistemologies and evolved over time.[13] The question of the presence of African intellectual traditions of enslaved people at universities has important ramifications for the history of subversive ideas in higher learning. Traces of African culture and intellectual traditions are found in the material culture enslaved people left on campus.

African Cultural Groundings

Archeological investigations at William and Mary have yielded artifacts left by enslaved people on campus. A 2001 study documents the discovery from the historical campus near the Wren building of Colonoware fragments, cowrie shells, and several marbles—of which one has an "X" or cross sketched on its surface.[14] According to the report, the artifacts are dated to the late eighteenth to early nineteenth century. The artifacts would correspond to the lives of enslaved individuals documented at the college around the year 1780. They include Winfield, Dick, Pompey, Adam, Nedd, Lucy, Kate, Nanny, and Effy.[15] The artifacts may have belonged to one or many of them.[16] Analyzing these artifacts in the context of African intellectual traditions, specifically cultural and religious practices, reveals the symbolism and significance these objects may have had for enslaved people and are potential evidence of their own knowledge and understanding of the world.

Among the discoveries were fragments of Colonoware, or ceramic bowls or pots. Archeologists have shown that Colonoware was made by enslaved Africans generally and specifically during the colonial era in the Chesapeake and in Williamsburg. Enslaved people used Colonoware for cooking. Higgins writes, "The Colonoware sherds are from locally made, coarse earthenware food preparation vessels. This type is frequently found in kitchen/service yard contexts and is often associated with slave occupations." Discovered in the kitchen and food service yard of the old campus, the fragments are linked to enslaved people who performed such labor. Beyond food preparation, enslaved people also used Colonoware in a variety of healing practices. According to Leland Ferguson, people of African descent used Colonoware bowls in which they crafted medicinal and herbal remedies for illness or injury. In the tradition of the Bakongo people of West Central Africa, small Colonoware bowls were objects that held items of tremendous symbolic cosmological significance. The bowl and a collection of items such as leaves, shells, clay, and stones, among others, comprised what is known as *nkisi*, or sacred medicines, and were used for various purposes, including bodily and spiritual health and attempts to control the energies between the spiritual realm and that of the living. *Minkisi* is a complex system of ritual healing in which practitioners seek remedies to matters of the living among ancestors. Depending on the nature of the situation, practitioners use charms, herbs or roots, or divination for the health of body and spirit. The practice is reflective of Bakongo cosmology in which the realm of the living, of the dead, and of the divine are intimately intertwined. As the shards were discovered in the kitchen area of the college, it is likely enslaved people used Colonoware for food service. However, since the kitchen area also functioned as the living quarters for enslaved people at the college, such personal usage of Colonoware that *nkisi* represents cannot be ruled out conclusively. Evidence of Colonoware at William and Mary provides multiple examples of enslaved people's knowledge on campus, namely, the knowledge of craftsmanship and the function of these items for preparing food for themselves and others they were forced to serve. That such objects potentially served in treating injuries or illnesses or other ritual practices demonstrates the utility and value of such vessels in the healing process and is indicative of medicinal and cosmological knowledge among enslaved people as well.[17] The discovery of Colonoware on campus is evidence of enslaved people's knowledge and the utilitarian and cultural significance they placed on such items. Colonoware items were vessels, literally and figuratively, of enslaved people's knowledge and were at once the product, and held the product, of that knowledge.

Most revealing from the archeological study was the discovery of two cowrie shells and the marble incised with an "X," which together provide further evidence of African-influenced intellectual traditions and cosmological understanding. Cowrie shells have a long history of utility as items with exchange value, serving as currency dating to 3000 BC in China. In predynastic Egypt, cowrie shells were used as amulets to increase women's fertility, and in the fourteenth century, they were currency in the Mali Empire. A transformation in the shells' significance occurred in the modern era when European slave merchants imported millions of cowrie shells to West Africa for commerce and trading in enslaved people. African polities, such as the Benin Kingdom in the sixteenth century, adopted the shells as currency. But cowrie shells also have alternative meanings and functions beyond currency among peoples of African descent. Historically, for African people cowrie shells have held religious and cultural meaning as items of adornment, as amulets, and for divination.[18] Cowrie shells have been discovered in multiple sites that enslaved people occupied in North America and the Caribbean, indicating their cultural or socioeconomic function among enslaved people. In the context of enslaved people at William and Mary, the two shells may have served any of these functions; however, they likely served as amulets.[19] For example, Africans from the Bight of Benin, specifically the Yoruba, associated cowrie shells with Olokun, the deity of the ocean and of all water masses, which were "the source of all life, wealth, and prosperity." They believed the shells were gifts bestowed upon them that symbolized abundance, fertility, and self-realization.[20] Cowrie shells also had other meanings in Yoruba cosmology. The Yoruba used them in rituals for protection against enemies and evil forces and to foster harmonious social relations among people and deities. Such use would have significant resonance among the enslaved in thwarting various manifestations of violence in their daily lives on campus. Cowrie shells were also used in mortuary rituals, in transitioning the deceased into the afterlife. Other cosmological meanings of the shells included fostering spiritual connections with ancestors and use in worship.[21] For the enslaved, cowries would have helped cultivate their connections to ancestors and their homelands in Africa, a signal of tremendous cosmological meaning.

A fascinating line of inquiry into the meaning enslaved people at William and Mary placed on the two cowrie shells lies in the site of their discovery. According to the 2001 report, the shells were discovered in the kitchen or service yard area of the historic college. As mentioned earlier, this was an area of food preparation and, in turn, refuse resulting from such activity.[22] Yoruba cosmology is again instructive in explaining the presence of cowrie shells in such contexts. Akinwumi Ogundiran shows that for the Yoruba, middens were not simply sites of discarded trash but also areas frequented by malevolent forces, or *ajogun*. These forces, Ogundiran writes, "persistently threaten the peace of the world, the stability of communities, and the aspirations of individuals," and "are blamed for the afflictions faced by individuals and corporate groups, be they death, loss, or any other kind of misfortune." The Yoruba countered such forces by appeasing *ajogun* with sacrificial offerings in rituals of individual purification with the aim of exchanging an affliction for an improved condition. As the Yoruba believed cowrie symbolized, among other things, physical and spiritual well-being, they would be offered as sacrificial objects and thrown into middens as an offering to appease *ajogun.*[23] An enslaved person at William and Mary may have made such an offering and thrown the shells into the midden at the college to remedy a specific illness or injury or to seek redress for their captivity in college slavery. Thus the shells would have assumed an altered meaning, as they represent an African-influenced response to enslavement in North America. Given that the shells were discovered in the kitchen/ service area of the historic college, that enslaved people occupied those spaces, and the potential meanings enslaved people placed on cowries, it is likely that cowrie shells are indicative of an African epistemology and cosmology on campus, an alternative understanding of the world wherein the human, the ancestral, and the spiritual were intimately connected. The shells represented an understanding of Black life, culture, and a way of knowing that subverted European conceptions of knowledge in American higher learning.

The stone marble incised with an "X" is perhaps the clearest evidence of enslaved people's epistemology and culture on campus. The "X" or cross incised on a spherical object resembles a cross-in-circle motif. Such etchings on marbles, as well as on other items, including Colonoware, have been found in multiple sites enslaved people occupied in North America. Archeologists have argued that such symbols are evidence of African cultural forms and reflect "traditional African cosmology and conjuring."[24] The symbol matches the *tendwa nza Kongo*, the cosmogram of the Bakongo people. *Tendwa nza Kongo* encapsulates the cosmology of the Bakongo in vivid ways, depicting how the worlds of the physical, natural, ancestral, and divine were inextricably intertwined and circular in nature. The Bakongo cosmogram is rich with complexity and meaning. The upper point of the vertical line represented *Nzambi a Mpungu*, the creator of the earth, and the lower point of the vertical line, the realm of the ancestors. Dividing these two worlds is the *kalunga*, or water, which is represented by the horizontal line, or *yowa*. The four points of the cross represent "four moments of the sun"; the top symbolizes the masculine, the North, the height of one's human life, and the bottom represents the female element, the South, the height of one's otherworldly strength. The horizontal points represent sunrise on the right and sunset on the left, which takes place in both realms above and below the horizontal line. The cosmogram also has natural elements; the upper and lower points represent mountains, separated by water through which human beings and ancestors pass. And the perception of the sun's counterclockwise motion through the sky forms the circle of the cosmogram. Ultimately, the symbol represents and fosters the interconnectedness of the living, the natural, the ancestral, and the divine. Rather than a linear notion of life to death or of time, for the Bakongo an individual's life has no end but instead is a cycle, and death is a transition in the process of change.[25]

For an enslaved person at William and Mary, the cosmogram-marble represented an understanding of themselves and their people in the universe and linked them to their ancestors and their African homelands. It may have been used as a charm or in conjuring in order to harness the powers of each realm the cosmogram represented to achieve a desired end. The presence of the cosmogram-marble is evidence of the knowledge of enslaved people, a subversive epistemology indicative of slave culture, an emblem of Africana life and humanity, and evidence of slave resistance. That enslaved people practiced African cultural forms and intellectual traditions of cosmology helped to preserve what Robinson terms the "ontological totality," the fullness of Africana humanity, the preservation of knowledge of what came before capture and enslavement, and what it meant to be an African person, and specifically in this context, an African person held in captivity and enslaved on a college campus.[26] Like the cowrie shells, the cosmogram would have taken on new meaning in the context of college slavery in North America. For enslaved people at the College of William and Mary, the incised marble represented, among other things, a world of the past and a world that was yet to come. Could the cosmogram, pervasive in African culture in North America, and its encapsulation on a stone marble have been a token of an enslaved person's faith and spirituality that they carried with them, an emblem signifying their birth, death, rebirth, and connection with their ancestors and the divine? Could such an item have helped them envision a world to come, a world in which they would be free and where they would live a new life?

Interpreting these artifacts linked to enslaved people at William and Mary through the lens of African cultures and cosmology, an intellectual history of enslaved people on campus emerges. The artifacts represent a Black epistemology that was subversive to European traditions of knowledge that were foundational to the early colleges of North America. Enslaved people's epistemologies helped them make sense of their world and reveal a continued connection to the history of their people and homeland. These epistemologies are evidence of slave resistance on campus, and evidence of an intellectual tradition that was not comprehended by whites in the academy. It contrasted with Euro-American notions of philosophy, religion, science, and humanity. For among the enslaved, such notions from whites had little value to their inner lives and worldviews. This was evidence of Black life, humanity, and ways of knowing. African-influenced epistemologies on campus were central to the advent of Black thought and abolition on campus as dissenting forces. As succeeding chapters will show, Black student abolitionists and other Black agitators who critiqued higher learning would draw on African knowledge, particularly African history, in their demands for freedom. The presence of African epistemology—cosmology and culture—among enslaved people on campus helped to create a tradition of Black knowing and resistance in higher learning that has had a lasting influence up to the present day and is deeply connected to the Black student movements of the mid-twentieth century and of the more recent past. The African ways of knowing among enslaved people on campus also contribute to a long history of Black Studies and its encounter with the university in the West. The knowledge of enslaved people manifested African cultural forms on campus, and it produced other forms of resistance as well.[27]

Fugitive Slave Resistance to College Slaving

Slave culture and Africana ways of knowing explain why some enslaved people fought to escape from college slavery. One of the earliest examples of fugitive slave resistance at colleges comes from the story of Jack, an enslaved boy who ran away in 1698. Jack was enslaved to a college trustee at William and Mary, Reverend Samuel Gray. Along with the college itself, the original trustees of William and Mary owned enslaved people. Jack escaped but was unsuccessful in gaining his freedom. He was captured and returned to Gray, who tortured and ultimately murdered him for absconding. Gray had Jack flogged and subsequently struck him, which drew blood from Jack's head. The punishment continued as Gray burned Jack with a hot iron and subsequently tied him to a tree where he ordered another slave to whip him. As a result of these heinous actions, Jack died shortly thereafter. Gray was arrested and tried in court where he exculpated his actions, concluding, "Such accidents will happen every now and then." Gray, the college trustee, was eventually acquitted of murdering Jack and continued his career in the ministry.[28] This episode is indicative of the anti-Black social and intellectual environment that was fostered at William and Mary. While Jack's life was cruelly ended at the hands of Gray, his act of running away highlights his resistance to a slaveholding college trustee. Jack sought to live differently, as a human being on his own terms. Enslaved people at William and Mary resisted college slaving in the early decades of the institution's existence.

Enslaved people also absconded from student slaveholders. During the mid-eighteenth century, King's College was founded and maintained on profits from the transatlantic slave trade. Early trustees of the college were slave traders, and the college was directly tied to the pocketbooks of slave merchants. Many of the early students came from wealthy slave-trading families such as the Livingstons and Wattses, who helped found the college.[29] By the 1750s, colonial New York City had the third-largest urban population of enslaved people in North America, and the colony itself had the largest population of slaves north of Maryland.[30] King's students were part of this broader slaving context, and many owned enslaved people. While most King's students did not live at the college during this time, enslaved people accompanied them to the city and po-tentially to campus when school was in session.[31] Samuel Bayard gradu-ated in 1760, but in 1758, while a student at King's, he posted an ad for Robin. Robin escaped and was about thirty-six years old. He was bilin-gual, speaking both Dutch and English. Bayard wrote from the city and offered a reward of twenty shillings if Robin were captured there or forty shillings if captured elsewhere. Little is known about Robin's life, and his ultimate fate is unknown. After graduation, Bayard was a deputy secre-tary to the colony and a court registrar. After the British imprisoned him during the Revolution, he became a loyalist, joining the King's Orange Rangers in the 1780s.[32] The historical record disproportionately details Bayard's life at the expense of Robin's. What is clear is that Robin fled his owner, who was a college student. The political implications of his es-cape are significant as they undermined Bayard's financial power, which enabled him to attend King's, and it reveals that enslaved people resisted college slaving in New York City. In striking for his liberty, Robin contributed to the rise of abolitionist dissent in higher learning.

King's students also sold enslaved people. Robert R. Livingston, a member of the slave merchant family who were benefactors of the college, sold Tom, an enslaved man, to Henry White. During the transaction, however, Tom escaped. Tom was about twenty-two years old and was "very black." The ad explains that Tom was well dressed, as he had a long jacket, a coat, thick breeches, a white shirt, stockings, and silver buckles in his shoes. At the time of the sale, Livingston was either a student at King's or soon to matriculate there. Livingston perhaps sold Tom to finance his King's education. Livingston graduated AB in 1765, MA in 1768, and went on to become involved in state and national politics.[33] As a student, however, Livingston was a slaveholder and trader, which facilitated his King's education. Tom likely saw the transaction as an opportune moment to strike for his freedom, and he seized it. Using the described clothing for his escape, Tom's resistance knowledge was revealed.

In 1766, Cato, an enslaved man, escaped from King's student Charles Doughty. Cato was around thirty-four years old and "had lost his upper teeth." He escaped with a jacket, a waistcoat, and two pairs of breeches. He was also bilingual. He spoke English and Dutch. Doughty offered forty shillings for Cato's capture. Doughty graduated in 1768 and went on to receive a medical degree from King's Medical School in 1772. He was a loyalist during the Revolution and seemingly relocated to Britain. Cato's ultimate fate is unclear.[34] Like Robin, Cato resisted his student slaveowner and directly undermined his economic power. While King's College was intimately connected to slave economies, enslaved people resisted the individuals who owned them while attending the college. Using language skills and clothing to facilitate his escape, Cato's resistance knowledge fueled his freedom struggle. In this light, fugitive slaves were agents of abolition and their escapes contributed to the development of abolitionist dissent in higher learning.

Striking at an opportune moment of uncertainty wrought by escalating tensions between American colonists and the British at the outset of the American Revolution, thousands of enslaved people ran away, planned revolts, and otherwise struggled for freedom. In Virginia alone, upwards of thirty thousand enslaved people are estimated to have es-

caped from their owners. Lord Dunmore's Proclamation of 1775, grant-
ing freedom to enslaved people fleeing rebel owners in exchange for
military service for Britain, acknowledged what was already occurring:
enslaved people escaping to British lines. A military provision, Dunmore's Proclamation elicited anger from patriot slaveholders, which, in
addition to other factors, fueled their desire for independence. Regardless of the proclivities of either the British or the American colonists, for
enslaved people the Revolution was indeed a war about slavery; for them
it was a war for Black freedom. Slaveholding colleges were not immune
to this context. Indeed, William and Mary's president, James Madison,
feared that enslaved people at the college were planning to flee to occupying British forces. "The College is entirely broken up," he observed.
"It is particularly necessary to move the few Negroes we have, as I know
nothing but a lucky accident prevented most of them from joining the
enemy." To prevent such escapes, Madison had college slaves relocated
to Richmond in order to protect the college's assets in human chattel.[35]

The resistance of enslaved people acquired new resonance at colleges
after the Revolution, as their actions embodied notions of freedom and
equality, ideals on which the nation was ostensibly founded. Enslaved
people's resistance was a critique of the narrow and compromised definition of those ideals. In 1792, James, who was enslaved to the college
steward at William and Mary, escaped from campus. A runaway ad describes James as "bold and daring," having fled with a forged pass, and
the steward believed that he would try to hire himself out.[36] The college steward was in charge of maintenance on campus, and stewards at
William and Mary often owned or rented enslaved people to perform
various tasks such as cleaning dormitories and recitation rooms, building fires, and acting as the personal servants of professors.[37] James was
among them as he fled campus, producing a critique of college slaving.
The forged pass is evidence of James's critical freedom knowledge.

Some of the most vivid examples of enslaved people challenging
college slaving after the Revolution unfolded at Georgetown College.
The Catholic Jesuits, faculty, and officers of the college owned slaves as
well as multiple plantations in Maryland that funded the college and
its missions. The college also rented enslaved people from local white
slaveholding women. From its founding in 1791 through the early decades of the nineteenth century, enslaved labor sustained Georgetown.[38]

Like enslaved people at William and Mary and among King's student slaveholders, enslaved people at Georgetown resisted college slaving. In the summer of 1800, the Neale family rented to the college Stephen and Tempey, an enslaved man and woman, to cover the cost of Francis Neale's education. Leonard Neale was the second president of Georgetown, and his brother Francis entered the college as a student in 1800. Both had managed Jesuit plantations in Maryland and had experience in buying, selling, and violently disciplining enslaved people.[39] Shortly after renting them, Stephen and Tempey "boath Ran away." By escaping college slaving, Stephen and Tempey deprived the Neales and the college the capital their labor would have provided.[40] While historians know about the Neales, less is known about the immediate fate of Stephen and Tempey. Both enslaved men and women resisted college slaving by running away. While the specific details of their lives remain unknown, their political act of fleeing college slaving gave rise to abolitionist dissent at Georgetown.

Enslaved people at Georgetown's plantations continued to run away. Five years later, Leonard Neale wrote to his brother Francis at St. Inigo's plantation. He revealed that "Spalding has runned away." Spalding likely fled from the plantations at White Marsh, where Leonard had been visiting. The letter also reveals that two other escaped slaves had been captured. Leonard wrote, "In regard to Stephen, I would advise you to keep him at St. Inigo's, but to dispose of the unhappy Girl." The passage likely referred to the fugitive slave Stephen, and "the unhappy girl" was possibly Tempey, both of whom had escaped five years earlier.[41] If the letter is any indication, Stephen was forced to labor at St. Inigo's plantation and the callous instruction to "dispose of" Tempey likely meant that she was sold away. Given Neale's description, it is likely that Stephen and Tempey were captured together. The logic of slaveholding, buying and selling human beings, was apparent among college officials, a product of the proslavery intellectual culture the college fostered. In contrast, Stephen, Tempey, and Spalding's actions represent the struggle for Black freedom and humanity, a subversive force on the boundaries of the college.

Other enslaved women like Tempey ran away from Georgetown or purchased the freedom of family members. In the 1790s, Henny labored at the Jesuits' Bohemia plantation. Her labor and the crops she cultivated funded the college. Not much is known about Henny's life except one line in the college financial records. The Jesuits sold Henny for fifteen pounds sterling in April 1796. But some time before then, Henny had been sick and ran away.[42] Nothing is recorded regarding Henny's age, her family, or where she was sold, let alone her own thoughts. But the only entry documenting Henny's life and actions in the historical record speaks volumes. She rejected her legal status and absconded from college slavery, refusing to labor for the Jesuits and the college. Henny's resistance to college slaving demonstrates that enslaved women's fugitivity played an important role in the history of abolitionist dissent and colleges. Enslaved people manufactured their freedom in other ways as well. On September 19, 1803, Nancy purchased her daughter Sophia's freedom for fifty dollars. Sophia was enslaved at St. Thomas Manor. Nancy paid eighteen dollars and fifteen cents as an initial payment.[43] Nancy may have remained enslaved, but she had gained enough money to free her daughter. Perhaps at a later time, Nancy became free as well. Instead of choosing fugitivity, Nancy acquired enough money to make her daughter's freedom legal. It likely kept their family together and prevented separation via the slave trade. Buying a family member's freedom was another way enslaved people resisted slavery at Georgetown, creating an alternative archive of Black freedom dreams.

One final example of slave resistance at Georgetown reveals the precarious situation fugitive slaves faced. In 1807, Jeremiah Neale sold to the college "a Negro Man named Isaac" for three hundred dollars. Neale made this transaction to cover the expenses of his son James, who had enrolled at Georgetown.[44] Isaac's market value essentially defrayed the costs of James's education, and since the college now owned Isaac, it would profit from his forced labor. After Isaac was sold to Georgetown, he refused to accept his slave status and on January 29, 1814, Isaac escaped from the college. The Reverend John McElroy, a college clerk, noted the escape in his journal. The escape, however, was short-lived. The following day, Isaac was captured and imprisoned in Baltimore. The college paid seven dollars and fifty cents for jail fees. McElroy noted that a Reverend Neale then sold Isaac to a slaveholder in Hartford County, Maryland. McElroy must have acted quickly, as an ad detailing Isaac's escape was printed in the *Daily National Intelligencer* on February 1, 1814, after Isaac had been sold to another slaveowner. The ad provides some details regarding Isaac's life. He was about twenty-three years old and could read well. McElroy believed that he fled to Pennsylvania, where he was raised. If that was indeed the case, Isaac's familial ties may have prompted him to flee the college in the hope of reuniting with loved ones.[45] By attempting to escape college slaving, Isaac, Tempey, Henny, and Stephen rejected their respective enslaved statuses at Georgetown and evidenced not only slave resistance but Black thought. Isaac, Tempey, and Stephen yearned to be free and to create lives for themselves and their families. Their escapes manifested Black humanity in a world of higher learning that attempted, unsuccessfully, to reduce their lives to chattel. Even though they were not ultimately successful in their escapes, their stories reveal that enslaved people resisted college slaving, and their actions represent alternative sources of Black freedom knowledge on the boundaries of the college.

Fugitive slave resistance remained a constant force of abolitionist dissent at American colleges in the early decades of the nineteenth century, especially in southern states. The University of North Carolina at Chapel Hill (UNC) provides one such example. Established in 1795, UNC was the first public university in the United States. When UNC opened and until the Civil War, enslaved people labored at the college and in the surrounding community. Slavery was also part of the intellectual culture on campus. In the early years of the university, students debated questions regarding the legitimacy of slavery and whether it should be abolished. One historian of the university notes, "On the slavery question, the members on the whole took the Southern view." Professors and college presidents also owned slaves. Professor Elisha Mitchell bought an enslaved girl in 1818 as a nurse for his infant son and a Professor Olmsted also owned slaves. The university also bought, sold, and owned enslaved people. UNC officials were also involved in colonization. The president of the university, Joseph Caldwell, was also the president of the Chapel Hill auxiliary colonization society and a life member of the ACS. Some UNC members, however, held antislavery positions, most notably William Gaston, who gave an antislavery speech in 1832, and some students held antislavery positions in their debate societies.[46] Within this context, enslaved people made their positions clear by running away, an important force for abolition.

In January 1805, Pompey, an enslaved man, fled his owner, William Simms. He was twenty-eight years old when he traveled to Chapel Hill and adopted the alias of Cook Evans while "at the University and its vicinity." Why Evans fled to Chapel Hill or the university is unclear. He may have had family or relatives who were enslaved workers at the university, or he may have attempted to hire himself out in the community. Evans was captured, however, and held at the university for a time. Evans subsequently was able to escape custody on campus and ran away again. Indicating Evans's resourcefulness, his owner could not describe his clothing, "as he will in all probability change his dress." Evans's strategy of changing clothes to deter his capture was another example of the intellectual world of enslaved people, knowledge derived from struggle. Evans's body was also marked from slavery. He had scars on his nose and on his left hand, likely indications that he had resisted in the past and drew the ire of Simms. His owner offered fifteen dollars for Evans's capture if he was brought to his estate and ten dollars for jailing him. While Evans's ultimate fate is unknown, he contested his legal status at Chapel Hill. When he was subsequently captured, the university became a site of his reenslavement. In striking to be free on multiple occasions, Evans used his own ways of knowing to resist college slaving at UNC.[47]

On January 31, 1820, Tom, an enslaved adolescent who was about fifteen years old, fled to Chapel Hill. Tom had attempted to pass as a free person and was hired to cut wood for the college. After a short time, Tom was captured on campus. It is unclear how his enslaved status was discovered. Tom subsequently escaped from the university. According to his owner, he wore dark, homespun clothes and had a scar above his eye. Tom's owner believed he would change his name, "or disown his master's name." Rejecting the name forced on him, Tom exercised a level of self-determination. The owner offered ten dollars if Tom was returned to him or five dollars if he was jailed. Tom escaped his owner and tried to earn a wage at the college, but like Evans he was captured on campus. UNC was a site of captivity for fugitive slaves. At a young age Tom refused to be enslaved and escaped from college slavery.[48]

Enslaved people whom UNC and professors owned or rented also struck for their freedom. On November 20, 1829, James escaped from college slaving. He had been enslaved as a college servant for four years. He fled on horseback and took clothing with him. The college steward believed James would go to Richmond or Norfolk on his way north.

Twenty dollars was offered for his capture. James rejected the conditions under which he lived when he ran away.[49]

On March 5, 1835, Needham and Summer, two enslaved men, escaped from Professor Elisha Mitchell. Needham was about thirty-five years old and Summer was forty-six when they escaped. Needham was partially bald and had a scar near his right eye. Summer only had one eye and had two upper teeth missing. The professor offered a fifty-dollar reward for their capture and return to the university. Perhaps the two men were related or became friends and bonded over their desire to be free. They rejected their enslavement to a college professor and ran away together.[50]

Enslaved women whom UNC faculty owned also ran away. In June 1804, Jenny and her two daughters, Docia and Elsae, absconded from William Kirkland, who purchased them from David Ker, a professor and UNC's first president. Kirkland owned a plantation near Hillsborough, North Carolina, about twelve miles north of the college. His transactions reveal further evidence that UNC professors profited from the internal slave trade. Kirkland offered a thirty-dollar reward for their capture. Jenny was about thirty-five to forty years old and was described as a "very artful" and "cunning woman" who could "write a little." Kirkland suspected that Jenny wrote a pass for her daughters and herself. Docia was fifteen, and described as a "very bright mulatto (almost white)." Elsae was twelve, and described as a "dark mulatto." Elsae was also scarred from enslavement. She had a mark under her eye which was a result of a candle burn. Ker brought Jenny and her daughters to Chapel Hill from Fayetteville, North Carolina, to which Kirkland speculated they had fled. Fayetteville was over seventy miles south of Chapel Hill. Fleeing with her children would have been a perilous journey. Yet, the escape shows Jenny's courage and determination for her and her daughters to be free. Their powerful desire to be free as a family kept them together. By running away together, Jenny was preventing their separation by sale and also protecting them from slaveholders. Knowledge about what happened to Jenny, Docia, and Elsae requires further research. Perhaps they made it to freedom. Jenny's story demonstrates that enslaved people rejected the proclivities of slaveholding professors. More importantly, it reveals their freedom dreams, their desire to be together, to protect each other, and to live on their own terms. Refusing to be separated from each other and striking for their freedom, Jenny and her daughters, Docia and Elsae, contributed to the growth of the abolitionist dissent in higher learning. They made demands for a new humanity.[51]

From the early colleges' very inception, enslaved people resisted college slaving. Their resistance provides a window into their world, in which they rejected commodification, formulated strategies to escape, asserted Black humanity, and struggled to be free. They sought to live in a different world free from the subjugation they faced at the colleges. Through their resistance, Black freedom was being proposed and demanded as an alternative to the slaving order. It is evidence of enslaved people's freedom dreams, their epistemologies of Black life and living. Regardless of fugitive slaves' ultimate fates, their actions subverted college slaving and were manifestations of Black freedom knowledge on the boundaries of colleges.

Enslaved People Who Sought Higher Learning

Enslaved people also sought higher learning on their own terms, marking a change in how enslaved people used and conceptualized higher learning as a means to foster Black knowledge and freedom. The cases of Titus Basfield, Henry Highland Garnet, and James W. C. Pennington are representative of this tendency. On October 28, 1833, Titus Basfield began a course of study at Franklin College in New Athens, Ohio. It was a momentous, yet improbable day for the new student. Born in Virginia around 1806 to his parents, who were enslaved, Basfield grew up experiencing the horrors of slavery. He, his mother, and his sister were separated from his father and sold to a slave trader who relocated them to Tennessee. Basfield was then forcibly sold away from his sister and later his mother. He was sold eight different times over the course of his early life, living enslaved in Tennessee and Alabama. One of his early owners, Basfield recounts, was a "very religious man" who sent him to school along with his own children. This educational experience had a profound impact on his life. Basfield explained, "Here my mind acquired a thirst for learning that never was satisfied." Basfield developed a deep desire for knowledge. Over the course of his early life, he received some fortuitous help from sympathetic whites, and his own drive for learning led him to Franklin College. Basfield became a student abolitionist.[52]

Titus Basfield cultivated a passion for higher learning while he was enslaved. "Although dragged from place to place for years, and shifted from hand to hand," he explained, "yet I acquired a taste for learning, imbibed at the first school I ever attended, which had not, with all the changes, rugged paths, hardships, and difficulties, been erased! In all these discouraging circumstances, my mind remained fixed upon education." Basfield remarked that the Reids, the people who owned him, favored his pursuit of education. Basfield obtained a spelling book and constantly studied it, sometimes aided by the Reid children. With their assistance, Basfield pursued a largely independent education. Over time he learned to read and anxiously studied the New Testament. "I often read until past midnight," he recalled, "and frequently rose up in the morning so early as to read several chapters; in the heat of the day, when respite was allowed for horses, I would generally read a number of chapters." After mastering the Bible, Basfied began attending various local religious services and was drawn to a sect of seceding Presbyterians who were sympathetic to the plight of the enslaved. His religious experiences propelled him to pursue his own ministry after attending the prayer services of David Carson, a local minister of the Associate Presbytery. Basfield's desire for learning and his relationship with Carson altered the rest of his life.

Basfield's relationship with Carson led him to Franklin College. After Basfield attended his services, Carson baptized him into the church. Recognizing Basfield's religious convictions and studiousness, Carson acquired the aid of his congregants and raised enough money to manumit Basfield. On March 22, 1830, Basfield became a free person, but he remained indebted to Carson. In turn, he studied intensively with the minister and appealed to the synod to help defer the manumission costs. Carson pressured Basfield to assure the clergy that he would emigrate to Liberia on the completion of his religious training. "Carson did insist," Basfield explained, "that I should have written more pointed on one particular, that was, to say positively that I would go to Liberia." This admission indicates that Carson favored Basfield's education as a colonizationist missionary. Basfield, however, refused the proposition. He continued, "I told him that I would not, under present impressions, conscientiously, nor according to my limited knowledge of things in [the] future, make such a promise." Carson relented, and Basfield never traveled to Liberia. In the fall of 1833, Basfield ventured with Carson to New Athens, Ohio, where Carson had been appointed a professor at Canonsburg Seminary; however, shortly thereafter, Carson died. Basfield was going to study with Carson at the seminary, but with his mentor gone, he looked elsewhere for instruction. The nearby Franklin College was the solution. The founder and a professor at the college was John Walker, who like Carson was a minister in the Associate Presbyterian Church, but Walker was an abolitionist. Proximity and the denominational connection most likely led Basfield to Franklin College.

Basfield entered into Franklin on October 28, 1833. It was a monumental time for him as he continued his formal training for the ministry. He lived with John Walker and worked for the college, building fires daily and sweeping the college halls. Basfield was also the sexton of Walker's Unity meeting house. In this role, Basfield earned twenty-five dollars for his labors and an extra ten dollars while working during college vacations. Basfield explained his daily regimen: "I did my own cooking and washing, swept the College every morning and slacked the fires every evening, and still kept with my class." He continued, "In the evening I would look over my lesson, and then retire to bed; and frequently rise at two o'clock, go down, regulate the rooms, stir up the fires and return; review my lesson, prepare and eat my breakfast, and attend and answer to my name at nine o'clock." Such was the typical day for the Black scholar. This routine of physical labor and study, however, took its toll on Basfield. He contemplated giving up his intellectual pursuits. But he resolved to continue. He wrote, "I would however take courage again; and with a determination to reach the highest summit of the hill of science, went forward with indefatigable ardor, completed my course." In 1837 Basfield earned his degree and entered into theological training at Canonsbury Seminary in November 1837. Upon the completion of his studies, he was ordained an Associate Presbyterian minister and moved to London, Canada, where he founded a mission for fugitive slaves.[53]

Basfield's journey from enslavement to being a college-educated minister was extraordinarily consequential. Over the course of his life, he consistently did whatever he could to continue his learning. With some fortuitous help, Basfield's achievements were largely a result of his determination and desire for higher learning. Not only did his life as a student exemplify abolitionist arguments, but his later work among fugitive slaves continued the work of Black liberation.[54] Basfield's life as a student abolitionist and later career working with escaped slaves had tremendous historical significance. It demonstrates that he used his learning to help other people of African descent in building lives in freedom.

Other former slaves who pursued higher learning include James W. C. Pennington and Henry Highland Garnet. They began their life's work for Black freedom as fugitive slaves and sought higher learning. Pennington's life was one of constant learning and study.[55] During his escape to free soil, Pennington reached the home of Quaker abolitionist William Wright, where he began learning to read and write as well as arithmetic and astronomy, which were his favorite subjects. He had been interested in education while enslaved as a blacksmith, and Wright helped facilitate his learning. Throughout Pennington's escape, eluding slave catchers and staying with other Quakers, he spent free moments studying. Upon reaching New York City, Pennington immersed himself in the city's Black communities, became active in organized abolition, and was a regular member of the Black convention's annual meetings. He also continued his education and attended Sabbath schools. Part of Pennington's learning was autodidactic; he studied logic, rhetoric, and the Greek Testament without a teacher. But Pennington gained an education through his participation in Black organizing spaces. He decided to pursue the ministry and planned to continue his academic training. In 1834, Pennington applied to Yale's Theological Seminary but was denied admission because of racism. He was allowed to study informally there, with permission to attend lectures. Pennington's admissions request, which directly protested the racial exclusivity of formal higher learning, mirrored the experience of many Black students who were rejected at American colleges and seminaries during the 1830s, a topic that is explored in subsequent chapters. In a later critique of racism in American institutions, he described his time at Yale as a "visitorship," as he was prohibited from participating in class discussions and denied access to the library. In 1838, Pennington's self-education on the boundaries of Yale resulted in his ordination as a minister of a church on Long Island. While he was working as a minister and teacher, Pennington's thirst for knowledge remained strong. In 1845, he contemplated applying to Dartmouth College, though a publicized incident of hostility towards Black admissions there altered his path. He instead traveled to Jamaica under the auspices of the Union Missionary Society. Pennington also published several works, including his autobiography and a pamphlet commemorating emancipation in the British West Indies.[56] One of his most important writings was a history of Black people.

In 1841, Pennington published a textbook on the history of Black people that included a systematic dismantling of academic theories of the day positing African inferiority. It was a Black abolitionist critique of higher learning. Pennington wrote the book for a specific audience: "The book is offered to families, and to students and lecturers in history." With this aim, Pennington was developing an idea for the purpose of studying Black history for Black people. Pennington hoped Black people using the text would develop knowledge and understanding of their ancestors and their true past. In turn, this kind of knowing a long past of African history and humanity would help propel the cause for Black liberation. He hoped it would produce "a right state of feeling on the total subject of HUMAN RIGHTS." Pennington believed that Black people understanding their history on their own terms was necessary to inform their work for Black freedom. The central threads of the book are refuting biblical arguments for enslaving people of African descent and disproving scientific racism, two arguments that were tethered to the academy and the Protestant sects. Disproving the religious justification for racial slavery known as "the curse of Ham," Pennington wrote, "A class of men have gained the high reputation of attempting gravely to theorise themselves into the right to oppress, and to hate and abuse their fellow men! Those theorists are ministers and professors of the faith of the Son of God. They have not only thus desecrated their holy profession, but they have taken a part of God's word and construed it into a commission to shed the innocent blood of his creatures." Pennington summarized, "The depravity of the human heart is often seen in men's fondness for theory to justify their sins." Pennington dismantled proslavery arguments construing scripture as authorizing the oppression of Black people and critiqued the ministry and professors who formulated such ideas to justify oppression. Pennington understood how knowledge was weaponized for political and economic gain. In a chapter on complexion, Pennington engaged the racist theorists Hanneman, who claimed that Black complexions were a curse, and Meekel, who said that one's complexion reflected the color of one's brain. Pennington responded that their "reasoning, or rather guessing, has been an issue of foolery." He also chided Benjamin Rush's notion that complexion was a result of a hereditary disease that could be cured with acid. Environment and climate, Pennington asserted "without hesitation," explained the color of one's skin, and he cited works to support his argument. Not only was this a debate over ideas, but environmentalism was logical and convincing for Pennington. He quipped, "I would far sooner be a black man with common sense, than a white man with a head full of nonsense."

Pennington's arguments went further than critique. In responding to the question of African inferiority, he asserted, "My position is that the notion of inferiority is not only false, but absurd, and therefore ought to be abandoned." In the very act of writing his book, Pennington observed, "I am to be understood as disputing the idea of our inferiority by a direct effort of my own reasoning powers." He proceeded to give an overview of African history, what he termed "facts and incidents from the history of our intellect." Recounting the historical significance of African civilizations from antiquity, Pennington traced the origins of science and the arts to Egypt and Ethiopia, signaling that the origins of human civilization emanated from Africa and African people. "The arts and sciences had their origin with our ancestors, and from them have flown forth to the world. They gave them to Greece, Greece to Rome, and Rome to others." He also proved that "Egyptians were black people," cementing the argument of African contributions to knowledge. He also listed people of African descent who distinguished themselves intellectually during the era of slavery. He summarized, "God is not only the all glorious author, then, of the black man's mind as well as of that of the white man, but he has produced it in the *same way identically*." There was no order of human beings based on inferiority, only one human species whose individual intellects were divinely inspired and could be cultivated the same way for everyone. Pennington's use of "our" when referring to intellect and ancestors is an indication of his situating himself among Africans of the world and his desire for collective liberation. Pennington's argument fused theology, morality, philosophy, history, and science together to produce a significant argument for Black life and history as well as human equality and against the vogue of academic scientific racism. For Pennington, the imperative of abolition necessarily followed. He did not mince words, insisting that it was necessary to "discharge the Africans" and "compensate them for false enslavement." He paired Black freedom with compensation for the crime of slavery.[57]

Pennington's book is a significant text of Black Studies and Black intellectual history. Not only did it refute contemporary academic thought, scientific racism, but it struck at the very intellectual foundation of American colleges. It was a sustained treatise that centered Black humanity and history, ideas and traditions that were anathema to the colleges, their intellectual traditions, and their symbiotic relationship with the political economy of slaving. It represented an alternative philosophy of history and theory of the modern world. Relegated to the boundaries of higher learning by white American intellectuals and their traditions, Pennington represented a Black radical epistemology and was part of an alternative intellectual tradition that was subversive to the academy and the slavocracy.[58] That he proposed his book to be used by families and students is of tremendous significance, as he hoped that it would produce an understanding of Black history and humanity for Black people. In turn, that knowledge and shared history would inform their work in fighting to realize a different world. Pennington's work reveals how Black social movements created knowledge, and, significantly, how this knowledge came from Black people in the community and not the academy. He understood how scholars weaponized knowledge to oppress and refuted their ideas with force. By drawing on African history, Pennington made an early contribution to a long history of Black Studies and its challenge to academia in the West. The works of Pennington represent a significant force of abolitionist dissent and Black thought. They gave meaning to Black higher learning as an idea and harbinger of freedom. He created knowledge for liberation.

Pennington's intellectual work was recognized overseas. In December 1849, he was bestowed an honorary degree of doctor of divinity from the University of Heidelberg, which was recognition of Pennington's work as an intellectual and minister. The conferral of a doctoral degree on Pennington was a further refutation of racism in American colleges and the exclusion of Black people from them. Pennington argued that the degree was not for himself but for Black people as a whole and ultimately a tool for abolition. He wrote,

It is proper to notice this as the first instance in which this method of encouraging Sacred Literature has been applied to my people. For although
I am informed, that the degree was conferred, "with full cognizance of
my writings, personal character, and merits," yet I know I am only to be
regarded as receiving it in trust for my People, and as an encouragement
to the Sons of Ham to rise with others in the acquisition of learning: in
this view I accept of it in behalf of the Negro Race throughout the world,
and especially in America, where we are, at this moment, passing through
a crisis, and maintaining a conflict of the most fearful character, where
our opponents are attempting to doom us to eternal bondage upon Biblical authority.

Throughout Pennington's steadfast pursuit of learning, he participated in the abolition movement as a minister, agitator, writer, and
lecturer. In his autobiography, Pennington explained the tremendous
significance of education in his life. He lamented that the most griev-
ous sin slaveholders committed was preventing enslaved people from
learning. His life's work was dedicated not only to his own intellectual
improvement but also to that of his countless students. Pennington was
a teacher and taught in Black schools in Long Island, New Haven, and
Hartford. He worked to ensure that other Black people did not have his
experience of growing up without education.[59] Never officially attending an institution of higher learning, Pennington was among the most
academically accomplished of the Black student abolitionists. Defined
by the social structure as a fugitive slave, Pennington was a student, a
scholar, and a teacher. He fought institutional racism and refuted the
racist ideas that emerged from universities in the antebellum period. In
his writings and teachings, he helped to provide tools for education for
his people.

Like Pennington, Garnet escaped slavery and sought higher learning,
but his journey differed from Pennington's. At age nine, Garnet escaped
with his family, fleeing successively from Maryland, Wilmington, Delaware, and New Hope, Pennsylvania, finally arriving in New York City,
where he became a beneficiary of Black institutions, attending the African Free School, receiving private tutoring, and becoming a mentee of
Theodore Wright.[60] Wright's influence propelled Garnet to a career in
the ministry, and he pursued college education.

In 1835, Garnet's career as a student continued in Canaan, New Hampshire. After attending Black institutions in New York City, Garnet, along with fellow Black classmates Alexander Crummell, Thomas S. Sidney, Thomas Paul Jr., and Julia Williams, attended Noyes Academy, an institution founded on abolitionist principles. The Black students soon endured racist violence as a mob attacked and eventually destroyed the school.[61] The actions of Garnet and others at Noyes were putting abolition into practice, and the attack laid bare the virulent racism embedded in New England communities. The contingent of Black students went on to study instead at Oneida Institute, an abolitionist institution open to Black students. At Oneida, Garnet became fully immersed in abolition and was part of a community of Black and white students dedicated to the movement. From 1833 to 1843, Oneida Institute admitted the largest number of Black students over that span of any institution and represented the nexus of abolition as institutional policy and foundational to the curriculum.[62] During seasonal vacations, Garnet lectured and recited antislavery poems at the Phoenix Society in New York City. He also helped found, along with Sidney and others, the Colored Young Men's Society in New York City, which aimed to flood the state legislature with petitions demanding Black suffrage. Along with Crummell, he spoke on August 1, 1838, in Utica to commemorate emancipation in the British West Indies. A year later, Garnet spoke at a similar event in Troy, New York. He was still a student when he delivered the speech, and it is the earliest surviving document of Garnet's writings. While cultivating a literary education was personally satisfying for Garnet, he emphasized the greater importance of Emancipation Day. "However sweet the music of the streams that murmur through the academic groves, may seem to be, yet far sweeter are the anthems of freedom. It is the distant voices of freeborn souls that have brought me hither." Garnet evoked the role of ancestors in his life who shaped who he was. He went on to give a brief history of the historic occasion and chided those who claimed that economic ruin and violence would follow emancipation.[63]

The height of Garnet's student abolitionist career came in 1840, when he delivered a lecture at the annual meeting of the American Antislavery Society. His address was an emphatic call for Black citizenship. Drawing on the role of Black soldiers in the American Revolution and the War of 1812, the centrality of enslaved labor in forming the bedrock of the US economy, and the establishment of Black religious institutions, Garnet asserted plainly and with force, "We claim the right of American citizenship." Garnet highlighted as well that enslaved people provided the financial capital for sons of slaveholders to attend college. Enslaved people "contributed greatly in supporting the science and literature of the South. For poor Tom and Dick are sold far away, in order that my young lord Frederick William may be sent to college."[64] Garnet's address situated him as a young agitator in abolition. Significantly, he was among the Black thinkers who identified and critiqued slavery's direct connections to colleges and other American institutions. Garnet's critique of higher learning also extended to restrictions on Black admissions as he led other Oneida students in protesting the exclusion of Crummell at General Theological Seminary and demanded equality in theological training. Garnet became active in the movement as a student, demanding political rights and citizenship for African Americans, lecturing in literary societies, and participating in Emancipation Day commemorations. He drew on the British example to bolster the cause of abolition in the United States, crafting an international argument for emancipation.[65] Garnet represented a rising generation of Black abolitionists who cut their teeth on agitation as young students pursuing higher learning and who crafted original critiques of American colleges for their complicity in the slaving economy.

The resistance of enslaved people was central to the advent and evolution of abolition and Black thought as dissenting forces in higher learning. The African-influenced cultural practices and cosmology of enslaved people represent the presence of a subversive, Black epistemology on the boundaries of the early academy. The culture enslaved people produced helped to explain why some enslaved people fought to escape college slavery. Collectively, the fugitive slaves— women, men, and children who fled college slavery—were agents of abolition, their actions evidence of their freedom knowledge. By the early 1830s, fugitive slaves also sought higher learning, helping to fuel the growth of student abolitionism. By resisting slavery and actively seeking higher learning, both within and on the boundaries of institutions, they became Black intellectuals who harnessed their skills and knowledge in service to the movement. They became part of a generation of Black thinkers who crafted arguments condemning slavery and racism but also made original arguments for Black higher learning. In academic spaces conspicuously defined by white patriarchal supremacy, former slaves redefined who could be a college student, and redefined the contours of academic thought. Basfield's desire for learning facilitated his manumission, and he became a minister who aided fugitive slaves in Canada. Among other achievements, Pennington crafted an original rebuttal of scientific racism, which was intimately tied to the academy, and wrote a history of Black people, connecting them to Africa and Kemet so Black people could know themselves and their ancestors. Garnet critiqued the grip slaveholders had financially and ideologically on colleges as well as championed the right of enslaved people to overthrow slavery. By grounding themselves in the study of African people and the problems they faced, and working to create a new humanity, Basfield, Pennington, and Garnet were shaped by African cultural groundings in community. They fought for the collective liberation of Black people. As Sterling Stuckey observed, even without direct acknowledgment, the actions of Black intellectuals in the antebellum period bore the markings of African cultural influences.[66] While serious engagement with African cultural and spiritual forms eluded many Black intellectuals in the antebellum United States, they used what was available to them—Christianity, notions of rights, etc.—and molded them to the needs of Black people. African cultural forms, however, remained prominent among the African majority in the United States: enslaved people. The arguments from fugitive slave student abolitionists helped define the meaning of Black freedom ideology and of abolitionist dissent and Black thought at colleges. Their work in the movement showed that they used their education to advance the freedom of all Black people. Slave culture, slave resistance, and Black freedom knowledge were subversive intellectual and social forces within and on the boundaries of American colleges. They represent a historical iteration of Black Studies encountering academia. They helped provide the substance of the meaning of Black higher learning as a tool for liberation.

4

The White Abolitionist Insurgency

On June 26, 1833, white students at Amherst College prepared for an important debate. They discussed whether "colonization or anti-slavery" merited their support. After discussing the topic over multiple meetings, ultimately a large majority of students favored colonization. The period in between meetings was pivotal. Students attended a July Fourth colonizationist sermon after which they immediately formed the Amherst College and Amherst Colonization Society. The society announced its auxiliary status to the Hampshire County Colonization Society, led by Amherst faculty. Officers of the society were students, including Henry Ward Beecher as treasurer. Amherst professor Samuel Worcester was president and local lawyer and future Amherst College treasurer, Edward Dickinson, was secretary. After an initial donation of $11.25 from students, the organ's donations swelled to seventy dollars by the end of July.[1] As chapter 2 illustrates, the colonization movement was well represented at Amherst College. It was not until 1833, however, that an organization was formed on campus in conjunction with the local community. The college colonization society helped shape the outcome of the student debate, but another crucial development unfolded as well. On July 19, eight students established an antislavery society as an auxiliary to the New England Anti-Slavery Society (NEASS). Rejecting colonization, the group advocated immediate emancipation and racial equality.[2] The formation of the student antislavery society was a significant development in the summer of 1833. It challenged the colonizationist consensus at the college and represented a new phase of student politics on campus, one that produced a radical student movement for Black freedom.

In the 1830s, the abolition movement entered a new phase, and Black and white college students were integral to its evolution. By the time Amherst student abolitionists organized in July 1833, two other student antislavery societies had been established elsewhere. White students at

Western Reserve College organized in October 1832 and, by the following January, so too did students at Andover Theological Seminary (ATS).
Other student organizations emerged in July 1833 as well at the Oneida
Institute, Waterville (Colby) College, and Bowdoin College.[3] This chapter examines the emergence and proliferation of student antislavery
societies in the 1830s. At a time when the abolition movement was ex-
panding, colleges and seminaries became important battlegrounds over
abolition, colonization, and slavery. Abolitionist leaders recognized the
potential students had as promoters of the movement at institutions
dominated by the ACS. In turn, students engaged the new abolitionist
literature such as *The Liberator* and Garrison's *Thoughts on Colonization*,
both of which had Black antecedents, and debated the merits of colonization and abolition. As a result, students from Maine to Ohio converted
to abolition and established their own organizations. Their activism
precipitated ideological confrontations with colonizationist faculty who
sought to suppress their agitation, which they deemed fanatical and detrimental to the academy. The reactionary backlash student abolitionism elicited helped merge the question of civil liberties with abolitionist
protest. Many faculty perceived abolition simply as anathema, as it undermined colonization as well as institutional ties to proslavery donors.
In other words, abolition represented a radical challenge to college authorities and the very ideological and financial foundations on which
the institutions rested. At stake was nothing less than the very meaning
of colleges, their function, and the role of students in society. The student debates over abolition and colonization helped reveal the failure of
the ACS in initiating emancipation in any significant way and further
exposed its racism. Student abolitionists represented crucial challenges
in proximity to the ACS in higher learning.

College and seminary students were an important demographic that
underpinned abolitionist organizations like the NEASS and the American Antislavery Society (AASS). They participated in national meetings
and helped develop organizational platforms. Students also authored
their own treatises explaining their positions against the onslaught of
colonizationist and proslavery backlash to their agitation. They signed
antislavery petitions in the famous campaigns of the mid-1830s led
largely by women. Widespread student participation in early second-
wave abolition provides a new look at the abolitionist constituency and

explains how the movement expanded. Student abolitionists were significant members of the antislavery bulwark that emerged in the 1830s. Students themselves became radicalized through studying abolitionist ideology. As they organized on campus, students confronted the limitations of colleges in fostering abolitionist activity, namely because of the intransigence of faculty and presidents who controlled the colleges and their ideological and epistemic orientations. The advent of widespread student abolition in the 1830s reveals the tensions between radical dissent and institutional power at colleges. It ultimately reveals the limitations of working within institutions inextricably intertwined with systems of oppression to realize Black liberation.

Through their agitation, white student abolitionists of the 1830s joined the field of activism cultivated by Black student abolitionists in the 1820s and fugitive slaves and further manifested the utility of college education for promoting Black freedom and human equality. Black and white student abolitionists of the 1830s also marked an evolution in the idea of student involvement in antislavery that Phillis Wheatley and Peter Peckard conceptualized in the 1780s. By forming their own antislavery societies and helping to build a mass movement, Black and white student abolitionists became important grassroots agitators whose actions had transnational reverberations.

This chapter will trace the development of student abolition in the early 1830s from the initial stirrings at a series of institutions from Maine to Ohio. The widespread nature of student antislavery from 1832 to the summer of 1833 demonstrates that students from Lane Seminary were not atypical in their abolitionism and indeed students elsewhere organized antislavery societies prior to the tumultuous Lane controversy in 1834–1835. The Lane story should be seen as a culmination of early student abolitionist agitation, not its beginning. Rather than examine one college or seminary exclusively, this chapter will examine the impact of the movement at multiple northern colleges and analyze the activities of student contributions to abolition.[4] In fact, the student antislavery origins of the Lane Debates and subsequent establishment of Oberlin College cannot be fully understood without the broader context of student abolitionism that preceded them both. The Lane story, however, is indeed significant. The student rebellion elicited a national debate over students' role in the slavery controversy. In the wake of the Lane Debates, faculty elsewhere aimed to prevent similar controversies over abolition at their own institutions. It had a very different impact on students. The Lane Controversy inspired and emboldened students to organize, and they cited civil liberties to defend their work. As large numbers of students began participating in abolition, they converted their campuses into sites of protest for Black liberation. As white agitators, they were inspired by a movement created by Black people and contributed to Black abolitionists' conceptualization of college education as facilitating Black freedom and equality. For the first time in US history, an organized student movement supporting Black freedom had emerged.

The history of student antislavery societies in the 1830s marked a crucial development in student abolitionism. White students in large droves joined the ranks of a radical movement. Simultaneously, Black students were increasingly barred from colleges. The crucial gains of Black students in the 1820s were met with reactionary white violence towards Black education across northern states. In some cases, a select few Black students enrolled at colleges, the focus of subsequent chapters. These developments, white student antislavery societies and Black struggles for higher learning, in some cases converged, but they mostly unfolded in parallel to one another. Both forces were part and parcel of abolitionist dissent at colleges. While some white student abolitionists included Black educational equality in their abolitionist positions, many did not make direct appeals for their own institutions to admit Black students. And institutions themselves did not adopt ideas coming out of the movement. This marks a crucial distinction from student abolition at places like Amherst and colleges like Oneida Institute and Oberlin that admitted Black students. In fact, it was difficult for student abolitionism to even exist at places like Amherst because of the entrenchment of colonization on campus. The fact that student abolitionists did not transform colleges into centers of racial egalitarianism was not a failure of student protest and abolition more generally but rather explains the intransigence of a culture of white supremacy at most colleges in the antebellum period. The context in which students engaged questions of abolition helps explain the emergence of their protests.

The transformation of the abolition movement and the religious culture of the Second Great Awakening provided important fodder for student engagement with abolitionist ideology. When white evangelicals came to support abolition through their religious conversions, they joined an already existing movement.[5] The religious grounding for evangelical abolitionists was the immediate repudiation of all sin. Christians, they believed, had to individually repent from sin and also remedy sinfulness in society. This led some white evangelicals to abolition, for they saw in slavery a series of grave sins plaguing society. Evangelical revivalism was widespread at colleges and helped prepare students for the ministry.[6] While the religious revivals of the 1810s led students to the ACS, evangelical revivalism in the early 1830s helped bring a new generation of students to abolition.

The rise of antebellum abolition was a result of the coalescence of Black and white agitation that rejected colonization and demanded Black freedom via immediate emancipation and Black rights. The precedents set by slave rebellions, Black abolitionist newspapers and pamphlets such as *Freedom's Journal*, the short-lived *Rights for All*, and David Walker's *Appeal* provided the ideological foundations for the immediatist turn. Within this context emerged William Lloyd Garrison, who came to promote abolition through conversations with Black abolitionists. The publication of his newspaper *The Liberator* was the product of this Black protest context, and few abolitionist newspapers rivaled its significance. Garrison became a prominent figure, and his *Thoughts on Colonization* was one of his significant contributions. It converted new members to the movement. The evangelical context of contemporary religious life and the transformation of abolition led students to engage and assess abolitionist arguments alongside colonization. For many students, this engagement came in their literary societies, which were spaces where they engaged political and social questions of the day. They held debates, which provided students a more expansive education beyond the classroom.[7] It was often in this extracurricular context that students engaged the concept of immediate emancipation and Black rights. As previous chapters have shown, abolition and Black thought were external to the college and emerged as dissenting forces therein as a result of free and enslaved Black people's actions and ideology. In the early 1830s, white students expanded the dissenting movement's insurgency on campus. White students first organized around this idea in the fall of 1832 in Hudson, Ohio.

Student Abolition Emergent

The first college controversy over immediatism and colonization was at Western Reserve College. Like other colleges in the 1820s, Western Reserve students and faculty were colonizationists. Professor and college president Charles B. Storrs was a leader in the local colonization society. A student group donated forty dollars to the ACS late in 1831.[8] But abolitionist arguments began circulating on campus in February 1831. After the winter recess Isaac Bigelow, a student from Massachusetts, returned to campus and brought with him copies of Garrison's *Liberator*, which had first been published a month earlier. Bigelow shared the newspaper with other students and Storrs. By the summer of 1832, Storrs, along with professor of mathematics and natural philosophy Elizur Wright Jr. and professor of sacred literature Beriah Green, had converted to abolition.[9]

Wright published a series of essays in the local newspaper lauding Garrison's arguments. Wright argued that slavery was sinful and thus required eradication immediately as Christians do not gradually stop sinning; they do so immediately. Wright emphasized the positive effects immediate abolition would have on society, such as eliminating the possibility of slave rebellions. If emancipated, African Americans would not seek vengeance on their oppressors, he argued, but rather would welcome freedom with gratitude. The continuation of slavery held greater risks. There were multiple historical examples, Wright explained, of the oppressed "rising in terrible vengeance upon their oppressors," such as "St. Domingo, and our own revolution." For Wright, unlike college colonizationists, immediatism and Black rights were the solution to the threat of slave rebellions, not the removal of Black people from the polity. Wright also cited the "swelling lists of runaways in the southern papers" as more reason to support abolition. Enslaved people's resistance to bondage and demands for freedom moved Wright to adopt abolition. He also condemned slaveholders' unmitigated sexual exploitation of enslaved women. "The moral character of the whites is rapidly deteriorating," he reasoned, as the enslaved population grows and "a large proportion are the illegitimate offspring of WHITE fathers!" Wright unveiled the hypocrisy of anti-abolitionist arguments citing racial mixing as detrimental to whites when slaveholders conspicuously raped Black women. These sins had to end immediately, Wright reasoned, and neither gradualism nor colonization were adequate responses. Wright's early arguments promoting abolition were molded by slave resistance and Black women's rights to their bodily autonomy.[10]

Wright's abolitionist essays denouncing colonization continued into December 1832. In response, the editor, Warren Isham, who was a colonizationist, refused to print them. Isham felt the pressure of the local community, and trustees of the college, who were also colonizationists, owned the newspaper. Wright's abolitionism began to alarm college officials.[11] His essays spread abolition on the Western Reserve and provided the basis for his influential tract, *The Sin of Slavery and Its Remedy*. He wrote to Garrison, revealing that his *Thoughts on Colonization* propelled his conversion to abolition and describing the efforts of colonizationists to shun his writings.[12] He was among the earliest scholars in the United States to endorse immediate emancipation, and his arguments were an intellectual thrust for abolition.

As Wright penned abolitionist essays in the local paper, Green facilitated the discussion of abolition in his teaching. The controversy in the community between Wright and colonizationists inspired students to assess the arguments of abolition and colonization. Students themselves proposed a debate, which they held in October or early November as part of the college course. They had formed an abolition society in October 1832 and students like Bigelow had already been reading *The Liberator*. A letter from the college, likely from a student, appeared in Garrison's paper, where the author volunteered to become an agent for the paper in Ohio and asked Garrison to send more abolitionist publications. Green observed the discussion "arose in the regular disputations of the college." After students proposed the debate, Green readily obliged them. His account suggests that many still backed colonization. "I was not a little alarmed, not to say shocked with the ground, which was assumed to maintain the doctrine and defend the designs of this society," Green wrote in reference to the ACS. Student colonizationists sympathized with slaveholders and absolved them from blame for inheriting slavery. But central to students' pro-colonization argument was racist ideology. These students insisted "that against the colored Americans, a *prejudice*, arising from his complexion, was universally cherished, as effective and invincible, as a *constitutional tendency*, which must forever exclude him from the affectionate regard, and withhold from him the

rights and privileges, of his white neighbors." For these student colonizationists, Black people could never be equal to whites, an inherently racist
claim and longstanding argument of college colonizationists. Green then
highlighted a central flaw of their thinking. Colonizationists acknowledged the pernicious effects of racism in society, but instead of working
to eliminate it, Green observed, they were "yielding to its giant power,
and adapting their plans to the satisfying of its exorbitant demands."[13]
By embracing racist thought, the students believed they were helping
Black people. Instead, they were complicit in sustaining and advancing
an ideology that underpinned the slave system and nominal freedom of
northern Black communities.

Even though some students extolled colonization during the debate,
others favored abolition. In a letter to the abolitionist Simeon Jocelyn,
Green reported, "A good deal of interest has been awakened in the College among the students, on the subject of African emancipation. The
matter has . . . been pretty thoroughly discussed. A number of students
take the ground maintained by the New England Anti-Slavery Society."
Green hoped the number of student abolitionists would increase. By November 1832, students at the college were divided over abolition and colonization, and each group had its own college society. Green mentioned
that faculty and students had a copy of Garrison's *Thoughts on Colonization*, a few issues of *The Liberator*, and a publication from the British
abolitionist Charles Stuart, as well as records, speeches, and the official
journal of the ACS, the same combination of documents Lane students
would use in their debates two years later.[14] After witnessing the arguments from student colonizationists, Green began lecturing on abolition.

Over the course of four weeks, Green preached a series of abolition sermons in the college chapel. They offered a guide to abolitionist agitation for students. They also represent an intellectual rebuke of
colonizationist and proslavery arguments of scholars in northern and
southern colleges.[15] Green chided colonizationists for proffering a gradualist approach to ending slavery on grounds of expediency, which was
tantamount to appeasing slaving. For Green, expediency was compro-
mising with sin. Green quipped, let colonizationists go into the South
and preach gradualism to enslaved people who suffered daily. Green
condemned "the loathsome crime of slave-holding," as slaveholders bla-
tantly disregarded family relations and subverted "the bonds of wedded

life." Green observed, "The enslaved husband sees his wife daily exposed to the violence and pollution of unbridled lust and unchecked licentiousness!" Echoing Wright, Green condemned the sexual exploitation of enslaved women and supported their rights and marriages. In addition to such violence, the slaveholding interest sought to strengthen the institution by withholding from the slave the "knowledge of his rights." The injustices extended to free African Americans, Green argued, who were "subject to gross contempt and shocking abuse." The philanthropist, Green believed, was required to fix the evils of slavery and prejudice. Green used the phrase "human rights" in comparing biblical figures fighting injustices and abolitionists fighting racial prejudice; both acted in favor of God's law. He cautioned students that a reformer's appeal to principle rather than expediency would be met with ridicule but reassured them that God and justice were on their side.[16]

Green further attacked the racist logic of colonization and slaveholding. He criticized the colonizationist Yale professor Benjamin Silliman, who argued that the British were to blame for introducing slavery into the colonies, appeasing the current slaving regime. Green believed that notion was filled with "absurdity and impiety." "Let the slaveholder know," Green asserted, "Heaven will one day teach him, that he is more deeply guilty than his predecessors in the crime."[17] He further chided colonizationists for arguing that abolition would be worse in its effect than perpetuating slavery. Green quoted the ACS leader Gurley's remarks: "We wish it to be distinctly understood, that we consider slavery to be an evil, which cannot without producing evils greater than itself, be abolished, except by cautious, deliberate, and gradual measures." Colonizationists mollified slaveholders with anti-abolitionist arguments. In the colonizationist plan, Gurley argued, "the rights and interests of all parties" must be taken into consideration. Green exposed colonization for sympathizing with slaveholders and proposing a plan for emancipation that would cause the least harm to the very perpetrators of the crime. Because of these arguments, Green observed, colonizationists like Gurley were nothing more than slaveholding apologists.[18]

Green's sermons reveal a theological philosophy of abolitionist dissent. He exposed the flaws and prejudices of the colonizationist program and the hypocrisy and sin of slaveholding. Green demonstrated how, in effect, colonization resulted in complicity with slavery. In this light, Green's sermons were a lesson in political and social protest and encouraged students to never compromise on the established principles of human equality. Green observed, "The mind, in the first place, acts upon human rights and interests, unawed—free from embarrassing constraint." While the logic and force of Green's arguments would naturally lead students to support abolition, his intent was not to force ideas on them; he was not dogmatic. Rather, he revealed the pervasiveness of racism in society, pushing students to consider their roles in either perpetuating or counteracting it.[19] Green's 1832 sermons built on the British abolitionist Peter Peckard's arguments from the 1780s. As dissenting scholars, Green and Peckard believed in educating students on moral and political issues related to human equality and abolition. In effect, Green continued the example set by Phillis Wheatley and Peckard, who envisioned students becoming involved in abolition. Green's lectures also represented an epistemological challenge to the white-washed knowledge fostered in colleges. Abolitionist dissent in this case was being taught on campus, a significant development in higher learning. By the end of 1832, Western Reserve College had a strong abolitionist presence due to professors and students.

Green's sermons and Wright's essays had a formative impact on students. Students sent a letter to the local paper, signed "Abolition Friends," revealing their affinity with the movement. They believed that the "letter and the spirit of the Bible condemn slave holding in all its forms" and that no man-made law or "constitution of government" should be followed that contradicts God's law. For these students the US Constitution was illegitimate for supporting slavery. They also asserted, "All men in the United States, of whatever color, have naturally, and by the laws of God, the same right to our civil and religious privileges." Revealing their knowledge of emancipation in other countries, they admonished slaveholders and politicians for not abolishing slavery. "The results of emancipation in St. Domingo, and Mexico, take away all excuse for slaveholding in our nation," the students argued.[20] In December, Wright informed Theodore Weld that "more than 20 of the students may be reckoned thorough abolitionists." Concerned local colonizationists wrote of the developments at the college to Gurley: "A large portion of the students . . . have become, 'all of a sudden,' thorough-going *Abolitionists*." In December, students, along with Green and Wright, established the Western Reserve College Anti-Slavery Society. While they believed in enacting emancipation without violence, the society resolved that enslaved people "have an hundred fold more provocation to rise in arms, than our Fathers had in 1776." They condemned racism and colonization and promoted immediatism, the slave's right to rebel, and Black rights. Garrison printed a copy of the college society's constitution. After Wright was shunned in the local press, he wrote to Garrison, who published his letters reporting on the developments at the college and local community. Garrison praised the efforts of Wright, Green, and the students for joining the movement and denounced their censure by the local press and trustees.[21]

But this insurgency was soon challenged. The abolitionists at Western Reverse College were met with a white backlash from local colonizationists, including the board of trustees. Green was "urged to desist immediately" because of his abolitionist activity. Concerned locals condemned Green for "offering philosophy and politics" in the college chapel. College trustees led by David Hudson said that Green's abolitionist arguments were "known to be adverse to the feelings of a large majority of the Trustees, and [are] calling forth expressions of dissatisfaction from the parents of students in College, and from the friends of the Institution in every part of the Reserve."[22] In their eyes, abolition posed a threat to the political and social relations of society. Fearful of losing benefactors, students, and support from the community, the colonizationist trustees met to discuss the respective futures of Green and Wright. They believed that they were neglecting their duties as professors for lecturing and writing on abolition. Storrs, however, backed Green and Wright, and he lectured on abolition locally as well. The controversy that arose at the college threw into question the very utility of the college in society and whether individuals in academia could be involved in social movements for Black freedom. Of course, colonizationists condemned Green for bringing politics onto campus when they had been perfectly content with students and faculty supporting colonization prior to the abolitionist ascendance. Their claims that the college was being politicized therefore were hypocritical and were motivated by racism, as they disagreed with the fundamental tenets of abolition—Black freedom immediately and human equality. The example of student abolitionists and abolitionist scholars at Western Reserve demonstrates the potential and possibilities for using the campus as a space to study and organize around radical ideas. Student and faculty cooperation led to discussions that resulted in spurring participation in the movement. It also reveals the obstacles abolitionists faced from white reactionary forces within institutions and the local community. Abolition ideology and agitation were antithetical not only to colonization but also to the intellectual orientation of the college. The advent of abolition at Western Reserve was significant at the time. No other college students or faculty publicly advocated abolition or formed college abolition societies. Indeed, the abolition society at the college was one of the first white abolitionist organizations in the Old Northwest in the early 1830s.

The controversy continued into the summer of 1833. Storrs gave a long abolitionist address in May, which aggravated his health problems. He contracted tuberculosis and took a leave from his duties. He never returned to the college, as he died on September 15. The abolitionist press lauded Storrs as leader and christened him a martyr of the movement. John Greenleaf Whittier wrote a poem eulogizing him. Wright and Green knew that the trustees were attempting to force them out, and they planned for their futures. Green published his sermons early in the spring of 1833 and entertained an offer for the presidency of a college in western New York, the Oneida Institute. Wright traveled east in the spring and prepared for a public debate with colonizationists. By August of 1833, it was clear that Wright's and Green's days at the college were numbered. In one last jab at the colonizationists, Wright organized a parody of the controversy over abolition at commencement. Students lampooned colonizationists and their arguments. To top it all off, Wright invited George B. Vashon, the Black abolitionist from Pittsburgh, to join the festivities. They attended commencement and adorned the platform together. The day after commencement, Wright submitted his resignation. All three abolitionist scholars had left the college by the fall of 1833. Colonizationist trustees and other locals claimed victory for their departures, reporting that they had prevented the college from becoming "a Seminary for educating Abolition Missionaries."[23] Abolition, however, was not completely extinguished from the college. Sixty-three students petitioned college officials to continue discussing abolition as a matter of free discussion. Tutor Ralph Walker, along with the students, kept abolition alive. At least six student abolitionists withdrew and enrolled at the newly established Oberlin Institute. Student abolitionism from Western Reserve was thus part of Oberlin's early history and shaped its reputation.[24] The departure of abolitionists from the college took its toll, but the trustees could not fully suppress abolitionist dissent there.

The rise of abolition at Western Reserve College spurred the conversion of someone who would become a pivotal leader in the movement. Theodore Weld visited Hudson in the fall of 1832 at the height of the abolitionist fervor at the college. His conversations with Green, Wright, and Storrs resulted in his conversion to abolition. "Since I saw you my soul has been in travail upon that subject," Weld wrote to Wright, and proclaimed, "Abolition *immediate universal* is my desire and prayer to God." Weld was determined to act on his beliefs, for he believed that "*Faith without WORKS is dead.*"[25] Weld was a student at Oneida Institute when he met Wright, and he played a role in getting Beriah Green to join Oneida. Green resigned from Western Reserve in June 1833 and arrived in Whitesboro in August. Green accepted the position under the stipulation that the college allow the admission of Black students.[26] Green sought to implement his vision, outlined in his sermons, in providing young men an activist education in abolitionist ideology. Green's leadership would fundamentally transform Oneida into an abolitionist college. By the time he arrived in Whitesboro, however, the seeds of abolition had already been sown by students.

Founded in 1827, the Oneida Institute in Whitesboro, New York, was the product of the evangelical revivalism of Charles Grandison Finney and the manual-labor vision of George Washington Gale. The manual-labor model of education paired classical education with a regimen of physical work, which typically sustained the operation of the institution. The labor regimen allowed poor students to enroll at places like Oneida as the program deferred costs for their education and was a mode of physical exercise. Other institutions such as Amherst and Andover Theological Seminary adopted voluntary manual-labor programs. At Oneida, it was a requirement.[27] Among the first students to enroll at Oneida was Weld, who led the organization for the Promotion of Manual Labor in Literary Institutions. Oneida students had a millennial vision. They labored and trained for the ministry and became involved in temperance, missions, and other reform activities.[28] It was not until the summer of 1833, however, that students took up the question of abolition.

The abolitionist press reported the organization of a student antislavery society at Oneida in early August. How students formed the society, however, is not well known.[29] On a summer day in June, students were tasked with shoveling gravel for the maintenance of a county road in lieu of paying a road tax. As the teams hauling gravel were few and far between and idleness was frowned upon under the manual-labor system, students decided to fill the time by organizing a debate. The question proposed was "the right of the slaves to receive their freedom without going to Africa." Students derisively asked who would argue the affirmative position. One student who had read issues of *The Liberator* and the first report of the NEAS agreed to argue the immediatist position. The student was Hiram Foote. Enslaved people had a right to immediate freedom, Foote reasoned. Denouncing colonization, he added, "Nor have we any right to compel him to cross the ocean to find liberty." Foote met counterarguments asserting the supposed dangers that would follow emancipation by providing historical evidence. He cited examples of emancipation without a so-called race war in Mexico, Guadeloupe, and also Haiti prior to French attempts to reenslave freed people. Since they had not finished the discussion before resuming their work, Foote told students that his arguments could be found in abolitionist publications. That night, one participant recalled, students filled the Oneida library and read through issues of *The Liberator*. The event was remembered as the "Gravel Debate."[30] The result was the formation of a student antislavery society in July, consisting of thirty-five students, most of whom converted from colonization. "The presentation of truth" of abolition had a tremendous impact on students. A student writing to the *Emancipator* believed that similar results would be replicated if people weighed the merits of the respective arguments. In contrast, a colonization society was formed as well. It survived for a time, but by the following March, the society had disbanded. The constitution of the student antislavery society mirrored that of NEAS. The Gravel Debate produced the first official abolition society of the second wave in New York, and it was a student organization.[31] When Green arrived at Oneida, abolition was ascendant, and he fueled its flame.

What brought Green to Oneida, however, spurred a handful of students to follow Weld to Lane Seminary. By 1832, Weld was targeting Lane as the center of his manual-labor, evangelical mission in the West. Weld and other students believed that Oneida had lost its religious zeal under Gale's leadership. Gale subsequently left Oneida and continued his career in Illinois. These factors pulled Weld and his followers west. After his visit with, and conversion by, the abolitionist scholars at Western Reserve, his evangelical mission became inseparable from abolition.

The student abolitionist origins of the Lane Controversy and the establishment of Oberlin College are rooted in the histories of abolition at Oneida Institute and Western Reserve College. Oneida students followed Weld, who had become their leader, and were determined to spread abolition in the West.[32] Some of the students had already finished at Oneida when they left for Lane. For example, Sereno W. Streeter left in 1830, enrolled at Lane in 1833, and participated in the Lane Debates. By 1834, twenty-four Oneida students enrolled at Lane. As of November 1833, Hiram Foote and other students who participated in the Gravel Debate anchored the student antislavery society at Oneida. All twenty-four students who followed Weld subsequently participated in the Lane Debates.[33] In short, the abolitionist conversion of Oneida students and their subsequent enrollment at Lane in the fall of 1833 played a significant role in the Lane Controversy over abolition and, by extension, the rise of Oberlin College as an abolitionist outpost.[34] The broader context of student antislavery mobilization was filled with potential for the movement.

While Weld and students prepared for the debates at Lane, simultaneously, students in New England were having their own debates and organizing antislavery societies. Students at Andover Theological Seminary and Waterville, Amherst, and Bowdoin colleges, became enthralled with the immediatism question well before the events at Lane. A group of Waterville students corresponded with Garrison and accepted copies of *The Liberator* in November 1832. In May 1833, the same students supported political abolition as they affirmed the question, "Ought Congress to interfere in the abolition of slavery?" A month later in Waterville, Garrison addressed the students, which spurred the creation of a student antislavery society on July 4, 1833. The opening lines to their constitution revised the Declaration of Independence: "Believing that all men are born free and equal, and possess certain unalienable rights, among which are life, liberty, and the pursuit of happiness . . ." But they included a crucial abolitionist principle that "in no case consistently with reason, religion, and the immutable principles of justice, can man be the property of man." The student abolitionists asserted the principle of human equality and used it to condemn the chattel principle that underpinned American slavery. They resolved to abolish slavery and "obtain for them [African Americans] in this their native land, equal civil and political rights and privileges with the whites."[35] The students crafted a radical politics and established an organization for Black freedom in rural Maine. They reportedly celebrated July Fourth as abolitionists.

Controversy ensued soon after the emergence of student abolition at Waterville. The abolitionist celebrations were met with rebuke from college president Jeremiah Chaplin. The following day, he scolded students for their boisterous conduct, which he believed was unbecoming of future ministers in training. A week later, Chaplin gave a chapel address where he further reflected on the July Fourth celebration. "The manner in which you passed the evening has still left a painful impression on our minds," he told students. While never directly addressing abolition, Chaplin argued for restrained, chaste recognition of Independence Day, which was a veiled critique of students' support for abolition and their new organization. The reprimand continued as Chaplin maintained that a college education set them apart from the populace and their actions were beneath their station. He went further, and attacked students' character, explaining, "For you to pride yourselves on doing that which a boor, a savage, or a brute, may do as well as you, is truly contemptible." Then, in a refrain many college leaders would echo as students became involved in abolition, Chaplin assessed the impact such conduct would have on the college. He believed that it would diminish the college's reputation, lose its patrons, and reduce it to ruins.[36] Notably, Chaplin said nothing of organized abolition or Black rights, the substance of the celebration. Indeed, throughout the sermon, he described the student celebration as antithetical to religion, morality, and college education. He made no distinction between the students' alleged conduct and the cause they celebrated. In condemning the students' actions and refraining from mentioning abolition, Chaplin was likely trying to prevent any direct conflict over the issue and instead made the event about student conduct and religious impropriety.

Chaplin's admonition elicited a swift response from the students. Student abolitionists joined with other students at the college and demanded redress. They petitioned faculty, stating, "We feel that we were injured, individually and collectively," and that "our proceedings on the evening of the Fourth of July, were misrepresented." They singled out Chaplin's remarks as insulting. "The epithets which were applied to us were harsh severe and undeserved." They demanded an explanation. What began as a student celebration of organized abolition became a question of the students' character and their relationship to the president. Chaplin's condemnation produced a student backlash. They warned, "We think that the interest of the college requires that an explanation be made."[37]

The student petition divided the faculty, which consisted of Chaplin and three others. Two professors, Calvin Newton and George Washington Keely, sided with the students and opposed Chaplin and his ally, Thomas Jefferson Conant. Newton was an abolitionist, which explains his support for the students. Further exacerbating the division was Chaplin's resolve to expel individual students for their behavior. What followed was a dramatic change. Facing the student backlash, which Newton and Keely supported, Chaplin resigned his office, and Conant did as well. Chaplin refused to withdraw or qualify his critique of the student abolitionist celebration. In an attempt to save face, the trustees organized a committee to reconcile faculty differences but to no avail. Revealingly, the committee reported that if Chaplin and Conant returned, "most of the students would then leave."[38]

The root cause of the events that precipitated the resignation of the college president and a faculty member was the student abolitionist celebration. The summer of 1833 at Waterville College reveals the students' resolve to adhere to their abolitionist positions and their refusal to submit to Chaplin's attack on their character. It also illustrates the impact of student resistance to institutional power. Rather than protest through mass exodus from the college, students effectively forced Chaplin's resignation. In this case, student radicalism carved out space on campus to promote abolition. The event emboldened the Waterville students, and they continued their agitation for Black freedom.

While the Waterville controversy unfolded, students at Amherst and Andover began to promote abolition as well. In early 1833, a small band of Andover students formed an antislavery society. In January 1833, David T. Kimball Jr. represented the Andover Auxiliary Anti-Slavery Society at the first meeting of the New England Anti-Slavery Society. This group of

Andover students believed that slavery was a violation of humanity, morality, and religion. They asserted that "justice and humanity, requires the slaves should be immediately emancipated and restored to their natural rights and privileges." Colonization was inadequate, as they believed the ACS gave "security and permanency to the slave system" and therefore was "unworthy of support."[39] The emergence of student abolitionists at Andover signified dissent from within the colonizationist stronghold and a significant ideological challenge to the institutional consensus.[40]

Over the succeeding months in 1833, abolition spread on campus. Lewis F. Laine, the secretary of the student abolition society, corresponded with Arthur Tappan, the influential philanthropist who converted to abolition. Tappan lauded the students' efforts, writing, "Your Society may be eminently instrumental in dissipating prejudice, and pouring light upon the intellect of millions of our countrymen who are held in bondage."[41] Recognizing abolition's threat to the ACS, the student colonizationists responded with a letter requesting the view of the president of the seminary, Ebenezer Porter. Porter believed that immediate emancipation was impossible because only slaveholders could bring about emancipation. As much as he disliked slavery, Porter claimed, "I cannot hope to see its extinction till the measures requisite for such a result shall be taken by the masters themselves." He also condemned any attempt of enslaved people asserting their rights, deploying a familiar colonizationist argument against slave resistance. If enslaved people were set free, he explained in racist overtones, they would "live by plunder" and, "ripe for treason and violence, would organize an army of outlaws" to wreak havoc on whites. For Porter, emancipation would be worse than the continuation of slavery. Revealing to southern benefactors his decided opposition to abolition, Porter's reply to students was published widely and received approbation from southern newspapers while abolitionists rebuked Porter's position.[42] Despite the emergence of abolition at ATS and elsewhere, the president and the majority of students remained wedded to colonization. And yet, as one writer observed, the "abolitionists at Andover are driving the advocates of prejudice, gradualism, 'exile,' and slavery into close quarters."[43]

As Porter advocated colonization, the Andover student abolitionists published a forceful tract demanding abolition. Kimball and Laine sarcastically penned the "Apology for Anti-Slavery." Their arguments had offended the colonizationists, but they did not apologize for their abolitionism. They affirmed their society's status as an auxiliary to the NEAS, and their advocacy for "the enfranchisement and elevation of the colored people in all parts of the country" was an indication of their radicalism. Contrary to their detractors' claims, their work was as much needed in northern states as in the southern slaveholding ones. "We attack the spirit of slavery, which in reference to the colored people is to be found in every portion of our union," they argued. They cited the recent racist violence perpetrated by colonizationists against Prudence Crandall's school for Black girls in Connecticut as evidence and praised Black educational programs. They recognized that racism in the North was an appendage of slavery in the South, both of which had to be destroyed. Their solution was political antislavery measures. They provided an antislavery reading of the Constitution, believing that it upheld slavery in states where it existed but empowered Congress to abolish it in federally controlled territories, including Washington, DC. They also condemned the religious argument of proslavery apologists that encouraged enslaved people to be obedient to their owners. To the young aspiring ministers, this was heretical, for it only perpetuated the moral wrong and sin of slaving. They felt that it was their right to advocate abolition because every white American was implicated in sustaining slavery if they were not fighting to abolish it. They called on the church to condemn slavery. "We think slavery is an evil which the church, in its proper capacity, should weigh and discuss." The only religious denominations to officially and actively oppose slavery were Black churches. By 1833, none of the white-dominated sects had done so. The Presbytery synod offered opposition to slavery in 1818, but most religious bodies either sanctioned slavery or backed the ACS. In terms of religious argument, the student abolitionist tract marked a significant ideological shift among young white evangelicals. They believed that clergy should play a fundamental role in promoting abolition. They also adopted an argument for abolition in order to quell the possibility of slave rebellion. Like Green, abolition and Black rights were the solution to the possibility of rebellion, not colonization.

The most forceful aspect of the student abolitionist tract was their definition of immediate emancipation. They defined it as "the abolition, at once, of that which is morally wrong—wrong not merely in the abstract" but "in present and in all circumstances." Notably, they condemned all forms of slavery and did not include customary qualifications for slavery and criminal infractions. They demanded the removal "of every thing which, in the present condition of the slave, can be accounted oppression." They invoked the golden rule and stated plainly, "We shall place the negro on an equality with the white man." They also explained the specific rights they believed Black people should have:

> We desire to see changed whatever in the present system is morally wrong. We plead for the abrogation of the laws which regard the slave as property, and withhold from him the right of acquiring and transmitting property; for wresting the rod of oppression from the hands of an irresponsible master; for securing the inviolability of the marriage relation, for prohibiting the forcible separation of husbands and wives, of parents and children, for imparting to the negro the same rights and means of elevation and improvement granted to the white man. . . . This is what we mean by immediate abolition.

The students' definition of abolition proposed a transformation of society and supported equal rights for Black people. They denounced the chattel principle and demanded the protection of families, a direct condemnation of the internal slave trade that tore apart Black families. They also demanded that the "right of education" be extended to enslaved people. Andover student abolitionists were thus part of a growing contingent of abolitionists supporting Black education. Illuminating a transnational understanding of emancipatory processes in other countries, the students cited the examples of Mexico, the republics of South America, and the recent example of British emancipation in the Caribbean to assuage opposition to emancipation. They also cited the safety of abolition in Haiti before French attempts to reintroduce slavery occurred. The student abolitionists articulated a clear, radical perspective and used international examples of emancipation to support Black freedom.

The student abolitionists also explicitly attacked colonization. They explained that while students discussed their distinct perspectives, the student colonizationists did not engage the substance of the critiques or arguments from the abolitionists and instead would cite their "calendar of saints" who supported the ACS to justify their arguments. The fundamental problem with student colonizationists, they believed, was their views towards Black people. They explained, "We can have no fellowship with the sentiments of those who consider the black color as a contamination of European descent, and who more than insinuate that the blacks were not made to live with people of lighter complexion." The Andover abolitionists highlighted the racist ideology that underpinned student colonizationists' positions as the crucial distinction from abolition. White fears of "amalgamation," the students wrote, were absurd, and they highlighted the hypocrisy of such claims. "We should think that the amalgamation going on at the south, to which the present system of slavery is so favorable, might serve to neutralize these horrors," they quipped. The students condemned the ACS for fueling racism and for sustaining the very prejudices that prevented Black freedom in the United States. The student abolitionists challenged racist ideology that underpinned society and its colleges.

The indictment went further. After seventeen years of the ACS program's existence, hardly any progress had been made towards general emancipation. The conditions of northern free Black communities had not improved and indeed in some cases had only worsened under the influence of colonization as the violent attacks on Crandall's school attested, and as other examples of white colonizationist violence towards Black communities in places like Cincinnati illustrated. The lack of Black rights had produced the very problem the colonizationists sought to remedy, but instead of working to codify Black rights, they upheld and deepened racial prejudices plaguing the country. The Andover student abolitionists presented a sophisticated analysis championing racial equality with cutting-edge abolitionist arguments.

The students' "Apology" represented a significant rebuttal to colonization at the preeminent theological seminary in New England. The students vindicated their convictions and assured their opponents that they were "harmless fanatics" and adhered to the "gospel of peace" in their activism.[44] The controversy at Lane Seminary was still in the making. Indeed, Weld had only begun planning for such a debate, which took place six months after the Andover abolitionists published their pamphlet.

The Andover Apology was widely printed in the press.[45] Signifying the radical nature and significance of the students' pamphlet, white southern sympathizers attacked them in newspapers. The editor of the

United States Telegraph derogatorily stated that the Andover abolitionists took the lead among northern abolitionists as defenders of "amalgamation." The editor feared that the Andover professors would frown upon such sentiments and that the "young fanatics will thus have stronger inducement to make their practice square with their professions." An editor of the *Virginia Times* was furious that Andover students, "whose studies are curiously compounded of divinity and anti-slavery, [were] disciples of Garrison and Wright." The writer exclaimed, "These young gentlemen have no fellowship with our sentiments!"[46] The reactions to the Andover Apology revealed a crack in the foundation of a traditional seminary education, colonization, and laid bare the politicization of higher learning. Intolerable to most whites was Andover student abolitionists using their religious training in agitating for Black freedom.

As the beginning of this chapter explains, a group of Amherst students organized for abolition as well. In 1832, a student reviewed Garrison's *Thoughts on Colonization* for a campus newspaper. The reviewer believed that Garrison's assessment of colonization was impartial and his zeal justified. Garrison's arguments "will have great weight" and "will influence without doubt many of the warmest advocates of the Colonization Society," he opined.[47] Garrison's pamphlet provided fodder for students as they organized on campus. After they formed their society in July of 1833, leading abolitionists took note. The following month, Arnold Buffum, vice president and traveling lecturer for the NEAS, visited the college and discussed abolition with students. He gave two speeches in the community, both attended by students. Buffum reported that he met with many "fine young men, who . . . will be scattered over the country, exercising a powerful influence in the community, and in the various learned professions." Buffum recognized the potential the students could have in their postgraduate lives as abolitionists. Buffum's discussions and speeches emboldened the students' convictions. In their subsequent society meetings, the students expressed their "abhorrence of the barbarous treatment of Miss Crandall" and voted in defense of her school for Black girls and young women. Amherst students and their Andover colleagues' interests aligned in their advocacy for Black education. They also clearly opposed colonization as they believed expatriation was morally wrong because "it gave countenance and sanction to the unholy prejudices against [Black people]" and removal "weakens the strength of the whole." Amherst student abolitionists' convictions aligned with those of many Black abolitionists.[48] The Amherst resolutions echoed the Andover Apology and marked a bookend to a year of tremendous abolitionist activity at northern colleges and seminaries. Their affirmation of abolition came just a week after the organization of the first national abolition society.

Beginning to develop at northern institutions was a cadre of white student abolitionists. Starting in the fall of 1832 at Western Reserve and Andover, Oneida, Amherst, Waterville, and also at Bowdoin, student antislavery societies emerged as part of a coalescing movement—all of which predated the Lane Debates. Students engaged in radical politics, organized at their respective institutions, and fostered connections to the broader movement. Representing an abolitionist insurgency, they challenged the control of the ACS on campus and the authoritative power of faculty. The backlash against the Andover Apology revealed white fears of students becoming active in abolition. At stake was nothing short of the utility of college education. The growth of student antislavery societies revealed a widespread shift among some white students towards an activist education that supported Black freedom and equality, including Black education.

The proliferation of student antislavery societies culminated in the organization of the AASS. In December 1833, Black and white abolitionists met in Philadelphia to establish the national abolition society. The event was an important moment of interracial activism for Black rights. Convention members also promoted women's involvement in the movement. College students participated and helped shape the agenda. Thirty-two students from Waterville College sent a letter of approval of the proceedings, and Calvin Newton became a manager of the national society. Albert G. Tenney sent expressions of his support, and Patrick H. Greenleaf attended the meeting; both represented Bowdoin College, where students had established an antislavery society five months earlier. The abolitionist scholars who had taught at Western Reserve College were also well represented. Beriah Green, by then president of Oneida Institute, was elected president of the convention, Elizur Wright became the corresponding secretary of the organization, and delegates paid tribute to Storrs. The student abolitionists from Andover, David T. Kimball Jr. and Daniel E. Jewett, participated in the convention as well. Garrison praised them for their agitation "in that hot-bed of Colonization," the ATS. The founding of the American Anti-Slavery Society had deep ties to abolitionist dissent at colleges. Student abolitionists and select faculty represented an important constituency for the new organization; not only were they members, but they challenged racist thought at colleges across the North. The role of student abolitionists likely prompted the official approval of a resolution of the convention raised by Charles Denison that "the youth of our country, male and female, . . . form auxiliary Anti-Slavery Societies."[49] The presence of the student abolitionists and the existing college antislavery societies affirmed the resolution. Students proved to be an important constituency of the AASS and help explain the rise of interracial abolition in the early 1830s. Convention officials also received a letter of encouragement from Theodore Weld at Lane Seminary, where he was preparing for a debate.

After Lane: The Backlash to Student Abolition

The controversy over abolition at Lane Seminary (Cincinnati, Ohio) in 1834–1835 was a significant moment in the history of the abolition movement. Students gathered to debate two questions spanning eighteen meetings: "Ought the people of the Slaveholding States to abolish slavery immediately?" and "Are the doctrines, tendencies, and measures of the American Colonization Society and the influence of its principal supporters, such as render it worthy of the patronage of the Christian public?" James Bradley, a Black student who freed himself from enslavement by buying his freedom, provided significant testimony on his life experience to critique slavery and demand abolition. By the end of the debates, students led by Bradley and Weld, some of whom were sons of slaveholders, overwhelmingly supported abolition, and they began working with Black people in Cincinnati in building schools and lyceums, and attending church services together. This activity enraged white people in the city, and the president of the seminary, Lyman Beecher, along with other faculty and trustees, enforced sanctions on the students, prohibiting their interracial abolitionist work. Rather than submit to institutional leaders' policies designed to stymie their freedom work, the majority of Lane students withdrew from the seminary and continued organizing with Black people. After 1835, many of the conflicts over student abolitionist organizing unfolded in reference to the Lane Debates and withdrawal of students.[50]

As the Lane Debates and subsequent controversy unfolded, students elsewhere remained active in abolition. In May 1834, six students from Amherst College, including Edward C. Pritchett, attended the annual meeting of the NEAS. Elijah Beckwith and James A. Thome were also student representatives from Western Reserve College and Lane Seminary, respectively. Beckwith's organ donated twenty-eight dollars to the AASS. The Amherst delegates provided a brief history of their organization and reported that its membership numbers had grown to over fifty. The notion that colonization and abolition could coexist as one antislavery force was absurd to them because of important ideological differences. "All men of right principles see this to be impossible," they explained because colonization promoted gradualism and abolitionists advocated "immediate abolition, which is common sense." They also explained their efforts in working with African Americans in Amherst for Black education.[51] Student abolitionists continued fostering connections between their organizations and national antislavery societies. The relationship was symbiotic. Students were agents challenging colonization on campuses and in their local communities whereas their participation in the national organization connected them to the broader movement that informed and affirmed their work.

By the fall of 1834, news of the Lane Controversy had enveloped the world of higher learning. College presidents were adamant about stifling abolitionist dissent and preventing similar student revolts in their own institutions. A meeting of college and seminary officials unanimously agreed that "the times imperiously demanded that all anti-slavery agitation should be suppressed by laws" similar to those proposed at Lane. College officials resolved to make anti-abolition formal institutional policy. They believed that student abolition was too controversial and would ostracize students from the South who provided key finances to their institutions, evidence of slavery's connections to northern colleges. Student abolitionism was also antithetical to colonization and contradicted faculty's outlook on the future of the United States as a white country.[52] These developments illuminate further the radical implications of abolitionist dissent and the challenge it posed to the economic, intellectual, and social nature of the colleges.

Amherst student abolitionists recognized the potential threat faculty power posed to their activities. In August 1834, they voted unanimously to affirm the principles of their society. The timing of the vote suggests they were aware of the stirring backlash of suppression. Yet, they remained steadfast in their convictions. Students also continued their subscriptions to movement publications and listened to a peer's testimony detailing a recent trip to the South, where he witnessed the oppression of enslaved people.[53] The students continued their activities despite growing opposition to student abolitionism.

By the fall of 1834, Amherst student abolitionists were directly under siege. Colonizationist Heman Humphrey and other faculty demanded that the student society disband. Humphrey's sanction precipitated a fascinating exchange between students and faculty that illuminates the ways in which abolition challenged power relations in the academy. The Amherst controversy unfolded in parallel to the Lane rebellion, and student abolitionist organs at ATS and Hamilton College dissolved around this time as well. In October, the students unanimously rejected Humphrey's suggestion to cease their work. Student leaders, including Leander Thompson, authored a rebuke to Humphrey. Their declaration affirmed abolition as a moral, religious, and political movement. The students could not overlook the cause of the enslaved. "We look again over two millions of our Countrymen—we hear the clanking of their chains. We listen to their moving pleas for deliverance," the students wrote. They believed it was their duty to follow the golden rule. Disbanding their organ, they believed, would violate their moral obligations and vocation. The students' organization had also grown to upwards of seventy members. Signifying their evangelical abolitionism, they argued that slaveholders were guilty of the sin of enslaving people "whose birthright is liberty and who possess immortal minds created to be free." Abolition must come; "Fiat Justitia, ruat Coelum" (Let justice be done though the heavens fall). They also evoked the legacy of Storrs, signifying the influence of the Western Reserve example on the students. They resolved to continue campaigning for Black freedom.

Amherst student abolitionists were uncompromising in their vision, as they believed justice should be done regardless of the circumstances or consequences. In their eyes, the American political, social, and economic conditions that underpinned slavery merited destruction. Believing that abolition "is the cause of God—the cause of humanity—the cause of the bible," the students could not in good conscience dissolve their society. Their refusal was a principled stand against slavery and racism. Their position was significant, though they left the task of dissolution to the faculty. If the student society had to disband, the charge to do so would come from the top, not from the students, who in turn would acquiesce to the faculty's decision.[54] While the students were less defiant than the Lane Rebels, they did not compromise their convictions.

During the succeeding weeks, the students continued meeting. Despite the threat of faculty sanctions, their protests were emboldened and evolved into political action. Society members amended their organization's constitution by adopting the language of the Lane student antislavery society. They clearly understood that southern slavery and northern prejudice were intertwined. They advocated "the emancipation of the slave from the oppression of the master" and "the emancipation of the free coloured man from the oppression of public sentiment." Their central aim was to effect "the elevation of both to an intellectual, moral, and political equality with the whites." The students also recognized the success of the Lane Debates in converting opponents to abolition as they believed appealing to "the minds of all our fellow citizens in the spirit of love" would convince them that Black freedom was paramount. Significantly, the students followed a call from the NEAS and resolved to petition Congress to abolish slavery in Washington, DC. A special committee including Pritchett, who attended the NEAS annual meeting that year, was appointed to procure signatures for their antislavery petition within the college and town.[55] Despite threats from faculty to disband their organization, they applied their convictions, crafted in the movement, to formal political agitation. The Amherst students helped facilitate the movement's engagement in formal politics, believing that Congress was empowered to abolish slavery in the nation's capital.

From November 1834 to January 1835, the student abolitionists corresponded with the faculty over their organization's future. The faculty continued to pressure the students to voluntarily disband, introducing regulations on their meetings that reduced the society to a prayer group. No debates or writing to editors was allowed. Faculty claimed that they were protecting the college from internal and external strife. In effect, they were pressuring students to censor themselves on the question of

Black freedom. The sanctions were crippling, yet the students refused to give in. They continued meeting, and their rift with faculty was made public.[56] As the conflict unfolded at Amherst, news of the Lane Debates, the student-faculty conflict that followed, and the mass exodus of students became well known. Amherst students and faculty would have been well aware of these events. Perhaps the Lane abolitionists' defiant actions added to the Amherst students' bold yet measured convictions.

Humphrey responded to the students' defiance in February. The timing was significant, as he drew on developments at ATS to bolster his argument to censor students' abolitionist activity. In early February, Andover students disbanded both their colonizationist and their abolitionist societies. They feared that their agitation "might interfere with the rigorous prosecution of our studies, and with that harmony which ought to prevail among us." The students' decision came in the wake of a visit to the town of Andover from the British abolitionist lecturer George Thompson, whose visit polarized the students. At the direction of Leonard Woods and other Andover faculty, the students disbanded their organizations. Woods also lamented the events at other institutions where slavery had been discussed and made the subject of "associated action," a veiled reference to the Lane student withdrawals. For Woods, the slavery question was such a divisive topic, it "cannot be introduced into our public institutions, as a subject of special discussion at the present time, without interfering more or less, with the duties of Instructors, and without essential injury to the improvement and future usefulness of the students."[57] Woods believed that student abolitionism was injurious to the seminary and antithetical to students' education. In response to the growth of student abolition and events at Lane, Woods convinced students to cease all activity related to slavery and Black freedom.

Humphrey cited this development to justify his position. Representing the faculty, Humphrey wrote, "We fully accord with the opinion recently expressed by the whole body of students in the Andover Theological Seminary, that in the present agitated state of the public mind, it is inexpedient to keep up any organization, under the name of Anti-Slavery, Colonization, or the like, at our Literary and Theological Institutions." Humphrey believed that this was the position of officials at other institutions, and the Amherst antislavery society was the only one he knew that existed "in any respectable College" in the country. Humphrey ordered that their society "must cease to exist."[58] The Amherst student colonizationists had by that time disbanded, but they could simply join the local organization, which Amherst faculty led. There was no local antislavery society for the students to join. Following Andover's example, Humphrey censored the student abolitionists.

Students met to chart a way forward. Joseph Haven Jr., one of the student leaders, expressed his indignation, saying, "We are no longer 'Anti-Slavery Brethren,' Resolved that we *are* and *will be forever Anti-Slavery Men.*" While their organization was no more, the students remained steadfast abolitionists. They continued to receive *The Liberator* and *Emancipator*, which would be made available privately in a student's room. Months later, one student, John Farwell, wrote in June 1835, "Feel as much interested in Anti-Slavery as ever," but observed that he and his fellow students only "pay our monthly subscriptions and talk among ourselves." Another student, Frederick Augustus Fiske, wrote to the abolitionist Amos Phelps encouraging him to lecture in Amherst. Fiske was sorry to inform Phelps that abolition in the town of Amherst was "not in a very flourishing state." The colonizationist professor Samuel Worcester, he explained, "had his people under his thumb" and, regarding antislavery, had done "nearly all their thinking and talking for them." A lecture from Phelps was sorely needed, Fiske believed, and the student abolitionists would welcome him. The state of abolition at the college, Fiske wrote, was invigorated by the attendance of students like Pritchett at the anniversary meetings in Boston and New York. Pritchett also pledged to raise over one hundred dollars for the AASS. Fiske explained that if a town antislavery society formed, "many of the students of the College will probably join it."[59] While the students complied with the faculty demand to dissolve their organization, the faculty could not extinguish the students' abolitionist spirit. They remained active in the movement beyond the campus, illustrating the restrictive nature of Amherst as an institutional space for organizing for Black freedom. They continued their subscriptions, read abolition newspapers, attended conventions, corresponded with lecturers, and devised ways to organize abolition in the community.

Student abolitionism was representative of the movement's broader impact on society. Abolition challenged the political economy of slavery as well as organized colonization. Student abolition was a direct challenge to college colonizationists. At Andover, faculty actively buoyed anti-abolitionist sentiment. This mirrored the broader reactionary backlash against abolition across the country, exemplified in the proliferation of anti-abolition mob violence in northern cities and towns, the suppression of abolitionist newspapers and pamphlets in the South, and the advent of the "gag rule" in Congress.[60] Colonizationist faculty and colleges as institutions were part of this reactionary wave of anti-abolitionism. But student abolitionists continued their dissent beyond campus. The implication of Woods's and Humphrey's prohibition on students agitating for abolition reveals the problem of moderation on the slavery issue. While they opposed slavery in principle, their actions appeased the slave power. Their complacency with attacks on abolition was de facto acquiescence to slavery as normative. Their actions upheld racist ideologies. They also believed that abolition was beyond the scope of antebellum college education because it was controversial among many whites. They feared that their institutions would lose public support, including money from white southerners connected to slavery. The Andover and Amherst officials believed in protecting the prosperity of their institutions rather than in supporting, or allowing students to support, a movement to end the enslavement of human beings. They opposed a movement for Black freedom. Woods's arguments included the biblical example of Paul instructing slave obedience to their masters, lending credence to the religious argument upholding slavery. Southern slaveholders would have been pleased with the Andover theologian. Indeed, the censure of student abolitionism demonstrated the reach and influence of the slave power in northern institutions. Slaveholders and their sympathizers had a grip on colleges and attempted to dictate the parameters of study and debate on campus. The opposition of most faculty to abolition was a formidable obstacle to the movement and particularly for student abolitionists. Such dynamics—the institutional power of administrators and faculty beholden to capital and the ideologies tethered to it, on the one hand, and insurgent dissenting movements for a new humanity among students and some faculty on the other—resonate across the history of the university and continue in our own time.

The Stakes of the Controversy

The controversy over abolition at colleges and seminaries was deftly represented in an editorial exchange in May 1834 between James Hall and Theodore Weld. Hall was the editor of the *Western Monthly Magazine and Literary Journal*. A former judge and politician from Illinois, Hall moved to Cincinnati in the 1830s and chided student involvement in abolition. He believed that no seminary or college should foster such sentiments. He wrote, "There certainly ought to be some spot hallowed from the contests of party, sacredly protected from the contamination of the malignant passions, where the mind might be imbued with the lessons of truth, and peace, and honor, unalloyed with prejudice. Such sanctuaries should all our seminaries of learning be." Hall singled out the student abolitionists at Lane for their actions when conventional wisdom had ruled abolition absurd. "The calm wisdom of the nation has long since settled down in the opinion that this subject should be left to the providence of God," he claimed, and not to the proclivities of "boys at school wearing paper caps, flourishing wooden swords." Hall mocked students for their dedication to Black freedom and dismissed them as youthful idealists. He went on to explain his version of the function of colleges and the purpose of higher learning.

Hall's objective was to shield colleges from the abolition movement. According to Hall, "Colleges are public property: they are intended for the general good, and are parts of a great system of beneficent institutions, the objects of which are the education of the youth, the dissemination of useful knowledge, and the creation of a pure and elevated public sentiment." Colleges served the public good, he claimed, and "must possess the public confidence." To maximize the purpose and usefulness of them, he claimed, colleges must appeal to the widest audiences for patronage. But when a college assumes a partisan character, according to Hall, "its sphere of operation will be limited, and its usefulness diminished." An institution that served a specific political interest diminished its influence in society, he believed. Hall explicitly argued that students' public support for abolition was "at variance with those of a great body of people in some of the states" and as a result their "charity becomes limited." In other words, a college or seminary that fostered abolition "deprive[s] the institution of the confidence of parents in the

slaveholding states." Hall's position was clear. Abolition obstructed college revenue streams from slaveholding patronage. His editorial neglected to mention the politicized nature of slavery and its ideological
grasp on colleges, an inherently political position that contradicted his
own argument for college neutrality. Acknowledging such contradictions assumed Black humanity. Hall could not accept such terms. The
contradictions in his argument mounted, as he went on to praise the
ACS as "one of the noblest devices of Christian benevolence and enlightened patriotism" worthy of public patronage. Hall overlooked these
explicitly political assertions because the political economy of slavery
underpinned society and its institutions, and the ACS was seen as the
only respectable solution to slavery. For Hall and many other whites, the
ACS's conservative outlook made it the only reputable organization, as
it touted opposition to slavery while aligning with their racist ideology.
And yet Hall continued, "No good can be gained" from political discussions "by students, or by the establishment of political clubs in colleges."
For Hall, the question of slavery was simply too serious for students to
consider. "Surely a topic of such grave magnitude . . . connected with the
whole scheme of civil subordination is not one to be made the theme of
sophomoric declamation." According to Hall, the possibility of colleges
and seminaries becoming sites of political debate over topics like slavery
was "preposterous." Such institutions should be "kept pure from the contamination of irritating topics, and the influence of peculiar doctrines
in politics."[61] In Hall's view, colleges should simply continue operating
as they had been, receiving money from slaveholders, and students and
faculty should continue supporting the ACS. Any kind of political challenge to these systems was not to be tolerated at colleges. His position
was rooted in white supremacy, assuming slavery and profits from it as
natural and attempting to set the terms of the debate of what was and
was not political. His call for apolitical colleges was inherently political
and endorsed slavery and the ACS.

Hall also noted that the abolitionists directly attacked the platform of
the ACS and saw the connection to colleges and seminaries. He asked,
"Is it [the abolition movement] intended to forestall the opinions of
young men in theological seminaries in relation to colonization?" Hall
perceived student involvement in abolition as a political conspiracy. "Are
the sympathies of these young gentlemen to be worked upon in refer-

ence to the abstract question of slavery, while a cunning agent is enlisting their prejudices, and preparing them to divulge the doctrines of party?" Hall believed that abolitionists were indoctrinating "embryo clergymen" to spread abolition across the country. This was a "cunningly devised scheme," Hall quipped, but he assured his readers that "the indignation of the public will put it down, and the united voice of all moderate and reflecting men . . . will be raised to admonish these gentlemen, to mind their own business, and their books." Hall condemned the introduction into colleges of abolition or any controversial topic because he believed it was antithetical to the purpose of college education and would be disruptive to society. Even though students might ultimately promote abolition, he concluded that public sentiment would check the schemes of abolitionists.[62] He clearly articulated a perspective of colleges steeped in the racist outlook of the ACS and dedicated to upholding slavery.

Hall's views were the logical extension of the Western intellectual foundations of the colleges. He sought to protect slavery and racist ideology, which had underpinned academe for over a century by this time. As the movement for Black freedom gained traction and challenged those systems, Hall cried foul and sought to cloister the college from abolition. He acknowledged the challenge abolition posed to the social and economic foundation of American society and its colleges. Hall's meditation on the proper political role of colleges in society reveals his belief in their significance in shaping political and social issues. Hall's position aligned with that of many college officials as they contended with the radical challenge of student abolition.

Weld countered Hall's criticism of student abolition. Rebuking Hall's derisive characterization of students, Weld showed that the vast majority of Lane students were in their twenties and some in their early thirties. "Thirty of the theological class are over twenty-six years old, fourteen over twenty-eight, and nine are between thirty and thirty five," Weld wrote. He retorted, "So much for the babyhood of theological students." Far from a result of uninformed, passionate impulse, the abolitionist sentiment of the Lane students was based on their study of various arguments related to slavery, abolition, and colonization, and they drew their own conclusions. He outlined the proceedings of the Lane Debates and emphasized that rather than sowing seeds of discord, "harmony and brotherly love prevailed not only during the debate, but still remains unbroken." Weld was writing in May of 1834, before the controversy with the faculty ensued. To that point, according to Weld, five students had left the seminary, but their withdrawals had nothing to do with the rise of abolition among students. In fact, eighteen students had enrolled or expressed interest in joining the seminary after the debates. Rather than fomenting chaos among students, as the detractors claimed, abolition increased enrollment at the seminary.

And yet, Weld lamented, Hall called for silence on such a divisive issue. "What! Are our theological seminaries to be awed into silence upon great questions of human duty?" he asked, and continued, "Are they to be bribed over to the interests of an unholy public sentiment, by promises of patronage, or by threats of its withdrawal?" Weld condemned colleges' monied interests with the slave power. Should students be "tutored into passivity," or should all topics of discussion be banned "except upon the *popular side*?" he asked. Are students to avoid all issues that "involve human interests" in order to pacify popular sentiment? Weld was making an argument for an activist education regardless of public perception or financial ties. Indeed, the state of public opinion on slavery was all the more cause for students to discuss slavery. Those "who preach in the nineteenth century must know the nineteenth century," he asserted. Students were obligated to discuss political and social questions facing the society in which they lived. He focused on Hall's hypocrisy and argued that all sorts of political questions had been discussed in colleges. "Colonization discussions have been held, and colonization societies have long existed in almost all our institutions of learning," and there was no public outcry among whites against it. Temperance, moral societies, antigambling and antidueling societies "have been rife for years in our institutions of learning," Weld wrote. The only difference with the ascendance of abolition in these places was that many whites, especially white benefactors, objected to its principles. "So long as discussions upon the subject of slavery conduced to results in accordance with your views, your horizon, it would seem, was unclouded with portents of ominous boding." As long as students supported Hall's politics, Weld observed, he had no issue with political organizations at colleges. "But recent discussions have produced convictions about slavery, which disown affinity with yours," Weld charged, "and have led to the adoption of measures at war with your views of expediency and now forsooth disaster and downfall assail the cause of education." Weld laid bare the contradictions in Hall's essay and skewered his arguments, which benefited the slavocracy and the politics of racism exemplified in established social relations. He also condemned Hall's position regarding public sentiment reacting to forestall abolition. That type of rhetoric led to anti-abolition mob violence. Weld recognized it as such, writing "This is precisely the inflammatory language, word for word, which was used by certain demagogue prints in the city of New York last October." Weld had put his finger on the suppressionist actions of mob violence as violations of free discussion and abolitionist dissent. "Has it come to this? Is free inquiry to be paralyzed by the terror of pains and penalties?"[63] When it came to discussing Black freedom, the vaunted rights of the Constitution and the law of the land could be denied with impunity by the power of white mobs.

Weld's essay countered Hall, and the exchange revealed the stakes of abolition at institutions of higher learning. Hall's arguments represented the type of college education that was firmly entrenched at eurocentric American colleges and seminaries. It was an education for the so-called common good, buttressed by white-supremacist ideology, and in practice was exemplified by college colonizationists: remove free Black people from the country while sustaining financial ties to slaveholding patronage in northern institutions. In contrast, Weld articulated an activist education that facilitated study in social and political issues and fostered student agitation for Black freedom. His view of advanced education was to allow any and all discussion on political topics and let students decide for themselves their own positions, not to be dictated by donors and public sentiment. He believed that his formula for extended study and discussion of slavery would produce abolitionists, as it had done at Lane. Weld's outlook was in the lineage of that of Phillis Wheatley, Black students, white student abolitionists, and others like Beriah Green. It was a vision of an education with the central tenet of Black freedom and humanity that was long in the making, and Weld was working to popularize it. This type of education underpinned the cause of humanity, supporting the idea that the freedom of enslaved and free Black people superseded avarice and money making and the institutions that underpinned them. The Hall-Weld exchange laid bare the opposing positions regarding slavery and abolition that unfolded at colleges in the 1830s. In short, Weld summarized, Hall's objective had been to "muzzle discussion upon the subject of slavery, especially in institutions of learning." But Hall's efforts were for naught. As Weld explained to Hall, "You are too late, sir. Discussion has begun."[64] Indeed, discussion had begun, and students were leading the charge for abolition at colleges from Maine to Ohio.

Beyond the Campus

As the 1830s unfolded, students themselves developed arguments about their rights to organize and discuss abolition on campus and participate in social movements. As a result of their radicalism and defiance, some student abolitionists were expelled or withdrew. Rather than acquiesce to the racist proclivities of faculty, they recognized the limitations of advocating Black freedom in institutions that were averse to it. In turn, many moved beyond the campus and continued to work for abolition. The direction the movement would take beyond the 1830s was in part due to the positions of student abolitionists.

In the wake of the Chaplin resignation at Waterville College, students remained active in the movement. In October 1834, a group of students, including Hartly W. Day and George LeRow, attended the Maine Anti-Slavery Convention in Augusta. In April, students helped found the Waterville Anti-Slavery Society, a local organization in the community. Fifty-four of the eighty-two members were students. Day and LeRow were the organization's recording and corresponding secretaries, respectively. LeRow was also the local organ's representative for the NEAS.[65] The Waterville community had a strong abolitionist presence due to the students' organizing. After a lecture in the local Baptist church, several more students joined the antislavery society, and LeRow collected subscriptions from nearly forty students for an antislavery newspaper. In a letter to Garrison, LeRow wrote, "The cause of human rights is prospering in this region." Included in this letter was a list of books LeRow was returning to Garrison, among them "Wheatley's Poems."[66] LeRow and other students read the poems of Phillis Wheatley Peters, which helped theorize student abolition and fostered abolitionist dissent at colleges. The students embodied the idea. That they engaged Wheatley's work is an indication of her lasting influence on abolition. Student abolition was gaining momentum and poised to spread the movement. LeRow quipped, "Our students will be scattered all over the state this winter, and what a host of fires these 'fire brands' will kindle!" LeRow fostered connections with leaders in the movement, linking students and the local Waterville antislavery society to the broader movement. Student abolition was ascendant in rural Maine and logically progressed beyond the campus as the backlash against student abolition was beginning to unfold.

Indeed, Waterville students encountered the backlash in November 1834. LeRow wrote to Phelps, "I have got my dismission from here" and "President Babcock is, I understand, much pleased to think so much Abolition is to leave him! Poor man!" According to LeRow, the college president sought to purge abolition from the campus. LeRow planned to go to New York, where he would continue working for antislavery organizations.[67] Other Waterville students involved in abolition, such as Hartly Day, Samuel W. Field, and Nathan Oliver, among others, left as well.[68] While the specific reasons why the students left the college may have varied, their dedication to abolition and obstacles posed by Babcock likely played a decisive role in their withdrawals.

Student abolitionist withdrawals occurred elsewhere as well. The revolt at Lane Seminary, where 95 of 103 students left in the fall of 1834, coincided with the Waterville dismissals. A year later, forty-seven students at ATS withdrew, including student abolitionists Royal Reed, Charles T. Torrey, and James M. McKim. Torrey's most recent biographer argues that his involvement in abolition during his time at Andover propelled him to abolitionist work. Torrey famously died in prison for aiding fugitive slaves. McKim became a major figure in the Underground Railroad in Philadelphia. Reed was involved in local organizing while other Andover students, Jonathan Blanchard and Abner Warner, became lecturers for the AASS.[69] Backlash to student abolitionism was a northern phenomenon, and the dismissal or withdrawal of student abolitionists was part of widespread faculty use of institutional power to subdue abolitionist dissent at colleges. Suppressing student abolition was thus part of the larger anti-abolitionist backlash during the mid-1830s. White students championing a movement for Black freedom was unconscionable to faculty. The tensions reveal the radical nature of abolition in academe.

Facing repression on campus, white student abolition evolved, in at least two ways. Students argued that they had a right to discuss moral and political issues on campus. "The question of human rights" and their "undeniable right and duty to avouch for the cause of immediate abolition" spurred students at Hamilton College to organize an antislavery society in 1835. Referencing the events at Lane, Andover, and Amherst, they wrote, "Experience has taught us the fallacy and ridiculous absurdity of all objections to free discussion at colleges." Student abolitionists at Union College concurred. "Students, in a special manner," they declared, "are called to the consideration of all subjects tending to the melioration of the condition of man," and "We take it as an axiom, that students, as every one else, have a business to do with all that pertains to the moral state of man." They believed that the precepts of the Declaration of Independence were "applicable to all mankind as to ourselves." The denial of Black freedom was a dangerous precedent. While their situations were categorically distinct, the white students saw the plight of free Black people and the slaves' cause as intertwined with their own rights. At a time when the slave power challenged the freedoms of anyone opposed to slavery and racism, the students' rallying cry was "all who have not sacrificed principle on the altar of ambition and avarice, are called to rescue liberty from her destroyers, and the resuscitation of human rights from their graves."[70] Echoing Weld but coming from the students themselves, a concept of student protest as a political philosophy and student abolition as a specific duty was developed by Hamilton and Union student abolitionists. Against the slave power and its attendant array of abuses, they fashioned a politics of solidarity with Black people with a conception of the right to protest for human rights and human equality.

White student abolition evolved in another direction, extending beyond the campus into direct engagement in formal politics. Student abolitionists were involved in the petition campaigns to Congress. From 1836 to 1838, Hamilton College students signed five petitions, three of which were from students themselves while two others were a town and county petition. The petitions were clear articulations of antislavery politics, using formal politics and the Constitution against slavery, particularly outlawing it in areas controlled by the federal government. Students called on Congress to abolish slavery and the slave trade in Washington, DC, and in the territories under its jurisdiction, prohibit the internal and coastal slave trades among the states, and prevent the exportation of enslaved people from the United States and its controlled territories to Texas or other foreign states. The first petition students signed in 1836 included a critique of the Fugitive Slave Law (1793) and its use to enslave free African Americans with impunity at the will of slavecatchers. They supported abolition in the capital because "persons have been imprisoned in the District on mere suspicion of their being runaways, and not being proved to be such, have been sold into per-petual slavery for the *payment of their jail fines!*" They demanded pro-tections for free Black people from such actions. At least thirty-nine students signed the petition. Students also signed an 1837 petition from Kirkland County against the annexation of Texas because it would vio-late Mexico's sovereignty and Texas would provide the slaving interest in the United States with disproportionate political power, subverting the interests of the free states. Sixty-six women and fifty-eight men from the area signed the petition along with students.[71] As in Waterville, stu-dent abolitionists joined the local community in their collective anti-slavery work.

The Hamilton students' own petitions drew the ire of faculty and state officials. In March 1837, students sent an antislavery petition to the New York state legislature demanding the full abolition of slavery in the state, which set in motion a conflict between student abolitionism and state power. Slavery had been abolished gradually in New York, culminat-ing in 1827, but under the state's provisions a number of Black people remained enslaved. There was also no law prohibiting slaveholders from residing temporarily in the state with enslaved people.[72] Students be-lieved that the current laws had to be abolished and replaced with ones codifying universal Black freedom. The student petition was a response to Whig congressmen Charles O. Shepard, who proposed an abolition bill to fully eradicate slavery in the state and called for petitions to sup-port it. In response, the students sent a petition, and the state assembly recorded receiving it on March 23: "The sundry students of Hamilton College, praying for the more effectual abolition of slavery in this State, was read, and committed to a committee." On March 24, the Senate took notice. Democratic senator Levi Beardsley motioned to reconsider appropriating five thousand dollars annually for five years to the col-lege because "a petition had been presented to the Assembly, from 60 students of that institution in favor of abolitionism." Beardsley was disgusted by the thought of funding Hamilton and disavowed "pampering institutions which were the hot beds of such fanaticism." The motion to pause funding initially passed, but the senators ultimately passed legislation appropriating the funds to the college only after the president of Hamilton, Joseph Penney, hand delivered to the legislature the faculty's response condemning the students' abolitionist politics and declared ignorance of the petition. Only with the rejection of student abolition by the college president would the legislature fund the institution. The student abolitionist petition exposed the fact that the political and institutional power of the legislature and the college were unified against Black freedom. Undeterred, the students signed another petition in September 1837 and drafted an original petition the following January to the US House of Representatives demanding abolition and the restriction of slavery's extension in federally controlled areas. Fifty-five students signed it.[73] In total, Hamilton student abolitionists signed five different petitions, including the one sent to the state legislature. Their petitions preceded, and continued after, the controversy with the legislature.

Many students signed antislavery petitions during the campaigns in the first and second halves of the 1830s. Petitioners answered the call of the NEAS in 1834 to demand the abolition of slavery in Washington, DC. As mentioned above, Amherst students formed a committee led by Pritchett in November 1834 to circulate a petition for signatures at the college and in the town. At Waterville, George LeRow wrote to Amos Phelps asking where he could send petitions the students there had signed. "I want something in the *Liberator* about petitions to Congress," LeRow asserted, because "we have got some up 'round here and want to know where to send them." These early student petitions represented pockets of abolition at rural colleges in New England. They also demonstrate that students were aware of broader trends in the movement and indeed shaped those trends. In response to the petition campaign, proslavery senators from South Carolina Henry Pinckney and John C. Calhoun led congressional efforts to ignore or gag the petitions. The infamous "gag rule" laid bare the influence of the slave power in the federal government. Abolitionists countered this antidemocratic measure and continued petitioning. The Hamilton student abolitionists' petitions were part of this second wave of student petitions. In 1837, John Quincy Adams presented a petition against the annexation of Texas signed by ninety-eight students from Bowdoin College. Student abolitionists were part of grassroots abolitionist organizing and along with women abolitionists helped anchor the antislavery petition campaigns of the 1830s.[74]

Finally, white student abolition moved beyond the campus and turned to third-party politics. Student abolitionists were a constituency of the Liberty Party, an abolitionist political party. By the late 1830s, Amherst student abolitionists successfully reorganized on campus. Over the course of three evenings in November 1841, they debated the question, "Is the present organization of the Liberty Party expedient?" The issue was so passionately debated that on the third night, not only did the members of the student antislavery organization participate, but it was open to everyone at the college. "A large number of students were present," and throughout the proceedings, "a degree of candor and good feeling, hitherto unknown in this college in debating questions of this nature," characterized the discussion. After three hours of debate the entire group assembled voted in favor of the Liberty Party. "This we record as a decided triumph of Abolition over Slaveocracy in this institution," the secretary of the society cheered.[75] It was a decided victory for the political abolitionist third party. An achievement almost impossible only five years earlier, Amherst students had effectively spread abolitionist sentiment on campus, and many of the students became Libertyites.[76]

Other students came to similar positions. In late 1840, students at Yale advocated "consistent political action" for "the immediate, unconditional, and total annihilation of American slavery." Along with other youth, students formed the New Haven Young Men's Anti-Slavery Society and identified the slave power's grip on national politics as a cancerous sore plaguing the nation. They singled out for criticism the Fugitive Slave Act and proslavery expansionist warfare in western territories. The slave power required "our State Legislatures to descend to the inhuman and degrading office of hunting and catching its self-emancipated negroes," they wrote, condemning fugitive slave renditions. It also appropriated "our money to build its prisons, our men to carry on a horrible frontier warfare" at the direction of a "proslavery Executive, for the protection of crimes with which they tell us we have nothing to do." The students understood the influence of the slave power over the entire country, the laws built into the fabric of the nation to uphold slavery, and the imperialist outlook of proslavery politicians that fueled western expansion. And the northern Whigs and Democrats were complicit, they believed, in perpetuating the slave power's dominance in American politics. "The political parties of the *North* have joined hand in hand for the support of the Slave Power, thus proving recreant in the cause of *Freedom*, and the true interests of the *Republic*, and forfeiting all claims to the confidence or co-operations of *Freemen*." The students publicly withdrew their support of the Whig and Democratic parties.[77] Predating the official organization of the Liberty Party, the students in the New Haven Young Men's Anti-Slavery Society were political abolitionists.

In August 1840, four months before Yale students announced their political antislavery stance, students from Hamilton College attended a political abolitionist meeting in Syracuse, New York. Henry Kendall and Frederick Jackson of Hamilton College were official members of the convention, where resolutions were passed advancing Black men's voting rights and voting only for the "Freedman's party" ticket, an early manifestation of the Liberty ticket.[78] In February 1842, a student from Hanover College condemned the Indiana legislature for tabling a motion to support jury trials for captured fugitive slaves. He wrote to the *Emancipator* in outrage, announcing, "I cordially sympathize with the Liberty Party, and bid them God speed!"[79] In September 1842, Alvan Stewart addressed the antislavery society at Bangor Seminary on "Ballot box Theology."[80] He spoke on the importance of future ministers preaching on voting the abolitionist ticket. An important catalyst for pushing the Hanover student and the Yale students to abolitionist politics was the controversy over fugitive slaves. They believed in personal liberty laws and the right to habeas corpus in fugitive slave cases. In this respect, slave resistance propelled students to abolitionist politics. Student abolitionists were among those promoting abolitionist politics as the movement entered the fraught terrain of electoral politics.

As abolitionists organized for Black freedom, a minority of white college students from across the northern states joined the movement. Students assessed the arguments for abolition and colonization. Moral and evangelical arguments for immediate emancipation and human equality proved persuasive. While evangelicalism was significant, students' arguments for abolition quickly adopted a political outlook, as they advocated Black political rights and Black education. The advent of student antislavery societies marked the proliferation of abolitionist insurgency on campuses, signifying a prominent challenge to the slaving and settler-colonial logics of the American academy. Rather than embrace slavery, colonization, or the racism that underpinned the academy and society, student protesters championed an ideology and movement that centered Black freedom and humanity. Striking a major blow to the intellectual foundations of the college, student abolition precipitated opposition from faculty who worked to stifle abolitionist dissent. It exposed the financial links between slaving and northern colleges. Significantly, student abolitionism was a prominent phenomenon prior to the Lane Debates. The Lane Controversy thus can be seen as a culmination of the student abolitionist controversies at places like Western Reserve, Waterville, ATS, and Amherst that preceded it. Indeed, student abolitionists wrote their own pamphlets exposing colleges as citadels of racism and outlining their convictions for human rights and equality. The Lane Controversy was also a pivot, as subsequent controversies over abolitionist dissent at colleges unfolded in reference to them. By the mid-1830s, abolition on college campuses became a controversy over the freedom of discussion and the freedom to organize. It threw into question the very meaning of college education. As faculty implemented restrictive sanctions on debate, student abolitionists increasingly recognized the limitations of colleges as institutional spaces restricting their agitation. In turn, students participated in abolition beyond the confines of their campuses, becoming involved in the petition campaigns and the organization of third-party abolitionist politics. An important shortcoming of many of the white student abolitionist men of the 1830s not explored in this chapter but still important was their disavowal of women's rights as part of the abolitionist agenda.[81] The emergence and growth of second-wave abolition marked a turning point in the movement and in society, when college education was being used for the purpose of Black liberation. These developments were the result of the Black struggle for freedom and of student protest. The abolition movement of the 1830s was also, in part, a student movement.

5

Developing Black Higher Learning

In 1829, David Walker published one of the most influential tracts in Black history. Walker's *Appeal, in Four Articles, Together with a Preamble, to the Colored Citizens of the World, but in Particular, and Very Expressly to Those of the United States of America* was a revolutionary treatise that examined the historic conditions of the enslavement of Black people in the United States at the hands of white Christians, the oppression slavery and racism produced, the appropriation of Christianity to subjugate Black people, and the grave moral failure of the American Colonization Society, among other things. The urgency of the *Appeal* was for the liberation of all Black people in the world, through force if necessary. To usher in freedom, Walker believed, Black people had to be united. Learning would produce unity and facilitate world-historic change. Refuting Thomas Jefferson's racist claims in *Notes on the State of Virginia* was the duty of Black people themselves, he reasoned. Walker instructed, "You have to prove to the Americans and the world that we are MEN, and not brutes as we have been represented, and by millions treated. Remember, to let the aim of your labours among your brethren, and particularly the youths, be the dissemination of education and religion." The education Walker envisioned would reveal the injustices and causes under which Black people lived. In turn, Black people would learn a version of Christianity, positioning themselves as God's chosen people to remake the world by eliminating human oppression. Walker's vision of Black education was inextricably intertwined with liberation, and he believed the former would facilitate the latter.[1] It was a revolutionary vision Black abolitionists worked to realize using higher learning. Black students manifested Walker's outlook, which is further evidence of a nascent idea of Black Studies and its historical encounter with the American college.

In an essay on David Walker and his *Appeal*, Cedric Robinson argued that Walker could be considered a progenitor of Black Studies. Robinson

made connections between Walker's ideas in the 1820s and the founding of academic Black Studies in the mid-twentieth century, the link
being that the purpose of education was the liberation of Black people.
Elsewhere, Robinson succinctly captured this element of Walker's vision:
"Education had to have revolutionary emancipation as its central virtue."
Vincent Harding made a similar observation about Walker's *Appeal* that
speaks to a purpose of Black Studies: "Essentially, he was demonstrating
several of the major functions of radical teaching among dominated African peoples: to raise questions about the reasons for their oppression,
to speak the truth concerning both oppressed and oppressor, to clarify
as fully as possible the contradictions inherent in both communities,
and to indicate the possible uses of these contradictions in the struggle
for freedom." Building on Harding's and Robinson's conceptualization of
Walker's idea of Black Studies, this chapter and chapter 6 will continue
to recover a nascent notion of Black Studies and its encounter with colleges during the era in which Walker lived. This development marked a
continuation of Black Studies encountering colleges, traced in previous
chapters, that began with slave culture on campus and the writings of
Black students in the 1820s. There was a movement that came in the
wake of Walker's *Appeal* in which Black abolitionists sought to realize
Walker's vision of education for liberation. Black intellectuals and, importantly, Black students embodied his vision in their determination to
acquire higher learning and become active in the liberation struggle.
When selected Black students received formal higher learning, they
were most effective in their subsequent years as teachers, ministers, and
organizers in the movement. Importantly, they had to be accepted as
such by Black communities. In order for Black students and their training in higher learning to have meaning beyond the individual, Black
communities had to accept them as ministers or teachers in their own
institutions. Otherwise, such educational training, divorced from the
social and historical context of Black experiences, had little relevance
to the Black majority. The necessity of a symbiotic relationship between
Black higher learning and its purpose as a tool for realizing collective
freedom in Black communities was revealed in the antebellum period.[2]

The antebellum struggle for Black freedom was fought in and on the
boundaries of colleges. Alongside government, political parties, law,
churches, transportation, schools, and other public accommodations,

colleges, seminaries, and universities were social and intellectual bat-tlegrounds. Black abolitionists understood colleges to be spaces where Black students could refute racist ideas at their source and that higher learning was another tool to demonstrate Black humanity and produce equality. They believed that Black higher learning was a harbinger of political and social change. The struggle for Black higher learning was an effort to realize Walker's vision.

In the 1830s, a new insurgency of Black students made academia con-tested terrain. At institutions where white faculty advocated racial exclu-sion, sharpened emergent notions of scientific racism, and maintained financial ties to slaveholders, young Black women and men challenged slavery and racism and remade the very meaning of higher learning. Black students were agents of abolition on campus. Through their strug-gle they helped redefine the purpose of higher learning that had per-colated among the early Black students described in chapter 1 and had expanded among whites, as detailed in chapter 4. Rather than produce future leaders who replicated and perpetuated racial oppression, Black students were forerunners in introducing the utility of college educa-tion for Black liberation. Not only did they develop novel ideas about the meaning of higher learning; they made arguments based on Black interpretations of history, religion, and science to demonstrate Black hu-manity and the imperative of liberation. They produced a nascent idea of Black Studies. Black students themselves produced knowledge for the movement.[3] Their presence on campuses and academic successes strengthened arguments for human equality. While their goal for aboli-tion overlapped with that of white student abolitionists, Black students were fighting for something white students already had: the opportunity for learning at colleges and living as free people. As Black students pur-sued higher learning and faced exclusionary practices from faculty and students, the radical challenge Black students posed to existing social, racial, and intellectual hierarchies was revealed. As a result, Black stu-dent abolitionists extended the struggle from the 1820s and produced new ways of thinking about higher learning.

Black abolitionists' arguments for higher learning were part of their larger advocacy of self- and collective improvement. Some scholars have emphasized the limitations of self-improvement because it was insuf-ficient in achieving racial equality and, in some cases, resulted in the

ostracism of Black intellectuals from Black communities.[4] These arguments have limitations and fall short of considering the meaning of self-
elevation and higher learning for Black people like Walker. That such
strategies had limited impact in changing social structures reveals more
about the intransigence of white supremacy and the failure of whites to
alter a dominant racist culture than about the failure of Black people
seeking to learn and uplift themselves and their communities. The ostracism of selected Black intellectuals is evidence of a cultural stratification
in Black communities that ultimately obstructed unity in the struggle
for the liberation of all Black people. Learning for the community was
Walker's vision and the vision of some Black abolitionists. They saw
higher learning not simply as the realm for a few gifted people or race
leaders, but increasingly as a means of improving the lives of all Black
people regardless of background, as Walker envisioned. This can be seen
in their advocacy of classical learning, manual labor, *and* training in
the mechanical arts, an expansive notion of higher learning wherein
the mind, body, and spirit—the whole person—would be cultivated
in preparation for meaningful life in a world of Black freedom. Black
higher learning was antithetical to the colleges and the society they underpinned. It represented an alternative to college education based exclusively on the individual. For Black people in the community, learning
and self-elevation were important strategies of self-determination in the
fight for a new humanity.

Black thought on higher learning evolved as the antebellum abolition movement took shape. As chapter 1 shows, Black protests for higher
learning began in the early decades of the nineteenth century, but it was
not until the late 1820s and the transformed abolition movement that
arguments for Black higher learning gained ideological cohesion. As the
founding of denominational colleges and the development of American
higher learning continued, Black abolitionists developed their own ideas
about college learning. Central to that vision was a college for Black
learning that would foster a diasporic Black intelligentsia who would
lead the struggle for freedom. When plans for the proposed African College were thwarted by racist whites, Black abolitionists continued fighting for higher learning. In turn, Black students increasingly protested
for admissions at white colleges and seminaries but were often met with
rejections due to the prominence of white southern patronage and the

pervasiveness of racism, which were indicative of slavery's reach into northern institutions. Black abolitionists responded and critiqued slavery and racism's influence on colleges.

Black women also made demands for racial and women's equality in education. Maria Stewart championed higher learning for Black women, as did Sarah Parker Remond, Lucy Stanton, and many others. Black women had the most expansive vision for higher learning, one that would facilitate their freedom. Their claims for learning and rights conflicted with the sexism of many male student abolitionists. Stewart, a protégée of Walker, played a similar role as her mentor in that she conceptualized women's higher learning as a facilitator of Black women's liberation. Black women would manifest her vision on campus and build on her arguments.

Despite rejections at institutions across northern states, Black abolitionists continued to organize and develop strategies for making formal Black higher learning a reality. Black and white abolitionists had a lengthy debate over Black admissions at white colleges during the 1836 meeting of the New England Anti-Slavery Society, signifying the importance of the issue for the movement. Emerging from the convention was a greater understanding of the social and political significance of Black higher learning as a tool for both disproving racist ideas and procuring learned ministers, teachers, and organizers who would help unite Black people in transforming society. In turn, the broader movement began to exert pressure on colleges to admit Black students.

The history of Black higher learning in the antebellum period reveals a heretofore understudied strand of the history of Black Studies among Black abolitionists. Black thinkers and student abolitionists sought to use the realm of higher learning for Black liberation, as a tool to dismantle the most insidious argument of racist whites, that Black people were inferior. Black abolitionists and formally trained Black intellectuals would further expose this lie. But disagreements over realizing Black higher learning arose and reflected divergences in the movement over integration, women's rights, and Black separatism. Black student abolitionism was a generative force for abolition.[5] Indeed, some significant figures, both well known and less so, began their life's work in the movement in their pursuit of higher learning as student abolitionists. Higher learning became an important facet of the meaning and realization of

Black freedom. This repurposing of higher learning was largely due to the efforts of Black students. Black higher learning in the antebellum period was a novel idea historically and became a significant concept for the Black freedom struggle for generations to come.

Arguments for Black Higher Learning and Protests for Admissions

Black abolitionists believed that higher learning was a central node of the abolitionist project and an important tool that would procure meaningful freedom. Beginning in the 1820s, Black abolitionists conceptualized an idea for Black higher learning. The function of colleges was to train missionaries and teachers, and the ministry was the main profession into which most college- and seminary-educated men entered. Black abolitionists envisioned similar trajectories for young Black men. They sought formal training for Black ministers, who would in turn become activist clergy, disseminate knowledge, and preach the lessons of the gospel to congregants, a strategy that was believed would benefit everyone in the community. Formally educated Black ministers thus would also be teachers and symbols of learning. Many Black student men were formally trained ministers.

Alongside Black churches, literary societies, schools, and other autonomous spaces of Black learning, Black newspapers were vehicles for advancing learning. In the second issue of *Freedom's Journal*, editors Samuel Cornish and John B. Russwurm, a student abolitionist himself, signaled the importance of education for uplift and presented their newspaper as a tool for education. Cornish and Russwurm announced that their newspaper was intended "for the moral, religious, civil, and literary improvements of our injured race." They explained that "the diffusion of knowledge and raising our community into respectability, are the principal motives" of the newspaper. Two years later, Cornish chided American philanthropists for supporting a proposed institution dedicated to training teachers and other professionals in Greece when such a facility for African Americans was desperately needed within the United States. Advocates of such a plan, Cornish reasoned, were simply neglecting a domestic problem that merited their support more than a foreign one. He specifically singled out his own denomination, the Presbyterian

Church, for criticism. "There are nearly three millions of colored people in these United States, and connected with the Presbyterian Church, which is the most efficient in this country, in works of charity, there is not a single institution existing for the education of colored youths or young men." Cornish believed that formally educated Black ministers were required to spread the gospel and knowledge among African Americans. He criticized the efforts of the church for barely instructing Black ministers while "the white man, taken from the plough, and the bench, &c. is carried through the college course and then sent three or four years to the Seminary." Presenting a critique of racial exclusion in academia, Cornish reasoned that Black ministers needed to be educated in colleges and seminaries as well and the church should fund the endeavor. An educated ministry, he believed, would help cultivate "piety, virtue, and usefulness." To battle prejudice, Cornish summarized, "education is the strongest bulwark."

Four months later, Cornish called on Black people to create their own institution of learning. "Why have we not a system of education established among us, connecting by one strong chain the common, the grammar, the collegiate and the professional school, where everything relating to a polished and useful education may be taught"?[6] Cornish urged Black people to found their own college. His proposal and advocacy for Black higher learning were ambitious and radical. They constituted another critique of white higher learning in the United States. His proposal explained how higher learning would provide Black people with powerful tools to dismantle northern prejudice, assert Black humanity, and uplift Black people, striking at the heart of proslavery thought and the epistemic foundations of colleges.

By 1829, Cornish had emerged as a leading figure in the fight for Black higher learning. His work continued beyond his newspaper writings. He became a leading proponent of the "African College" in New Haven. The proposal for a Black college represented a watershed in the history of Black education in the United States.[7] The college proposal came from abolitionists. In 1829, Simeon Jocelyn, a white minister and a teacher at a Black school in New Haven, introduced a proposal and joined forces with the Reverend Peter Williams Jr., a Black minister, abolitionist, and teacher in New York City. By June of 1831, Jocelyn and other abolitionists presented the plan for the African College to the First Annual Meeting of the People of Colour in Philadelphia. The convention unanimously endorsed the college proposal and appointed Cornish as a general agent to collect donations. Members of the convention also dictated that the new college would be governed by seven trustees, four Black and three white. Recognizing the plan's significance, members "resolved at whatever Labor or Expense, to establish, and maintain an institution, in which their sons of the present and future generations may obtain a classical education and the mechanical arts in general."[8] They saw the African College as institutionalizing Black thought and abolition. The proposal was the first of its kind. Moreover, the gendered language of the convention made clear that this was a radical step for Black men. No mention was made of Black girls or women students. Emerging from the Black convention was an interracial effort to build a college for an expansive education. It was a significant moment for conceptualizing Black higher learning, with limitations.

The revolutionary proposal for the African College, however, was met with an immediate backlash. New Haven whites, including colonizationists, elites, working people, and students and faculty from Yale, all opposed the construction of such a college in New Haven, believing that it posed a direct threat to slavery. At a city meeting, they resolved "that the propagation of the sentiments favorable to the immediate emancipation of the slaves in disregard of the civil institutions of the States in which they belong, and as an auxiliary thereto the contemporaneous founding of Colleges for educating colored people, is an unwarrantable and dangerous interference with the internal concerns of other States, and ought to be discouraged."[9] They also opposed the plan to accept Black students from the Caribbean. White opponents charged that Black West Indians would foment slave revolts and transmit radicalism to the United States. The college would be open to Black people from the Atlantic world and thus could help create a Black diasporic intellectual culture. In short, oppositional whites perceived Black higher learning to be a direct threat to slavery and to the nation's political and economic institutions and social relations. The city resolution also came in the wake of Nat Turner's Rebellion. The white press considered Turner's education a factor in the slave uprising.[10] Educating more Black people at a college, these whites believed, increased the chance of further revolts. The opposition also marked a significant evolution in the ACS. As noted in chapters 1 and 2, college colonizationists embraced the education of Black missionaries if they would leave the country. The African College, a project of abolitionists, Black and white, who had long opposed the ACS and demanded Black citizenship, threatened the ACS's emphasis on Black removal.

The proposal reveals the radical nature of Black higher learning. It was a threat to the racial order. An African college presupposed Black intellectual culture, which was inconceivable to most whites and contrary to the intellectual foundations of their colleges. A community of college-educated Black people from the United States and the Caribbean would bolster Black freedom demands. In other words, the African College represented the development of Black higher learning as a liberatory project. It was a proposal that would institutionalize Walker's vision.

As the abolition movement evolved in the 1830s, Black abolitionists made higher learning part of the terrain on which the struggle for freedom and equality would be fought. From its earliest meetings, the Black convention movement made Black higher learning paramount. The African College signified a radical challenge to slavery and American racism. In response, white New Haveners struck down the proposal and refused to allow such an institution in their city. The radicalism exemplified in Nat Turner's revolt, the arguments in David Walker's *Appeal*, and the emergence of Garrison's *Liberator*, which all coincided with the proposal, are not to blame for the college's demise, as some historians have argued. The college never came to fruition because racist whites rejected it. To blame the failure of the proposal on the radicalization of abolition is tantamount to criticizing Black people resisting oppression. Placing the blame on abolition fundamentally overlooks, even distorts, social relations of power and essentially exonerates racist whites who opposed the plan.[11] The African College project was an evolution in the Black abolitionist imagination. Black abolitionists began to embrace Black higher learning as a critical component of the movement.[12] Despite the outcome in New Haven, abolitionists continued the fight for Black higher learning.

The backlash against the African College, however, initiated a wave of white reactionary opposition to Black higher learning and Black education more generally. The most infamous examples include the attack on Prudence Crandall's seminary for Black girls and women in Canterbury, Connecticut, and the destruction of Noyes Academy in Canaan, New

Hampshire. In 1833, Black girls and women from the surrounding region attended Crandall's school. She was tried in court for violating state laws prohibiting the education of Black people from outside of Connecticut. Crandall, however, continued teaching, but whites violently attacked the school, intimidating her students by hurling stones at the building and throwing refuse at students. Crandall had no choice but to close the school for the students' safety. Sarah Harris was one of the students, and she and her sister Mary went on to become important teachers and abolitionists. The attack on Noyes Academy in 1835 came after Black students enrolled and was perpetrated by whites who ultimately destroyed the academy. The assault on Black education was part of the proliferation of anti-abolition mob violence that was rampant in the 1830s.[13]

Included among this reactionary violence was the exclusion of Black students at colleges and seminaries. In the early 1830s, anti-Black sentiment arose at Wesleyan University in Middletown, Connecticut. The university opened in 1831 and was envisioned as a national institution for training Methodist ministers. A denomination that had significant ties to southern slaveholders, the Methodist university attracted white youth from the South. One of the university's earliest students, however, was Charles B. Ray, a twenty-five-year-old Black man from Falmouth, Massachusetts. Ray was the son of free Black parents. His father was a mail carrier. His mother was self-educated. She had access to a local minister's library and read most of the titles, setting an example of study and learning for her son. Ray's early schooling was in Falmouth. After experiencing a religious conversion in his early twenties, he decided to pursue the ministry. He attended an academy in Wilbraham, where he met Wilbur Fisk, the principal of the academy, who had been appointed president of the new university in Middletown. Ray's connection with Fisk facilitated his formal admission into Wesleyan in the fall of 1832.[14]

By December, however, Ray had left the university. As soon as Ray arrived at Wesleyan, southern students became irate. "The connection of Mr. R[ay] with the Institution occasioned discontent from the first. It prevailed, however, *chiefly among students from the South*," read one student's report of the events. Tensions escalated when Ray began boarding on campus, which "brought matters immediately to a crisis." Threatening to withdraw, white students petitioned Fisk to remove Ray from the university. Initially Fisk defended Ray, attempting to convince students that he should stay, but he was unsuccessful. Instead, he took the issue to the board of trustees. Meanwhile, the anti-Black students met and drafted a petition demanding that the trustees expel Ray. Other students wished to see Ray remain at the university. Amidst the turmoil, Ray resolved to leave the university before any formal decision was announced, protecting himself from the racist hostility. The anti-Black racism Ray encountered was so hostile, he believed it was necessary to leave the campus. Ray had pierced the boundaries of a white institution, which provoked a racist backlash among white-supremacist students. In the wake of Ray's withdrawal, Wesleyan students established a student colonization society, an organization where they preached what they practiced.[15]

The racial hostility Ray experienced at Wesleyan arose simultaneously with the controversies over colonization and abolition at many colleges, as shown in chapter 4. While those controversies centered on whether white students could discuss slavery or actively promote abolition at colleges, Black student abolitionists faced a different challenge: exclusion from, and virulent racism on, campus. This development marked an important shift from earlier episodic successes of Black students in the 1820s, as white reactionary opposition to abolition manifested in active exclusion of Black people from colleges. During the 1830s, white student abolitionist agitation merged with the abolitionist demand for racial equality in higher learning, which highlights dual forces of abolitionist dissent at colleges: white student agitation and Black admission protests.[16] The contending forces of white southern patronage, racist ideology, and Black freedom claims clashed in Middletown and gave way to whites' racist views. Financial ties to slavery helped the ACS make Wesleyan a stronghold of white supremacy in the early 1830s. After the events, the board of trustees implemented policy that further institutionalized white supremacy. They resolved that "none but male white persons shall be admitted as students at this institution." While the official resolution was overturned three years later, the damage had been done. Wesleyan retained a reputation for hostility towards African Americans throughout the antebellum period. Indeed, Fisk became a prominent colonizationist and the target of abolitionist criticism.[17]

During Ray's brief stint in Middletown, he became acquainted with a young Amos G. Beman, who had his own experience with racism at Wesleyan University. Beman was the son of Jehiel Beman, a pastor of the African Methodist Episcopal Cross Street Church in Middletown. In 1831, the Bemans were involved in protests against the ACS. The younger Beman, at nineteen years old, served as secretary at an antislavery meeting in Cross Street Church. Beman thus had an early education in Black protest and abolition from his family and the community. Two years later, armed with a consciousness formed in Black community, he began pursuing advanced learning in preparation for the ministry. He turned to the local university but was banned from formal admission. Instead, he studied privately with a white student, Samuel Dole, who was an abolitionist. Beman recited three times per week in Dole's room. Beman later recalled that "insults and jeers from the students were frequently encountered," but he continued his course of learning undaunted. Emboldened by their racist activism against Ray just months earlier, white students moved beyond verbal attack against Black students. One morning while Beman was on campus, students dumped water on him, and he was "completely drenched." It was a violent act, and it signified the evolution of the students' racist actions. Students then held a meeting during which they demanded that Dole cease tutoring Beman on campus. Dole seemingly agreed, which quelled the student unrest temporarily. Dole, however, continued studying with Beman in his room. After word of Dole's persistence became known among southern students, they penned a letter to Beman, threatening to forcibly remove him from campus. "To young Beman," students wrote, "A no. of students of this university, deeming it derogatory to themselves, as well as to the university, to have you and other colored people recite here, do hereby warn you to desist from such a course, and if you fail to comply with this peacable [*sic*] request, we swear, by the ETER-NAL GODS! that we will resort to *forcible* means to put a stop to it." Twelve students signed the letter. Emboldened by the removal of Ray, white students threatened Beman with physical violence. Indeed, the episode with Beman marked an escalation in violent anti-Black protest at the university. As a result, Beman quit his pursuit of higher learning. Dole showed the letter to two professors, who reacted indifferently. One cited the racist policy the trustees had enacted, which conveyed approval of the students' actions. The faculty's indifference was tacit support for the students' actions.[18]

The experiences of Ray and Beman were painful ones, as they encountered the malice of American racism in higher learning. Ray's episode had such a profound impact on him that four years later, when he should have been graduating, he recounted the events at an antislavery meeting in New York. He spoke about the effects of the experience: "I stand here this evening a victim of this withering, soul-killing prejudice." He explained the initial joy he felt about the opportunity to study at the university. He recalled, "I rejoiced in view of the prospect which spread out before me, of a favorable opportunity of acquiring moral and intellectual cultivation, requisite to the responsible work of the holy ministry." He went on to summarize the episode, explaining that his hopes were quickly dashed: "Mr. Chairman, I have not language justly to portray the emotions that agitated my lacerated bosom, when by the repelling influence of prejudice exercised by my supposed 'Christian brethren,' and fellow students, I was compelled to abandon the University, and with it all the hope of acquiring a liberal education; for then I found the colleges throughout the land closed against me. In an instant all my fond hopes were blasted. The only consolation I found in this dark hour, was in pouring my sorrows into the bosom of the God of the poor and the oppressed."[19]

Ray spoke passionately and critically about his experiences at the hands of racist students in higher learning. After he left Wesleyan, multiple colleges refused him admission, revealing the pervasive nature of anti-Black racism at northern colleges. He turned to the religion of the oppressed, to Black Christianity, for sustenance. This negative experience in his quest for higher learning propelled Ray to a lifetime of abolitionist work.[20] He traveled to New York City, where he was introduced to Theodore Wright, another abolitionist who had been active in the movement during his student days. When Ray gave his speech in 1836, Wright was present and would have identified with the malicious racism in higher learning, having been physically assaulted at Princeton earlier that year. Ray immersed himself in the vibrant Black communities of New York City. He worked initially as a boot maker, but in 1837, he became a traveling agent for the *Colored American*, the Black abolitionist newspaper founded by Philip A. Bell and Cornish. In the 1840s, Ray also served as a minister at Bethesda Congregational Church in New York City, which he helped establish for materially poor Black people.

He was also involved in the Black convention movement in New York and became active in the New York Vigilance Committee, aiding fugitive slaves. In short, Ray began his work in the movement as a student abolitionist, and his negative experience in higher learning was a catalyst for his working in community towards Black freedom.[21]

After Amos Beman left Middletown, he too embarked on a life of work in abolition. For two years, he taught at Hartford's only Black school. In 1835 he resumed his pursuit of formal education for the ministry, enrolling for a year at Oneida Institute. His classmates at the time included Garnet and Crummell. After Oneida, Beman resumed teaching in Hartford. In 1839 he was elected to the pastorate at the Temple Street African Congregational Church in New Haven, where he preached for the next twenty years and turned his church into a base for abolitionist organizing. Beman was involved in the Black convention movement, aided fugitive slaves, advocated Black men's voting rights, protested the Fugitive Slave Act of 1850, and promoted temperance and moral reform.[22] He recounted his Wesleyan experience later in his life at an 1854 antislavery meeting in Middletown. He published the violent threat from the twelve students and a selection from Dole, letting the documents "speak for themselves." He also observed the vibrant abolitionist presence that had since formed in Middletown, and the convention at which he spoke was a testament to its legacy.[23] Throughout his life, Beman fought slavery and racism. His upbringing in the Black community and his negative experience at Wesleyan as a student abolitionist placed him on a path to serving Black people in the struggle for freedom. By cultivating critical knowledge through experience and working in Black movement spaces, Ray and Beman practiced the tenets of Black Studies.

Ray's and Beman's respective rejections were part of a larger wave of anti-Black exclusion at colleges in the 1830s. A handful of qualified Black students had their admissions requests, which functioned as protests, denied at colleges and seminaries. The Black abolitionist minister William C. Munroe had sought admission at Bowdoin, Amherst, and Dartmouth Colleges but was "met with immediate rejection, or was offered admittance only on such degrading terms, as no one who had any sense of the rights of man would accept." After initially admitting Russwurm, Jones, and Mitchell, respectively, each of those institutions regressed on Black admissions in the early 1830s. Reverend Peter Williams Jr. helped lead the efforts in preparing young Black students for college. In 1834 he reported, "I was anxious that some of our youth should have the opportunity of acquiring a liberal education, and felt that it was my duty to strive to rear up some well qualified colored ministers." Williams worked with Cornish and others in supporting the African Free Schools in New York and taught Latin and Greek at a school for Black youth in Manhattan. Williams continued, "I selected two lads of great promise, and made every possible effort to get them a collegiate education. But the Colleges were all closed against them." One of the students was a young James McCune Smith, who was excluded from Geneva College and the Medical College at Columbia. A young Black man from Kentucky, who was formerly enslaved and aspired to become a Presbyterian minister, was rejected at Centre College in Kentucky. A similar episode occurred in Ripley, Ohio, where a young Black student was refused admission from a college there.[24]

More rejections came from General Theological Seminary in New York City. As Craig Wilder has shown, Isaiah DeGrasse, a student of African American and South Asian ancestry, was the first to be rejected. On October 10, 1836, DeGrasse passed entrance examinations required by the seminary, demonstrating his qualifications for candidacy. A month earlier, he had received a degree with honors from Newark College in Delaware and had previously studied at Hobart College. The following day, DeGrasse confronted the racist bar in higher learning. He recorded in his diary that the bishop of the Episcopalian seminary, Benjamin Onderdonk, "was dissatisfied with the step I had taken in entering the Seminary" because he thought "the South, from whence they receive much support, will object to my entering." On October 12, DeGrasse wrote, the bishop advised him to "vacate the room and silently withdraw myself from the Seminary." Within two days of passing entrance exams, DeGrasse was being forced from the institution. The bishop informed DeGrasse that he could study at the seminary but not as an official student. DeGrasse adamantly refused, writing, "Never, never will I do so!" He further denounced the offer as "so utterly repugnant to my feelings as a man, that I cannot consent to adopt it." DeGrasse was deeply insulted by the bishop's offer. His qualifications were equal to those of any white student and merited equal status. Cited as reasons DeGrasse should leave were the southern influence over the seminary and the potential for student withdrawals. Since the bishop argued that these reasons justified DeGrasse's exclusion, DeGrasse highlighted the bishop's complicity in racism. "It is my present opinion," DeGrasse reflected, "that Bishop Onderdonk is wrong in yielding to the 'unrighteous prejudice' (his [Onderdonk's] words) of the community. If the prejudice be wrong, I think he ought to oppose it without regard to consequences. If such men as he countenance it, they become partakers in the consequences." DeGrasse identified the problem with white northerners who critiqued prejudice but whose actions ultimately reinforced it. In citing white southern patronage as reason to reject DeGrasse, Onderdonk bowed to the slave power, clinging to its financial support. DeGrasse experienced what many Black students faced in their pursuit of higher learning. They clashed with white college authorities who faced south for funding and used their allegiance to the South to enforce white supremacy in their institutions, and thereby became complicit in sustaining slavery and northern racism. Refusing to accept what he believed were insulting conditions for study, DeGrasse left the seminary. On October 13, DeGrasse painfully recorded in his diary, "This day I am driven in the presence of all the students of the Seminary, and the sight of high Heaven, from the School of the Prophets."[25]

DeGrasse went on to study with Rev. Williams, who ordained him into the ministry. DeGrasse became a pastor to Black congregations in Long Island, and taught at an Episcopal school. He also gave lectures on African American Christianity and was a member of the committee, along with Cornish, Williams, and Theodore Wright, that oversaw the African Schools in New York. In 1840, he received an honorary master of arts degree from Newark, and in the fall of that year, became a missionary to Kingston, Jamaica. The following January, DeGrasse tragically died of yellow fever at the age of twenty-seven.[26] During his life, DeGrasse challenged the boundaries of northern colleges and seminaries. Ironically, he attended college in a slave state and yet was forced to leave a seminary in a (nominally) free one. His entrance into the seminary had radical implications, as he refuted racist stereotypes, demonstrated Black intellectual achievement, and showed that Black people were eminently qualified for the ministry. Like other abolitionists, DeGrasse exposed the grip slaveholders had on northern colleges and seminaries and put forth a critique of institutionalized racism in higher learning. He was rejected because of the radical challenge he posed to the slave power. As with other Black students, his experience with racism in higher learning was formative and propelled him to an activist life in the ministry and the movement.

Maria Stewart and Black Women's Higher Learning

Black women abolitionists were integral to the process of conceptualizing Black higher learning as a liberating force. Their theorizations went beyond those of most men, Black or white. During the antebellum phase of abolition, Black women advocated equal higher learning for young women and girls. In the early 1830s, Maria Stewart argued for an education for and by Black women, which she believed would yield political rights. Black women students at selected northern institutions took up Stewart's call and brought to fruition an expanded notion of student abolitionism that advocated Black women's rights. They redefined the meaning of student abolitionism for racial and gender equality both on campus and in the public sphere.[27]

In 1833, at the African Masonic Hall in Boston, Maria Stewart spoke in favor of Black higher learning. Stewart cultivated knowledge in Sabbath schools during her youth and was mentored by David Walker. She called on African Americans to "turn their attention to knowledge and improvement; for knowledge is power." Study and learning were the means to freedom and equality. Stewart recognized that there were indeed many intelligent Black men in the United States but asked, "Where can we find amongst ourselves the man of science, or a philosopher, or an able statesman, or counsellor of law?" Stewart was advocating formal education for Black men. "Give the man of color an equal opportunity with the white, from cradle to manhood, and from manhood to the grave, and you would discover the dignified statesman, the man of science, and the philosopher." Acknowledging the rampant racism in higher learning that prevented formal Black education, Stewart implored Black people to contribute their money "for schools and seminaries of learning for our children and youth." She saw education, including higher learning and Black institution building as the most effective path towards Black rights. If African Americans had these opportunities, Stewart asserted, "I would defy the government of these United States to deprive us any longer of our rights." She condemned colonizationists as hypocrites and called on them to make use of their resources to improve the conditions of African Americans in the United States, not in another land. "If the colonizationists are real friends to Africa let them expend the money which they collect in erecting a college to educate her injured sons in this land of gospel light and liberty," she challenged. Throughout the address, Stewart linked higher learning, and educational equality more generally, to freedom and equal citizenship. She also called on Black men to petition Congress for the abolition of slavery in Washington, DC, and to be granted "the rights and privileges of common free citizens." The address is also filled with biblical references, signifying Stewart's mastery of theological arguments and engagement with scripture. Indeed, her speech, as a written document and piece of oratory, demonstrated a Black feminist intellectuality.[28] While this oration addressed Black men's higher learning, in an earlier speech, Stewart advocated Black women's higher learning.

In her earliest published writings, political rights and equality in education were central to Stewart's ideas. In "Religion and the Pure Principles of Morality," Stewart's main goal was to "arouse you [African Americans] to exertion, and to enforce upon your minds the great necessity of turning your attention to knowledge and improvement." Stewart believed that the cultivation of knowledge and religious piety were the harbingers of Black freedom for all Black people, enslaved or free. She singled out Black women specifically as central to this political project. "O ye daughters of Africa, awake! awake! Arise! No longer sleep nor slumber, distinguish yourselves. Show forth to the world that ye are endowed with noble and exalted faculties." Gaining an education would not only enable their own freedom, Steward posited, but Black women would also instill in their children a desire for learning. "Let every female become united," she proclaimed, "and let us raise a fund ourselves, and at the end of one year and a half, we might be able to lay the corner stone for the building of a High School, that the higher branches of knowledge might be enjoyed by us." This plan of Black women's education would facilitate political recognition. "That day," Steward insisted, "the hissing and reproach among the nations of the earth against us will cease." She encouraged women to work fearlessly, to "possess the spirit of independence," and to showcase their knowledge. Stewart called on women to "sue for your rights and privileges. Know the reason that you cannot attain them. Weary them with your importunities."[29] Stewart's vision for Black women's education was clear from the outset: foster education among themselves and their children in a Black school, an act of self-determination, and participate politically to claim their rights and freedom. In other words, education provided the foundation for Black women's claims for liberation. She thus called for a political education, based on Black women's self-determination, that would advance the cause of Black women's freedom.

Stewart built on these arguments for women's educational and political rights in her 1833 farewell address in Boston. Defending herself from criticisms she received for speaking publicly to men and women, Stewart cited examples of women from the Bible to justify her role as public speaker, positioning herself among them as having been divinely inspired to do their work. She summarized, "Holy women ministered onto Christ and the apostles; and women of refinement in all ages, more or less, have had a voice in moral, religious, and political subjects." She went on to survey examples of women from the Middle Ages who were accomplished intellectuals and public figures. In this earlier time, Stewart wrote, "We might then have seen women preaching and mixing themselves in controversies. Women occupying the chairs of Philosophy and Justice, women writing in Greek, and studying Hebrew." She cited an example of a thirteenth-century woman "who devoted herself to the study of the Latin language and of the laws" and who at age twenty-six "took the degree of Doctor of Laws." She continued, "Her great reputation raised her to a chair, where she taught the law to a prodigious concourse of scholars from all nations." In doing so, "she joined the charms and accomplishments of a woman to all the knowledge of a man," asserting human equality. Stewart then rhetorically asked her audience why women were excluded from harnessing the benefits of advanced learning. After citing these precedents in history, she instructed her audience to foster an environment where Black women were active politically in the public sphere.[30] While this was not explicitly acknowledged in her speech, Stewart positioned herself in African traditions of womanhood in defiance of Western gender constructions.[31] Stewart's forceful arguments connecting women's learning with social activism put Black women's higher learning on the abolitionist agenda. By invoking bibli-

cal precedents, she vindicated her position as a public speaker and intellectual. In explaining women's scholarly achievements, she critiqued
American colleges for excluding women despite evidence of women's intellectual equality with men. As a Black intellectual, Stewart transcended
the world of white higher learning, as she embodied refutations to white
notions at the time of who could be a scholar. Like the figure evoked in
her address, Stewart may well have been a doctor of laws and teacher of
scholars in another time and place. She was, however, a teacher among
her people. Due to the exclusionary nature of the colleges, it was thus up
to women themselves, Stewart believed, in acts of self-determination, to
advance their own education and learning, which would translate into
political rights. Her arguments for women's education as a political project were in line with those of other Black abolitionists who saw higher
learning as a harbinger of freedom, but Stewart was among the earliest
to insert Black women specifically into the equation. With her lectures
on Black higher learning and lifetime of work, Stewart joined the tradition of Black women abolitionists such as Phillis Wheatley, Lucy Terry
Prince, and Betsy Stockton, in making the terrain of higher learning an
area of critique and protest for a new humanity. Stewart's arguments and
advocacy were taken up by a generation of Black women who sought to
acquire higher learning in the antebellum period.

The NEAS Takes on Black Admissions

Despite the barriers they faced, Black abolitionists' advocacy for Black
higher learning continued through the 1830s. Cornish remained a proponent of formally educated Black ministers. He lamented the persistent
dearth of them: "We know of but two who have been given a classical
education, while nine-tenths of the white candidates have been brought
into the office through a thorough course of training" with church spon-
sorship. Other commentators provided similar critiques and highlighted
the dire need for equal training for Black ministers and other professions.[32] Cornish's concerns and Black abolitionist protests for higher
learning gained wider attention in the movement. Responding to Black
student men's admission rejections in the 1830s, Black and white abolitionists debated the policies of New England colleges at the 1836 meeting
of the New England Anti-Slavery Society (NEAS). At the convention,

Theodore Wright condemned racism at colleges in his critique of northern prejudice. "No man can really understand this prejudice," Wright lectured the convention, without experiencing it themselves. Racism barred Black people from all levels of education, he asserted; it "has bolts in all the schools and colleges."[33] Wright's critique of American colleges elicited a robust discussion on higher learning the following day.

The central question prompted by Wright's address was whether any college east of Ohio besides the Oneida Institute accepted Black students. The white minister Cyrus Grosvenor first proposed a resolution applauding Oneida and called on abolitionists "to bestow their patronage and support" on it for its noble mission. Grosvenor's proposal came at a crucial moment, as the New York state legislature was threatening to withhold financial resources from Oneida because it was "the hot-bed of sedition." Grosvenor explained that Wright's speech the previous day had demonstrated the need for Black higher learning as a tactic to force changes in the dominant racist culture. Grosvenor reflected, "Yesterday, when I listened to the remarks of our brother Wright, I felt that the moral and intellectual claims of Africa had been practically defended." Grosvenor believed that Wright and other African Americans in higher learning were "doing more to break up the prejudice against the colored race" than could be done "by argument or appeal." Grosvenor added, "I want to see that power increased a thousand-fold, through the means of our literary institutions, by educated colored youths."[34] Wright's career as a student abolitionist and subsequent agitation had a powerful effect on the meeting. The protests of Black students and other Black abolitionists' arguments for higher learning were changing the movement.

Wright spoke again, responding to Grosvenor's resolution, and he emphasized the significance of Oneida as a critique of New England colleges. "This is practical abolition. This is laying the axe at the root of the tree," he explained. Opportunities for Black people to acquire "literature, science, and the mechanical arts" would give the lie to racist ideas. Wright praised the abolitionist education students received at Oneida. "God is there," he observed, "teaching abolition, by training the young men together, white and colored." He believed an education in abolition, in principle and in practice, with Black and white students, exemplified in the Oneida model, needed replication. Wright's and Grosvenor's arguments were an indictment of New England colleges for refusing to state publicly whether they would admit Black students. Wright put it bluntly: "It is pretended there is no regulation in New England Colleges which excludes colored students." He highlighted his attempts to enroll Black students at colleges: "I have carried pupils to these colleges. The professors will say, there is no rule to exclude you, but we think you had better not apply." Admission practices at New England colleges were clear. While there was no official rule barring Black students from any institution, it was de facto policy premised on northern racism and connections to slavery that prevented Black students from entering them. While some members questioned the restrictions at New England colleges, citing cases of Black students being admitted in the 1820s, examples of exclusion in the 1830s revealed otherwise.[35] Other abolitionists highlighted the persistent racial barriers at colleges in New England. Reverend Moses Thacher summarized, "The New England colleges might not exclude colored students, but they encouraged a prejudice which created an atmosphere in which a colored student could not live." He continued, "So long as it [American prejudice] existed in our colleges, no colored student could be admitted there to equal advantages with white pupils." A Reverend Fitch of Boston concurred and went further, illustrating the influence of the slave power at northern colleges. New England colleges "don't like to have it known that they admit colored pupils, for fear of losing Southern students." He quipped, "Like many other people, they are good abolitionists, so far as it will not hurt their trade." Finally, Mr. Caples of Boston, a Black abolitionist, gave a stirring statement regarding the terms of admissions. "If I enter the Institution, I want to enter as a man, and go through as a man." If Black students were accepted under the condition that they perform menial labor, "brushing boots and making fires for the students," then they could "never rise up like men." Black students must be admitted as equals, he argued. Elizur Wright Jr. followed, explaining how he had inquired about Black admissions at every college in New England and each had refused to state whether it would accept Black students. The resolution, Wright asserted, "would be a test by which to ascertain whether any college but Oneida could be opened to the colored student."[36]

These abolitionists raised a significant issue: singular examples of Black admissions at New England colleges did not extinguish racial barriers or hostility in those places. The conditions Black students endured were indeed racist, as illustrated in the experiences of Ray, Beman, and DeGrasse.

It would take more than selective admissions to transform New England colleges, and the Oneida example presented a working model. At the same time, from the perspective of Black students, their admissions represented the radical possibilities that Black higher learning had for the movement and their communities. It was this tension between the intransigence of white faculty in their refusal to accept Black students in large numbers, largely due to racism and the reliance of colleges on the economy of slaving, and the radical challenge Black students posed to the colleges that constantly played out over the course of the antebellum period.

The conversation surrounding Grosvenor's resolution reveals the impact Black students and other Black abolitionists advocating equality in higher learning had on abolition. Their agitation shaped the agenda of a major organization and further revealed the political significance of Black higher learning. It was long in the making, as the important work and persistent agitation of Theodore Wright, Maria Stewart, Peter Williams Jr., and Samuel Cornish, among others, combined to make Black higher learning central to the movement's agenda in the 1830s. The ideas for Black higher learning and the students challenging racism in northern institutions came from Black communities and institutions. When Black students came to campus, they brought themselves and a consciousness shaped by, in, and for Black community. Members at the NEAS unanimously passed Grosvenor's resolution as a tactic to exert pressure on northern colleges. Indeed, it would be a test to which New England college officials would respond when subsequent Black students made demands for admission. The strategy also represents a shift in tactics for some abolitionists from building a separate Black college to demanding entrance into existing white colleges, which would remain a topic of debate among Black abolitionists.

When Black students were excluded from northern colleges, many sought higher learning abroad, specifically in Britain. James McCune Smith, Alexander Crummell, and Sarah Parker Remond, to name only a few, exemplify this tendency. The academic achievements of Black students abroad both were framed as critiques of American colleges and represented Black people's demands for freedom on the world stage. British universities like Cambridge and Glasgow, however, remained tethered to slavery regardless of Black student enrollment.[37] As students, McCune Smith, Remond, and Crummell were all involved in the British abolition movement, lecturing and teaching Britons about the struggles of Black people in the United States. Upon returning to New York City, McCune Smith dedicated the rest of his life to abolition and helping Black people. He was the resident physician at a Black orphanage in New York, used his pen to refute racism in the intellectual sphere, and was a fixture in Black movement organizations.[38] After finishing at Bedford College in London and completing a series of lectures across England, Remond went on to study in Italy and became an obstetrician, where she lived out her days working in women's health.[39] As with other Black students, Crummell's intellectual journey and life experiences informed his orientation to the university. Along with McCune Smith, Garnet, and many others, he was a product of the New York African Free Schools and participated in the Black convention movement. Black learning spaces and activist formations shaped his consciousness. Through experience and study, Crummell developed keen insights into the question of Black education across the diaspora.[40] While in England, Crummell gave a speech at the British and Foreign Antislavery Society meeting in May of 1851, in which he explained his motivations for traveling to Liberia. He argued that the status of enslaved and free Black populations was intimately linked and that Black learning would be a tool for collective liberation. "As the free coloured population go up in scale of intelligence, increase in mental capacity, and demonstrate their intellectual power," he explained, "the whole fabric of slavery proportionately crumbles and totters." But, he recounted, "in the Northern States the prejudice of the whites prevents a full participation in the advantages of schools and colleges." Barriers to formal learning and study for Africans in America remained prominent. Black educational formations had to be expanded among the populace. Such teaching should take place in Africa as well, Crummell reasoned. He remarked, "Africa is to be evangelized only by preaching the Gospel. No mere trading-institutions, no colonies, and no colonisation schemes are able to redeem and elevate the vast population of that continent." Crummell believed that Christian teachings, not imperial or colonial interests, should spread on the continent.[41]

Four months after his lecture, Crummell traveled to Liberia, where he worked as a teacher and minister among colonists and Indigenous Africans. He joined in the tradition of early Black students who traveled to West Africa to work among the people, including Russwurm, who had spent most of his adult life in Liberia. He had died in 1851, just two years prior to Crummell's arrival.[42] It is unclear whether Crummell knew that Edward Jones was working as a teacher at Fourah Bay College in Sierra Leone. Crummell's anti-imperialist argument informed his work as a teacher, but the ideological inconsistency of spreading Christianity as a harbinger of civilization was a significant shortcoming. It conflicted with African cultural and religious practices. He would teach at Liberia College for several years before returning to the United States in the late nineteenth century. Crummell's emphasis on Black self-determination and working in the interests of all Black people was his lasting contribution to the struggle. His vision for Black learning prior to his departure to England and Liberia holds a significant place in the history of independent Black educational formations, a topic to be explored in the next chapter.

Black abolitionist demands for higher learning reveal a robust understanding of the function of education for Black liberation. Black thinkers like Cornish saw higher learning primarily through the lens of religion, as a means to formally educate Black ministers, who would teach the lessons of scripture in Black communities with the intention of uniting Black people in the struggle. Serving as teachers and intellectuals, Black ministers would also combat proslavery Christianity and the complicity of northern churches with slavery and prejudice. This was Walker's vision put into practice. It was what Black abolitionists strove to accomplish in the proposal for the African College and subsequent admission demands from Black students. The question whether to integrate existing colleges or create Black institutions would continue as a topic of debate among Black abolitionists, as the next chapter will show.

Maria Stewart expanded on Cornish's vision and added to Walker's plan a call for higher learning as a tool for Black women's freedom. While Stewart condemned the exclusion of Black women from institutions of higher learning, she encouraged women to create their own institutions and educate themselves. They did not need white institutions to gain a political education. Stewart herself was evidence of this fact. She believed that when no spaces were open to them, Black women needed to create their own spaces; and indeed they did so for their own cultivation of knowledge. Stewart thought beyond the logics of higher learning in formal institutions and proposed a form of Black study, forming autonomous spaces created in community with Black women to learn, to develop ways of knowing, and to foster a political consciousness that would lead to Black women's liberation. Black women manifested this idea in literary societies and other spaces where they learned together.

Black students themselves helped create the idea of Black higher learning. In their demands for admission, they became grassroots agitators for the abolitionist project. After their negative experiences in attempting to wield higher learning for their own purposes, Ray, Beman, and DeGrasse became teachers, ministers, and workers in the struggle. Black students' participation in abolition and the arguments they made while on campus challenged the social and intellectual hierarchies colleges upheld. Beyond their mere presence on campus, Black students' actions struck fear in college authorities and risked the financial resources emanating from slaveholders. While some Black students struggled to transform the United States, others pursued emigration. As the 1850s unfolded, Black students like Crummell and Garnet and also Martin Delany pursued emigration as an alternative to the American project, revealing the emergence of a nascent Black intelligentsia diasporic culture connected to notions of Black nationalism and a nascent Pan-Africanism.

Black student abolitionism was an expansive, transatlantic phenomena. Black students studying abroad were emissaries of Black freedom claims. They created a nascent Pan-African coalition of intellectuals who advanced the Black freedom struggle in the United States, West Africa, and Europe. As Black abolitionists developed new ideas for the purpose and meaning of higher learning, they exposed the racism embedded in American colleges and their connections to the slave economy. Undeterred by the social structure, Black people continued developing the mission David Walker helped formulate in his *Appeal*, the cultivation of education and religion among Black people to foster unity in the struggle to transform the world. The ways to achieve that goal, however, were less clear. But Black students and other Black abolitionists created a novel concept: linking learning and study to the movement for Black freedom. This was the meaning of Black higher learning. Black students thus added to the production of knowledge and tactics in the struggle. As the movement progressed, Black students continued protesting the boundaries of colleges through admission demands, which slowly began to yield different outcomes, while other Black abolitionists continued contemplating the creation of a Black college.

6

The Making of a Tradition

In July 1854, Frederick Douglass was invited to speak at the commencement ceremonies at Western Reserve College. Douglass highlighted the
irony of the occasion, as he, someone who was formerly enslaved and
never attended college, was asked to lecture. "I engage to-day for the
first time in the exercises of any College Commencement. It is a new
chapter in my humble experience." He proceeded with caution, explaining, "It was with much distrust and hesitation that he [speaking in the
third person] accepted the invitation." He took advantage of the situation, however, and hoped to engender the "generous indulgence" of the
audience with his remarks. In the midst of the unfolding sectional crisis,
Douglass observed, the relation between Black and white people in the
United States was "the vital question of the age," and as to the solution,
"the scholars of America will have to take an important and controlling part." Douglass explained the magnitude of the task for scholars,
for whom there was no neutral ground: "He who is not for us is against
us." In turn, Douglass surveyed scholarly positions on the question and
engaged the academic field in vogue at the time, the pseudoscience
of race, polygenesis, and the theory of diverse human origins. Referring explicitly to leading thinkers on the subject, including Josiah Nott,
Louis Agassiz, and Samuel Morton, Douglass observed sarcastically, "It
is strange that there should arise a phalanx of learned men—speaking
in the name of science—to forbid the magnificent reunion of mankind
in one brotherhood." It was not a coincidence that such theories came
from white men in positions of power, whose arguments slaveholders
and proslavery politicians deployed in the debates over the Kansas-
Nebraska controversy over slavery's extension. Rebutting the scientific
racists, Douglass drew on African history and culture, showing that the
ancient Egyptians were Africans, the arts and sciences emerged from
Africa, and the languages of the peoples of West, East, and Southern
Africa were similar to that of North Africans. Rather than ordering

human beings into hierarchies, an idea central to Western intellectual traditions, Douglass was drawing on the deep well of Africana intellectual genealogies to present an alternative conceptualization of world history that centered African history and the common humanity of all people. Douglass continued with an observation as resonant in our times as the 1850s: "A mortifying proof is here given, that the moral growth of a nation, or an age, does not always keep pace with the increase of knowledge, and suggests the necessity of means to increase human love with human learning." Douglass laid bare the fallacy of human progress and knowledge production marching lockstep with time. He debunked the scientific racism of the era with logical force and power. Douglass's central claim was that Black people were human beings and of common ancestry with all of humankind, which necessarily demanded the abolition of slavery and racial oppression. For Douglass, the destiny of the United States was tied to the destiny of Black people; either slavery and prejudice would be removed, ushering in a new era for humanity, or divine retribution would tear the country asunder for its sins. He left the audience to choose where they would align their affinities.[1]

Douglass speaking on the boundaries of the college and his address dismantling racist academic thought mirrored the experiences, both socially and intellectually, of Black students of the antebellum era. Like Douglass at the commencement, Black students were in but not of the American college, and their searing critiques of the academy's obsession with scientific racism anticipated Douglass's arguments. Along with students' writings, as will be shown below, Douglass's address is evidence of a nascent Black Studies challenging white academia and presenting alternative conceptions of humanity and world history rooted in African genealogies. His emphasis on increasing human love with human learning continues to resonate and has eluded university officials over time.

As restrictions to Black student admissions mounted, Black abolitionists continued to pressure colleges to admit Black students. As a result, several Black students broke through the racial barriers at selected institutions. Andrew Harris, Thomas Paul Jr., and Lucy Stanton went through the college course at predominantly white institutions and graduated with degrees. Not only were they agents of abolition on their respective campuses; they wrote critiques of racism in higher learning and made demands for Black women's rights. In addition to their academic work,

Black students were involved in the movement beyond the campus. They gave lectures at local and national antislavery meetings, taught in Black schools, preached in Black congregations, and promoted unity for Black freedom. Harris, Paul, and Stanton used their learning and knowledge for the benefit of Black communities, manifesting David Walker's and Maria Stewart's combined vision of learning and liberation. In producing knowledge through and for the struggle, Black students continued to manifest a nascent form of Black Studies.

The experiences of Harris, Paul, and Stanton, in conjunction with that of their peers who attended white institutions, reveals that Black students were socially and intellectually in but not of the colleges they attended. W. E. B. Du Bois used this formulation in describing his time at Harvard in the late nineteenth century, and it aptly captures the experiences of the generation of Black students before him.[2] Black students were often the only Black person on campus and frequently encountered racism from white peers and faculty. As this work has shown, they also faced hostile intellectual environments, as evidenced by the pervasiveness of the ACS, scientific racism, and sexism at the colleges, products of the Western intellectual foundations of the academy. In short, throughout the antebellum period, the colleges largely remained white male spaces underpinned by knowledge produced by white men, which was used to justify the oppression of Black people and others. This was the context Black students were up against as they entered the colleges as formal students. For Black women students like Stanton, Black feminist perspectives were doubly subversive.[3] While Black students represented insurgencies of Black thought and abolition on campus, their experiences reveal the necessity of Black institutions and self-determination.

The struggle for Black students entering white colleges as equals and the social and intellectual power dynamics therein spurred further debate among Black abolitionists on the most effective strategies to diffuse Black higher learning among the masses. The question of integrating existing colleges or building their own institutions persisted. Though the African College proposal was struck down in 1831, the impetus for such an institution remained a central topic of the Black convention movement.[4] By the late 1840s and early 1850s, a handful of Black people graduated from colleges, but progress was slow. By 1850, nowhere were

Black students admitted in large numbers, with the exception of Oberlin. But as indicated by the debates among Black abolitionists, Oberlin was insufficient in offering advanced learning for African Americans.[5] Oberlin was not a Black institution. As a result of the dearth of Black admissions, Black abolitionists continued to advocate the construction of an African College with an expansive curriculum that went beyond educating ministers. Black abolitionists' formulation of higher learning continued to include classical learning, manual labor, and the mechanical arts. The proposal for a Black college during the Black conventions in the late 1840s and early 1850s aimed to educate and train Black workers in the skilled trades as well as intellectuals in the changing political and economic context of the industrializing North. Significantly, the final version of the proposal called for a coeducational institution. Proposals for a Black college remained a radical idea for Black higher learning, as Black colleges paired learning with self-determination. Black people understood the inadequacy of Black students studying in hostile environments that were white colleges. These institutions were incapable of addressing the problems Black people faced because the colleges were part of the problem. While the African College ultimately did not come to fruition in the immediate term, it laid the foundation for proposals of what would become historically Black colleges and universities (HBCUs), as well as the Black University concept. The ideological foundations of HBCUs have their origins in the Black abolitionist idea of Black higher learning in the antebellum period. Black abolitionists in this period understood the significance of Black institutions and self-determination for changing their circumstances.

Black Men Student Abolitionists in White Colleges

When abolitionists debated whether New England colleges would admit Black students at the 1836 NEAS convention, a Black student was going through the college course at Burlington College, which later became the University of Vermont (UV). Andrew Harris entered the sophomore class in the fall of 1835. Harris was born in 1814 to Black parents in upstate New York, and his early life is somewhat opaque. He was adopted at the age of two by a Presbyterian minister in Cayuga, New York, near Seneca Falls. In adolescence, Harris attended the Geneva

Lyceum, an educational institution dedicated to preparatory training for aspiring young ministers. Harris was also a leader in the local Sabbath school. His experiences in education and religion shaped his worldview, and the youth grew interested in pursuing college learning.[6]

Before Harris entered the university, he was refused admission at other colleges. One such experience was at Union College in 1834. His admission protest came at the height of anti-abolition mob violence sweeping northern states. The Union faculty cited this context in their decision, informing Harris that "under other circumstances, they would have received him, but in the present state of public feeling, they decline[ed]." The broader racist backlash against abolition held sway over the Union faculty. The college's president, Eliphalet Nott, was also an anti-abolitionist and a leader in the New York state colonization society. Harris ventured further north and looked to Middlebury College but was denied admission there as well. By 1834, Middlebury faculty and trustees were members of the state colonization society. By rejecting Harris, these officials aligned with other college colonizationists who refused to admit Black students in the 1830s unless they promised to leave the country, extending their ideas about racial exclusion to the college itself.[7] College officials understood Black admissions as manifestations of the abolition movement, and they explicitly closed the doors to Harris on those grounds, reinforcing opposition to abolition. The rejections of Harris reflected the experiences of other Black students and further demonstrate the anti-Black nature of American colleges in the 1830s.

Despite the difficulties in finding a college open to him, Harris kept trying and applied to the faculty at the University of Vermont in 1835. The university was in a languishing state; a fire had destroyed one of two academic buildings, and only two students graduated in the class of 1833.[8] Harris applied to an institution struggling to stay afloat. In response to Harris's application, the faculty initially expressed wariness, citing the social climate that was hostile to abolition. And yet, Harris's qualifications and his desire to "preach the gospel to the poor" ultimately swayed university president John Wheeler and the faculty to admit him. His devotion to the ministry and the university's dire need for student enrollment to remain solvent seemingly won the day. Harris's preparatory education and his persistent efforts for college learning yielded significant results. Harris refused to accept the decisions at Union and

Middlebury, and his admission protest at UV was successful. He entered the university as a student abolitionist.[9]

Harris began his studies as a sophomore during the fall of 1835, a testament to his academic credentials, but he soon faced racism. For the first twelve months, Harris was forced to recite his lessons apart from the student body. "A few of the students refused to recite with him," read one report documenting Harris's time at the university. After twelve months of segregated learning, Harris entered the regular course with white students. Faculty could no longer justify his exclusion since Harris was "at the head of his class" academically. While one writer observed that "none of the faculty were abolitionists," they were modifying their views about Black people because of Harris's academic progression. This was one of the effects of Black higher learning: it chipped away at white supremacy. Another account explained that while Harris was "allowed more priveleges [sic]" while at the university, "he was not suffered to stand on the same footing with the other students."[10] A classmate later recalled that Harris "struggled hard against accumulated disadvantages, and that worst of all annoyance of a student's life—pecuniary embarrassments; but he nobly overcame them all." Harris endured racist conduct from white faculty and students while he attended the university. Indeed, the faculty's initial hesitance in admitting Harris was an indication of its anti-Black social and intellectual atmosphere. Wheeler was also a staunch colonizationist, having lectured for the state society as early as 1825. He remained a fervent ACS member well into the 1850s, becoming president of the state organ from 1852 to 1861.[11] Exclusion and other manifestations of racism were forces Harris combated as he went through his studies. He defied the odds and progressed through the course, passing his exams each year. Through his academic progression, Harris was making an impact on campus as a student abolitionist.

After his first year at the university, Harris traveled to Troy, New York, and his experiences with Black people there left an indelible mark on his life trajectory. Harris went there during the winter recess to teach at a Black school. Harris arrived at a period of mobilization in the town's Black community. In 1835, Black people and especially Black women led fundraising efforts for the construction of a new church and a school, which needed a teacher.[12] In November 1836, Harris was introduced at a meeting of Troy's Black community and was chosen secretary. The meeting, in part, was intended to introduce Harris as the new teacher for the winter term. A resolution read, "We cordially welcome among us Andrew Harris, of Vermont, who comes to take charge of our school. We pledge him our cordial cooperation, and regard him, as the teacher of our children, equally with our pastor and spiritual leaders, as entitled to our prayers and persevering support." As a student abolitionist, Harris was accepted as a teacher in Troy's Black community. The community bestowed legitimacy on him as an intellectual with formal training who would use his skills in service of teaching in their institutions. The following February, Harris was a featured speaker at the fourth anniversary of the Female Benevolent Society, an event dedicated to honoring the work of Black women in the community. The next month, Harris helped organize a six-night series of lectures on intellectual and moral improvement. The first topic was the significance of education, and Harris was the featured speaker. A report described Harris's talk: "There was never a more salutary impression made upon a colored audience in this city." After the lecture, members of the community donated to the school. After four months of teaching, Harris received seventy-eight dollars, indicating community approval. Harris also spoke on honoring the Sabbath and on temperance.[13] During his time away from the university, Harris was fully immersed in the Black community at Troy, which accepted him as a teacher and lecturer. His activities there were a welcomed respite from the hostilities he had endured at the university. The work was vital to Harris's growth as a student abolitionist. He was putting the skills and knowledge he acquired in college learning to work in the service of the local Black community and the abolition movement more broadly, carrying out David Walker's vision. In the community's institutions, Black people studied and learned together to advance their freedom. In those autonomous spaces of Black study, the utility of Black higher learning was revealed: it had to be used in community with Black people for it to have meaning. Together they fostered a vision for creating a different world.

Harris's influence extended beyond the Troy community as well. In March 1837, he spoke at the meeting of the Union Society of the Colored People of Albany, Troy, and Vicinity, held in Albany. Harris helped organize this new organization, which was dedicated to "combining the whole strength of our people in the several cities and towns in this vicinity, for our improvements in 'Morals, Education, and the Mechanical Arts.'" The organization emphasized the unity of Black communities and the importance of these objectives for their children, for posterity, and to "hasten the redemption of two and a half millions of our enslaved brethren."[14] Harris helped organize and unify local Black communities for learning and working towards the liberation of all Black people. He also served as the organization's recording secretary. One of the resolutions was critical of social-structure renderings of Black people and spoke to the significance of Black learning: "The question is forever settled, that our children and youth are not deficient in native capacity, for high improvement in any department of literature and science. The only deficiency is to be found in the want of opportunity and sufficient inducements for improvement." Harris symbolized this argument as a student abolitionist and teacher and helped shape the organization's platform. It was the objective of the organization to inspire Black people to study and learn, as they believed "virtue and intelligence constitute the sure foundation on which we are to rise." Harris also gave "an eloquent and efficient speech" at the meeting, which emphasized "*education, and a more general attention to the mechanic arts.*" Members of the organization believed that this outlook of moral reform, education, piety, and especially skills in the crafts would facilitate a transformation in their lives. The recurring theme of mechanical arts constituted recognition that learning skilled trades was equally as important as classical education. This expansive framework would appeal to a wide constituency of Black people seeking to improve their lives materially and intellectually.[15] As Harris's work illustrates, as a college student he quickly became an important Black abolitionist in eastern upstate New York. With his contributions, the community made education a central pillar of realizing freedom. As a formally trained intellectual, Harris was using his education in the service of organizing Black people and collectively making demands for a new humanity. In this way, Harris and Black people in upstate New York were practicing Black Studies, acquiring knowledge through collective experience, learning, and organizing. Together they manifested Walker's and Stewart's visions of using learning and knowledge to work towards liberation.

After this flurry of abolitionist activity, Harris returned to the university and progressed through his studies. While Harris already had been a student abolitionist when he entered the university, his experience working with Black people was formative. His activities in Troy and Albany helped shape Harris into a teacher, orator, and organizer, which marked an evolution in his work as a student abolitionist.[16] Harris also became an agent for the abolitionist newspaper *The Colored American*, the only agent in Vermont.[17] Aside from his work for the newspaper, his activity in Vermont was limited to his impact at the university. His traveling to Troy suggests that Harris sought to work elsewhere than Burlington. He continued to face racism at the university; a culmination of such treatment is evident in the commencement proceedings of Harris's class. Harris graduated in 1838 but was excluded from participating in the ceremony. Customarily, every student of the graduating class gave an oration at UV. Harris was prohibited from doing so, and he was also barred from receiving his diploma after white students threatened to boycott the proceedings.[18] Racist hostilities persisted throughout Harris's time at the university until the very end. In spite of that reality, Harris defiantly accomplished his goal of gaining the degree on July 31, 1838. He then left Vermont, never to return.

In a little over a week, Harris was in New York City with Daniel Payne and was being introduced to abolitionists. Harris met Theodore Wright, who became an important mentor to him. He also visited a temperance society, a Sabbath school where he gave remarks and was warmly received by its members, and the American Antislavery Society (AASS) office. Harris then traveled to Philadelphia, where he met members of the city's Black community, including James Forten, Robert Purvis, and Stephen Gloucester, as well as Charles Gardner. Harris also spoke before a meeting of the city's chapter of the American Moral Reform Society. Payne's report of the events formally introduced Harris to the readership of *The Colored American*: "Mr. Andrew Harris is a graduate of the University of Vermont. His personal appearance is very modest—his mental character not of the florid, but solid kind. This seems evident from his public speeches, which evince more of the discriminating logician, than the fanciful poet. His piety seems pure and ardent. Throughout the debates of the Society, he displayed great decision of moral character. In a word, his real worth, mental, moral and literary, will not fail to secure the high esteem of all who may become familiarly acquainted with him."[19] Harris exemplified what Cornish and Wright had been agitating for, formally trained ministers who would help lead Black congregations. The remainder of their trip to Philadelphia included a visit to the Minerva Association, a women's literary society. In Philadelphia, Harris was at home with the intellectuals and agitators of the city's Black community. The following year, Harris would make it his permanent home.[20] Harris's career as a student abolitionist propelled him into important positions in the movement at the local and national levels.

In 1839, Harris's abolitionist pedigree was peaking. He was a featured speaker at the annual meeting of the American Antislavery Society. He proposed the resolution "that the Degradation and Crime which exists among the Colored People, are a result of the wrongs under which they labor." Those wrongs, Harris explained, were southern slavery and northern racism, which were inextricably intertwined. In a speech, he lamented the violence of slavery and the separation of families. "But slavery does not stop here. It presses down upon the free people of color," he argued. The crux of the speech was critiques of racism in the North. He turned immediately to discrimination at colleges and the hypocrisy of arguments explaining Black degradation: "The colored people are also charged with want of desire for education and improvement; yet, if a colored man comes to the door of our institutions of learning, with desires ever so strong, the lords of these institutions rise up and shut the door; and then you say we have not the desire nor the ability to acquire education. Thus, while the white youth enjoy all these advantages, we are excluded and shut out, and must remain ignorant." Harris spoke directly of his experiences of being rejected at Union and Middlebury colleges. He explained how Black people desired to learn and acquire formal learning but racist whites shut them out. By 1839, a growing number of Black men identified with Harris's critique of northern colleges. He included a swipe at the avariciousness of capitalists as he proclaimed, "The bible says the love of money is the root of all evil, and if the love of money is a predominant passion anywhere it is in this land." At the same time, he believed that the love of slavery and prejudice among whites outweighed their love of money, as he was able to pay for a seat on a train but was forced to sit in the luggage car. Harris ended his address by offering a parting shot at colonizationists. Asserting his solidarity with Black people, Harris reflected, "Yet, with all the oppression and odium that is heaped upon us here, I for one would rather stand and endure it all, choosing rather to suffer affliction with my people, than to emigrate to a foreign shore."[21]

Harris gave an important address in front of a leading abolitionist organization. Drawing on his experiences with racism at northern colleges, Harris made racial exclusion in higher learning central to Black critiques of northern racism. He refuted the claim that Black people were not helping themselves by improving their conditions. Harris's own life proved it a lie, as did the efforts of the Black community at Troy and elsewhere. He also made a significant critique of capitalism and avarice. One abolitionist paper characterized Harris's lecture as "an eloquent and convincing statement," and another asserted that Harris spoke "honorably" and with "freedom and force."[22] After his speech, Harris became a well-known freedom worker. He helped formulate the Black abolitionist critique of higher learning, and his student abolitionist work had a significant impact on the movement.

Harris remained active in abolition during the early 1840s and sided with the other Black ministers in severing ties with the Garrisonians over electoral politics and women's rights. At the AASS meeting of 1839, Harris voted against including women's names alongside men's on the official role of the proceedings. The following year, he attended the annual meeting again but seceded with other Black clergymen to form the American and Foreign Anti-Slavery Society (AFASS). They embraced abolitionist politics and generally opposed advocating women's rights. Harris is listed as a founding member of the AFASS. He was also active in the Anti-Slavery Society of Eastern Pennsylvania. In the latter organization, however, women voted alongside Harris on supporting antislavery politics, suggesting fluidity in his sentiments. In 1841, Harris was the Philadelphia delegate to the annual meeting of the AFASS and also attended the inaugural nominating convention of the Liberty Party's ticket for the presidential election of 1844.[23] In addition to these activities, Harris was highly active in a slew of local and state abolitionist activities, including participating in fundraising drives for *The Colored American* and joining the New York Vigilance Committee to aid fugitive slaves. In August 1841, Harris returned to Troy and joined Garnet, Ray, Wright, and Crummell in attending the New York State Convention, where he advocated Black voting rights and citizenship.[24] Harris was among the Black abolitionists who demanded Black legal and political rights.[25]

Harris may have been the only Black student abolitionist attending a New England college at the time of the NEAS 1836 debate. As a result of the pressure abolitionists applied to them, New England colleges very slowly began to admit Black students on an individual basis. For the rest of the antebellum period, colleges such as Middlebury and Dartmouth accepted an individual Black student in various incoming classes in the regular college course. In the wake of the NEAS 1836 convention, the abolitionist pressure was felt at Dartmouth.

In 1837, Thomas Paul Jr. officially enrolled in Dartmouth's regular college course. Born to the Reverend Thomas Paul and Catherine Paul of Boston, the younger Thomas was a second-generation abolitionist. Susan Paul, his sister, was a teacher and leader in the Boston Female Antislavery Society. His father was a Baptist minister and friends with David Walker, Maria Stewart, and Prince Saunders. Paul Jr. was a beneficiary of Boston's Black institutions and was probably taught by Russwurm at the African Free School. Paul, however, was also forced to withdraw from a Latin school because of racism. After completing his early education, Paul apprenticed at *The Liberator*.[26] From a young age, Paul grew up in a Black community, and his consciousness was shaped by his family and community members. The education he received from family and Black schools prepared him for work in the movement as a young person, a foundation on which he would draw in pursuing higher learning. Prior to Dartmouth, Paul attended Noyes Academy in Canaan, New Hampshire, and experienced the racist backlash against the academy.[27] Following the experience at Canaan, Paul went to Hanover to continue his pursuit of higher learning.

Paul matriculated at Dartmouth College because of his academic qualifications, but he also received support from white student abolitionists. Dartmouth was one of the few colleges where white students facilitated a Black student's admission. Prior to 1837, antislavery emerged slowly at Dartmouth. In January 1834, the president of the college, Nathanial Lord, publicly rebuked a report listing him as a member of the AASS, though he held some sympathies for immediatism. Lord, however, initially sought to quell any antislavery agitation on campus. During his tour of New Hampshire, antislavery lecturer Nathanial Southard planned to give an address at the college and sent a letter to Lord in advance, hoping the president would inform the students. When Southard arrived at Dartmouth, he discovered that Lord never told the students and left without giving a speech.[28] It was not until 1835 that Dartmouth students organized an antislavery society. A contingent of students coming from Phillips Academy in Andover, Massachusetts, was an important catalyst.[29] An address in the college chapel from the Reverend Henry Wood in December 1835 also fostered antislavery at the college, drawing the approbation of white students who subsequently had the speech published. The following April, it became publicly known that white Dartmouth students "not having the fear of Lane Seminary and of the Andover Theological Institution before their eyes," organized an antislavery society with over sixty members.[30] In August, they wrote to Theodore Weld, requesting he lecture at the college. "A large minority of the students" and some faculty were abolitionists, they informed Weld, but many had not yet "become persuaded of their duty to act" or were not "acquainted with the means of acting." Abolitionist sentiment was rife at Dartmouth, but the students believed Weld could push them to a more active position. Weld did not journey to Hanover and instead, a few months later, the antislavery agent David Root lectured at Dartmouth for three successive nights. One report read, "The faculty of Dartmouth College, and the students generally, with many of the village inhabitants, attended." As a result of Root's efforts, "the cause of antislavery has there received a new and very encouraging impulse."[31] Over the course of a year abolition began to spread in Dartmouth, and it was within this context that Thomas Paul Jr. was admitted in April 1837.

Paul's entry into Dartmouth marked a transformation in abolition at the college. While white students had been active in the movement, Paul's admittance as an equal student exemplified abolition in practice, a step towards racial equality on campus. When Paul was accepted, eighty-eight white students were members of the Dartmouth antislavery society. Paul's admission protest and his example as a qualified candidate, combined with the presence of white student abolitionism, facilitated his matriculation. In fact, white student abolitionists demanded that the faculty admit Paul; otherwise, one account explained, "there would probably have been an abandonment of the Institution similar to what took place at the Lane Seminary two years since." The white student abolitionists threatened to leave the college if Paul was not admitted. By spring 1837, the students understood how to put abolition into practice. The episode was reminiscent of the case of Edward Mitchell and the victory of interracial student abolitionism twelve years earlier.[32] The event reveals a unique example of student abolitionism successfully challenging, indeed superseding, faculty decisions. Like other Black student abolitionists, Paul had applied to several colleges in New England and New York but received rejections; but he persevered. The pressure of Black abolitionists and the NEAS was felt at Dartmouth and bore fruit in this example. Paul's admission marked a new chapter of abolition at Dartmouth.

The social climate during Paul's time at the college, however, was mixed. Paul was a galvanizing presence, hardening some racist students' convictions while inspiring other students to work for Black freedom. In one case, Paul was excluded from a student literary society. Signifying the persistence of proslavery influence at Dartmouth, a white southern student received instruction from his family to leave the college because Paul was there. Another report claimed that admissions increased at the college. During Paul's time at Dartmouth, many of the students became involved in abolition beyond the campus. They attended meetings of the AASS, and their student society was listed among its auxiliaries throughout the late 1830s. Dartmouth student abolitionists also participated in the petition campaigns. In 1838, student names comprised the majority of the 152 signatures on an antislavery petition to the New Hampshire legislature. They were also a driving force in forming the Young Men's Antislavery Society in New Hampshire, which among its resolutions endorsed political abolition via voting for candidates who explicitly opposed slavery, praised emancipation in the British West Indies, and supported the right to petition. They twice included the phrase "human rights" in their platform.[33] In 1840, the Black abolitionist minister John W. Lewis spoke at the college on invitation from the students. He explained that he had spoken with Paul, lauding his example as a virtuous Black scholar.[34] That Lewis spoke at the college signifies the prominence of antislavery sentiment there. While episodes of reactionary racism manifested at Dartmouth after his admission, Paul also spurred greater abolitionist activity on campus.

Paul himself was active in the broader movement throughout his time at the college. Like Harris in Troy, during winter terms Paul traveled back to Boston to teach Black children. He donated to the Massachusetts

Antislavery Society and also participated with other Black abolitionists like Charles Remond and William C. Nell in celebrations of emancipation in the Caribbean.[35]

Paul's most significant moment as a student abolitionist came in January 1841 when he was a featured speaker at the Massachusetts Antislavery Society. The address reveals the knowledge Black student abolitionists produced to refute racism in higher learning. He offered a full-fledged assault on the slavocracy and its sympathizers: "They present the rare spectacle of a nation boasting of equal rights while a large part of the population are the most oppressed and degraded beings" on earth. While white Americans' ancestors fled the tyranny of the old world, they had built up "a still more horrid one" in the United States, where Indigenous peoples and enslaved Africans and their descendants were brutalized. He condemned the imperialist, capitalist motives for westward expansion and the dispossession of Indigenous peoples that facilitated the spread of slavery. Critiquing slaveholders, he wrote, "If they have driven the poor Indian . . . from the home of their fathers, it is only to make room for the still more imbruted slave, and to introduce a civilization which has been a curse to half of mankind. And thus they have become guilty of the double atrocity of immolating two races of men upon the bloody altars of their avarice and ambition." In a few lines, Paul had identified and condemned the violent hypocrisy of the American project. Through settler colonialism and slavery, white people created a civilization built on racism, violence, exploitation, and wealth accumulation. It was a damning indictment based on a Black radical analysis. Like other abolitionists, Paul identified the slave's cause and the abuse of Indigenous people as intertwined. He emphasized that American civilization facilitates racism, "a curse to mankind" that blocked the path to equality in various aspects of life, notably in college education. He wrote, "The road to the hill of science is guarded by a fiend," American racism. Paul used Black histories of struggle to make claims for a different world. He evoked the work of Black people in the past, "the voices of our revolutionary forefathers, who fought long and hard for the freedom of their country." Paul identified abolition's transnational scope, citing examples of emancipation in the Caribbean. He drew on the Haitian Revolution: "The free Haytien's voice is heard above the roar of the Atlantic, telling us, if we would avoid the horrors of a servile war, we must let the oppressed go free." As a student abolitionist, Paul produced a radical critique of the United States from a Black world perspective. He tied the formation of the country to racism in higher learning. Both issues were intertwined. It is noteworthy that he drew on the legacy of the Haitian Revolution to enforce his argument for a new humanity. Paul's oration, together with Russwurm's commencement address, demonstrates the significance of the Haitian Revolution in the ideology of Black student abolitionism. Enslaved people would resist until freedom came.

Paul's speech went even further. It was also a critique of the emerging theories that supposedly accounted for human differences, which were intimately tied to the American academy. Anticipating Douglass's oration, Paul observed the weakness of the argument made by scientific racists, whose claim that one man could be considered inferior to another was based "upon no better grounds than a dissimilarity in their outward conformation." He emphasized the absurdity of the argument and applied a critique to slavery. The conditions under which people labored were not sufficient to classify them as a distinct group of people inferior to those who oppressed them. "If you cannot raise mortals to the skies, can you drag angels down?" he asked rhetorically. Likewise, "If you cannot metamorphose a brute into a man, can you make a man a brute? Why then *treat* him as such?" he reasoned. Paul's oration was an insurgent force in higher learning. He critiqued the emergent pseudo-science of race being crafted in the university and used to uphold pro-slavery ideology. Paul's ideas represent a nascent idea of Black Studies encountering the academy through his Black radical analysis.

Paul closed his address imagining Black freedom and a political strategy. He hoped that abolition would reach "the oppressed of every clime" and "afford protection and security alike to patrician and plebian, to freeman and slave." He called on voters to adamantly oppose "demagogues and designing politicians" and those seeking "offices of preferment and personal aggrandizement" and instead to endorse those who demonstrated their commitment to "integrity and disinterested love of liberty," who would dismantle enslavement and racial oppression.[36] Paul embraced all tools at the movement's disposal, including the ballot and, importantly, women's rights. Paul's address represents the radical challenge Black student abolitionists posed to the slavocracy and its colleges.

Like Harris, Paul helped formulate an original critique of the American college and the society of which it was a part. In turn, he promoted ideas for Black freedom based on Black history, knowledge derived from resistance, and a critical understanding of the problems Black people faced.

A report described the significant impact of Paul's address on the antislavery meeting.[37] Paul made his mark on the movement. His erudite speech was the highlight of his student abolitionist career. It was a critical analysis coupled with solutions. The following August, Paul received the BA degree. During commencement he delivered an address on "Napoleon's estimate of himself on the island of St. Helena," a topic assigned to him. The notice of Paul's graduation occupied a column in *The Liberator*. Garrison likely wrote it and referred Paul for employment as a teacher or writer.[38] Paul went on to teach in Black schools and continued his work in the movement, including aiding fugitive slaves like George Latimer.[39]

Black Women Student Abolitionists

Black women students attended a handful of colleges in the antebellum period. Kabria Baumgartner's important work demonstrates that Black women abolitionists protested racial exclusion at women's seminaries. In some cases, Black women succeeded and attended Seward Seminary and Clinton Female Seminary, where they learned alongside white women.[40] The most well-known institution where students were admitted regardless of complexion or sex was Oberlin College. However, even with Oberlin's relatively expansive policy, Black women and men comprised only 4 percent of the overall student population before 1860. With a minority of the student population being of African descent, Black students' experiences of social equality at the college were mixed.[41] But Black students within the institution were radicals in the movement. Black women at Oberlin specifically were among the earliest official women students at a white college, and their positions on gender and abolition went beyond the positions of the white male faculty. Black women students used higher learning for their own purposes and cultivated a Black feminist perspective.[42] Black women at Oberlin were among those who manifested Maria Stewart's vision of Black women developing a political education.

Women of African descent began studying at Oberlin in the late 1830s and continued through the rest of the antebellum period. A total of thirty-two Black students earned collegiate degrees from Oberlin before 1865, fifteen women and seventeen men. Many more attended the college or its preparatory department than graduated. The early Black women at Oberlin marked an evolution in the protests of Black women in higher learning. They built on the legacy of Phillis Wheatley, Lucy Terry Prince, and Betsy Stockton. In 1837, Harriet Hunter began studying at Oberlin. She came from Canada, but her family was originally from Cincinnati, and the Cincinnati Female Antislavery Society paid for her college fees. Another student, Rebecca Morgan, studied there as well, but after marrying an Oberlin-trained minister, she left the college. Other Black women who studied but did not graduate included the African missionary Sarah Margru Kinson of the *Amistad* captives, Mary and Emily Emondson, who escaped from the slave ship *Pearl*, and two of the three Gloucester sisters from New York, Eloise and Adelaide; their sister Emma completed the degree in 1856.[43] Regardless of their degree statuses, these women were important Black students, and their education propelled them to lives of work in Black communities.

The earliest Black woman to graduate with a degree from Oberlin was Lucy Stanton. Born in Cleveland in 1831 to Margaret and Samuel Stanton, the latter a barber, Stanton was raised in an abolitionist household. Lucy's father passed away when she was two years old, and Margaret later married John Brown, who had been Samuel's business partner. Brown's household was a refuge for fugitive slaves, and as early as age ten, young Lucy helped aid escaped slaves. Part of the abolitionist vision of Stanton's parents included education for their children. Lucy attended a local school, but after she was expelled by racist whites, her stepfather helped build a separate school for her and Cleveland's Black children, which prepared Stanton for Oberlin. Stanton was raised in an activist Black family where she was involved in the freedom struggle as a young person. Her family and the Black community of Cleveland shaped her consciousness as she entered Oberlin in 1846 and embarked on a student abolitionist career.[44]

Stanton was one of the few Black students in attendance at Oberlin at the time. Ninety-seven percent of the student body was white, and according to Lawson and Merrill, only about ten to fifteen Black students attended at the same time as Stanton. The lopsided numbers did not deter Stanton academically. She progressed through her studies and became active in student literary societies. Upwards of sixteen Black women participated in women's literary societies, making them integrated organizations, though separate from men's societies. Stanton presented a series of essays in the Ladies Literary Society, including "The Female Missionary," "Scenes from the South," and "Be Not Unequally Yoked." In presenting these original essays, Stanton practiced oratory and argumentation and, as Lasser reveals, she did so without full text notes, a practice typically used by men. Stanton was well respected among Oberlin women, who praised her work in the society and elected her president of the organization in July of 1850.[45] Her work as a Black woman student defied gendered arguments about woman's proper sphere and racist notions of Black women's status in society. Instead, she shaped a Black feminist sensibility based on study, protest, and knowledge that translated into the public sphere.

Stanton showcased Black feminist thought and oratory in a commencement address. In four years she finished the literary degree, which was distinct from the bachelor of arts, as it did not require Greek, Latin, or advanced mathematics. However, it was recognized as a college degree.[46] Stanton's accomplishments were honored at Oberlin. She gave an oration at the 1850 commencement, and it was an abolitionist speech entitled "A Plea for the Oppressed." Stanton called for a rededication of the abolition movement. She lamented that "the Anti-Slavery pulse beats faintly," and "the right of suffrage is denied." Similarly to other Black students, Stanton argued that since "the freedom of the slave and the gaining of our rights, social and political, are inseparably connected," then "let all the friends of humanity plead for those who may not plead their own cause." She described slavery as a state of war: "Those who rob their fellow-men of home, of liberty, of education, of life, are really at war against them." She continued by addressing various constituencies, first politicians and then white women. "Statesmen," she asked, "will you not advocate the cause of the down-trodden, remembering that the spirit of liberty is abroad in the land?" She instructed them to endorse abolition and to "fear not loss of property or station" but rather to understand "it is a higher honor to embalm your name in the hearts of a grateful people than to contend for the paltry honors of party preferment." Stanton was

an astute political agitator, presenting an idea of electoral politics necessarily representing and reflecting the masses, not a leadership class.
Stanton instructed politicians to use the principle of liberty and equality
as their guide, not propertied interests or party politics. She then critiqued slaveholders' violations of Black families in slavery. She defended
enslaved women, their right to bodily autonomy, to their children, and
to their families. Stanton used vignettes of slavery's abuses to arouse
greater agitation for Black freedom among politicians, reformers, and
white women. It was the job of women, she summarized, to instill the
principles of freedom and love "in the nursery" and "in the social circle."
Stanton ended the address on a high note. "Truth and right must prevail.
The bondman shall go free." She looked to the future, imagining the day
of jubilee, of "universal freedom," when "the shout of joy gushes from
the heart of earth's freed millions!" and proclaimed that together heaven
and earth would celebrate the feat.[47] Stanton envisioned the scene of
liberation to come, providing a window into her freedom dreams.[48]

Stanton's address was a momentous occasion. It was a call for abolition at a most urgent time in 1850. Although she did not explicitly advocate women's rights, such a call was arguably an implied message. As
a young Black woman, Stanton gave a public commencement address
based on Black feminist thought, defying gendered notions of women's
proper sphere of influence. She envisioned a new society. It was an act
of abolition and political activism, a demonstration publicly of Black
women's claims to freedom. She was the embodiment of Black feminism,
and the dual message of racial and women's equality was not lost on the
audience. Observers that day praised the oration. While applause was
prohibited at commencement exercises, Stanton's address elicited "one
general, swelling burst of applause" from the crowd. The local newspaper published her address. Stanton subsequently gained the attention of
abolitionists. Martin Delany recognized Stanton as an important figure
in the movement and described her as "quite a young lady," who "has
her promise of life all before her, and bids fair to become a woman of
much usefulness in society."[49] Stanton became well known among abolitionists for her achievements and activist work as a student. Her address marked an evolution in student abolitionist activism, one that was
fashioned for the rights of Black women. She followed in the tradition of
Maria Stewart, who had proposed Black women's learning for freedom

over fifteen years earlier. In her life beyond Oberlin, Stanton worked in Black and women's organizations.[50] Stanton's address marked a significant moment. It represented a decisive blow to the intellectual and social foundations of academia. As a Black feminist thinker, Stanton used her training subversively for the movement.

Other Black women at Oberlin followed Stanton's example. In 1855, Mary Ann Darnes, a candidate for the literary degree, gave an address dedicating a flag to the Attucks Guards, a local Black militia in Cincinnati. Reflecting the growing militancy of Black abolitionists in the 1850s, she remarked, "The time is not far distant when the slave must be free" and continued, "if not by moral and intellectual means, it must be done by the sword." She implored the audience to honor the namesake of their regiment if duty calls: "Fight to the last for the great and noble principles of liberty and justice, to the glory of your fathers and the land of your birth." Darnes drew on the Black Revolutionary generation's legacy to encourage Black men to fight for freedom with force if necessary. Black women students also penned essays about marriage and the duties of husbands to their wives. Georgiana Mitchem, who was one of the first women candidates for the bachelor of arts, penned an essay entitled "The Model Husband," in which she advocated that husbands work equally with women in the home. "The Model husband rocks the cradle or wipes the dishes if his wife sees fit that he should and smiles meanwhile," she observed. "And most of all," she continued, "the model husband, when his wife asks for some change, gives it to her without demanding to what use she will put it." She also argued for protections for children and wives against physical abuse from husbands. Other Black women students attended the Black state conventions in Ohio and donated money to them. Sarah Stanley wrote an essay that was read before the 1856 convention. Echoing Darnes, Stanley called for "ACTION." She continued, "Let unanimity of action characterize us, let us reject absurd phantasy of non-intervention; let us leave conservatism behind, and substitute a radical, utilitarian spirit." As the sectional crisis intensified, Stanley recognized the growing urgency of united militant opposition to proslavery forces.[51] These examples are illustrative of the kind of freedom work in which Black women students were involved on, as well as beyond, the campus. From orations advocating violent force to achieve freedom to gender equality in the home, Black women students were at the cutting edge of Black radicalism. They were producing knowledge through study and struggle to facilitate Black women's freedom, another marker of a nascent Black Studies project. Indeed, they represented a collective of Black women intellectuals who came of age in the 1850s and participated in the movement during the Civil War and beyond.[52]

As the struggle for Black freedom progressed in the antebellum decades, Black students were among its most significant agitators. In their admissions protests and writings, they critiqued the hold of white supremacy and the slavocracy on colleges and seminaries. With the backing of Black communities, when a selective few gained admission, they manifested Black thought at colleges as a subversive epistemology. They brought the movement to the campus. They critiqued the limitations of the American project and used their knowledge to make arguments for Black freedom, for the creation of a different world. Black students were most effective beyond the campus in their roles as organizers and teachers in Black communities. In those spaces, a radical idea of Black higher learning took hold, where it was used to hasten the movement for collective Black freedom.

Black students refuted the notion of colleges promoting the so-called common good and instead made arguments for a new humanity. Through study and struggle, Black student abolitionist men and women created a student movement in the antebellum period that redefined the purpose of higher learning to promote Black freedom. It was not coincidental that featured speakers at national abolitionist meetings in the 1830s were, or had been, Black students. After completing his medical training in Glasgow, James McCune Smith was a featured speaker at the 1838 AASS annual meeting. The following year Harris spoke at the 1839 annual meeting after finishing his degree. In 1840, Henry Highland Garnet, while still a student at Oneida, spoke at the AASS as well. And as noted above, Paul spoke at the 1841 meeting of the MASS.[53] It was Black women like Stanton and Darnes who created new ideas that underpinned their crucial work and pushed the movement to its fullest realization. It was Black women who demanded that the movement recognize and champion their rights and freedom.

Black students were a growing constituency of agitators casting deafening blows to racist ideology espoused by white academics and the financial ties to slavery maintained at their institutions. Shaped by

Black communities and a social movement for liberation, Black student abolitionists led a concerted assault on white academia. Their collective example of learning and study that drew on Black history, experiences, and resistance revealed a way to transform their lives and their people.

Arguments for a Black College Revisited

As the antebellum period progressed, Black higher learning remained at the forefront of the abolitionist project, but by the mid-1840s, the path forward remained in question. While Black students alongside other Black abolitionists challenged racial exclusion in northern white colleges, wider progress remained painfully slow. After a handful of students completed their degrees, the Black admissions movement received another setback. In spring 1845, four Black students from Philadelphia were rejected from Amherst, Williams, Middlebury, and the University of Vermont. Middlebury's president asserted that only Black students from Vermont or adjacent states would be accepted there. "Middlebury college is not designed especially for the education of the colored race," he continued. "We are not inclined particularly to encourage negroes from all parts of the country to resort here for education." A better manifestation of the ideological, epistemic racism nurtured in American colleges could hardly have been expressed. Middlebury leadership feared that white public reprisals would tarnish the college should it gain a reputation as an institution for African Americans. Instead, he enforced a racist barrier to the majority of Black students. The same request was made to Dartmouth, where Lord hesitantly agreed to accept the four students, writing, "We should not choose to have a flood of blacks at this College. But we should refuse none of proper character." He also believed that African Americans needed "cultivation, as a people, for centuries, before many of them will hold their way with long civilized Christian Saxons, if indeed this is ever to be expected, which I doubt."[54] Lord hesitantly accepted Black students at Dartmouth and retained a deeply racist outlook. Elsewhere, a Black student was refused an examination for admission at Brown University because of the institution's southern patronage.[55] So went the responses from leaders of New England colleges on Black admissions protests: outright rejections from most institutions and the spewing of racism from college presidents.

The anti-Black logics of the American college remained strong in New England's institutions in contrast to the gains of Black student abolitionists. While selected Black admissions were a relative improvement from widespread exclusion during the early 1830s, progress attributable to the efforts of Black students and their communities, multiple Black students at most colleges would not be tolerated. Black abolitionists responded to this context with a renewed proposal for a Black college, which prompted a debate over the efficacy of separate Black institutions or attempts to transform existing ones, mirroring broader debates within the movement on integration versus Black self-determination.

Black abolitionists who cut their teeth in the movement as students were on both sides of the debate. Alexander Crummell and James McCune Smith led the call for a Black college, a revitalization of the efforts made in New Haven during the early 1830s. At the 1847 national meeting of the Black convention at Troy, New York, Crummell presented a report calling for a separate Black college that included an extraordinary conceptualization of Black higher learning. He believed that such an institution would have numerous advantages. It would inspire more Black people to advanced learning, which he believed would lead to high enrollments, and produce Black professors who would facilitate Black student success. Crummell argued, "The colored youth, under care of colored teachers, associating with those of his own complexion and condition, would not feel depressed as likely to be in other institutions, surrounded by those whom he had always regarded as opposed to his equality." Black students at a Black college with Black teachers would be able to learn without racist treatment from their peers or white teachers. "Colored colleges," therefore, Crummell reasoned, "were the most favorable to his mental growth." While many supported the plan, it also elicited opposition from a contingent of delegates including Douglass, Ray, and Garnet. They believed that such a plan was impractical, primarily because the proposal in New Haven had failed. They also believed in the necessity of Black students attending predominantly white institutions because "it was their glorious privilege to contend for equality, to secure every point gained, and still press on for more." The presence of a Black student at white institutions, they believed, would "disarm opposition, show himself an equal, and, in despite of cold looks and repulsive treatment, hew out a path to eminence and respect . . . and become himself among good scholars the very best." For them, Black students at white colleges would demonstrate Black achievement, presenting an argument for racial equality even if it meant enduring racism. Their plan was a continuation of what had been unfolding since the early 1830s. They also highlighted that some white institutions admitted Black students and such efforts would be better directed at transforming those institutions. Notably, the gender politics of this proposal were clear, as the planners envisioned the college for Black men with Black women excluded.[56]

Crummell, however, argued that with a few exceptions, "The education of the mind of colored youth, up to this time, has been shamefully limited, contracted." He surveyed the state of Black education and offered an illuminating assessment of colleges and Black people. "The colleges of New England and the West, which are opened to us, do not meet the needs of our people." Most significantly, Crummell identified a crucial pitfall of the white colleges Black men attended. "*While at college [they] are separated from their people, inasmuch as there is no point of interest, or of contact, between the colleges of our country and the colored people of the Union, but rather utmost distance.*" Herein lay the fatal flaw of white colleges in the antebellum period. They removed and separated Black students from Black communities. The American college was not designed in the interests of Black people; in fact, it had served as the obverse. American colleges were antithetical to Black life and humanity. The college, by and large, was socially, intellectually, and epistemically anti-Black. Crummell reasoned that colleges removed Black men from their communities to the detriment of the individual and the community. Crummell continued, "Such is the force and urgency of caste, penetrating every phase of life, social, ecclesiastical, civil and domestic, that college life has its peculiar restraints to young men, thrown in the midst of hundreds, who have concealed repugnance to colored men, and with few, and perhaps none, to sympathize." Crummell's assessment fit the experiences of Black students; they entered institutions that were socially and intellectually averse to Black humanity. In response, Crummell believed that Black colleges should foster connections between students and Black communities, an extraordinary concept. Crummell wanted to institutionalize Black thought at a college that would serve the interests of Black communities.[57] This was another early iteration of Black Studies, collective learning and liberation, that would fluctuate over subsequent generations. The paltry state of Black higher learning for Crummell and McCune Smith demanded action, and they proposed a radical vision for institutionalizing Black higher learning situated in community. Again, Walker's vision echoed.

Crummell advocated a "System of Intellectual Culture" wherein all avenues of study, be they scholarly or the mechanical arts, would be pursued by African Americans. He summarized, "Whatever means and availabilities for mental culture can be obtained it is our duty to seek and secure them. The education of our people should be carried on in the most earnest manner, with the largest expectations, to the development of all the powers, and by the appropriation of all the means that nature and scholarship may afford." The solution, the committee believed, was to mobilize every avenue and resource to maximize Black learning, for "our people." "Argument will not suffice. When capacity, undoubted capacity, is exhibited, then, and then alone, will the contempt and the outrages" end, Crummell believed. A Black college for Black people based on the manual labor system was the committee's solution, dedicated to the health and cultivation of the Black mind, body, and spirit. So important was this plan that it occupied the "leading and most prominent object" of the committee's concerns. The result would be "an early generation of scholars, capable of treading the platform of science, erudition and learning, with as much conscious ability, as any men in the land."[58] The proposal marked the importance Black abolitionists placed on higher learning situated in and for community.

After some debate, the delegates voted twenty-six to seventeen in favor of the Black college proposal. It is noteworthy that Crummell and McCune Smith favored a separate college, as they both had experienced the scourge of racism in higher learning in their early lives. And ironically, Crummell would follow McCune Smith in studying abroad for a university education after the convention, taking his argument for higher learning to Britain. A committee was appointed to further develop the plan and solicit necessary funding. Black abolitionists and former student abolitionists were well represented on it, including McCune Smith, Crummell, Ray, Pennington, and Beman. The longstanding proponent of Black higher learning, Samuel Cornish, was appointed to the committee as well.[59] The endorsement of the proposal indicated that the majority believed Black higher learning was in a meager state, even with Oberlin and selected matriculations elsewhere, rendering a Black college necessary. The proposal reflected the ongoing emphasis Black abolitionists placed on higher learning and their belief in its significance as a powerful tool in fighting oppression through self-determination and fostering Black knowledge. Importantly, the Black college would cultivate study among Black people as a means to liberation for Black communities. The idea of a college being connected to Black communities was enormously consequential for defining the purpose of Black higher learning. A separate Black college was the solution to manifest their vision.

The Black college plan of 1847 evolved in subsequent meetings of the Black conventions. Charles Reason, Frederick Douglass (who changed his position), and James McCune Smith led the charge for the establishment of what became known as an industrial college. From 1853 to 1855, Douglass and McCune Smith placed more emphasis on the education of Black tradesmen than earlier proposals had done. In the report on education at the 1853 National Convention, Reason emphasized the need to equalize scholarly and trades education in one institution. The committee believed "it desirable that a more thorough plan be established that will combine the literary course of the schools, scientific agricultural knowledge, theoretic mechanics, and engineering." Alongside math, Latin, and medicine, Reason advocated "Industrial pursuits" because of their "general usefulness" and "marketable demand." The central aim was to educate Black people in the skilled trades. Marking a departure from the 1847 proposal, the institution would be coeducational, as they outlined a "Department of Industry for Females" where young Black women and girls would learn various trades as well. Reason envisioned the fruits of such an endeavor, where "the triple tide of wealth, intelligence, and virtue" would be everywhere represented among African Americans.[60] The focus on a trades education reveals the continued expression of an expansive educational vision. Learning a trade would facilitate economic independence. The growing emphasis on such training is less a departure from scholarly pursuits than it was representative of the shift in broader political culture. The advent of organized antislavery politics like the Liberty Party and Free Soil Party represented the growing popularization of free labor ideology.[61] Black abolitionists recognized this changing context and the new types of jobs becoming available as a result of the increasingly industrialized northern economy in urban areas and the continued importance of agrarian labor in the countryside, both of which required skills training. Learning in the mechanical arts would prepare African Americans for this changing economic and political context. The plan for the industrial college marked an evolution of the meaning of Black higher learning in response to broader political and economic trends and also a continuation of African American participation in political culture. In other words, an industrial education would help create a class of Black workers ready to earn a wage or work for themselves and also participate in electoral politics. In theory, it would propel African Americans to rise above the limited economic opportunities available to them because of racism and become self-sustaining economic and political actors.

The 1853 education committee's focus on mechanical training paired with a traditional, though less emphasized literary course of college education represents an important shift in Black thought towards higher learning. After advocating Black college education for over two decades, more Black abolitionists began to identify the limitations of an exclusively literary education and preparing young men for the ministry. Douglass summarized this shift in a letter that was added to the education report at the 1853 convention. In response to Harriet Beecher Stowe, who inquired as to the best way she could support the movement, Douglass offered an overview of Black higher learning. Several Black men had received a college education, but "few have found themselves educated far above a living condition, there being no methods by which they could turn their learning to account." Those who acquired a college degree, Douglass argued, had limited opportunities to earn a living and were materially poor, since many professions were closed to them. Many became ministers, Douglass observed, but while an educated ministry was important, he believed it was equally important to have educated congregations. In essence, Cornish's model from the late 1820s–1830s of having an educated ministry was insufficient. Douglass explained that racism foreclosed Black intellectuals from the professions and many African Americans did not see college training as useful for their communities. For many living in a dominant culture of racism, more immediate concerns of combating poverty and violence and acquiring the basic means of survival took precedence over college learning. As a result,

Douglass observed, higher learning among Black men was often paired with emigration. Douglass meditated on this trend:

> It would seem that education and emigration go together with us; for as soon as a man rises amongst us, capable, by his genius and learning, to do us great service, just so soon he finds that he can serve himself better by going elsewhere. In proof of this, I might instance the Russwurms—the Garnetts—the Wards—the Crummells and others—all men of superior ability and attainments, and capable of removing mountains of preju-dice against their race, by their simple presence in this country; but these gentlemen, finding themselves embarrassed here by the peculiar disad-vantages to which I have referred—disadvantages in part growing out of their education—being repelled by ignorance on the one hand, and prejudice on the other and having no taste to continue a contest against such odds, they have sought more congenial climes, but I cannot blame them; for, with an equal amount of education, and the hard lot which was theirs, I might follow their example.

If we take Douglass's perspective at face value, he believed that formally educated Black men became ostracized because of their exclusion from professional occupations and Black communities' disinterest in the intellectual's plight, both of which factors combined to drive them away from the United States. This may have been true for some. However, leaving the United States to work with African people abroad was a critique of the racist social structures of America and an act of self-determination, not a shortcoming to Black higher learning, as Douglass framed it. To this point, Douglass of course opposed emigrationist plans, which informed his critique. But the bind Douglass highlights is one of Black intellectuals adopting white models of higher education, an education for social and economic mobility into a professional class. He lamented the fact that Black student abolitionists who emigrated did not become a part of educated classes of mainstream, i.e., white, America. This was precisely what other Black student abolitionists did not do, as evidenced by many highlighted in this book who worked in and for, and were accepted by, Black communities in the United States and abroad, however limited their ideological outlook. But Douglass believed that a Black institution, the industrial college, would facilitate the spread of learning more efficiently and in a diverse form rather than produce examples of Black college-educated individuals. The commitments of college graduates, and who and what colleges were for, mattered.

Douglass comes closer to the vision of Black higher learning grounded in collective liberation in his description of the industrial college. He believed that it would be "a college where colored youth can be instructed to use their hands, as well as their heads—where they can be put in possession of the means of getting a living." Such an institution, as with previous proposals, was grounded in abolition. "The most telling, the most killing refutation of slavery," Douglass opined, "is the presentation of an industrious, enterprising, upright, thrifty, and intelligent free black population. Such a population, I believe, would rise in the Northern States, under the fostering care of such a College as that supposed." A population, not individuals or specific leaders, was to rise and benefit from such an institution. At the end of the report, the political implications of the industrial college came to the fore. The convention believed it would serve "as a means to a great end, viz: the equality in political rights, and in civil and social privileges with the rest of the American people."[62]

The proposal for the coeducational industrial college took shape throughout 1854; however, within a year, the plan was abandoned. Delegates at the 1855 national convention meeting in Philadelphia voted down pursuing the project because of a scarcity in funds and because other institutions for Black learning existed.[63] The industrial college for Black youth never came to fruition. By 1855, circumstances in Black higher learning had changed along the lines the Philadelphia committee outlined.

Early Historically Black Colleges

Even though Crummell's and other abolitionists' plans to build a Black college did not come to fruition, other organizations built colleges for Black people. Before 1860, these academic formations were the Institute for Colored Youth (ICY) in Philadelphia, founded in 1837; Ashmun Institute, established near Oxford, Pennsylvania, in 1854 (renamed Lincoln University in 1866); and Wilberforce University, founded in Xenia, Ohio, in 1856. Although these colleges focused on classical learning with the function of preparing students for the ministry and other professions, they were the first to be built specifically for Black students. Like other Black institutions, these colleges provided space for Black people to learn, organize, resist, and advance the cause of abolition and human equality. Jelani Favors terms this element of HBCUs as the "second curriculum."[64] Black students at these Black colleges manifested the Black abolitionist vision for higher learning.

The function of these colleges reflected the ideology of their specific founders and leaders. Promoting colonization was at the center of the Ashmun Institute, which was founded by white Presbyterians and members of the ACS. According to Russell Irvine, Ashmun "was perceived as nothing more than as an adjunct to the broader colonizationist campaign."[65] The colonizationist leaders of Ashmun like John Dickey imbued the institution with racist paternalistic ideology from the outset. At the opening ceremonies of the institution, a speaker remarked about Black people in the United States, "Will the race rise to social equality and partake of political privileges with classes in the same community? This is equally improbable."[66] Conversely, Black freedom and human equality were the grounding ethos for the ICY and Wilberforce University. Whereas the Ashmun Institute was controlled by whites, the ICY and Wilberforce had Black people among the leadership and faculty. The ICY emerged out of autonomous Black studying circles, employed Black faculty, and actively fostered Black student participation in the freedom struggle. Charles Reason, Sarah Mapps Douglass and her cousin Grace Mapps, Ebenezer Bassett, and Robert Campbell served on the faculty. They were all involved in the abolition movement and infused their work at the ICY with education for liberation.[67] Wilberforce was structured on "a general program of education to help bring about the much desired abolition of the slave system."[68] Unlike ICY, Wilberforce was the product of the African Methodist Episcopal (AME) Church, whose leaders believed that their ministers required college training.[69] AME Church members in Ohio joined other Methodist Episcopalians to secure land and facilities to build a university. The proposed name of the institution was "The Ohio African University," but the board of managers ultimately decided on "Wilberforce University," named after the British abolitionist William Wilberforce. Four of the original twenty-four trustees were Black men, Rev. Daniel Payne, Lewis Woodson, Alfred Anderson, and Ishmael Keith.[70] Black leaders helped shape Black colleges as institutions for self-determination.

Like their Black student abolitionists predecessors, Black students in each of the early HBCUs contributed to the freedom struggle. Living through the tumultuous 1850s and the Civil War, they understood the meaning of their work through the lens of Black emigration or the struggle to transform the United States for Black freedom. Four students enrolled at Ashmun in 1857, when Black emigrationism was on the rise. The *Dred Scott* decision declaring that Black people had no rights or legal standing in the polity further entrenched the deeply racialized social structures of American society and led many Black abolitionists to reconsider emigration.[71] In May 1859, three graduates from Ashmun became ordained ministers and left for Liberia, including Armistead Miller. The day of the departure, Miller proclaimed, "I am going home— home, Africa is my home. . . . Yes, Africa was dark and benighted, but the gospel would enlighten her, and make her a nation among the nations."[72] Claiming Africa, not the United States, as his home, he believed his work among African people would transform their lives. While the graduates seemingly followed the colonizationist program in their careers, they did so shorn of the racist idea that Africans were unequal to whites. For Black missionaries, their work was a question of culture, not racialist logics. Both formulations, while distinct, are problematic. As with Russwurm before them, bringing notions of Western civilization to change African ways of life was a function of imperialism and colonialism, making their work fraught. From 1857 to 1866, out of forty-six known recorded students, forty-two remained in the United States. Thirty-two students and alumni served in the Union Army during the Civil War, working to free their people from enslavement and to create better lives for themselves and their families. Many became ministers in Black communities and teachers in freedpeople's schools in the South during Reconstruction.[73]

Black students at ICY and Wilberforce followed paths similar to those of Ashmun students, save for emigration. Graduates of ICY in the 1850s included Mary Ayers, Jacob White Jr., Martha Farbeaux, and Octavius Catto. While a student, White lectured against purchasing slave-produced goods and confronted Governor James Pollock, who visited the school in 1855, on the question of Black citizenship. White, Farbeaux, and Catto taught at ICY after they graduated. Favors shows that students were among those who defended fugitive slaves in the streets. "We had at that time a lot of young fellows who stood together and . . . gave good account in many broils [involving] fugitive slave cases," one alumnus wrote. After the Civil War, the new leader of the ICY, Fanny Jackson Coppin, carried on the tradition of instilling ICY students with the lessons of self-determination and racial uplift.[74] Wilberforce students followed a similar trajectory. Some of the early students had been formerly enslaved. Like the graduates from Ashmun, ICY and Wilberforce students would go on to teach in Black schools in the South after the Civil War.

After the war, the AME Church took full possession of Wilberforce University, making it the first private HBCU fully controlled by and operated for Black people.[75] Wilberforce's example of Black self-determination attracted to Xenia Black families who wanted their children to attend the institution. Among the notable early Black students at Wilberforce was Hallie Quinn Brown. Born to Frances Jane Brown of Virginia, who had been enslaved and freed as a young child, and Thomas Arthur Brown of Maryland, who had been enslaved and purchased his and his sister's, brother's, and father's freedom, young Hallie was one of six children. The Brown family lived in Pittsburgh and was immersed in the freedom struggle. The Brown home often housed people escaping enslavement, including whole families at times. Young Hallie's consciousness was thus shaped by her family's freedom work. The Browns would eventually move to Xenia, for the express purpose of enrolling Hallie and her siblings at Wilberforce. The Brown family fostered a symbiotic relationship with Wilberforce students. As Hallie recounted, her mother "befriended scores of poor, worthy students and for thirty years brought into her home young men and women to 'work for their board' but treated as members of the family, many of whom are today of sterling character and worth in the arena of life." Frances Jane Brown was a leading member of the College Aid Society, an organization that assisted materially poor Wilberforce students.[76] A better encapsulation of the meaning of Black higher learning connected to community could hardly be conveyed. Black education at Wilberforce was sustained by the Black community surrounding the institution. Hallie Quinn Brown entered Wilberforce University in the early 1870s and finished a bachelor of science degree in 1873. Brown subsequently embarked on a life of teaching and working in the freedom struggle for Black and women's rights. She taught in Mississippi and served as dean of Allen University. In 1892 she became a principal at Tuskegee Institute, and the following year, returned to Wilberforce as a professor of elocution. She was instrumental in founding the National Association of Colored Women and was involved in other branches of the freedom movement.[77] In 1926, she authored and published the landmark text, *Homespun Heroines and Other Women of Distinction*, a volume of biographies of Black women. Hallie Quinn Brown's life carried on the legacy and meaning of Black higher learning. She was the beneficiary, and extended the meaning, of Black higher learning. Learning for community and liberation guided Brown's work in the Black institutions she worked in and helped build. The story of the Brown family's connections to Wilberforce was an example of Crummell's plan come to life, a plan that built on the ideas of Walker and Stewart.

Not inherent to institutions themselves, the Black abolitionist vision for higher learning was instilled in these early HBCUs by Black people. Students continued in the tradition fostered by Black student abolitionists before them, using education for liberation.

* * *

Black abolitionists and students were original critics of American higher learning and its connections to slavery and racism. They conceptualized novel ideas about the utility of higher learning for advancing the cause of Black freedom. Black higher learning demonstrated Black humanity and intellectual traditions while also fostering study, learning, and unity among Black people seeking freedom. Throughout the antebellum period, Black abolitionists consistently made the terrain of higher learning contested ground, a battle over the meaning of humanity and Black life. They developed a series of ideas and tactics, from Black admissions protests to refuting racist academic theories to creating proposals and ideas for separate Black institutions. Shaped by their families and communities, Black students brought a critical consciousness to campus and contributed to a student movement for abolition. They were at the forefront of the abolitionist assault on proslavery ideology and the ACS in higher learning. In turn, they wielded their learning and knowledge for the betterment of Black communities in their work as teachers, ministers, and organizers. They were forerunners in using the college in subversive ways for advancing Black freedom. Crummell's vision of a Black college directly connected to the needs of Black people was an early formulation of the Black University concept. The Black abolitionist pursuit of higher learning is part of a long history of Black Studies and its encounter with the university in the United States. Together, Black people crafted an idea of higher learning that centered people over profits, human interests over capital, and Black humanity over European traditions of knowledge. They envisioned a world where Black knowledge and life were valued, a world where they and their progeny would be free. They envisioned a world of human flourishing. Centering the perspectives and actions of enslaved Africans, Black intellectuals, and students from the past provides an alternative history of slavery and universities, one in which slavery and racism and Black freedom and humanity were contested in higher learning. It illuminates the significance of dissenting Black voices and their visions for building a different world.

Black students and other Black abolitionists were original theorists on the utility of higher learning for creating a new humanity. The Black abolitionist vision of higher learning was one generation's attempt to wield the power of study and learning to meet the needs of their moment. It was one strategy for living on their terms. They are part of a genealogy that is unbroken. Subsequent student movements for Black liberation, including those of today, are heirs to this radical tradition of Black thought and protest from the antebellum period.

Epilogue

Sketching the Legacy

The legacy of the Black abolitionist vision of higher learning has reso-nated among Black thinkers and students for generations. That legacy remains central to critiques of the university in our own time. Black people continued to shape the meaning and purpose of higher learning for liberation in new ways after the US Civil War and the widespread establishment of historically Black colleges and universities (HBCUs). These new institutions exemplified the centrality of education to con-ceptions of freedom among Black people. The legacy manifested in the years following Reconstruction's overthrow, when Black teachers taught in Black schools. The legacy continued into the early twentieth century when Black students at HBCUs protested institutional practices that forced them to accept a subordinate status within the racist hierarchy of the United States. Instead, they made arguments for determining the nature of their educational experience and their right to shape the intel-lectual environment of the campus. Building on Crummell's idea of a Black college, Black thinkers developed the Black University concept, further envisioning an institutional space shorn of Western conceits and centering community. The legacy continued to evolve by the mid-twentieth century, when Black students demanded a new intellectual environment in historically white universities. The impetus to create Black Studies departments came from the Black student movement. Black students' demands for Black Studies was the manifestation of Black Power in higher learning, a radical social movement whose mem-bers made systemic critiques of white supremacy and the institutions upholding it, and envisioned other possibilities for Black life and soci-ety. The establishment of academic Black Studies in universities was a watershed moment; it marked the advent of a field of study that came from an external force, a social movement consisting of Black folks who extended Africana learning traditions to the campus. That struggle was a continuation of a tradition in the making of Black higher learning both as a critique of universities and as part of a vision for study and learning as a means to Black liberation. When Black students made demands for Black Studies, they became part of a tradition that included enslaved Africans, Black abolitionists, and students from the nineteenth century. Indeed, the Black Studies movement was one generation's response to the university slavery and settler colonialism had made. In this light, one component of the Black Studies movement was, and continues to be, a critique of slavery's legacy in the academy. Just as slavery's legacy and racist ideology in universities changed over time, so too did Black resistance and demands for Black forms of knowledge and learning. Critical engagement with universities' connections to slavery did not begin in the late 1990s and early 2000s, as some projects or studies might have it. Black people, students, and intellectuals have long understood the university's historical connections to oppressive systems and ideas since the era of slavery, and their resistance to oppression in higher learning has persisted and evolved over time.[1] That tradition continues today and represents an alternative history to the university, its historical ties to slavery, and its legacies.[2]

The Black abolitionist vision for higher learning as a tool for Black liberation lived well beyond the 1850s. With the revolutionary transformations wrought by the General Strike in the Civil War, the movement for Black higher learning became a national project. The demand for learning at all levels could now be voiced publicly in the South, and it was a critical element of freedpeople's definition of freedom. During Reconstruction, the founding of HBCUs was part of the wider proliferation of a southern educational system that was largely built by newly freed people.[3] The rise of schools for Black people in the US South, including HBCUs, marked the historical convergence between the studying and learning of enslaved people for the purpose of realizing liberation that had long taken place largely in secret and the institutional prerogatives for formalizing Black education. While such institutionalization was necessary, the Black masses struggled to fully determine, on their own terms, the contours of the institutional forms Black learning would take. In that process, the intervention of white philanthropy and ideas about education clashed with the views of the Black masses and some Black leaders. For the Black masses, learning and study were to facilitate the political and economic freedoms of their communities. They were to facilitate Black freedom, to which self-determination and autonomy were critical. This outlook conflicted with the interests of white capitalists, who largely funded HBCUs and were determined to craft the function of Black higher learning for educating menial laborers, creating a subordinate class of Black workers for the benefit of capital on the grounds that Black people were supposedly only fit for such work. Black philanthropists and northern missionaries supported the educational foundation of HBCUs as fostering Black political and civil rights.[4] From the outset of establishing HBCUs, a duality emerged regarding the purpose and function of HBCUs that has largely characterized their historical trajectory: the struggle between institutional interests dictated by white philanthropists and their allies versus the vision of Black students, dissenting Black thinkers, and the Black masses. The struggles of the latter are in the tradition of the Black abolitionist vision for higher learning. The continuation of this legacy in the late nineteenth century is encapsulated in a period of W. E. B. Du Bois's early life.

The purpose of Black higher learning as a tool for the liberation of all Black people after Reconstruction is recounted from an episode of Du Bois's time as a Fisk student and his relationship to rural Black folks in Tennessee. Du Bois attended Fisk University from 1885 to 1888, and during vacations from the academic year, students spent their time teaching Black children and adults in schools across the state. Like other Fisk men, Du Bois searched for such work and eventually located a school in a rural community near Alexandria. The fusion of Black higher learning represented in Du Bois and in Black people accepting him as a teacher represents the Black abolitionist legacy of the purpose of higher learning. Significantly, Du Bois described how the yearning for education came from Black people themselves. Recounting the context, Du Bois explained that Josie, a local young Black woman, upon "hearing of my errand, told me anxiously that they wanted a school over the hill, that but once since the war had a teacher been there; that she herself longed to learn,—and thus she ran on, talking fast and loud, with much earnestness and energy."[5] A rural community of Black people yearned for learning, and the prospect of having a Black teacher was a significant development. They would bestow legitimacy on Du Bois as a college-educated teacher.

He observed the austere school building, "a log hut," and described the first day he began teaching. "It was a hot morning late in July when the school opened. I trembled when I heard the patter of little feet down the dusty road, and saw the growing row of dark solemn faces and bright eager eyes facing me," he recalled. The ages of students ranged from very young to teenagers. In attendance was Josie, who Du Bois said was about twenty and had dreams of attending school in Nashville. He described many of the students and explained their studies: "There they sat, nearly thirty of them, on the rough benches, their faces shading from a pale cream to a deep brown, the little feet bare and swinging, the eyes full of expectation, with here and there a twinkle of mischief, and the hands grasping Webster's blue-back spelling-book. I loved my school, and the fine faith the children had in the wisdom of their teacher was truly marvelous. We read and spelled together, wrote a little, picked flowers, sang, and listened to stories of the world beyond the hill." What Du Bois and the students were doing was Black Studies; they were learning and studying together in order to know and in that way to be. This was a manifestation of what freedom meant to Black folks, the ability to learn about and understand the world as Black people. Du Bois taught there for two summers. It was his introduction to the lives of rural southern Black folk. He explained how on Sundays he ventured to nearby Black churches and experienced "old time religion" and witnessed "the soft melody and mighty cadences of Negro song" that "fluttered and thundered." Du Bois learned as much from the people and Black culture, especially the spirituals, as he taught them. They were teaching him as well; they were in fact learning together. He observed the larger context and meaning of their world as they experienced it:

I have called my tiny community a world, and so its isolation made it; and yet there was among us but a half-awakened common consciousness, sprung from common joy and grief, at burial, birth, or wedding; from a common hardship in poverty, poor land, and low wages; and, above all, from the sight of the Veil that hung between us and Opportunity. All this caused us to think some thoughts together; but these, when ripe for speech, were spoken in various languages. Those whose eyes twenty-five and more years before had seen "the glory of the coming of the Lord," saw in every present hindrance or help a dark fatalism bound to bring all things right in His own good time. . . . There were, however, some—such as Josie, Jim, and Ben—to whom War, Hell, and Slavery were but childhood tales, whose young appetites had been whetted to an edge by school and story and half-awakened thought. Ill could they be content, born without and beyond the World. And their weak wings beat against their barriers,—barriers of caste, of youth, of life.

Through these passages, Du Bois revealed a culture of Black life, its complexities, how Black folk made sense of the world, their aspirations, cosmology, spirituality, and the virulent contradictions they faced, what it meant to be Black and encounter the color line. It was in this context that the purpose of learning among Black people emerged. It was an important tool for which they were building a different world that was to come. For those who experienced freedom from chattel bondage, their world had indeed changed, and they believed a new day was still coming. And the next generation felt that acutely. Yes, they were no longer enslaved, but they were not yet free either. Their learning awakened a yearning for more, to live fully and deeply, which was thwarted by the color line.

Significantly, in this episode from Du Bois's life, the meaning of Black higher learning comes into focus and indeed gains ideological specificity. What Du Bois was beginning to realize through this experience of teaching and learning with Black people was the meaning of higher learning for the community. By accepting Du Bois as their teacher, Black folk bestowed legitimacy on him as a young intellectual. Without acceptance from the community, the impact of Du Bois as a Black college student and teacher would have been negligible. The question that arose was, How would higher learning and education generally be meaningful to Black folk? For Black people, higher learning had to be adapted to their lived experiences, their traditions and knowledge of the world. In other words, Black people adopted higher learning to help them make further sense of the world and how they experienced it. For example, Du Bois wrote of the skepticism of some in the community about "book-learning" and explained how he attempted to make his teaching applicable to the people. "I put Cicero 'pro Archia Poeta' into the simplest English with local applications, and usually convinced them—for a week or so."[6] In one sense, this is what Crummell was striving for in his call for creating a Black college that was situated within Black communities so as not to remove Black students from the people and the communities from which they came so that everyone would benefit. In this story from Du Bois's student days, the purpose and utility of Black higher learning and the meaning of Black education more generally were revealed to this generation. For Black people, education at any level could not be a replication of education defined by whiteness and Western traditions of knowledge. Black people themselves had to define the terms of their education; they had to apply it to their historical circumstances as a people for it to have meaning and utility. Thus higher learning and education necessarily had to be Black higher learning and Black education.[7]

The spirit of the Black abolitionist vision of higher learning continued to emerge through time among Black students at HBCUs who protested and questioned the meaning of their learning experience. In the 1920s, students organized protests at Fisk University over strict policies regulating student life on campus. After being appointed to the presidency of Fisk in 1915, the white sociologist Fayette McKenzie sought to secure the patronage of organized philanthropy that was dedicated to upholding white-supremacist hierarchy. After securing one million dollars in donations, McKenzie in turn implemented a series of repressive rules on campus. Student government, the *Fisk Herald*—the oldest Black student newspaper at HBCUs at the time—and sports were all disbanded and any form of dissent was prohibited. A request for creating a campus chapter of the NAACP was denied, and a strict student conduct policy was implemented dictating, among other things, that young men and women could not meet or walk together on campus without permission and the presence of a chaperone. A strict dress code was implemented for young women, who protested it. The students argued that such policies were designed to accommodate the white South and force Black students to accept the racism of the dominant culture. In November 1924, students began to protest McKenzie and his policies, shouting, "Away with the czar!" and "Down with the tyrant!" The students printed their demands and posted them around campus; they included reinstituting the student newspaper and student council, autonomy in debate and literary societies, the reinstitution of sports teams, and the organization of sororities and fraternities. These were all essential elements of student life that existed at other colleges, and Black students at Fisk demanded they have the same right to such organizations and practices. They refused to accept conditions that aligned with the prerogatives of the white South bent on repressing Black life and freedom.

The student protests continued through the winter, and McKenzie remained steadfast in his opposition to the students. Alumni and a few board members sided with the students, as did Du Bois, who helped publicize the protests. All the while, the Black community in Nashville supported the students as well, especially after McKenzie called the local police to respond to student protests on campus. In the middle of the night, fifty police arrived after a demonstration was over, eliciting a strong rebuke from alumni and Black residents who were appalled at the prospect of fatal danger that came with the police. In response, twenty-five hundred Black residents met in the local AME church and denounced McKenzie's actions. They declared that his "usefulness as president of Fisk is at an end." The Black community in Nashville was in solidarity with the students. Some residents housed students who had been kicked off campus and helped to cover expenses they faced. The student protests continued, and about 150 students boycotted classes for ten weeks. Refuting the narrative McKenzie spread to save face, the students were adamant that their protests were organic and not instigated by outside forces. While Du Bois played an important role in the events, he admitted that he knew nothing of the students' protests until he read about them in the press. The inspiration came from the students themselves; "the uprising was spontaneous." Under pressure from students, alumni, and Black residents of Nashville, McKenzie resigned on April 16, 1925. As the board of trustees searched for new leadership, they implemented the students' demands.[8] The Fisk students had won an important victory in shaping the kind of university Fisk should be. They refused to acquiesce to the white South and the dictates of white philanthropy. In acts of self-determination, they forced the institution to change and realize their demands for learning and rights. Their protests helped define the meaning of Black student life and the nature of their college education. They made demands for Black life on their terms at the university. And the backing of the Black community of Nashville was pivotal, demonstrating the significance of the symbiotic relationship between Black communities and Black higher learning. Similar examples of Black student protest for self-determination on campuses unfolded at other HBCUs during the 1920s, including Howard, Hampton, Wilber-force, and Lincoln (PA).[9]

In addition to Black students, dissenting Black intellectuals also be-came a part of the legacy. In the wake of Black student protests, Du Bois's ideas for Black higher learning evolved. He would revisit the lessons he learned as a student from Black folk as well as from the student pro-tests of the 1920s. By the 1920s, Du Bois had made arguments for higher learning to create a "talented tenth," a group of Black intellectuals who would lead the masses in the freedom struggle. Du Bois was also clear that the talented tenth was part of a larger program of Black education that included liberal arts as well as other forms of learning. The crux of Du Bois's argument was that Black people should have the same learning and professional opportunities as whites but for the purpose of advanc-ing the freedom struggle and specifically for realizing political and civil rights for Black people.[10] After the talented tenth idea proved insuffi-cient and elitist, Du Bois's vision of Black higher learning, specifically the role of HBCUs, evolved and is exemplified in an address he delivered at Fisk in 1933.

Du Bois's argument marked a turning point in the conceptualization of Black higher learning and its purpose. Early iterations of the idea had been developed by Walker, Stewart, and Crummell, and practiced by the Black student abolitionist teachers John Newton Templeton, Andrew Harris, and Lucy Stanton and through the actions and experiences of Black people who accepted them as teachers. But Du Bois transformed the conceptualization of the role of Black colleges in society. "Negro Colleges," as Du Bois referred to HBCUs, necessarily had to be Black colleges; they could not simply be colleges. They had to be institutions organized around the historical and social circumstances of Black peo-ple. He explained, "A Negro university in the United States of America begins with Negroes. It uses that variety of English idiom which they understand; and above all, it is founded, or it should be founded, on a knowledge of the history of their people in Africa and the United States, and their present condition." He went on, "Without white-washing or translating wish into facts, it begins with that; and then it asks how shall these young men and women be trained to earn a living and live a life under the circumstances in which they find themselves or with such changing of those circumstances as time and work and determination will permit"? This was to be the central organizing principle, or the field, of the Black college. Interestingly, Du Bois briefly considered the contributions of previous ideas for Black education, the industrial model and liberal arts college learning, and argued that both had strengths and important limitations. Indeed, these models were the outgrowth of a holistic model of higher learning that Black abolitionists put forth in the antebellum period—classical learning, manual labor, and the mechanical arts. Du Bois explicitly expanded on these previous ideas:

> Starting with present conditions and using the facts and the knowledge of the present situation of American Negroes, the Negro university expands toward the possession and the conquest of all knowledge. It seeks from a beginning of the history of the Negro in America and in Africa to interpret all history; from a beginning of social development among Negro slaves and freedmen in America and Negro tribes and kingdoms in Africa, to interpret and understand the social development of all mankind in all ages. It seeks to reach modern science of matter and life from the surroundings and habits and aptitudes of American Negroes and thus lead up to understanding[s] of life and matter in the universe.

For Du Bois, this was to be the epistemic orientation, and function, of the Black college and university. It was a nascent idea of academic Black Studies. Indeed, such ideas and practices for studying Black life, culture, and history emanated from HBCUs.[11] Du Bois explained that the function of the Black college necessarily had to be grounded in the lived experiences of Black people. "The university must become not simply a center of knowledge but a center of applied knowledge and guide of action." For "if the college does not thus root itself in the group life and afterward apply its knowledge and culture to actual living, other social organs must replace the college in this function." Here we can see the influence of Black people and culture on Du Bois, specifically during his experience in teaching and learning with Black people as a Fisk student. In fact, he cited that experience explicitly in his address. He recalled how he had visited the rural community where he had taught forty years earlier. Du Bois wrote of the stark realities he observed. "There is no progress there. There is only space, disillusion, and death beside the same eternal hills. There where I first heard the 'Sorrow Songs' are the graves of men and women and children who had the making of a fine intelligent upstanding yeomanry. There remains but the half-starved farmer, the casual laborer, the unpaid servant. Why, in a land rich with wealth, muscle, and colleges?" Progress had not marched lockstep with time. Du Bois's idea of the Black college had to have meaning and purpose for Black people in rural Tennessee and everywhere. It could not be otherwise. The Black college had to be rooted in Black communities, in order for Black people to earn a living and to live meaningful lives.[12] Otherwise it would replicate an aristocracy of wealth and elitism bred and replicated at the Harvards and Yales of the country, further entrenching and exacerbating racial, class, and gendered oppression. The best model of learning to which Du Bois compared his vision of the Black College, indeed the model on which his vision was based, came from West African learning traditions. It was the example of the "bush school," in the tradition of the Yorubas and the Sudanese and Bantu-speaking people. During a visit to West Africa, Du Bois observed the tradition. His description merits full quotation:

> The education of the child began almost before it could walk. It went about with mother and father in their daily tasks, it learned the art of sowing, reaping, and hunting; it absorbed the wisdom and folklore of the tribe; it knew the lay of land and river. Then at the age of puberty it went into the bush and there for a season the boys were taught the secrets of sex and the girls in another school learned of motherhood and marriage. They came out of the bush with a ceremony of graduation, and immediately were given and taken in marriage. Even after that, their education went on. They sat in the council with their elders and learned the history and science and art of the tribe, and practiced all in their daily life. Thus education was completely integrated with life. There could be no uneducated people. There could be no education that was not at once for use in earning a living and for use in living a life. Out of this education and out of the life it typified came, as perfect expressions, song and dance and saga, ethics and religion.

The education of Black people, Du Bois argued, had to be based on a similar system of education where every person in the community learned from the community's social and intellectual traditions—a holistic education to earn a living and for living life. Du Bois stated plainly, "Thus the university, if it is to be firm, must hark back to the original ideal of the bush school. It must train the children of a nation for life and for making a living."[13] For Du Bois, the example mattered as much as its source. African traditions of learning and knowledge were to be central to the teachings and epistemology of Black colleges, fostering a Black world cultural consciousness. In conceptualizing the meaning and function of Black colleges, Du Bois revealed the purpose of study, learning, and knowledge as a requirement for meaningful Black life and freedom. Du Bois, himself the product of the Black abolitionist vision of higher learning, was part of a tradition of Black thinkers who transformed the meaning of higher learning for Black people. That tradition included the cultural forms and African epistemologies of enslaved people on campus, Walker's *Appeal*, the Black college proposal of 1831, Pennington's textbook on the history of African people, Stewart's political education for Black women, and Crummell's idea of Black higher learning in the community. It included Black student abolitionist writings on the Haitian Revolution and Black women students teaching their peers about the fullest meaning of human equality. Written in the context of the 1930s, Du Bois's speech updated and improved upon the Black abolitionist vision of higher learning for the twentieth century. His vision for Black higher learning resonated among Black students and thinkers in the freedom struggle of the 1960s and 1970s, and it remains a model to emulate.[14]

Du Bois's "Field and Function" argument is in part what the Black student movement for academic Black Studies sought to realize at universities writ large. The full history of Black student protests during the mid-twentieth-century iteration of the freedom struggle is capacious and multifaceted, and its complete telling is beyond the scope of our purposes here. However, the history of SNCC and the Black student movement for academic Black Studies is a significant chapter of the legacy of the Black abolitionist vision for higher learning. Indeed, the student movement for Black freedom in this period was the heir to the student abolitionist legacy recovered in this project. In the movement for academic Black Studies, Black students critiqued the Western epistemic foundation of the university that was rooted in and built on Indigenous dispossession, slavery, capitalism, and racist ideas. They critiqued the university that slavery and settler colonialism made. In the midst of the Black student revolution on white campuses, Paul E. Wisdom and Kenneth A. Shaw laid bare the state of the university in the mid-twentieth century: "What the universities have failed to realize in almost every case is that the American educational experience is a white experience, an experience based on white history, white tradition, white culture . . . an education designed primarily to produce a culturally sophisticated, middle class, white American." Black students, activists, and intellectuals brought this context to the fore and demonstrated how Black higher learning and Black education, while present in Black communities for generations, were historically dissenting traditions in the United States because of the larger context of white supremacy as the central ideology of American institutions. Historically white universities were hostile places socially and intellectually for Black people. Wesley Profit, a Black student who entered Harvard's freshman class of 1965, observed that Black students "were made to feel insecure in a thousand different ways. . . . We were an experiment of sorts, and a lot of us had experiences that were discomforting and a little bit alienating." Al Dempsey, a Black student from Georgia at Columbia in the late sixties, asserted that "the worst racism I have seen is here at Morningside Heights." Thirty-four Black women at Vassar, including Claudia Thomas, took over Main Building and issued this statement as part of their demands: "We refuse not only to waste four years of our lives, but to jeopardize four years of our lives becoming socialized to fit a white dominant cultural pattern. We refuse to have our ties to the black community systematically severed; to have our life styles, our ambitions, our visions of our selves made to conform solely to any white mold." Lenneal Henderson, a Black student at Berkeley, stated plainly of white students, "They never let you forget you were black." Asserting self-determination, Henderson continued, "We decided to remember we were black."[15]

A mass movement of Black students categorically rejected the white-supremacist logics of the university and instead transformed those spaces by demanding academic Black Studies. Black students acquired a critical lens from the families and communities they came from, through their social experiences, and the historical context in which they were living. In turn they developed a consciousness, an understanding that American society and its institutions were fundamentally flawed and compromised. They demanded space in the university for Black Studies as an academic arm of the freedom struggle. Academic Black Studies was the expression of Black self-determination and autonomy in the university, and it was an extension of what many Black people had been doing in study groups, in high schools, within communities, in churches, in the oral tradition, and in other spaces and forms of Black education—they studied the experiences, culture, and thought of African people throughout the world in order to know themselves and each other. They developed a historical consciousness of struggle as a basis for organizing to be free. Black Studies was an extension and expression of these other forms of knowledge and Black education *in* the university. It was a novel intervention in its formalization of academic study of Black thought and experiences as envisioned by Black students, faculty, and their allies. They demanded departments and autonomy in controlling them, including student participation in governance of the departments, the hiring of Black faculty, and the creation of a curriculum shaped collectively by students and faculty. Significantly, many of the proposals for Black Studies were grounded in ties to Black communities, an enduring theme of the purpose of Black higher learning dating back to some Black abolitionists. Indeed, the knowledge and works of Black people from the abolition movement and works about them would have a central place in Black Studies courses. The creation of Black Studies departments was a watershed moment in the history of the university, and it has had a lasting influence on the intellectual, social, and epistemic context of higher education. Its original orientation must be revived and extended. Without Black Studies, this book would not have been possible. As part of a tradition and a radical social movement for Black life and freedom, the Black student movement for Black Studies became part of the legacy of the Black abolitionist vision of higher learning.

Some of the direct successors who continued the work of Du Bois's "Field and Function" idea were Black intellectuals who theorized the creation of a Black university. In the late sixties and early seventies, Black thinkers convened conferences and penned essays developing the Black university concept. In 1968, a group of scholars, intellectuals, activists, and artists held a major conference at Howard University titled "Toward the Black University."[16] Two notable conceptualizations of the Black university came from Vincent Harding and Toni Cade Bambara. Harding positioned the emergence of the idea at that specific moment in time as an outgrowth of Black freedom movements that "were moving toward a demand for decolonization, independence and self-determination, as well as the building, reconstitution and control of our own institutions." He explained that Black people understood that there could be no sustained movement for liberation without Black people determining for themselves the terms of their education, which necessarily meant the "transformation and ultimate control of pre-college Black education, and the call for the Black University shared these same assumptions." Among the objectives that Harding argues constituted the Black University were that "its students are guided essentially by the central purpose of service to the Black community on every technical and personal level possible" and that it necessarily had to be tied "to the struggles of African people everywhere." The legacy of Du Bois as well as the Black abolitionist vision of higher learning as a liberatory project for all further manifested in Harding's writing: "The Black University would be seeking in every possible way to move with its surrounding community toward the radical change that is necessary in order for community and university to find a common new humanity."[17] Harding's writings were crucial in developing the notion of a Black university grounded in global Africana liberation.

Bambara's writings provided a road map for students, teachers, and community members to implement changes at City College, part of the City University of New York. As a professor at City College who sought to transform the institution, Bambara argued that an important step in building a Black University was to first establish a Center for Black and Hispanic Studies on campus, an autonomous space where students could develop an alternative curriculum in collaboration with faculty and community members, creating the foundation on which the Black University would be built. Importantly, Bambara was not telling the students what to do; rather, she was inviting them to think strategically and collectively about how to transform City College. She was clear that students had to lead. "What remains is work from you, students. It will do none of us any good if the Center is run by faculty, if the curriculum is designed wholly by faculty, if staff is hired merely by faculty." Organizing the center and presenting a plan to the chancellor for financial resources would be a collaborative effort. The center would have multiple functions. It would be a "buttress" to the existing curriculum, providing the student with "courses, workshops, seminars, or one-to-one relationships to help him anticipate the omissions or biases in any given course" and "offer counter theories, and suggest additions to the book-lists." Another core function of the center would be as "A Research Agency," getting works from Black authors back in print, and providing materials and guidelines for "teachers in grammar, high school, and colleges." It would also serve as a "Skills Bank," tapping into "resources in our community and use as instructors those grandmothers, those on the corner hard-heads, those students, those instructors, whoever happens to have the knowledge and expertise we desire, regardless of the number of or absence of degrees, publications, titles, honors, etc." Here was an example of the significance and necessity of autonomy, the ability of faculty and students to hire intellectuals from the community to teach at the college whom the university would not consider credentialed. For Bambara, the center's most important function was to be a "Course Offering Agency," which as such "would lead ultimately to the Black University."

Bambara went on to list several course ideas but emphasized again that students must direct and develop the curriculum collectively with faculty. The courses reveal a thorough grounding in Black Studies and other non-Western knowledge traditions. Possible courses included "an examination on the philosophy, the architects (Senghor, Diop, Cesaire), disseminators (Sartre, Toure), Afro-Americans (Hughes, etc.), critics (Baldwin), other practitioners (Caribbean and South America), [of] the movement and its current impact on the current renaissance all over the world where Black people reside"; nutrition focusing on "soul food" and "Caribbean cookery," with field work in local restaurants and instruction by "some cooks from soul restaurants, some grandmothers, and dieticians from southern and urban hospitals"; critical investigations of Western traditions of thought focusing on reason and man, which were implicated in producing "rationales for racialist convictions and imperialist adventures"; and "Eastern Ethics Through Literature," focusing on Buddhist, Hindu, Chinese, Arabic, and other writings that predated Western traditions of knowledge. Other courses based on Black intellectual traditions included a three-semester sequence on "comparative revolutions and colonial revolutions" as part of the core requirements for the BA, and root courses focusing on a "thoroughgoing way to move into our roots with Blacks in areas other than North America . . . part workshop, or studio dance, part lecture, part lecture-demonstration," a pedagogically innovative class on Black world traditions of dance and movement and their historical significance. A final course Bambara proposed was on what today would be called mass incarceration and, arguably, prison abolition: "A cold hard look at how the American judicial system has aided in the enslavement of our people." In these courses, Bambara was proposing a curriculum of Black Studies and other knowledge traditions, in which for many classes the thought and intellectual traditions of the African world comprised the core materials of study. It was a curriculum that would transform the intellectual culture of City College.[18] Bambara's "Realizing the Dream of a Black University" was a detailed road map to construct a collaborative, autonomous space for Black students, faculty, community members, and allies who would collectively design, teach, and learn from an alternative curriculum and develop a consciousness that would inform action and organizing, and ultimately transform the university. It is a proposal with applicability in our own time. While Harding provided a vision for a Black University, Bambara's proposal was for building a similar institution out of an autonomous Black and Brown space at City College. Both have tremendous value for us today. As Harding and Bambara built on and extended Du Bois's "Field and Function" argument and offered specificity for their own time and context, so should we today learn from and build upon Harding's and Bambara's ideas, in order to teach, to learn, and to transform.

There is a long history of Black resistance for life and meaning within and on the boundaries of higher learning that dates back to the construction of such institutions in North America. It is rooted in the epistemologies of African people who extended ideas about learning in and for community, of those held enslaved on campus and their cultural consciousness that encapsulated African ways of knowing, and the freedom dreams and knowledge of fugitive slaves resisting college slavery. It includes the insurgency of Black thought from intellectuals like Phillis Wheatley and Maria Stewart that disrupted the logics of the university, Black protests for admissions, the advent of alternative knowledge produced by studying slave resistance, the Haitian Revolution, and African history in the writings of Black students, the organizations of white students who helped underpin the abolition movement and made demands for Black freedom, and Black student abolitionists who produced original arguments critiquing racism and slavery in higher learning and whom Black communities accepted as teachers as they learned together and organized to build a different world. It includes the dissenting tradition at HBCUs, the symbiotic relationship among Black students, higher learning, and Black communities, and the ideas of Du Bois, Harding, Bambara, and, more recently, Greg Carr, among many others, for study, learning, and liberation. That tradition continues among Black thinkers and students who practice Black study and use the university in subversive ways.[19]

Black abolitionists developed the idea of Black higher learning in order to address the historical context of slavery and racist ideologies connected to it. They helped conceive of study and learning as tools for liberation. Their legacy lives on. Understanding that tradition necessarily requires disrupting chronological and temporal boundaries, as well as ideologies, that are central to Western disciplines such as history. The establishment of Black Studies departments was not identical to the Black abolitionist vision of higher learning. However, while context changed, the nature of the demands for Black higher learning across time have been informed by a tradition comprised of knowledge derived from struggle, a tradition of resistance and knowing that has insisted that knowledge and learning on the terms set by African people is a means for liberation and building a different world. The long history of Black Studies reveals that universities have historically been poor arbiters of diverse knowledge systems. In fact, an argument can be made that the university as an arbiter of Western epistemologies has been integral to producing the catastrophe of the human condition the world over today. The argument that universities have produced some good is insufficient; for such "good" has come at the grave expense of human life for centuries. The argument that universities have done some good seeks to compromise with the violence of neoliberalism, to benefit those who have benefited and continue to benefit from the exploitation of others. In this light, different epistemological orientations are needed beyond those beholden to neoliberalism and the violent logics of capitalism, imperialism, colonialism, militarism, white supremacy, patriarchy, and environmental destruction. For those interested in creating change and a better world, the university can no longer remain sutured to those in-terests. For if universities in their current iterations have benefited from and continue to perpetuate various forms of human oppression and en-vironmental degradation, it would follow that fundamental transforma-tions are required to resolve such historic and contemporary problems. Such transformation can emerge from a collective consciousness and culture where our common humanity and a responsible stewardship of nature are organizing, uncompromising principles. Learning and studying Africana intellectual traditions, and the outlook of Du Bois, an education to make a living and to live life that does not rely on the exploitation of others, or reproducing an elite or a so-called leadership class, can be guides. An honest historical interpretation shows that the current models of the university do not serve the interests of the major-ity of people. A specific tradition in Black Studies provides solutions. The works of Black Studies scholars in this tradition should be taught, learned from, studied, deeply engaged, and reengaged, alongside other knowledge traditions. For not only do the analyses that they have pro-duced provide grounds for resisting the current world system, but they have proposed, envisioned, and practiced other ways of being and other ways of relating to others, the world, and the environment. For some, these are familiar arguments. But for others there are and have been solutions, and they have existed in the grounding of community. Earlier generations have shown the way. For the living on this side, there is an obligation to the tradition now and for the future.

ACKNOWLEDGMENTS

Crafting an adequate section dedicated to the people who have helped me produce this work is a challenging but rewarding task. This project has been with me for several years and has evolved in profound and meaningful ways. First and foremost, it exists because of the people whom this book chronicles. I'm grateful to have learned about and from them, their struggles, their ideas and actions, and for being able to bring this history to light, however imperfect my abilities to do so may be. And I am grateful for a way of knowing and understanding this history from people in Africana Studies. I'm very fortunate and lucky for the opportunities I've had and the people I've met who have made a difference in the journey of creating this book.

Libraries, librarians, and archivists made this work possible. Stella, Jasmin, Shmyah, Shannon, and Musa Jatta of the Schomburg Center for Research in Black Culture from the summer of 2022 made my time there an invigorating and rewarding experience. The following archivists facilitated the research: Catherine Sutherland and Ronald Hyam, Magdalene College, Cambridge; Hubert Merrick, Colby College; Caroline Moseley, Bowdoin College; Katherine Collet, Hamilton College; Mary Kimberly, McGraw Historical Society; and Mariah Leavitt and Mike Kelly, Amherst College. Thank you to all the librarians, archivists, and staff for their assistance in tracking down sources and materials.

Several people were instrumental in helping me develop this project in its early stages. But before there was a project, there were Douglas Huff and Greg Kaster. They inspired me and believed in me. I started down this path because of them. Thank you, Doug. I wish Greg was here to read and discuss the book. We'll still have that lunch. I thank everyone in History and the W.E.B. Du Bois Department of Afro-American Studies at UMass–Amherst during my time there, including Emily Pipes, Janelle Bourgeois, Chuck Weisenberger, Julia Carroll, Chloe Spinks, Camesha Scruggs, Felicia Jamison, Andy Grim, Dan Chard,

Sarah Cornell, John Higginson, Joye Bowman, Jennifer Fronc, Sam Redman, Emily Hamilton, Brian Ogilvie, James Smethurst, John Bracey, Whitney Battle-Baptiste, Bob Williams, Nneka Dennie, Karla Zelaya, and many others. Brittany Frederick remains a steadfast confidante and friend. Mary Hicks was a formative advisor who helped to broaden my understanding of Black history beyond national borders. Feedback, advice, and guidance from Bruce Laurie and Hilary Moss was invaluable. Barbara Krauthamer's mentorship was and continues to be pivotal. My deepest appreciation goes to Manisha Sinha. She supported this project from the start, seeing it through from a seminar paper to beyond graduate school. She continues to support me in numerous ways. I'm grateful for her mentorship. My years in the valley would not have been possible without addressing larger issues of living. Gratitude goes to Nick Alverson, Erica Fagen, Amy Breimaier, Kayla Pittman, Bill O'Connell, and especially Jack and Bobbie Jemsek.

Along the way, I've had some fortuitous opportunities that have helped develop my understanding of the meaning of my writing and teaching. Susannah Ottaway, George Vrtis, and especially Thabiti Willis believed in me, as well as the students from the Ujamaa Collective and those who took my classes at Carleton College. Thabiti continues to be an interlocutor in this work and I'm grateful for his mentorship. I was fortunate to receive a fellowship from the Charles Warren Center at Harvard University, which provided valuable resources and time for revising the manuscript. The fellowship cohort was an important experience for sharpening my thinking on slavery and universities. I must thank Tiya Miles, Monnikue McCall, Sven Beckert, Evelynn Hammonds, and the entire cohort of fellows, including Chana Kai Lee. Thank you to Rowan Murphy and Andus Baker for my time in Cambridge; it will forever be special to me.

Many friends and colleagues have listened to me talk about this project, provided feedback on drafts, or shared helpful advice at crucial moments. Kabria Baumgartner, Ousmane Power-Greene, Bill Hart, John Bell, J. E. Young, the cohort at the Center for Historical Analysis at Rutgers in Spring 2023, Roberta Tabanelli, Valerie Kaussen, and Davarian Baldwin all have made this book better. Craig Wilder's work made this book possible. Over ten years ago we had a conversation, and since then he has supported me and generously shared his time and wisdom. Julia Bernier has helped me think about slavery, universities, and the implications in important ways. Crystal Webster continues to share advice and conversation about publishing and the meaning of this work. My life intersected with Crystal Donkor's at a critical juncture, and she is always there for all things related to work, life, and living. Students impact me in deep and profound ways; thank you Owen Madigan-Fried, Lindsay Okindo, Mariam Zewdu, Seth Eislund, Charles Hodge II, Kenny Douglas, Athieei Monydit, Ashi Jose, Ashanti Huye, Bri Schultz, Laila Hallom, Heaven Butler, Marion Johnson, Aidyn Gleason, KJ Byrd, and many others.

One of the most transformative moments in this journey began with an encounter in the summer of 2019. I had the good fortune of receiving a fellowship through the W.E.B. Du Bois Center at UMass and met Josh Myers. The time, care, and attention Josh exemplified in conversation about universities and Black Studies initiated a process of study and being in community that has altered my orientation to the world and the meaning of the work. This book has been profoundly shaped by him and the tradition of which he is a part. He introduced me to Cedric Robinson, whose work continues to have an enduring impact on my consciousness, writing, and teaching. These encounters also led me to Greg Carr, whose work, deep study, commitment to, and love for Black people have been profoundly transformative. Dr. Carr, Professor Karen Hunter, Miguel Byrd, and everyone in Knubia have sustained me and have transformed this work. Collectively, this tradition of Africana Studies has shown me the way. Thank you to those who are now ancestors: Cedric Robinson, Vincent Harding, June Jordan, Toni Cade Bambara, Sterling Brown, Sterling Stuckey, Mari Evans, Carter G. Woodson, and many others.

Important support for this project came from the Department of History, the Graduate School, and the Du Bois Center at UMass–Amherst, Massachusetts Historical Society, American Antiquarian Society, the Schomburg Center for Research in Black Culture, the Charles Warren Center at Harvard, the Center for Historical Analysis at Rutgers, and the College of Arts and Sciences at the University of Missouri. The National Council for Black Studies has been crucial for my intellectual growth. Thank you to all my colleagues and everyone in Black Studies at the University of Missouri for supporting me. It has been a pleasure to work with New York University Press. I am thankful for Clara Platter who began working with me at a pivotal moment and has been a steadfast supporter of this project ever since. Thank you to Clara, Emily Wright, the reviewers, and the team at NYU Press for making this process a smooth one.

The last word goes to family and friends. While this work has resulted in less time spent with them, they are as important to me and my life as ever. Adam Michel's enduring friendship has meant more to me than perhaps he realizes. Jamie, April, Zoe, and Jordan have only added to that friendship in wonderful ways. Shout out to the Nassau group. My many relatives, especially Dave Jirik, Sharif Ibrahim, and Rita Jirik, are always there to pick up right where we left off, no matter the time in between. My family make my trips to Minnesota meaningful. Jean Jirik's care, love, and prayers nourish me. My parents, Paul and Mary, have been there for me in so many crucial ways from the beginning. I cannot thank them enough. The gift of their example endures. And, to Candace. The words in this space are inadequate but will have to do for now. Thank you for you and for everything.

NOTES

INTRODUCTION

1 Jesse James Deconto and Alan Blinder, "'Silent Sam' Confederate Statue Is Toppled at University of North Carolina," *The New York Times*, August 21, 2018, www.nytimes.com; Deepika Jonnalagadda, "Students Endorse Reconciliation Fee in GU272 Referendum," *The Hoya*, April 12, 2019, www.thehoya.com; Adeel Hassan, "Georgetown Students Agree to Create Reparations Fund," *The New York Times*, April 12, 2019, www.nytimes.com; Janelle Harris Dixon, "Street Smart," *Howard Magazine* (Spring 2021), www.magazine.howard.edu; Elliot Kozuch, "HRC Mourns Merci Mack, Black Trans Woman Killed in Dallas," Human Rights Campaign, July 2, 2020, www.hrc.org; on other student protests, see Jaeah Lee, "Uncovering the Painful Truth About Racism on Campus," *Mother Jones*, November 20, 2015, www.motherjones.com.

2 The term "higher learning" is used to describe education at the college and seminary levels before 1860.

3 For new directions in Black intellectual history, see inter alia Brandon R. Byrd, Leslie M. Alexander, and Russell Rickford, eds., *Ideas in Unexpected Places: Reimagining Black Intellectual History* (Northwestern University Press, 2022).

4 For the phrase "new humanity" I am drawing on the work of Vincent Harding; see for example *There Is a River: The Black Struggle for Freedom in America* (Harcourt Brace, 1981), xxv, 137, 186, 308. For scholars who have used the term "student abolitionist" but applied it only to students at individual institutions, see Lewis S. Feuer, *The Conflict of Generations: The Character and Significance of Student Movements* (Basic Books, 1969), 8, 320–24; Milton C. Sernett, "First Honor: Oneida Institute's Role in the Fight Against American Racism and Slavery," *New York History* 66, no. 2 (April 1985): 110; Milton C. Sernett, *Abolition's Axe: Beriah Green, Oneida Institute, and the Black Freedom Struggle* (University of Syracuse Press, 1986), 104; J. Brent Morris, *Oberlin, Hotbed of Abolitionism: College, Community, and the Fight for Freedom and Equality in Antebellum America* (University of North Carolina Press, 2014), 3, 25, 82.

5 The term "student abolitionist" describes persons in the nineteenth century who studied formally or informally in schools, colleges, or elsewhere and who resisted slavery and racism in their writings or actions, including participation in abolitionist organizations. This study's focus is on higher learning specifically. The formulation of abolitionists as the activist wing of the antislavery movement is a

useful definition of who was an abolitionist. See David Brion Davis, *The Problem of Slavery in the Age of Revolution, 1770–1823* (Cornell University Press, 1975), 21–22. For a conceptualization of first-wave and second-wave abolition, see Manisha Sinha, *The Slave's Cause: A History of Abolition* (Yale University Press, 2016). On the first phase, compare Paul J. Polgar, *Standard Bearers of Equality: America's First Abolitionists* (University of North Carolina Press, 2019) and Timothy Messer-Kruse, *The Patriot's Dilemma: White Abolitionism and Black Banishment in the Founding of the United States* (Pluto Press, 2024).

6 "College slavery," or "slaving," a term that is indicative of an active practice that was always ongoing, is defined as a specific type of racial slavery in which the labor of enslaved people built, directly funded, or sustained colleges. College slaving included slaveholding colleges where enslaved people worked on campus or on college-owned plantations as well as for individual owners—students, faculty, and college officials who owned slaves. The distinction between institutionally owned slaves and individually owned slaves is important, but the impact of fugitivity in both cases was equivalent. Regardless of who owned an enslaved person, fugitivity challenged the political economy of slavery that sustained colleges. The labor of enslaved people often financed students' education, increased college endowments, and made professorships possible, and slave escapes from colleges or individual masters associated with them undermined the operation of the early colleges. College slavery was part of the larger system of enslavement in the Atlantic world. On the idea of slaving as historical process, see Joseph C. Miller, *The Problem of Slavery as History* (Yale University Press, 2012).

7 Greg Carr, "What Black Studies Is Not: Moving from Crisis to Liberation in Africana Intellectual Work," *Socialism and Democracy* 25, no. 1 (March 2011): 178–91, quotation from 178. Importantly, Carr argues that the field's origins in the US university are "traced to insurgent activity among African-descended academics at Historically Black Colleges and Universities" and highlights W. E. B. Du Bois, Oliver Cox, and Charles Johnson during the first half of the twentieth century as examples (181–82n6); see also James B. Stewart, "Black/Africana Studies, Then and Now: Reconstructing a Century of Intellectual Inquiry and Political Engagement, 1915–2015," *Journal of African American History* 100, no. 1 (Winter 2015): 87–118; Joshua Maurice Myers, "Reconceptualizing Intellectual Histories of Africana Studies: A Review of the Literature" (PhD dissertation, Temple University, 2013), chapters 5–7, 9, 11; Joshua Myers, *Cedric Robinson: The Time of the Black Radical Tradition* (Polity Press, 2021); Joshua Myers, *Of Black Study* (Pluto Press, 2023).

8 Lawrence Crouchett, "Early Black Studies Movements," *Journal of Black Studies* 2, no. 2 (December 1971): 189–200; for histories, textbooks, and theoretical conceptualizations of Black Studies, see inter alia Delores P. Aldridge and Carlene Young, eds., *Out of the Revolution: The Development of Africana Studies* (Lexington Books, 2000); Gloria T. Hull, Patricia Bell Scott, and Barbara Smith, *All the Women Are White, All the Blacks Are Men, but Some of Us Are Brave: Black Women's Studies* (Feminist Press, 1982); Maulana Karenga, *Introduction*

to Black Studies (University of Sankore Press, 1982); Nathaniel Norment Jr., ed., *The African American Studies Reader* (Carolina Academic Press, 2007); Molefi Kete Asante, *The Afrocentric Idea* (Temple University Press, 1987); Perry A. Hall, *In the Vineyard: Working in African American Studies* (University of Tennessee Press, 1999); Abdul Alkalimat, *The History of Black Studies* (Pluto Press, 2021); Martha Biondi, *The Black Revolution on Campus* (University of California Press, 2012).

9 In this study, a working definition of "Africana Studies" or "Black Studies," used interchangeably, is the study of African people, their histories and cultures, across time and space around the world with genealogical ties to the African continent. It centers the knowledge and intellectual traditions of African people on their own terms. Its function is to liberate all African-descended people, and all of humanity, and to transform the world. When referring to Black Studies or Black study, this work grounds its meaning in Greg Carr's definition and the field's purpose: study for liberation. On Black study, see Myers, *Of Black Study*, and Stefano Harney and Fred Moten, *The Undercommons: Fugitive Planning and Black Study* (Minor Compositions, 2013).

10 In formulating these ideas, my thinking has been shaped deeply by the work and teachings of Cedric Robinson and Josh Myers. The notion of knowledge derived from struggle is directly from Robinson. See Cedric J. Robinson, *Black Marxism: The Making of the Black Radical Tradition* (University of North Carolina Press, 2000), xxx; Myers, *Cedric Robinson*; Cedric J. Robinson, "Manichaeism and Multiculturalism," in *Mapping Multiculturalism*, ed. Avery Gordon and Christopher Newfield (University of Minnesota Press, 1996), 116–24.

11 Robin D. G. Kelley, *Freedom Dreams: The Black Radical Imagination* (Beacon, 2002), 8–12.

12 Craig Steven Wilder, *Ebony and Ivy: Race, Slavery, and the Troubled History of American Universities* (Bloomsbury Press, 2013).

13 Other institutions of higher learning such as women's seminaries and colleges founded and operated by abolitionists represent important counter-institutional histories to many of the oldest colleges and universities that exist in the United States today. However, many of them as institutions remained tethered to capital and a cultural orientation grounded in white supremacy. For an important study on abolitionist colleges, see John Frederick Bell, *Degrees of Equality: Abolitionist Colleges and the Politics of Race* (Louisiana State University Press, 2022).

14 Robin D. G. Kelley, "Black Study, Black Struggle" Forum, *Boston Review*, March 7, 2016; Harney and Moten, *The Undercommons*; for Du Bois's reflection, see W. E. B. Du Bois, "A Negro Student at Harvard at the End of the 19th Century," *Massachusetts Review* 1, no. 3 (Spring 1960): 443.

15 Robinson, "Manichaeism," 118.

16 As this study will show, there is a longer history, mainly among Black people and some whites, of critical engagement with slavery and universities during the era of slavery; however, conventional studies of this relationship are relatively new.

17 In 2001, a group of graduate students at Yale wrote a report detailing the university's connections to slavery and racism to counter a university pamphlet touting its relationship to antislavery. Two years later, Dr. Ruth Simmons as president of Brown University appointed a committee to study and publish results regarding the university's connections to slavery. Brown's study marked the first time a university officially sponsored an investigation into its slaving past and also provided recommendations for addressing slavery's legacies at the university and in the surrounding community. Six years after Brown's investigation, and three years after its report, other universities began their own official investigations. See Antony Dugdale et al., *Yale, Slavery, and Abolition* (The Amistad Committee, 2001); Brenda Allen et al., *Slavery and Justice: Report of the Brown University Steering Committee on Slavery and Justice* (Brown University, 2006); "The Lemon Project," William and Mary, www.wm.edu, accessed December 9, 2024; "President's Commission on Slavery and the University," University of Virginia, 2013, https://slavery.virginia.edu; "The Princeton and Slavery Project," Princeton University, https://slavery.princeton.edu, accessed December 9, 2024; "Columbia University and Slavery," Columbia University, https://columbiaandslavery.columbia. edu, accessed December 9, 2024; Sven Beckert, Katherine Stevens, and Students, *Harvard and Slavery: Seeking a Forgotten History* (Beckert and Stevens, 2011); Hilary Green, "The Hallowed Grounds Project," www.hngreenphd.com; Brooke Krancer, "Penn Slavery Project Report," student essay, Independent Study, University of Pennsylvania, November 25, 2017; Manlu Liu, "Penn Unveils New Findings on History with Slavery," *The Daily Pennsylvanian*, June 29, 2018, www.thedp.com; Isabel Togoh, "Cambridge University Is Investigating Its Links to Slavery: What Exactly Does That Mean?," *Huffington Post*, May 1, 2019, www.huffpost.com; Sally Weale, "Cambridge University to Study How It Profited from Colonial Slavery," *The Guardian*, April 29, 2019, www.theguardian.com; Lee, "Uncovering the Painful Truth About Racism on Campus"; Leslie M. Harris, James T. Campbell, and Alfred Brophy, eds., *Slavery and the University: Histories and Legacies* (University of Georgia Press, 2019), 1–18. For a list of institutions with links to digital projects, see "Universities Studying Slavery," University of Virginia, https://slavery.virginia. edu, accessed December 9, 2024.

18 Wilder, *Ebony and Ivy*; Alfred L. Brophy, *University, Court, and Slave: Pro-Slavery Thought in Southern Colleges and Courts and the Coming of the Civil War* (Oxford University Press, 2016); Jennifer Oast, *Institutional Slavery: Slaveholding Churches, Schools, Colleges, and Businesses in Virginia, 1680–1860* (Cambridge University Press, 2016); Daina Ramey Berry, *The Price for Their Pound of Flesh: The Value of the Enslaved, from Womb to Grave, in the Building of a Nation* (Beacon Press, 2017), chapter 6; Marisa J. Fuentes and Deborah Gray White, eds., *Scarlett and Black*. Volume 1, *Slavery and Dispossession in Rutgers History* (Rutgers University Press, 2016); also see essays by Alfred L. Brophy, Lolita Buckner Inniss, Kelley Fanto Deetz, Jody L. Allen, and Michael Sugure in *Forum on Slavery and Universities*, special issue, *Slavery and Abolition* 39, no. 2 (2018); Harris et al., *Slavery and*

the University; see the essays respectively from Tiya Miles, Chana Kai Lee, Hilary Green, Rhondda Robinson Thomas, and Leslie Harris in "Universities Studying Slavery Roundtable," *The Public Historian* 42, no. 4 (November 2020): 9–62; Maurie D. McInnis and Louis P. Nelson, eds., *Educated in Tyranny: Slavery at Thomas Jefferson's University* (University of Virginia Press, 2018); Rhondda Robinson Thomas, *Call My Name: Documenting the Black Experience in an American University Community* (University of Iowa Press, 2020); Lolita Buckner Innis, *The Princeton Fugitive Slave: The Trials of James Collins Johnson* (Fordham University Press, 2019); Rachel L. Swarns, *The 272: The Families Who Were Enslaved and Sold to Build the American Catholic Church* (Random House, 2023); Julia W. Bernier, "Georgetown and Slavery, from Plantation to Campus," *Journal of the Early Republic* 44, no. 1 (Spring 2024): 87–114; Adam Rothman and Elsa Barraza Mendoza, eds., *Facing Georgetown's History: A Reader on Slavery, Memory, and Reconciliation* (Georgetown University Press, 2021); for work on the connections between slavery and the advent of modern medicine, see Deidre Cooper Owens, *Medical Bondage: Race, Gender, and the Origins of American Gynecology* (University of Georgia Press, 2018); and Christopher Willoughby, *Masters of Health: Racial Science and Slavery in U.S. Medical Schools* (University of North Carolina Press, 2022).

19 Robert Lee and Tristian Ahtone, "Land-Grab Universities," *High Country News*, March 30, 2020; Abigail Boggs and Nick Mitchell, "Critical University Studies and the Crisis Consensus," *Feminist Studies* 44, no. 2 (2018): 432–63; Davarian L. Baldwin, *In the Shadow of the Ivory Tower: How Universities Are Plundering Our Cities* (Bold Type Books, 2021); Conor Tomás Reed, *New York Liberation School: Study and Movement for the People's University* (Common Notions, 2023); for universities and settler colonialism, see Leigh Patel, *No Study Without Struggle: Confronting Settler Colonialism in Higher Education* (Beacon Press, 2021) and Sharon Stein, *Unsettling the University: Confronting the Colonial Foundations of U.S. Higher Education* (Johns Hopkins University Press, 2022).

20 Wilder has a chapter on the controversy over colonization and antislavery at a selection of northern colleges, but the topic comprises one chapter at the end of his important book. For works on colleges and colonization, see Wilder, *Ebony and Ivy*, chapter 8; Wilder, "'Driven . . . from the School of the Prophets': The Colonizationist Ascendance at General Theological Seminary," *New York History* (Summer 2012): 157–85; William B. Hart, "'I Am a Man': Martin Henry Freeman (Middlebury College, 1849) and the Problems of Race, Manhood, and Colonization," in Harris et al., *Slavery and the University*, 148–78; Russell W. Irvine, *The African American Quest for Institutions of Higher Education Before the Civil War: The Forgotten Histories of the Ashmun Institute, Liberia College, and Avery College* (Edwin Mellen Press, 2010).

21 Richard Hofstader acknowledged that abolition was an important force at some colleges in the antebellum North, but he maintained that rather than providing sober academic leadership dedicated to "research, inquiry, and discussion," its

advocates fueled the slavery controversy. Russel B. Nye argued that "abolition did not become an important issue" at colleges and that "the suppression of abolitionist discussions was never a problem of overwhelming importance on Northern campuses." Richard Hofstader, *Academic Freedom in the Age of the College* (1955; Columbia University Press, 1961), 253–61, 261; Russel B. Nye, *Fettered Freedom: Civil Liberties and the Slavery Controversy, 1830–1860* (Michigan State University Press, 1963), 107, 116. Hoftstader's interpretation was mainly anachronistic and implied that abolitionists were ideological fanatics who contributed to his overall framing of antebellum denominational colleges as dysfunctional and retrogressive, or "Old Time Colleges," but he did recognize the prevalence of the slavery controversy at antebellum colleges. For the reception of antislavery in southern colleges, see Clement Eaton, *The Freedom of Thought Struggle in the Old South* (Harper and Row, 1964), chapter 9.

22 Lawrence T. Lesick, *The Lane Rebels: Evangelicalism and Antislavery in Antebellum America* (Scarecrow Press, 1980), 146; Lois W. Banner, "Religion and Reform in the Early Republic: The Role of Youth," *American Quarterly* 23, no. 5 (December 1971): 688; Feuer, *The Conflict of Generations*, 321–22. Feuer argued that Lane students constituted the only student movement in the antebellum era. His assertion that "no wave of empathy or identification with the slaves' lot swept Northern students" and that "they remained placid, and either indifferent or hostile to the abolitionist agitation" is incomplete and historically inaccurate.

23 Claude Moore Fuess, *Amherst: The Story of a New England College* (Little, Brown, 1935), 110–11; William S. Tyler, *History of Amherst College During Its First Half-Century, 1821–1871* (Clark W. Bryan, 1873), 245–51; Gilbert H. Barnes, *The Antislavery Impulse, 1830–1844* (Harbinger, 1933), chapters 6 and 7; Robert Samuel Fletcher, *A History of Oberlin College: From Its Foundation Through the Civil War*, 2 vols. (Arno Press, reprint, 1971); Herman R. Muelder, *Fighters for Freedom: The History of Anti-Slavery Activities of Men and Women Associated with Knox College* (Columbia University Press, 1959); J. Earl Thompson, "Abolitionism and Theological Education at Andover," *The New England Quarterly* 47, no. 2 (June 1974): 238–61; Lesick, *Lane Rebels*; Sernett, *Abolition's Axe*; Morris, *Oberlin*; Gary J. Kornblith and Carol Lasser, *Elusive Utopia: The Struggle for Racial Equality in Oberlin, Ohio* (Louisiana State University Press, 2018); an important exception is Bell, *Degrees of Equality*.

24 Betty Fladeland, "Who Were the Abolitionists?," *The Journal of Negro History* 49, no. 2 (April 1964): 99–115. Leonard Richards's classic study *Gentlemen of Property and Standing* offers compelling evidence that middling to wealthy whites tended to violently oppose abolitionists. See Leonard L. Richards, *Gentlemen of Property and Standing: Anti-Abolition Mobs in Jacksonian America* (Oxford University Press, 1970).

25 David Allmendinger persuasively demonstrated that white men college students who enrolled at denominational colleges in New England were often materially poor and from rural families. David F. Allmendinger, *Paupers and Scholars: The*

Transformation of Student Life in Nineteenth-Century New England (St. Martin's Press, 1975), 1–11. Lois Banner, in "Religion and Reform in the Early Republic," took seriously the role of youth in social reform and antislavery but only focused on the Lane Rebels. Cf. David H. Donald, "Toward a Reconsideration of Abolitionists," in *Lincoln Reconsidered: Essays on the Civil War Era* (Knopf, 1956).

26 Donald M. Scott's analysis of the professionalization of the New England ministry reveals how young white ministers coming of age in the 1830s dedicated themselves to immediatism because of its connections to evangelicalism but stopped short of examining the controversy over student participation in, or debates over, abolition at colleges. See Donald M. Scott, "Abolition as a Sacred Vocation," in *Antislavery Reconsidered: New Perspectives on the Abolitionists*, ed. Lewis Perry and Michael Fellman (Louisiana State University Press, 1979), 51–74; Donald M. Scott, *From Office to Profession: The New England Ministry, 1750–1850* (University of Pennsylvania Press, 1978), 76–94.

27 While historians have centered the significance of the evangelical revivalism of the Second Great Awakening in explaining why some whites converted to abolition, it did not create the abolition movement. Abolition was its own movement with Black roots that predated the rise of white evangelical revivalism and instead merged with it in the 1830s. On evangelicalism in the antebellum movement, see Barnes, *The Antislavery Impulse*; Dwight L. Dumond, *Antislavery Origins of the Civil War in the United States* (University of Michigan Press, 1939); David E. Swift, *Black Prophets of Justice: Activist Clergy Before the Civil War* (Louisiana State University Press, 1989); John R. McKivigan, *The War Against Proslavery Religion: Abolitionism and the Northern Churches, 1830–1865* (Cornell University Press, 1984); Rita Roberts, *Evangelicalism and the Politics of Reform in Northern Black Thought, 1776–1863* (Louisiana State University Press, 2010); also see Bertram Wyatt Brown, *Lewis Tappan and the Evangelical War Against Slavery* (Press of Case Western Reserve University, 1969); Douglas M. Strong, *Perfectionist Politics: Abolitionism and the Religious Tensions of American Democracy* (Syracuse University Press, 1999); and Robert Abzug, *Cosmos Crumbling: American Reform and the Religious Imagination* (Oxford University Press, 1994). On abolition as its own movement that preceded the Second Great Awakening, see Alice Dana Adams, *The Neglected Period of Anti-Slavery in America, 1808–1831* (Ginn, 1908); Sinha, *The Slave's Cause*; Benjamin Quarles, *Black Abolitionists* (Oxford University Press, 1969), 3–23; cf. Anne C. Loveland, "Evangelicalism and 'Immediate Emancipation' in American Antislavery Thought," *Journal of Southern History* 32, no. 2 (May 1966): 172–88; David Brion Davis, "The Emergence of Immediatism in British and American Antislavery Thought," *Mississippi Valley Historical Review* 49, no. 2 (September, 1962): 209–30.

28 Shirly J. Yee, *Black Women Abolitionists: A Study in Activism, 1828–1830* (University of Tennessee Press, 1992); Martha S. Jones, *All Bound Up Together: The Woman Question in African American Public Culture, 1830 1900* (University of North Carolina Press, 2007); Sinha, *The Slave's Cause*, 266–98.

29 Kabria Baumgartner, *In Pursuit of Knowledge: Black Women and Educational Activism in Antebellum America* (New York University Press, 2019); Vincent Carretta, ed., *Complete Writings by Phillis Wheatley* (Penguin Books, 2001); Marilyn Richardson, ed., *Maria W. Stewart, America's First Black Woman Political Writer: Essays and Speeches* (Indiana University Press, 1987); Ellen Nickenzie Lawson and Marlene D. Merrill, *The Three Sarahs: Documents of Antebellum Black College Women* (Edwin Mellen Press, 1984), 188–220; Sirpa Salenius, *An Abolitionist Abroad: Sarah Parker Remond in Cosmopolitan Europe* (University of Massachusetts Press, 2016); on Black women's activism in the antebellum United States, see the preceding note and Jessica Millward, *Finding Charity's Folk: Enslaved and Free Black Women in Maryland* (University of Georgia Press, 2015); Erica Armstrong Dunbar, *A Fragile Freedom: African American Women and Emancipation in the Antebellum City* (Yale University Press, 2008); Stephanie M. H. Camp, *Closer to Freedom: Enslaved Women and Everyday Resistance in the Plantation South* (University of North Carolina Press, 2004).

30 Manisha Sinha's work has refuted the characterization of abolitionists as incendiary fanatics, religious zealots, and bourgeois reformers. While the movement was interracial, significant differences among and within groups of abolitionists were important. See Sinha, *The Slave's Cause*; also see Jesse Olsavsky, *The Most Absolute Abolition: Runaways, Vigilance Committees, and the Rise of Revolutionary Abolitionism, 1835–1861* (Louisiana State University Press, 2022); cf. Andrew Delbanco, *The Abolitionist Imagination* (Harvard University Press, 2012), chapter 1. Also see Sinha, "The Problem of Abolition in the Age of Capitalism," *American Historical Review* 124, no. 1 (February 2019): 144–63.

31 The idea of universities as the third arm of American civilization comes from Wilder, *Ebony and Ivy*, 11.

32 It is imperative to distinguish between emancipation as a process dictated by the state versus abolition as a social movement. Conflating one with the other is disingenuous and obscures more than it reveals. See Thomas Holt's argument on parsing "abolition" in Thomas C. Holt, "Explaining Abolition," *Journal of Social History* 24, no. 2 (Winter 1990): 371–78, esp. 375–76. However, Holt's questions about how abolitionist ideology came to be embraced seemingly pertains to white views on the subject, as the questions posed largely ignore free and enslaved Black people who did not have to be convinced of slavery's evils. Sinha makes a similar argument about the differences between abolition the social movement and abolition the state process, here meaning the British state, and further distinguishes abolition from industrial capitalism and empire. These distinctions should be applied to the American state as well. See Sinha, "The Problem of Abolition in the Age of Capitalism," 159–60.

33 For a similar argument about Black higher learning, see Kabria Baumgartner, "Towers of Intellect: The Struggle for African American Higher Education in Antebellum New England," in *Slavery and the University*, 179–96.

34 Sinha, *The Slave's Cause*; Erica L. Ball, *To Live an Antislavery Life: Personal Politics and the Antebellum Black Middle Class* (University of Georgia Press, 2012); Kellie Carter Jackson, *Force and Freedom: Black Abolitionists and the Politics of Violence* (University of Pennsylvania Press, 2019); Elizabeth Stordeur Pryor, *Colored Travelers: Mobility and the Fight for Citizenship Before the Civil War* (University of North Carolina Press, 2016); Martha S. Jones, *Birthright Citizens: A History of Race and Rights in Antebellum America* (Cambridge University Press, 2018); Hilary J. Moss, *Schooling Citizens: The Struggle for African American Education in Antebellum America* (University of Chicago Press, 2009); Patrick Rael, *Black Identity and Black Protest in the Antebellum North* (University of North Carolina Press, 2002); James Oliver Horton and Lois E. Horton, *In Hope of Liberty: Culture, Community, and Protest Among Northern Free Blacks* (Oxford University Press, 1998).

35 For new work on the symbiotic relationship between Black education, broadly conceived, and the abolition movement, see Baumgartner, *In Pursuit of Knowledge*; Bell, *Degrees of Equality*; Crystal Lynn Webster, *Beyond the Boundaries of Childhood: African American Children in the Antebellum North* (University of North Carolina Press, 2021), 90–113; Michaël Roy, *Young Abolitionists: Children of the Antislavery Movement* (New York University Press, 2024), esp. 107–42; Jesse Olsavsky, "Runaway Slaves, Vigilance Committees, and the Pedagogy of Revolutionary Abolitionism, 1835–1863," in *A Global History of Runaways: Works, Mobility, and Capitalism*, ed. Marcus Rediker, Titas Chakraborty, and Matthias van Rossum (University of California Press, 2019), 216–34; Jesse Olsavsky, *The Most Absolute Abolition*, 87–124; Sarah L. H. Gronningsater, *The Rising Generation: Gradual Abolition, Black Legal Culture, and the Making of National Freedom* (University of Pennsylvania Press, 2024), 95–128.

36 Carter G. Woodson, *The Education of the Negro Prior to 1861* (Association for the Study of Negro Life and History, 1919); John Hope Franklin, *From Slavery to Freedom: A History of Negro Americans*, 3rd ed. (Knopf, 1967), 230–32; Baumgartner, *In Pursuit of Knowledge*; also see Benjamin Quarles, *Black Abolitionists*, 106–15; and Carleton Mabee, *Black Education in New York State: From Colonial to Modern Times* (Syracuse University Press, 1979); Moss, *Schooling Citizens*. For a significant study of Black higher learning before the Civil War, see Russell W. Irvine, *The African American Quest for Institutions of Higher Education Before the Civil War*.

37 Antebellum colleges were spaces of contestation that mirrored the society of which they were a part. See Kenneth Nivision, "'But a Step from the College to the Judicial Bench': College and Curriculum in New England's 'Age of Improvement,'" *History of Education Quarterly* 50, no. 4 (November 2010): 460–87; James Axtell, "The Death of the Liberal Arts College," *History of Education Quarterly* 11, no. 4 (Winter 1971): 339–52; Allmendinger, *Paupers and Scholars*; Roger Geiger, ed., *The American College and University in the Nineteenth Century* (Vanderbilt University Press, 2000). A focus on Black and white student abolitionists also answers a call of the historian Frederick Rudolph to study students on their own terms. See Frederick Rudolph, "Neglect of College Students as a Historical Tradition," in *The College and the Student*, ed. Lawrence E. Dennis and Joseph F. Kauffman (American Council on

Education, 1966), 47–58; Michael S. Hevel, "A Historiography of College Students 30 Years after Helen Horowitz's *Campus Life,*" *Higher Education Handbook of Theory and Research*, vol. 32 (Springer International Publishing, 2017), 419–84. Moreover, historians of higher education before the Civil War have sometimes mentioned or have outright neglected the politics of slavery, racism, abolition, and equality in their otherwise valuable studies of American colleges. See for example Roger L. Geiger, *The History of American Higher Education: Learning and Culture from the Founding to World War II* (Princeton University Press, 2016); John R. Thelin, *A History of American Higher Education*, 3rd ed. (Johns Hopkins University Press, 2019); Charles Dorn, *For the Common Good: A New History of Higher Education in America* (Cornell University Press, 2017), 33, 47–48, 55–56, 63.

38 See for example, Jelani M. Favors, *Shelter in a Time of Storm: How Black Colleges Fostered Generations of Leadership and Activism* (University of North Carolina Press, 2019); Joshua M. Myers, *We Are Worth Fighting For: A History of the Howard University Student Protest of 1989* (New York University Press, 2019); Joy Ann Williamson, *Radicalizing the Ebony Tower: Black Colleges and the Black Freedom Struggle in Mississippi* (Teacher's College Press, 2008); Stefan M. Bradley, *Upending the Ivory Tower: Civil Rights, Black Power, and the Ivy League* (New York University Press, 2018); Biondi, *The Black Revolution*; Ibram Rogers, *The Black Campus Movement: Black Students and the Radical Reconstitution of Higher Education, 1965–1972* (Palgrave, 2012).

39 Vincent Harding, *Beyond Chaos: Black History and the Search for the New Land* (Institute of Black World, 1970); Vincent Harding, *There Is a River*; Sylvia Wynter, "On How We Mistook the Map for the Territory, and Re-Imprisoned Ourselves in Our Unbearable Wrongness of Being, of Désêtre: Black Studies Toward the Human Project," in *Not Only the Master's Tools: African American Studies in Theory and Practice*, ed. Lewis R. Gordon and Jane Anna Gordon (Paradigm Publishers, 2006), 107–69; Sylvia Wynter, "'No Humans Involved': An Open Letter to My Colleagues," *Forum N.H.I.: Knowledge for the 21st Century* 1, no. 1 (Fall 1994): 1–17; W. E. B. Du Bois, *Black Reconstruction in America* (1935; Free Press, 1992); Gerald Horne, "W. E. B. Du Bois's Abolition Democracy," *The Nation*, May 3, 2022, www.thenation.com; L. D. Reddick, "A New Interpretation for Negro History," *The Journal of Negro History* 22, no. 1 (January 1937): 17, 17–28; Myers, *Of Black Study*, 42–51, 176–77; Sterling Stuckey, "Twilight of Our Past: Reflections on the Origins of Black History," *Amistad 2: Writings on Black History and Culture*, ed., John A. Williams and Charles F. Harris (Random House, 1971), 261–96. Nell Irvin Painter, *Exodusters: Black Migration to Kansas After Reconstruction* (Knopf, 1976); Robinson, *Black Marxism*; Cedric J. Robinson, *Black Movements in America* (Routledge, 1997); Carter G. Woodson, *The Miseducation of the Negro* (Associated Publishers, 1933), introduction and chapter 1. Vincent Harding also argued that those who study Black history have a moral debt to those Black people who created the struggle on which much intellectual work in the university is based. See Harding's important essay "Power from Our People: The Source of the Modern Revival of Black History," *The Black Scholar* 18, no. 1 (January/February 1987): 40–51. The term "common humanity" comes from Dr. Greg Carr.

CHAPTER 1. BLACK STUDENTS AND THE ACADEMY

1 While there is no recorded evidence of this event in the Williams College archives, scholars have maintained the credibility of the Prince admission case through oral accounts and contemporary knowledge of the individuals involved. See Sharon M. Harris, *Executing Race: Early American Women's Narratives of Race, Society, and the Law* (Ohio State University Press, 2005), chapter 6, 155–57; David R. Proper, "Lucy Terry Prince: 'Singer of History,'" *Contributions in Black Studies* 9 (1990–1992): 187–214, esp. 199–200; Manisha Sinha, *The Slave's Cause: A History of Abolition* (Yale University Press, 2016), 26–27; Gretchen Holbrook Gerzina, researched with Anthony Gerzina, *Mr. and Mrs. Prince: How an Extraordinary Eighteenth-Century Family Moved out of Slavery and into Legend* (Amistad, HarperCollins, 2008), 163–64, 206–7; George Sheldon, *A History of Deerfield, Massachusetts*, vol. 2 (Hall, 1896), 900–901; Calvin Durfee, *Williams Biographical Annals* (Lee and Shepard, 1871), 50–52; Leverett Wilson Spring, *A History of Williams College* (Houghton Mifflin, 1917), 138.

2 Cedric J. Robinson, *Black Movements in America* (Routledge, 1997), 44; Vincent Harding, *There Is a River: The Black Struggle for Freedom in America* (Harcourt, 1981), 82–84, 120, 132, 134.

3 Biographical works on early Black students include Winston James, *The Struggles of John Brown Russwurm: The Life and Writings of a Pan-Africanist Pioneer, 1799–1851* (New York University Press, 2010); Hugh Hawkins, "Edward Jones, Marginal Man," in *Black Apostles at Home and Abroad: Afro-Americans and the Christian Mission from the Revolution to Reconstruction*, ed. David Wills and Richard Newman (G.K. Hall, 1982), 243–53; Bella Gross, "Life and Times of Theodore S. Wright, 1797–1847," *Negro History Bulletin* 3, no. 9 (June 1940): 133–38, 144; Connie Perdreau, "John Newton Templeton: Dreamer of the Possible Dream," biographical sketch, Ohio University Archives General Collection, Ohio University Libraries: Mahn Center for Archives and Special Collections; Forrester A. Lee and James S. Pringle, *A Noble and Independent Course: The Life of the Reverend Edward Mitchell* (Dartmouth College Press, 2018).

4 According to John R. Thelin, less than 2 percent of the population received a college education in the early nineteenth century; John R. Thelin, *A History of American Higher Education* (Johns Hopkins University Press, 2004), 69.

5 Vincent P. Franklin, "Education for Colonization: Attempts to Educate Free Blacks in the United States for Emigration to Africa, 1823–1833," *Journal of Negro History* 43, no. 1 (Winter 1974): 91–103; Carter G. Woodson, *The Education of the Negro Prior to 1861* (1919; Arno Press, 2nd ed., 1968), 256–66.

6 Carter G. Woodson, *The Education of the Negro Prior to 1861*; V. P. Franklin, "'They Rose and Fell Together': African American Educators and Community Leadership, 1795–1954," *Journal of Education* 172, no. 3 (Fall 1990): 39–64; Hilary J. Moss, *Schooling Citizens: The Struggle for African American Education in Antebellum America* (University of Chicago Press, 2009). For examples of general

histories of higher education in the early nineteenth century, see Thelin, *A History of American Higher Education*; Charles Dorn, *For the Common Good: A New History of Higher Education in America* (Cornell University Press, 2017).

7 For Black women and higher learning see Kabria Baumgartner, *In Pursuit of Knowledge: Black Women and Educational Activism in Antebellum America* (New York University Press, 2019); Kabria Baumgartner, "'Cruel and Wicked Prejudice': Racial Exclusion and the Female Seminary Movement in the Antebellum North," in *Women's Higher Education in the United States: New Historical Perspectives*, ed. Margaret A. Nash (Palgrave, 2018), 45–68; see also Kabria Baumgartner, "Towers of Intellect: The Struggle for African American Higher Education in Antebellum New England," in *Slavery and the University: Histories and Legacies*, ed. Leslie M. Harris et al. (University of Georgia Press, 2019), 179–96.

8 Sinha, *The Slave's Cause*, chapter 6; J. R. Oldfield, *Transatlantic Abolitionism in the Age of Revolution: An International History of Anti-Slavery, c. 1787–1820* (Cambridge University Press, 2013); Richard S. Newman, *The Transformation of American Abolitionism: Fighting over Slavery in the Early Republic* (University of North Carolina Press, 2002); Alice Dana Adams, *The Neglected Period of Anti-Slavery in America (1808–1831)* (Ginn, 1908); Betty Fladeland, *Men and Brothers: Anglo-American Antislavery Cooperation* (University of Illinois Press, 1972); C. L. R. James, *The Black Jacobins: Toussaint L'Ouverture and the San Domingo Revolution* (Vintage, 1963); Ada Ferrer, *Freedom's Mirror: Cuba and Haiti in the Age of Revolution* (Cambridge University Press, 2014); Douglas R. Egerton, *Gabrielle's Rebellion: The Virginia Slave Conspiracies of 1800 and 1802* (University of North Carolina Press, 1993); Douglas R. Egerton, *He Shall Go Out Free: The Lives of Denmark Vesey* (Madison House, 1999); Edward B. Rugemer, *The Problem of Emancipation: The Caribbean Roots of the American Civil War* (Louisiana State University Press, 2008), 17–66.

9 James Oliver Horton and Lois E. Horton, *In Hope of Liberty: Culture, Community, and Protest Among Northern Free Blacks* (Oxford University Press, 1998); Elizabeth McHenry, *Forgotten Readers: Recovering the Lost History of African American Literary Societies* (Duke University Press, 2002); Julie Winch, *Philadelphia's Black Elite: Activism, Accommodation, and the Struggle for Autonomy* (Temple University Press, 1988); David E. Swift, *Black Prophets of Justice: Activist Clergy Before the Civil War* (Louisiana State University Press, 1989); Erica Armstrong Dunbar, *A Fragile Freedom: African American Women and Emancipation in the Antebellum City* (Yale University Press, 2008); Leslie M. Harris, *In the Shadow of Slavery: African Americans in New York City, 1626–1863* (University of Chicago Press, 2003); James Sidbury, *Becoming African in America: Race and Nation in the Early Black Atlantic* (Oxford University Press, 2007); Patrick Rael, *Black Identity and Black Protest in the Antebellum North* (University of North Carolina Press, 2002).

10 Horton and Horton, *In Hope of Liberty*, 150–54, 216–21, quotation from 150; Sinha, *The Slave's Cause*, 116–20, 133, 142; Moss, *Schooling Citizens*; Woodson, *The Education of the Negro Prior to 1861*.

11 Lawrence Crouchett, "Early Black Studies Movements," *Journal of Black Studies* 2, no. 2 (December, 1971): 189–200.

12 Stuckey, *Slave Culture: Nationalist Theory and the Foundations of Black America* (Oxford University Press, 1987), 73–83, 198–203. On the connection between culture and the development of consciousness, see Cedric J. Robinson, "Historical Consciousness and the Development of Revolutionary Theory," *Review of Afro-American Issues and Culture* 1, no. 3 (Fall 1979): 217–36.

13 Phillis Wheatley-Peters was an African, and likely came from Senegambia and the Fulani people, where Islam and indigenous African spiritual traditions coalesced. While American writers laud Wheatley's intellect in learning English and classical literature, they rarely begin with the fact that she would have participated in the learning traditions of her people prior to capture and enslavement. She was already an intellectual when she arrived in Boston, and her knowledge was honed by Fulani and Africana ways of knowing, culture, and traditions. See Greg Carr and Dana A. Williams, "Toward the Theoretical Practice of Conceptual Liberation: Using an Africana Studies Approach to Reading African American Literary Texts," in *Contemporary African American Literature: The Living Canon*, ed. Lovalerie King and Shirley Moody-Turner (Indiana University Press, 2013), 314–17; John C. Shields, *Phillis Wheatley's Poetics of Liberation: Backgrounds and Contexts* (University of Tennessee Press, 2008), 97–124; April C. E. Langley, *The Black Aesthetic Unbound: Theorizing the Dilemma of Eighteenth-Century African American Literature* (Ohio State University Press, 2008), 57–97; Babacar M'Baye, *The Trickster Comes West: Pan African Influence in Early Black Diasporan Narratives* (University Press of Mississippi, 2009), 21–69; June Jordan, "The Difficult Miracle of Black Poetry in America: Something like a Sonnet for Phillis Wheatley," in June Jordan, *Some of Us Did Not Die: New and Selected Essays* (Basic, 2002), 174–86; cf. David Waldstreicher, *The Odyssey of Phillis Wheatley: A Poet's Journey Through American Slavery and Independence* (Farrar, 2023), 21.

14 Phillis Wheatley, "To the University of Cambridge, in New-England," in *Blacks at Harvard: A Documentary History of African-American Experience at Harvard and Radcliffe*, ed. Werner Sollors, Caldwell Titcomb, and Thomas A. Underwood (New York University Press, 1993), 10.

15 Antonio T. Bly, "Wheatley's 'To the University of Cambridge, in New England,'" *The Explicator* 55, no. 4 (1997): 206; also see the respective interpretations of Wheatley's poem to Harvard students by Eric Ashely Hairston, Babacar M'Baye, and Mary McAleer Balkun in *New Essays on Phillis Wheatley*, ed. John C. Shields and Eric D. Lamore (University of Tennessee Press, 2011), 74–76, 286, 378.

16 These phrases are taken from the original version of the poem; see "To the University of Cambridge, Written in 1767," the Manuscript Poems of Phillis Wheatley, American Antiquarian Society, Worcester, MA; to compare the unpublished and published versions, see *The Collected Works of Phillis Wheatley*, ed. John C. Shields (Oxford University Press, 1988), 15–16, 196–97.

17 For the foregoing, see Michael E. Jirik, "Beyond Clarkson: Cambridge, Black Abolitionists, and the British Anti-Slave Trade Campaign," *Slavery & Abolition* 41, no. 4 (2020): 748–71.

18 Cherry Fletcher Bamberg, "Bristol Yamma and John Quamine in Rhode Island," *Rhode Island History* 73, no. 1 (January 2015): 5–31, esp. 15–22; Sinha, *The Slave's Cause*, 37–38, 131–32; Joseph A. Conforti, *Samuel Hopkins and the New Divinity Movement: Calvinism, the Congregational Ministry, and Reform in New England Between the Great Awakenings* (Christian University Press, 1981), 142–58; Joseph Yannielli, "African Americans on Campus, 1746–1876," essay on the Princeton and Slavery website, www.slavery.princeton.edu, accessed December 10, 2024. After Yamma and Quamine's time at Princeton, John Chavis studied there unofficially with Witherspoon and subsequently attended Liberty Hall Academy in Virginia, which later became Washington and Lee College. On Chavis's life, see Helen Chavis Othow, *John Chavis: African American Patriot, Preacher, Teacher, and Mentor (1763–1838)* (McFarland, 2001); Wilder, *Ebony and Ivy*, 143–44, 350n63, 98, 168; Frederick Chase, *A History of Dartmouth College and the Town of Hanover, New Hampshire*, vol. 1, ed. John King Lord (Wilson, 1891), 300–301; Gregory Nobles, "Betsy Stockton," essay on the Princeton and Slavery website, www.slavery.princeton.edu, accessed December 10, 2024; also see Gregory Nobles, *The Education of Betsy Stockton: An Odyssey of Slavery and Freedom* (University of Chicago Press, 2022); John Saillant, *Black Puritan, Black Republican: The Life and Thought of Lemuel Haynes, 1753–1833* (Oxford University Press, 2003), xi, 4–7, 72, 91, 84, 137, 143–44; Thomas E. Boyce, *Catalogue of the Officers and Alumni of Middlebury College, in Middlebury Vermont, 1800 to 1889* (Register, 1890), 9, 146; William B. Sprague, *Sketches of the Life and Character of the Rev. Lemuel Haynes, A.M.* (Harper, 1837), 166, 161, 168, 279; *Black Preacher to White America: The Collected Writings of Lemuel Haynes, 1774–1833*, ed. Richard Newman (Carlson, 1990), 171–74; Peter P. Hinks, "Timothy Dwight, Congregationalism, and Early Antislavery," in *The Problem of Evil: Slavery, Freedom, and the Ambiguities of American Reform*, ed. Steven Mintz and John Stauffer (University of Massachusetts–Amherst, 2007), 155–59; Sinha, *The Slave's Cause*, 44–48.

19 The census records in 1800 reveal that the Twilights were categorized as people of color. But by the following decade, Ichabod was no longer in the record and the census listed the family as "white." Census records are imperfect historical sources, as they are more representative of the census taker's perspective than they are of the individuals being recorded. Nevertheless, Twilight was of mixed ancestry, which likely included African heritage. See 1800 United States Census, Orange County, Vermont, Corinth, p. 525, NARA microfilm publication M32, Roll 51. Records of the Bureau of the Census, National Archives, Washington, DC; 1810 United States Census, Orange County, Vermont, Corinth, NARA microfilm publication M252.

20 Alana J. Abbott, "Alexander Twilight, 1795–1857," *Contemporary Black Biography*, vol. 125, ed. Margaret Mazurkiewicz (Gale Virtual Library, 2015), 156–58; Gregor

Hileman, "The Iron-Willed Black Schoolmaster and His Granite Academy," *Middlebury College Newsletter*, April 1974, 6, 12; Clark M. Ferrin, "Rev. Alexander Twilight," *Vermont Historical Gazetteer: A Magazine . . .* , vol. 3, ed. Abby M. Hemenway (Claremont, 1877), 101–4. Also see Michael T. Hahn, *Alexander Twilight: Vermont's African American Pioneer* (New England Press, 1998) and William B. Hart, "The Inscrutable Alexander Twilight, 1795–1857," *Vermont Almanac* 11 (2021): 217–19.

21 Boyce, *Catalogue of the Officers and Alumni of Middlebury College*, 56; Edgar J. Wiley, ed., *Catalogue of the Officers and Students of Middlebury College . . .* , *1800–1915* (Middlebury College, 1917), 69. Abbott, "Alexander Twilight," 157; David M. Stameshkin, *The Town's College: Middlebury College, 1800–1915* (Middlebury College Press, 1985), 68–71.

22 Ferrin, "Rev. Alexander Twilight," 102; Abbott, "Alexander Twilight," 157–58.

23 Stameshkin, *The Town's College*, 108–9, 305n31; Hileman, "The Iron-Willed Black Schoolmaster," 12.

24 Stameshkin, *The Town's College*, 179–80; William B. Hart, "'I Am a Man': Martin Henry Freeman (Middlebury College, 1849) and the Problem of Race, Manhood, and Colonization," in *Slavery and the University: Histories and Legacies*, ed. Leslie Harris et al. (University of Georgia Press, 2019), 148–78.

25 For studies of Jones's life, see Hugh Hawkins, "Edward Jones: First American Negro College Graduate?," *School and Society* 89 (1961): 375–76; Clarence G. Contee, "The Reverend Edward Jones, Missionary-Educator to Sierra Leone and 'First' Afro-American College Graduate, 1808? to 1865," *Negro History Bulletin* 38, no. 2 (February–March 1975): 356–57; Hugh Hawkins, "Edward Jones, Marginal Man," 243–53; Michael Crowder, "From Amherst to Fourah Bay: Principal Edward Jones," Bicentenary of the Founding of the Colony of Sierra Leone, 1787–1987, *International Symposium on Sierra Leone, May 19–21, 1987* (Fourah Bay College, University of Sierra Leone, 1987). An important work on Jones's time in Sierra Leone is Nemata Blyden, "Edward Jones: An African American in Sierra Leone," in *Moving On: Black Loyalists in the Afro-Atlantic World*, ed. John W. Pulis (Garland, 1999), 159–82. The most comprehensive study on Jones yet is Stephen Keith's undergraduate thesis, written for a BA in Black Studies: "The Life and Times of Edward Jones: Sower of the African Diaspora," student thesis, Amherst College, 1973, Amherst College Archives and Special Collections.

26 When Jehu Jones died in 1833, his estate was valued at around forty thousand dollars. Contee, "The Reverend Edward Jones," 356; Crowder, "From Amherst to Fourah Bay," 2–3; E. Horace Fitchett, "The Traditions of the Free Negro in Charleston, South Carolina," *Journal of Negro History* 25, no. 2 (April 1940): 139–52, esp. 143–44.

27 Keith, "The Life and Times of Edward Jones," 1–48; C. W. Birnie, "Education of the Negro in Charleston, South Carolina, Prior to the Civil War," *Journal of Negro History* 12, no. 1 (January 1927): 13–21; Russell W. Irvine, *The African American Quest for Institutions of Higher Education Before the Civil War: The Forgotten His-*

tories of the Ashmun Institute, Liberia College, and Avery College (Edwin Mellen Press, 2010), 44–45; *The Fifth Annual Report of the American Society for Colonizing the Free People of Color of the United States* (Davis, 1822), 14–16.

28 Nine other students in Jones's class entered the college at age twenty or younger. Six students, including Jones, were between fourteen and seventeen years old upon admission. *Biographical Record of the Alumni of Amherst College, During Its First Half Century, 1821–1871* (Amherst, 1883), 2, 6–35.

29 Over the course of four years, Jones's college education was as follows: Freshmen: Roman Antiquities, Arithmetic, Webster's Philosophical and Practical Grammar, Livy's first five books, Day's Algebra, Erving on Composition, Morse's Geography, and Graeca Majora the historical parts; Sophomore: Euclid, Hedge's Logic, Jamieson's Rhetoric, Horace, Latin, and parts of Day's Mathematics; Junior: Graeca Majora continued, Cicero, Paley's Evidences, Enfield's Philosophy, Chemistry, History, and Trigonometry; Senior: Stewart's Philosophy of the Mind, Anatomy, Paley's Moral Philosophy and His Natural Theology, Vattel's Law of Nations, and examinations prior to commencement. See the *Catalogue of Officers and Students* for the years 1822–1825.

30 For a speculative sketch of Jones's time at Amherst, see David W. Wills, "Remembering Edward Jones: First Black Graduate, Missionary Hero, and 'Genteel Young Man of Excellent Disposition,'" in *Amherst in the World*, ed. Martha Saxton (Amherst College, 2020), 29–51. There are reminiscences and remembrances of Jones from white people who knew him during his time at Amherst; however, these sources should be viewed with caution in terms of understanding who Jones was, as they are more reflective of white perceptions of Jones and his time at the college than of Jones's own perspective and thoughts. For a reading and interpretation of these sources and how Jones may have experienced his time at Amherst, see Michael E. Jirik, "Abolition and Academe: Struggles for Freedom and Equality in British and American Colleges, 1742–1855" (PhD dissertation, University of Massachusetts–Amherst, 2019), 193–206.

31 For anti-Black sentiments of students and faculty at Amherst College in the 1820s, see chapter 2.

32 *Amherst College, Order of Exercises at Commencement, 1826 August 23* (Adams, 1826); Hawkins, "Edward Jones, Marginal Man," 244; Crowder, "From Amherst to Fourah Bay," 10.

33 Winston James, *The Struggles of John Brown Russwurm: The Life and Writings of a Pan-Africanist Pioneer, 1799–1851* (New York University Press, 2010), 66–67, 274n28; Contee, "The Reverend Edward Jones," 356.

34 *The Sixth Annual Report of the American Society for Colonizing the Free People of Color of the United States* (Davis, 1823), 15–16.

35 "Missions to Africa," *African Repository and Colonial Journal* 2, no. 11 (January 1827): 347–48, quotation from 348 (hereafter *ARCJ*).

36 "Report," *ARCJ* 6, no. 9 (November 1830): 260–62; *General Catalogue of the Theological Seminary, Andover, Massachusetts, 1808–1908* (Todd, n.d.),

122–23; on the colonizationist African Schools, see "The African Mission School Society," *ARCJ* 4, no. 7 (September 1828): 193–208; Franklin, "Education for Colonization," 91–103; Woodson, *The Education of the Negro*, 256–66. Interestingly, Jones never joined the ACS or worked in Liberia. Years later, Jones critiqued the ACS project in Liberia, writing, "The colony of Liberia is at present in a very bad state. No work, no money, no food for many of the poor people," and instead "many of their best people are coming here" to Sierra Leone. See Jones, "The Chief of Sinners," *The Colored American*, January 20, 1838, 7. Other historians depict Jones's decision to go to Britain and then Sierra Leone as a shocking turn of events. See Hawkins, "Edward Jones, Marginal Man," 245–46; Crowder erroneously writes that Jones was "brought up as an Evangelical Congregationalist," Crowder, "From Amherst to Fourah Bay," 16, 18.

37 John B. Russwurm to Edward Jones, March 20, 1830, in C. Peter Ripley, ed., *Black Abolitionist Papers*, vol. 3 (University of North Carolina Press, 1991), 72, 74, 79n9; James, *The Struggles of John Brown Russwurm*, 66–67, 274n27–28.

38 Contee, "The Reverend Edward Jones," 356–57; Blyden, "Edward Jones," 165–75, 180n49, quotation from 172; Keith, "The Life and Times of Edward Jones," 114–33.

39 *House of Commons, Third Report from the Select Committee on the Slave Trade, Together with the Minutes of Evidence and Appendix* (1848), quotation from 115; Contee, "The Reverend Edward Jones," 357.

40 For a biography of Mitchell's life, see n3 of this chapter.

41 There is no published work on Templeton. For information on Templeton's life, I've relied on a biographical sketch from the Ohio University archives. Perdreau, "John Newton Templeton, Dreamer of the Possible Dream."

42 Betty Hollow, *Ohio University, 1804–2004: The Spirit of a Singular Place* (Ohio University Press, 2003), 2, 7–8; Samantha Seeley, *Race, Removal, and the Right to Remain: Migration and the Making of the United States* (University of North Carolina Press, 2021).

43 Perdreau, "John Newton Templeton."

44 *Ohio University Commencement, Wednesday, September 17, 1828* (1828); *General Catalogue of the Ohio University, from the Date of Its Charter in 1804 to 1875* (Ohio University, 1876), 69.

45 Quoted in Perdreau, "John Newton Templeton"; "Ohio University," *The Scioto Gazette*, December 3, 1828.

46 "Negro Eloquence," *The Scioto Gazette*, July 22, 1829.

47 "Ohio University"; "Intelligence," *ARCJ* 5, no. 8 (October 1829): 248.

48 David Nickens, "An Address to the People of Color in Chillicothe," *The Liberator*, August 11, 1832, 126; "Celebration," *The Liberator*, August 11, 1832, 126; Nikki M. Taylor, *Frontiers of Freedom: Cincinnati's Black Community, 1802–1868* (Ohio University Press, 2005), 88.

49 "Chillicothe Anti-Slavery Society," *The Liberator*, September 13, 1834.

50 Perdreau, "John Newton Templeton."

51 Notice of the organization was printed in "Communication for the Colored American," *The Colored American*, September 2, 1837.

52 "Communication for the Colored American."

53 "Preparatory Remarks," *The Colored American*, May 13, 1837.

54 "Pennsylvania Convention," *The Colored American*, July 1, 1837.

55 *Proceedings of the State Convention of the Colored Freeman of Pennsylvania, Held in Pittsburgh, on the 23d, 24th, and 25th of August, 1841* . . . , printed in *Proceedings of the Black State Conventions, 1840–1865*, vol. 1, ed. Philip S. Foner and George E. Walker (Temple University Press, 1979), 106–16.

56 Perdreau, "John Newton Templeton."

57 *Address of the Rev. Theodore S. Wright Before the Convention of the New York State Antislavery Society, on the Acceptance of the Annual Report, Held at Utica, September 20, 1837*, in *Negro Orators and Their Orations*, ed. Carter G. Woodson (1925; Russell, 1969), 87; Swift, *Black Prophets of Justice*, 48–49.

58 "Shameful Outrage at Princeton, N.J.," *The Emancipator*, October 27, 1836, 102; "The Outrage at Princeton," *The Liberator*, November 5, 1836, 180.

59 Alexander wrote the first history of the ACS, Archibald Alexander, *A History of Colonization on the West Coast of Africa* (Martin, 1846); James W. Alexander, *The Life of Archibald Alexander* (Presbyterian Board, 1857), 396–98; Swift, *Black Prophets of Justice*, 37–38. Also see James Moorhead, "Princeton Theological Seminary and Slavery"; Craig Hollander, "Princeton and the Colonization Movement"; and Kimberly Klein, "Princeton and the New Jersey Colonization Society," all on the Princeton and Slavery website, www.slavery.princeton.edu.

60 "To Our Patrons" and "Authorized Agents," *Freedom's Journal*, March 16, 1827, 1, 4; *Address of the Rev. Theodore S. Wright* in *Negro Orators*, 88.

61 Wright's father was listed as an agent of *Freedom's Journal* as well. "For the Freedom's Journal," and "Wilberforce," *Freedom's Journal*, September 7, 1827, 101–2, 103; "New York, September 21, 1827" and "Authorized Agents," *Freedom's Journal*, September 27, 1827, 110, 112; *Address of the Rev. Theodore S. Wright* in *Negro Orators*, 88; Swift, *Black Prophets of Justice*, 37–38, 49–50.

62 "Shameful Outrage at Princeton N.J.," *The Emancipator*, October 27, 1836; "Shameful Outrage at Princeton," *Zion's Watchman*, November 2, 1836; "The Outrage at Princeton," *The Liberator*, November 5, 1836; "Shameful Outrage at Princeton," *National Enquirer and Constitutional Advocate of Universal Liberty*, November 12, 1836; Swift, *Black Prophets of Justice*, 49; Joseph Yannielli, "White Supremacy at the Commencement of 1836," essay on the Princeton and Slavery website, www.slavery.princeton.edu.

63 Theodore S. Wright, "Prejudice," *The Liberator*, November 5, 1836.

64 Vincent Harding, *There Is a River: The Black Struggle for Freedom in America* (New York: Harcourt, 1981); Sinha, *The Slave's Cause*.

65 "Extract," *The Colored American*, November 11, 1837; "Notice, The Female Department of the Phoenix High School," *The Colored American*, September 16, 1837; Ripley, *Black Abolitionist Papers*, 3:81–88; Bella Gross, "Life and Times of Theodore

S. Wright, 1797–1847," *Negro History Bulletin* 3, no. 9 (June 1940): 133–38; Swift, *Black Prophets of Justice*, 47–76; Benjamin Quarles, *Black Abolitionists* (Oxford University Press, 1969), 68, 79, 184, and passim; Sinha, *The Slave's Cause*, 315; Eric Foner, *Gateway to Freedom: The Hidden History of the Underground Railroad* (Norton, 2015), 77, 99.

66 James, *The Struggles of John Brown Russwurm*, 1–16.

67 *Catalogue of the Officers and Students of Bowdoin College, Maine, October 1824* (Griffin, 1824); Nehemial Cleveland, *History of Bowdoin College with Biographical Sketches of the Graduates, from 1806 to 1879 Inclusive*, ed. Aldephus Spring Packard (Ripley, 1882), 353.

68 Russwurm to the Athanean Society, October 30, 1824, John Brown Russwurm Collection, box 1, folder 2, George J. Mitchell Department of Special Collections and Archives, Bowdoin College Library.

69 See the entries of August 6, 20, 1824, October 22, November 18, 1825, and March 3, 17, 1826, in *Records of the Peucinian Society*. Vol. 3, *1819–1831*, George J. Mitchell Department of Special Collections and Archives, Bowdoin College Library.

70 *Catalogue of the Officers and Students of Bowdoin College, Brunswick ME* (Griffin, 1825); *Ninth Annual Report of the American Society for Colonizing the Free People of Color of the United States* (Way, 1826), 63. Two of Russwurm's professors, Packard and William Smyth, however, went on to become active in abolition in the 1830s.

71 Mrs. T[homas] C. Upham, *Narrative of Phebe Ann Jacobs* (Stewart, 1850); Wilder, *Ebony and Ivy*, 144–45; Harriet Beecher Stowe, *A Key to Uncle Tom's Cabin* (Jewett, 1853), 25.

72 Each term he spent at Bowdoin, Russwurm boarded with a Mr. Pettengill. *Catalogue of the Officers and Students of Bowdoin College, Maine, October 1824*; *Catalogue of the Officers and Students of Bowdoin College, Maine, February 1825* (Griffin, 1825); *Catalogue of the Officers and Students of Bowdoin College, Brunswick, ME, 1825*; *Catalogue of the Officers and Students of Bowdoin College, February 1826* (Griffin, 1826); James, *The Struggles of John Brown Russwurm*, 18.

73 Quoted in James, *The Struggles of John Brown Russwurm*, 19.

74 [John Brown Russwurm], "Toussaint L'Overture, the Principal Chief in the Revolution of St. Domingo," c. 1825, p. 4, 13, African American History Collection, Box 2, William L. Clements Library, University of Michigan, Ann Arbor.

75 [Russwurm], "Toussaint L'Overture," 12, 22; James, *The Struggles of John Brown Russwurm*, 19, 21. Also note James's commentary on Russwurm's authorship of the essay and Russwurm's reliance on a contemporary history of the Haitian Revolution. See James, *The Struggles of John Brown Russwurm*, 261n63–64.

76 John Brown Russwurm, "The Conditions and Prospects of Hayti," 1826 Commencement Oration, printed in James, *The Struggles of John Brown Russwurm*, 132–34, quotations from 132, 133, and 134; for abolitionists drawing on the legacy of the Haitian Revolution, see Sinha, *The Slave's Cause*, 53–64. For reviews of Russwurm's oration in the press, see "Bowdoin College," *United States Telegraph*, Sep-

tember 18, 1826, reprint from the *Eastern Argus*, September 12, 1826; other notices include *New York Spectator*, September 22, 1826, reprint from the *Boston Gazette*; "Commencement at Bowdoin College," *New Hampshire Statesmen and Concord Register*, September 16, 1826; James, *The Struggles of John Brown Russwurm*, 23–24.

77 Cedric J. Robinson, *Black Marxism: The Making of the Black Radical Tradition* (1983; University of North Carolina Press, 2nd ed., 2000).

78 James, *The Struggles of John Brown Russwurm*, 25.

79 See James, *The Struggles of John Brown Russwurm*, 59–108, esp. 92–93, 97–98. Russwurm supported the ACS as a vehicle to advance Black freedom through a Western lens in West Africa. He did at times privately critique the ACS. See James, *The Struggles of John Brown Russwurm*, 71–72. Also see Sandra Sandiford Young, "John Brown Russwurm's Dilemma: Citizenship or Emigration?," in *Prophets of Protest: Reconsidering the History of American Abolitionism*, ed. Timothy Patrick McCarthy and John Stauffer (New Press, 2006), 90–113.

CHAPTER 2. COLONIZATION'S COLLEGES

1 *Memoirs of the American Missionaries, Formerly Connected with the Society of Inquiry Respecting Missions in the Andover Theological Seminary* . . . (Pierce, 1833), 29–34; *Seventh Annual Report of the American Society for Colonizing the Free People of Color of the United States* (Davis, 1824), 29–30; Hugh Davis, *Leonard Bacon: New England Reformer and Antislavery Moderate* (Louisiana State University Press, 1998), 34–36; P. J. Staudenraus, *The African Colonization Movement, 1816–1865* (Columbia University Press, 1961), 76–78. For a study that includes Andover Theological Seminary's role in the ACS but with a different interpretative framework from this chapter, see Gale L. Kenny, "Race, Sympathy, and Missionary Sensibility in the New England Colonization Movement," in *New Directions in the Study of African American Recolonization*, ed. Beverly C. Tomek and Matthew J. Hetrick (University Press of Florida, 2017), 33–49.

2 The multilevel institutional support the ACS received from colleges and seminaries was largely absent from the abolition movement, with few exceptions that came after 1830.

3 Craig Steven Wilder, *Ebony and Ivy: Race, Slavery, and the Troubled History of American Universities* (Bloomsbury Press, 2013), chapter 8; Wilder, "'Driven . . . from the School of the Prophets': Colonizationist Ascendance at General Theological Seminary," *New York History* 93, no. 3 (Summer 2012): 157–85; Marisa J. Fuentes and Deborah Gray White, eds., *Scarlet and Black: Slavery and Dispossession in Rutgers History*, vol. 1 (Rutgers University Press, 2016); William B. Hart, "'I Am a Man': Martin Henry Freeman (Middlebury College, 1849) and the Problems of Race, Manhood, and Colonization," in Leslie Harris et al., eds., *Slavery and the University: Histories and Legacies* (University of Georgia Press, 2019), 148–78; "Columbia and Colonization," Columbia and Slavery website, https://columbiaandslavery.columbia.edu; Craig Hollander, "Princeton and the Colonization Movement," Princeton and Slavery website, https://slavery.princeton.edu.

4 Ousmane Power-Greene, *Against Wind and Tide: African American Struggle Against the Colonization Movement* (New York University Press, 2014); Sinha, *The Slave's Cause*, 161–70; Claude A. Clegg III, *The Price of Liberty: African Americans and the Making of Liberia* (University of North Carolina Press, 2004), 34–36, passim. Cf. David Brion Davis, "Reconsidering the Colonization Movement: Leonard Bacon and the Problem of Evil," *Intellectual History Newsletter* 14 (1992): 3–17; David Brion Davis, *The Problem of Slavery in the Age of Emancipation* (Knopf, 2014), 84–86; Tomek and Hetrick, eds., *New Directions in the Study of African American Recolonization*, 17, 335, 343–44, 347n14.

5 Sinha, *The Slave's Cause*, 182–91; Padraig Riley, *Slavery and the Democratic Conscience: Political Life in Jeffersonian America* (University of Pennsylvania Press, 2016); Matthew Mason, *Slavery and Politics in the Early Republic* (University of North Carolina Press, 2006); Robert Pierce Forbes, *The Missouri Compromise and Its Aftermath: Slavery and the Meaning of America* (University of North Carolina Press, 2007).

6 Samantha Seeley, *Race, Removal, and the Right to Remain: Migration and the Making of the United States* (University of North Carolina Press, 2021); Adam Rothman, *Slave Country: American Expansion and the Origins of the Deep South* (Harvard University Press, 2005); John Craig Hammond, *Slavery, Freedom, and Expansion in the Early American West* (University of Virginia Press, 2007); Steven Deyle, *Carry Me Back: The Domestic Slave Trade in American Life* (Oxford University Press, 2005); Walter Johnson, *River of Dark Dreams: Slavery and Empire in the Cotton Kingdom* (Harvard University Press, 2013).

7 Craig Steven Wilder, "War and Priests: Catholic Colleges and Slavery in the Age of Revolution," in *Slavery's Capitalism: A New History of Economic Development*, ed. Sven Beckert and Seth Rockman (University of Pennsylvania Press, 2016), 228, 231–32; Wilder, *Ebony and Ivy*, chapter 5.

8 Joseph A. Conforti, *Samuel Hopkins and the New Divinity Movement: Calvinism, the Congregational Ministry, and Reform in New England Between the Great Awakenings* (Christian University Press, 1981), 175–93; Nathan O. Hatch, *The Democratization of American Christianity* (Yale University Press, 1989).

9 Donald G. Tewksbury, *The Founding of American Colleges and Universities Before the Civil War* (Columbia University Press, 1932), 119; Conforti, *Samuel Hopkins*, 176–88; Robert H. Abzug, *Cosmos Crumbling: American Reform and the Religious Imagination* (Oxford University Press, 1994), 6–7, 32–34; Lois W. Banner, "Religion and Reform in the Early Republic: The Role of Youth," *American Quarterly* 23, no. 5 (December 1971): 677–95.

10 Allmendinger, *Paupers and Scholars*, 1–6; Conforti, *Samuel Hopkins*, 186–87.

11 Presbyterians, Methodists, and Baptists also established their own colleges as the nineteenth century progressed. For colleges built in the early nineteenth century and their religious affiliation, see Tewksbury, *The Founding of American Colleges*, 93–95, 104–5, 115–16, and 121–22. Tewksbury's study is limited, however, as he only charted incorporated colleges that remained open beyond the Civil War and

thus his is not a comprehensive study of all American colleges before 1860. The legacy of the New Divinity and slavery is deeply fraught. Clergy subscribed to the doctrine of disinterested benevolence in multiple, often conflicting ways for slave-holding apologists, colonizationists, and abolitionists. See Kenneth P. Minkema and Harry S. Stout, "The Edwardsean Tradition and the Antislavery Debate, 1740–1865," *Journal of American History* 92 (June 2005): 47–74. American colleges provided unique terrain where these ideas and movements clashed.

12 Wilder, *Ebony and Ivy*, chapters 5, 6, and 7; P. J. Staudenraus, *The African Colonization Movement, 1816–1865* (Columbia University Press, 1961), 12–17; Nicholas Gyatt, *Bind Us Apart: How Enlightened Americans Invented Racial Segregation* (Basic Books, 2016).

13 Sinha, *The Slave's Cause*, 87–90; Douglas R. Egerton, "'Its Origin Is Not a Little Curious': A New Look at the American Colonization Society," *Journal of the Early Republic* 5, no. 4 (Winter 1985): 465–67, 471–75.

14 Finley became a trustee of the College of New Jersey in 1807 and was appointed director of the Theological Seminary in 1815. See *General Catalogue of Princeton University, 1746–1906* (Princeton University, 1908), 19, 50, 104; Staudenraus, *The African Colonization Movement*, 15–16.

15 Henry K. Rowe, *History of Andover Theological Seminary* (Todd, 1933), 10–22; Leonard Woods, *History of the Andover Theological Seminary* (Osgood, 1885), 199–201; Davis, *Leonard Bacon*, 20–23, 28; Banner, "Religion and Reform," 484–87.

16 *Memoirs of the American Missionaries, Formerly Connected with the Society of Inquiry Respecting Missions in the Andover Theological Seminary* . . . (Pierce, 1833), 13, 14.

17 Samuel J. Mills and John F. Schermerhorn, *A Correct View of That Part of the United States Which Lies West of the Allegheny Mountains with Regard to Religion and Morals* (Gleason, 1814), 4–52; Samuel J. Mills and Daniel Smith, *Report of a Missionary Tour Through That Part of the United States Which Lies West of the Allegheny Mountains* (Flagg, 1815), 5–47.

18 Gardiner Spring, *Memoirs of the Rev. Samuel J. Mills, Late Missionary to the South Western Section of the United States and Agent of the American Colonization Society* (Seymour, 1820), quotations from 24 and 61, emphasis in the original; *General Catalogue of the Officers and Graduates of Williams College* (Williams College, 1905), 35.

19 Spring, *Memoirs of the Rev. Samuel J. Mills*, 133, 115, 129, 122–29; Thomas C. Richards, *Samuel J. Mills, Missionary Pathfinder, Pioneer, and Promoter* (Pilgrim, 1906), 191.

20 "African Colonization. Princeton, Nov. 6, 1816," *Philadelphia Gazette*, December 18, 1816; *General Catalogue of Princeton University*, 111, 409.

21 Wilder, *Ebony and Ivy*, 248, 265.

22 *General Catalogue of the Theological Seminary, Andover, Massachusetts, 1808–1908* (Todd, n.d.), 42; "Obituary," *African Repository and Colonial Journal* 47, no. 10 (October 1871): 302; Spring, *Memoirs of the Rev. Samuel J. Mills*, 135–46; Archibald

Alexander, *A History of Colonization on the Western Coast of Africa* (Martien, 1846), 80; *The First Annual Report of the American Society for Colonizing the Free People of Color of the United States* (D. Rapine, 1818), 3, 6; "The Meeting on the Colonization of Free Blacks," *Daily National Intelligencer*, December 24, 1816; Staudenraus, *The African Colonization Movement*, 16–19, 28–29; Sinha, *The Slave's Cause*, 163–64.

23 Samuel J. Mills to Levi Parsons, March 1, 1817, in *Memoirs of the American Missionaries*, 217–18, 29.

24 Spring, *Memoirs of the Rev. Samuel J. Mills*, 227–28; *The First Annual Report of the American Society*, 11–13; "Obituary," 301–4; Staudenraus, *The African Colonization Movement*, 43–47.

25 Thomas S. Harding, *College Literary Societies: Their Contribution to Higher Education in the United States, 1815–1876* (Pageant, 1971), 349, 350; Davis, *Leonard Bacon*, 13; *The Third Annual Report of the American Society for Colonizing the Free People of Color of the United States* (Davis, 1820), 136, 139, 142; *Sixth Annual Report of the American Society*, 5; *Catalogue of the Officers and Graduates of Yale University, 1701–1910* (Tuttle, 1910), 1, 92; Kemp P. Battle, *History of the University of North Carolina, from Its Beginning to the Death of President Swain, 1789–1868*, vol. 1 (Edwards, 1907), 826; E. Merton Coulter, *College Life in the Old South* (MacMillan, 1928), 30–31; *Officers and Graduates of Columbia College, 1754–1894* (Columbia, 1894), 17, 19, 86, 100. Also see Sarah Schutz's essay on "Columbia and Colonization" on the Columbia and Slavery website, https://columbiaandslavery.columbia.edu, accessed December 11, 2024.

26 Power-Greene, *Against Wind and Tide*, 1–95; Sinha, *The Slave's Cause*, 160–71; Staudenraus, *The African Colonization Movement*, 73–76; Nicholas P. Wood, "The Missouri Crisis and the 'Changed Object' of the American Colonization Society," in *New Directions in the Study of African American Recolonization*, 146–65; Eric Burin, *Slavery and the Peculiar Solution: A History of the American Colonization Society* (University of Florida Press, 2008).

27 *Memoirs of the American Missionaries*, 29.

28 *Catalogue of the Officers and Graduates of Yale University, 1701–1910*, 91; Davis, *Leonard Bacon*, 32n35; Letter to Ralph Randolph Gurley, February 28, 1823, in *Memoirs of the American Missionaries*, quotation from 30.

29 Bacon, "Report of the Committee Appointed February 18, 1823, to Inquire Respecting the Black Population of the United States, April 22, 1823," *Memoirs of American Missionaries*, quotations from 296 and 297. This was the original version of Bacon's report, which came to be called "Report on Colonization." Hereafter cited as "Report on Colonization."

30 Bacon, "Report on Colonization," quotation from 298.

31 Bacon, "Report on Colonization," 305, 313, 309–10.

32 Few scholars have centered the impact of slave resistance in the development of Bacon's reactionary colonizationist ideology. See Davis, *The Problem of Slavery in the Age of Emancipation*, 149–50; Davis, *Leonard Bacon*, 33–34; Brandon Mills

has made the connection between slave resistance and its impact on coloniza-
tion more generally, and he also makes connections to Bacon's ideas, see Brandon
Mills, "Situating African Colonization Within the History of U.S. Expansion," in
New Directions in the Study of African American Recolonization, 166–83; Brandon
Mills, *The World Colonization Made: The Racial Geography of Early American Em-
pire* (University of Pennsylvania Press, 2020), for Bacon, 33–34.

33 Bacon, "Report on Colonization," quotations from 299, 301.

34 Bacon, "Report on Colonization," quotations from 301, 302, 305.

35 Bacon, "Report on Colonization," quotation from 303.

36 Bacon, "Report on Colonization," 304–14. A revealing objective that Bacon proposed was "a Seminary for the education of blacks previously to their leaving the
country." See Bacon, "Report on Colonization," 316. Bacon's call for Black education was one that Mills had made before his death. A few colonizationist schools
were eventually built, but they were short-lived. See V. P. Franklin, "Education for
Colonization: Attempts to Educate Free Blacks in the United States for Emigration to Africa, 1823–1833," *Journal of Negro History* 43, no. 1 (Winter 1974): 91–103.

37 Along with the impact of slave resistance, important influences on Bacon's colonizationist outlook included Jefferson's *Notes on the State of Virginia*. Hugh Davis
also observes that Bacon's experiences in the Society of Moral and Religious Instruction in Boston as well as two editorials by Jeremiah Evarts had an important
impact on Bacon. See Davis, *Leonard Bacon*, 31–33.

38 *Memoirs of American Missionaries*, 31–33; *Seventh Annual Report of the American
Society*, 29–30, 87–103; *Christian Spectator* 5, no. 9 (September 1823): 493–94;
Christian Spectator 5, no. 10 (October 1823): 540–51; Davis, *Leonard Bacon*, 35–41;
Davis, *The Problem of Slavery in the Age of Emancipation*, 377n2; Staudenraus, *The
African Colonization Movement*, 76–79.

39 *Eighth Annual Report of the American Society for Colonizing the Free People
of Color of the United States* (Davis, 1825), quotations from 15–16; *Princeton
Theological Seminary, General Catalogue* (Rodgers, 1872), 23; *African Reposi-
tory and Colonial Journal* 2, no. 2 (April 1826): 62–63; *African Repository and
Colonial Journal* 3, no. 12 (February 1828): 371, 377–79; *General Catalogue of the
Theological Seminary Andover, Massachusetts*, 77; *African Repository and Colo-
nial Journal* 1 (March 1825–January 1826): 252–53, 287–88, 351–52; *Ninth Annual
Report of the American Society*, 34, 63; *African Repository and Colonial Journal* 1,
no. 5 (July 1825): 157–58 (hereafter *ARCJ*); Staudenraus, *The African Colonization
Movement*, 106, 108, 122–23.

40 The exact amount they donated was sixty-six dollars and thirty-two cents. "Contributions," *ARCJ* 3, no. 12 (February 1828): 384; "Contributions," *ARCJ* 5, no. 8
(October 1829): 255; "Contributions," *ARCJ* 6, no. 8 (October 1830): 252; "Contributions," *ACRJ* 7, no. 11 (January 1832): 348; *Memoirs of American Missionaries*,
33–34; Harding, *College Literary Societies*, 349.

41 *Tenth Annual Report of the American Society for Colonizing the Free People of
Color of the United States* (Davis, 1827), 83, 91; *Catalogue of Officers, Gradu-*

ates, and Students of Western Reserve College and of Adelbert College, 1826–1916 (Western Reserve University Press, 1916), 5, 8; *The Literary Focus* 1, no. 1–3 (June–August 1827): 14, 25–28, 35–39, quotations from 26, 27, and 39.

42 *The Literary Register*, June 30, 1828, 71, 79; *The Literary Register*, October 6, 1828, 279; *The Literary Register*, December 1, 1828, 390; Thomas D. Matijasic, "Conservative Reform in the West: The African Colonization Movement in Ohio, 1826–1839" (PhD dissertation, Miami University, 1982), 130–34.

43 "Contributions," *ARCJ* 7, no. 11 (January 1832): 351; "Intelligence," *ARCJ* 7, no. 6 (August 1831): 185; "Agency of R.S. Finley," *ARCJ* 7, no. 7 (September 1831): 208; Harding, *College Literary Societies*, 384.

44 These institutions were also built on land stolen from Indigenous people. See for example Betty Hollow, *Ohio University, 1804–2004: The Spirit of a Singular Place* (Ohio University Press, 2003), 2, 7–8.

45 "Resolutions in Vermont," *ARCJ* 2, no. 7 (September 1826): 221; *Sixth Annual Report of the American Society*, 67; *Seventh Annual Report of the American Society*, 171; *Catalogue of the Officers and Alumni of Middlebury College*, 4.

46 *African Colonization, Proceedings of the Formation of the New York State Colonization Society* (Websters, 1829), 3–19, quotations from 10, 18, and 13. On Nott's fear of slave resistance, see especially 11, 12–14. He directly quotes Bacon on 13. Bacon, "Report on Colonization," 301, 302, and 305; *ARCJ* 5, no. 2 (April 1829): 58–59.

47 See, for example, *Biographical Record of the Alumni of Amherst College, During Its First Half-Century, 1821–1871* (Amherst, 1883), 10, 12, 13, 16, 17, 19, 24, 26, 27.

48 *General Catalogue of the Theological Seminary, Andover*, 72, 87; *General Catalogue of Amherst College . . . , 1821–1885* (Amherst College, 1885), 8.

49 Staudenraus, *The African Colonization Movement*, 130.

50 Samuel M. Worcester, ed., *Essays on Slavery* (Carter, 1826), 9–12, 13–16, quotation from 20, emphasis in the original. Worcester published his essays anonymously as "Vigornious." See David Brion Davis, *From Homicide to Slavery: Studies in American Culture* (Oxford University Press, 1986), 252.

51 Worcester, *Essays on Slavery*, 18, 19.

52 Worcester, *Essays on Slavery*, 22.

53 Worcester, *Essays on Slavery*, 24–26, quotations from 24 and 26.

54 Ebenezer G. Bradford, "Ought the Colonization Society to Be Patronized by the General Government?," 1827, Historical Manuscripts Collection, Box 7, Folder 2, Amherst College Archives and Special Collections; *Biographical Record of the Alumni of Amherst College*, 36.

55 Lucius F. Clark, "Africa," August 10, 1827, Historical Manuscripts Collection, Box 7, Folder 2, Amherst College Archives and Special Collections; *Biographical Record of the Alumni of Amherst College*, 37.

56 George W. Boggs, "Connection Between Christianity and Civil Liberty," August 13, 1827, Historical Manuscripts Collection, Box 7, Folder 2, Amherst College Archives and Special Collections; *Biographical Record of the Alumni of Amherst College*, 35–36.

57 Heman Humphrey, *Parallel Between Intemperance and the Slave Trade, an Address Delivered at Amherst College, July 4, 1828* (Adams, 1828), quotation from 27. The title is a misnomer as Humphrey continuously refers to intemperance as worse than the slave trade ever was, and the speech is filled with flagrant inaccuracies and is a highly selective presentation of the history of the transatlantic slave trade and racial slavery more generally. See 6, 15, 17, 18, 20, 23, 24, 28.

58 "Contributions," *ARCJ* 4, no. 6 (August 1828): 190.

59 In addition to Amherst, July 4 or commencement addresses on campuses and in the surrounding community resulted in student donations to the ACS at Jefferson College (PA), Centre College (KY), and Rutgers College (NJ). Williams College and Andover Theological Seminary also contributed annually following Fourth of July addresses. "Contributions," *ARCJ* 4, no. 8 (October 1828): 254; "Contributions," *ARCJ* 5, no. 8 and 10 (October and December 1829): 256, 319; "Contributions," *ARCJ* 6, no. 4 (June 1830): 127; *ARCJ* 7, no. 12 (February 1832): 374–75.

60 "Contributions," *ARCJ* 5, no. 5 (July 1829): 159; "Contributions," *ARCJ* 6, no. 1 and 8 (March and October 1830): 32, 250; *ARCJ* 7, no. 1, 6, 8 (March, August, October 1831): 28, 187, quotation from 243; *ARCJ* 8, no. 8 and 9 (October and November 1832), 282–83, quotation from 248; "Contributions," *ARCJ* 8, no. 11 (January 1833): 352; Staudenraus, *The African Colonization Movement*, 119–22, 126, 132–33.

61 Giles B. Kellogg, *An Oration Delivered July 4, 1829, Before the Anti-Slavery Society of Williams College* (Bannister, 1829), 14–22, quotations from 14, 15, 20, 21. Kellogg went on to become a lawyer in Troy, New York, and held positions in the local court system. He also became the editor of a Whig newspaper, the *Northern Budget. General Catalogue of the Officers and Graduates of Williams College*, 46; Durfee, *Williams Biographical Annals*, 94–95.

62 For a different framing of the common good, see Charles Dorn, *For the Common Good: A New History of Higher Education in America* (Cornell University Press, 2017).

CHAPTER 3. BLACK CULTURE, BLACK RESISTANCE

1 "Journal of the Meetings of the President and Masters of William and Mary College," *William and Mary College Quarterly, Historical Papers* 2 (William and Mary College, 1893–1894), 51; "College Negroes," *William and Mary College Quarterly, Historical Magazine* 16 (Whittet, 1908), 170; Craig Steven Wilder, *Ebony and Ivy: Race, Slavery, and the Troubled History of American Colleges* (Bloomsbury, 2013), 42–44, 118, 131, 135, 136; Terry L. Myers, "A First Look at the Worst: Slavery and Race Relations at the College of William and Mary," *William and Mary Bill of Rights Journal* 16, no. 4 (2008): 1141–68; Jennifer Oast, *Institutional Slavery: Slaveholding Churches, Schools, Colleges, and Businesses in Virginia, 1680–1860* (Cambridge University Press, 2016), 127, 131, 145, chapter 4.

2 Chana Kai Lee, "A Fraught Reckoning: Exploring the History of Slavery at the University of Georgia," *The Public Historian* 42, no. 4 (November 2020): 12–27, esp. 23–27; Cedric J. Robinson, "Manichaeism and Multiculturalism," in *Mapping*

Multiculturalism, ed. Avery Gordon and Christopher Newfield (University of Minnesota Press, 1996), 116–24; on the fraught nature of traditional archives for studying the lives of enslaved people, see for example Saidiya Hartman, "Venus in Two Acts," *Small Axe* 12, no. 2 (June 2008): 1–14; Marisa J. Fuentes, *Enslaved Women, Violence, and the Archive* (University of Pennsylvania Press, 2016). The problematic nature of university archives demands the use and study of other sources, including oral traditions, memory among descendants of enslaved people, and other interpretive frameworks and epistemologies. See for example, Mark Auslander, "'The Family Business': Slavery, Double Consciousness, and Objects of Memory at Emory University," in *Slavery and the University: Histories and Legacies*, ed. Leslie Harris et al. (University of Georgia Press, 2019), 277–97. On white faculty and students manufacturing racist ideology and proslavery thought in universities, see Wilder, *Ebony and Ivy*; Daina Ramey Berry, *The Price for Their Pound of Flesh: The Value of the Enslaved from Womb to Grave in the Building of a Nation* (Beacon Press, 2017), chapter 6; Oast, *Institutional Slavery*; Alfred L. Brophy, *University, Court, and Slave: Proslavery Academic Thought and Southern Jurisprudence, 1831–1861* (Oxford University Press, 2016); Deborah Gray White and Marisa Fuentes, eds., *Scarlet and Black: Slavery and Dispossession in Rutgers History*, vol. 1 (Rutgers University Press, 2016); also see the digital work and archives scholars and undergraduates have created at Brown, Columbia, Harvard, MIT, and Princeton, as well as other universities studying slavery.

3 This speaks to the limitations of the historical discipline as conceived of in the West. Other forms are necessary, as is using sources and materials that are extant and record, however fleetingly, the lives of enslaved people, such as fugitive slave advertisements. To be sure, the activities of enslaved people went beyond the purview of whites and were intentionally secretive, as a strategy to live and practice their own culture away from whites. See Stephanie Camp, *Closer to Freedom: Enslaved Women and Everyday Resistance in the Plantation South* (University of North Carolina Press, 2004), chapter 3; Sterling Stuckey, *Slave Culture: Nationalist Theory and the Foundations of Black America* (Oxford University Press, 1987), 24–25, 88.

4 As Amilcar Cabral wrote in the context of the nationalist liberation struggle in Guinea Bissau about the imperative of imperialists' attempts to suppress cultural development among dominated people, "It is generally within the culture that we find the seed of opposition." In the context of college slavery, and slavery more generally in the Americas, the consciousness and culture of enslaved people was the seed of their resistance and struggles against enslavement, not simply a reaction to the violence of enslavement. Quoted in *Return to the Source: Selected Speeches of Amilcar Cabral*, ed. African Information Services (Monthly Review Press, 1973), 43; Cedric J. Robinson, *Black Marxism: The Making of the Black Radical Tradition* (1983; University of North Carolina Press, 2000), 122.

5 Frederick Douglass, *Narrative of the Life of Frederick Douglass: An American Slave* (1845); "Brief Account of an Emancipated Slave," *The Oasis*, ed. Lydia Ma-

rie Child (Bacon, 1834), 106–12; Heather Andrea Williams, *Self-Taught: African American Education in Slavery and Freedom* (University of North Carolina Press, 2005), 7–29.

6 "Terms of order" comes from Cedric J. Robinson, *The Terms of Order: Political Science and the Myth of Leadership* (1980; University of North Carolina Press, 2016). Some historians have claimed that Black abolitionists' engagement with scientific racism, while well intentioned, also replicated false ideas about racial difference and engaged in intellectual malpractice, flattening the distinctions between them and the very racists they engaged. These arguments fall short of capturing historical context, social and intellectual dynamics of power, and the thrust of the arguments Black abolitionists made for human equality as the imperative for abolition. The ways Black abolitionists engaged science were antithetical to the ways racist scientists used it; they made arguments on moral and religious grounds for universal human freedom. They regularly began their arguments on the premise that all people were equal. They did not use science to argue for the exploitation or oppression of white people as scientific racists did against Black people. When engaging ideas about human difference, Black abolitionists argued that Black people had better value judgments, ethics, morals, and ideas than whites—not that they were inherently distinct or superior—while most white scholars of the era wielded nearly every possible realm of knowledge towards oppressing Black people, free or enslaved, as well as Indigenous people and others. Black intellectuals also used climate and environment to explain human differences but never argued that groups of human beings were inferior because of those differences. They did not argue that differences culturally or otherwise should equate to oppression. Black abolitionists thus refuted scientific racism as part of their larger assault on the slavocracy and racism on the grounds of Black humanity and human equality to demand abolition. See Manisha Sinha, "Of Scientific Racists and Black Abolitionists: The Forgotten Debate over Slavery and Race," in *To Make Their Own Way in the World: The Enduring Legacy of the Zealy Daguerreotypes*, ed. Ilisa Barbash, Molly Rogers, and Deborah Willis (Peabody Museum Press, 2020), 235–57; Manisha Sinha, *The Slave's Cause: A History of Abolition* (Yale University Press, 2016), 299–316; cf. Mia Bay, *The White Image in the Black Mind: African American Ideas About White People, 1830–1925* (Oxford University Press, 2000); Bruce Dain, *A Hideous Monster of the Mind: American Race Theory in the Early Republic* (Harvard University Press, 2002). See also Rachel Walker, "Facing Race: Popular Science and Black Intellectual Thought in Antebellum America," *Early American Studies* 19, no. 3 (Summer 2021): 601–40. While Walker shows that some Black abolitionists, such as Hosea Easton, used physiognomy to explain the intelligence and equality of Black people, they did so with a utilitarian purpose distinct from its use by contemporary white theorists. For another perspective, also see Patrick Rael, "A Common Nature, a United Destiny: African American Responses to Racial Science from the Revolution to the Civil War," in *Prophets of Protest: Reconsidering*

the History of American Abolitionism, ed. Timothy Patrick McCarthy and John Stauffer (New Press, 2006), 183–99.

7 The epistemology of enslaved Africans in the Atlantic world that underpinned a variety of resistance strategies—running away, maroonage, revolt, cultural and religious practices, and others—represents African ways of knowing that were/are historically distinct from eurocentric notions of Western civilization. The purpose of this chapter is to investigate this dynamic at the intellectual core of the West, the university, and the lives and worldviews of enslaved people in college slavery. For this formulation and dialectical framing, my thinking is deeply indebted to the work of Cedric Robinson and scholars and intellectuals in Black Studies. See for example, Robinson, *Black Marxism*, esp. 121–22, 167–71; W. E. B. Du Bois, "The Field and Function of the Negro College," in *The Education of Black People: Ten Critiques, 1906–1960*, ed. Herbert Aptheker (1973; Monthly Review Press, 2001), 111–34; Toni Cade Bambara, "Realizing the Dream of a Black University (1969)," in *Lost and Found: The CUNY Poetics Document Initiative*, ed. Makeba Lavan and Conor Tomas Reed, Series 7, Number 2, Part 1 (Fall 2017); June Jordan, "Black Studies: Bringing Back the Person (1969)," in June Jordan, *Civil Wars* (Beacon Press, 1981), 45–55; Sylvia Wynter, "A Black Studies Manifesto," *Forum N.H.I.: Knowledge for the 21st Century* 1, no. 1 (Fall 1994): 3–11; Joshua M. Myers, *We Are Worth Fighting For: A History of the Howard University Student Protest of 1989* (New York University Press, 2019). Over time, African ways of knowing changed and evolved, as people of African descent were born in the Americas and encountered other systems of knowledge and culture depending on context; however, the African influence was never extinguished. See Stuckey, *Slave Culture*; Michael A. Gomez, *Exchanging Our Country Marks: The Transformation of African Identities in the Colonial and Antebellum South* (University of North Carolina Press, 1998); Gwendolyn Midlo Hall, *Africans in Colonial Louisiana: The Development of Afro-Creole Culture in the Eighteenth Century* (Louisiana State University Press, 1992).

8 For scholars who argue that slave resistance was constitutive of the abolition movement, see W. E. B. Du Bois, *Black Reconstruction in America, 1860–1880* (1935; Free Press, 1998), 13; Vincent Harding, *There Is a River: The Black Struggle for Freedom in America* (Harcourt, 1981); Stuckey, *Slave Culture*; Manisha Sinha, *The Slave's Cause: A History of Abolition* (Yale University Press, 2016); Merton L. Dillion, *Slavery Attacked: Southern Slaves and Their Allies, 1619–1865* (Louisiana State University Press, 1990); Herbert Aptheker, *Abolitionism: A Revolutionary Movement* (Twayne, 1989); Edward B. Rugemer, "Slave Rebels and Abolitionists: The Black Atlantic and the Coming of the Civil War," *Journal of the Civil War Era* 2, no. 2 (June 2012): 179–202.

9 See for example, Camp, *Closer to Freedom*; also, the notion of the inner person for enslaved people would have applied in the context of college slavery as well, as the verse reveals: "Got one mind for white folks to see, / 'Nother for what I know is me, / He don't know, he don't know my mind," quoted in Gomez, *Exchanging Our Country Marks*, 10.

10 On enslaved people's labor as well as the violence they faced on campus, see
    Wilder, *Ebony and Ivy*, 128–38; Oast, *Institutional Slavery*, 126, 133–43, 174–87;
    Kelly Fanto Deetz, "Finding Dignity in a Landscape of Fear: Enslaved Women and
    Girls at the University of Virginia," *Slavery & Abolition* 39, no. 2 (2018): 251–66;
    Educated in Tyranny: Slavery at Thomas Jefferson's University, ed. Maurie D. McIn-
    nis and Louis P. Nelson (University of Virginia Press, 2019), 27–42, 97–113; Lee,
    "A Fraught Reckoning," 22–23; Hilary Green, "The Burden of the University of
    Alabama's Hallowed Grounds," *The Public Historian* 42, no. 4 (November 2020):
    34–40; Terry Meyers, "Slavery at the College of William and Mary," in *Encyclope-
    dia Virginia*, July 2021; A. James Fuller, "'I Whipped Him a Second Time, Very Se-
    verely': Basil Manly, Honor, and Slavery at the University of Alabama," in *Slavery
    and the University: Histories and Legacies*, ed. Leslie M. Harris et al. (University of
    Georgia Press, 2019), 114–30; Jesse Baker, Christopher Blakely, and Kendra Boyd,
    "His Name Was Will: Remembering Enslaved Individuals in Rutgers History," in
    Fuentes and White, *Scarle t and Black*, 71–74.
11 Robinson, *Black Marxism*, 121–22; Cedric Robinson, "Retracing Black Radical-
    ism," lecture, Western Michigan University, February 9, 2013.
12 Jacob H. Carruthers, *Intellectual Warfare* (Third World Press, 1999) 257–60; Layo
    Ogunlola, "The Precolonial Yoruba Education System: Catalyst Against Im-
    morality," *Yoruba Studies Review* 5, no. 1.2 (2020): 83–97; Timonthy A. Awoniyi,
    "Ọmọlúwàbí: The Fundamental Basis of Yoruba Traditional Education," in *Yoruba
    Oral Tradition*, ed. Wande Abimbola (University of Ife, 1975), 357–88; Beatrice
    Ndubuokwu Okwu, "Igbo Traditional Educational Thought and Practice: Pro-
    cesses and Products in Philosophic Perspective" (PhD dissertation, University
    of Connecticut, 1995), 3–8, 65–156; Wyatt MacGaffey, "Education, Religion, and
    Social Structure in Zaire," *Anthropology & Education Quarterly* 13, no. 3 (Autumn
    1982): 238–50; Joshua Maurice Myers, "Reconceptualizing Intellectual Histories of
    Africana Studies: A Review of the Literature" (PhD dissertation, Temple Univer-
    sity, 2013), 324–43; Du Bois, "The Field and Function," 111–34.
13 For example, if enslaved people adopted Christianity, they created an Africanized
    Christianity that fit their needs, but they did not displace African-based religious
    traditions and ways of knowing. See Gomez, *Exchanging Our Country Marks*,
    244–90; Stuckey, *Slave Culture*; see also James H. Sweet, *Domingos Álvares, Afri-
    can Healing, and the Intellectual History of the Atlantic World* (University of North
    Carolina Press, 2011), 4–8; Walter C. Rucker, *The River Flows On: Black Resistance,
    Culture, and Identity Formation in Early America* (Louisiana State University
    Press, 2006); Jason R. Young, *Rituals of Resistance: African Atlantic Religion in
    Kongo and the Lowcountry South in the Era of Slavery* (Louisiana State University
    Press, 2007).
14 Thomas F. Higgins III and Joseph R. Underwood, *Secrets of the Historic Campus:
    Archaeological Investigations in the Wren Yard at the College of William and Mary,
    1999–2000* (William and Mary Center for Archaeological Research, March 2001),
    71–72. A major thank you to Tom Higgins for his timely help.

15 The record indicates that Dick, Lucy, Kate, and Nanny were either elderly or in-
firm. The list reads, "Winfield, Daniell, Dick—almost an invalid, Pompey, Adam,
Nedd, old Lucy—almost an invalid, old Kate a invalid, Nanny a invalid, Effy not
much better." The list also includes enslaved people the college owned and hired
out for revenue; they were "Lemon, James, Letty, Charlott, Frankey, Betty and two
Gerrels" and "Molly, Mass, and Lucy"; "A List of Negros at College, c. 1780," Office
of Bursar Records, Special Collections, Swem Library, College of William and
Mary; Meyers, "Slavery at the College of William and Mary."

16 The question of how enslaved people used or gave meaning to these items, of
course, is difficult to answer with absolute certainty. However, reconstructing the
context of what the artifacts symbolized and their function among people of African descent in other contexts during the same era sheds light on the reasonable
plausibility, perhaps likelihood, that the artifacts in question had specific meaning
and functions for enslaved people on campus. Positivism has its limits, and strict
adherence to its qualities constructs barriers that constrain other forms and methods of historical inquiry and study. The aim here is to study the artifacts discovered on campus, and to interpret them as possible windows into enslaved people's
culture and knowledge and the implications for the history of the university.

17 Higgins and Underwood, *Secrets of the Historic Campus*, 8, 58, 64, 78, 92–93, quotation from 45; Patricia Samford, "The Archaeology of African-American Slavery
and Material Culture," *William and Mary Quarterly* 53, no. 1 (January 1996): 102–
4; Aaron E. Russell, "Material Culture and African-American Spirituality at the
Hermitage," *Historical Archaeology* 31, no. 2 (1997): 63, 71. Samford indicates that
Colonoware dating to the colonial era has been found at many former plantation sites throughout Virginia and was made by enslaved Africans, but there is
also evidence that Colonoware was crafted by Indigenous people as well. Thus
Colonoware at the college may have been made directly from Africans or they
may have used Colonoware created by others. Higgins makes a similar point but
also shows that in the Chesapeake and in Williamsburg specifically, enslaved
people themselves made such items, making it likely that enslaved people at the
college either made Colonoware themselves or used such items that were made
locally. Leland Ferguson shows that Colonoware discovered elsewhere in Virginia
has Indigenous, African, and European elements in style and construction; see
Leland Ferguson, *Uncommon Ground: Archaeology and Early African America,
1650–1800* (Smithsonian, 1992), 44–52; for Ferguson on Colonoware and healing
practices, see "Early African-American Pottery in South Carolina: A Complicated
Plainware," *African Diaspora Archaeology Newsletter* 10, no. 2 (2007): 1–15; on
nkisi, see for example, Robert Farris Thompson, *Flash of the Spirit: African and
Afro-American Art and Philosophy* (Vintage, 1983), 107, 117–31; on African medicinal practices among enslaved people, see Karol K. Weaver, *Medical Revolutionaries: The Enslaved Healers of Eighteenth-Century Saint Domingue* (University of
Illinois Press, 2006); Sharla M. Fett, *Working Cures: Healing, Health, and Power on
Southern Slave Plantations* (University of North Carolina Press, 2002).

18 Abigail Joy Moffett and Simon Hall, "Divining Value: Cowries, the Ancestral Realm, and the Global in Southern Africa," *Cambridge Archaeological Journal* 30, no. 2 (May 2019): 313–26, esp. 313–15; Akinwumi Ogundiran, "Of Small Things Remembered: Beads, Cowries, and Cultural Translations of the Atlantic Experience in Yorubaland," *The International Journal of African Historical Studies* 35, no. 2/3 (2002): 438–40; Bin Yang, *Cowrie Shells and Cowrie Money: A Global History* (New York: Routledge, 2019), 231; Ibo Changa, "Cowrie Shells," in *Encyclopedia of African Religions*, vol. 1, ed. Molefi Kete Asante and Ama Mazama (Sage, 2008), 180–84; Samford, "The Archaeology of African-American Slavery," 101.

19 Samford, "The Archaeology of African-American Slavery," 101, 110; Theresa A. Singleton, "The Archaeology of Slave Life," in *Before Freedom Came: African American Life in the Antebellum South*, ed. Edward D. C. Campbell with Kim S. Rice (University Press of Virginia, 1991), 157–58; Georgia L. Fox, *An Archaeology and History of a Caribbean Sugar Plantation on Antigua* (University of Florida Press, 2020), 174–75. It seems less likely that the shells were used for adornment as there is no indication that they were fastened together to form a necklace or other like objects. In terms of divination among the Yoruba, for example, sixteen cowrie shells were required for this ritual. See Ogundiran, "Of Small Things Remembered," 453. Barbara Heath speculates that enslaved people in colonial Virginia may have used cowrie shells as currency in local economies, see Barbara Heath, "Cowrie Shells, Global Trade, and Local Exchange: Piecing Together the Evidence of Colonial Virginia," *Historical Archaeology* 50, no. 2 (2016): 17–46, 37.

20 Ogundiran, "Of Small Things Remembered," 442. Ogundiran has convincingly shown how the socioeconomic and sociocultural meanings of cowrie shells among the Yoruba have shifted and changed over the course of the seventeenth through nineteenth centuries, see "Of Small Things Considered" as well as Ogundiran, "Cowries and Rituals of Self-Realization in the Yoruba Region, ca. 1600–1860," in *Materialities of Ritual in the Black Atlantic*, ed. Akinwumi Ogundiran and Paula Saunders (Indiana University Press, 2014), 68–86.

21 Ogundiran, "Cowries and Rituals," 74.

22 Higgins and Underwood, *Secrets of the Historic Campus*, 13, 21.

23 Ogundiran, "Cowries and Rituals," 83. Ogundiran further explains the connection between the shells and middens: "These sacrificial objects were recognized when found in these locations, and no sane person would pick them up because, by so doing, the person would be transferring the supplicant's affliction onto him- or herself."

24 Higgins and Underwood, *Secrets of the Historic Campus*, 71, 72, 92–93; Samford, "The Archaeology of African-American Slavery and Material Culture," 104–6; Russell, "Material Culture and African-American Spirituality," 64–65, 71; Ferguson, *Uncommon Ground*, 109–20; Thompson, *Flash of the Spirit*, 109–16.

25 This follows closely Gomez, *Exchanging Our Country Marks*, 141–49, esp. 148; Thompson, *Flash of the Spirit*, 106, 108, quoting MacGaffey; also see Stuckey, *Slave Culture*, 10–11, 34–37. It has been established that the cross in Bakongo culture was

conceptualized by the Bakongo themselves and was not introduced by external forces; its usage predated the arrival of Europeans. See Gomez, *Exchanging Our Country Marks*, 148; Gomez cites Wyatt MacGaffey, *Religion in Society in Central Africa: The BaKongo of Lower Zaire* (University of Chicago Press, 1986).

26 Robinson explains, "This was a revolutionary consciousness which proceeded from the whole historical experience of Black people and not merely from the social formations of capitalist slavery or the relations of production of colonialism." The ontological totality—"the mind, metaphysics, ideology, consciousness"—was a collective consciousness rooted in African history and cultural traditions that informed revolutionary Black resistance in the Americas. See Robinson, *Black Marxism*, 167–71.

27 The foregoing has been an attempt to recover the possible epistemologies and cultural forms of enslaved people at William and Mary. In the absence of positivistic evidence, attending to material culture and considering the potential meaning and utility of artifacts left by enslaved people can help imagine their worldviews on campus. The cultural and intellectual traditions of other enslaved people and people of African descent can help us reconstruct such possibilities, though not definitively. Colonoware was found at William and Mary in areas occupied by enslaved people. Can we infer that the range of possible uses for Colonoware included enslaved people using them to prepare remedies to injuries and illness that were informed by African knowledge? Can we surmise that cowrie shells held spiritual and cultural meaning for enslaved people at the college, as they did for other people of African descent? Can the practice of appeasing a deity by throwing cowrie shells into middens in Yorubaland and doing so into a midden at a college be a similar ritual practice? Could the Bakongo cosmogram, pervasive in African culture in North America, and its encapsulation on a stone marble have been a token of an enslaved person's faith in their religion that they carried with them, an emblem signifying their birth, death, rebirth, and connection with their ancestors and the divine? Could such an item have helped them envision a world to come, a world in which they would be free from enslavement and where they would live again? If we do not consider these possibilities, we lose the ability to imagine or even begin to image how enslaved people in college slavery may have made sense of their world. To not consider such possibilities would be to not consider the humanity of Black people from the past or their struggles for life and to be free, a proposition to which this study refuses to concede.

28 "Charter Granted by King William and Queen Mary, for the Founding of William and Mary College in Virginia," in Henry Hartwell et al., *The Present State of Virginia, and the College* (1727), 73; Philip A. Bruce, *Institutional History of Virginia in the Seventeenth Century: An Inquiry into the Religious, Moral, Educational, Legal, Military, and Political Conditions of the People*, vol. 1 (Putnam, 1910), 213–14; John Fiske, *Old Virginia and Her Neighbors*, vol. 2 (Houghton, 1897), 195; John Moncure, "Christ Church, Middlesex, County, Virginia," in *Colonial Churches in the*

Original Colony of Virginia, 2nd ed. (1907; Southern Churchman Company, 1908), 246; Wilder, *Ebony and Ivy*, 129; Oast, *Institutional Slavery*, 31.

29 Wilder, *Ebony and Ivy*, 48–49, 64–70.

30 Leslie M. Harris, *In the Shadow of Slavery: African Americans in New York City, 1626–1863* (University of Chicago Press, 2003), 29.

31 There was no student housing at King's during its early years. Once a dormitory was built in the 1760s, it only accommodated a small portion of the student body. Students typically lived near campus or boarded elsewhere. David C. Humphrey, *From King's College to Columbia, 1746–1800* (Columbia University Press, 1976), 204–5.

32 Samuel Bayard, "Runaway from Hobuck," *New York Mercury*, July 31, 1758; *Catalogue of Columbia College, in the City of New York, Embracing the Names of the Trustees, Officers, and Graduates* (1844), 21; Leonard F. Fuld, *King's College Alumni* (New York, 1913), 14. Many thanks to Jordan Brewington for her work on fugitive slave resistance to King's College slaveowners, Jordan Brewington, "'Run-Away from the Subscriber': Resistance Against King's College and Columbia Slave-Owning Students and Affiliates from the Class of 1760 to 1805," student paper, Columbia University and Slavery Seminar, 2016.

33 Henry White, "Run-Away from the Subscriber," *New York Gazette*, January 19, 1761; *Catalogue of Columbia College*, 22, 23; Fuld, *King's College Alumni*, 27–28.

34 Charles Doughty, "Run-Away from Charles Doughty," *New York Mercury*, May 12, 1766; *Catalogue of Columbia College*, 23; Fuld, *King's College Alumni*, 36.

35 Cedric J. Robinson, *Black Movements in America* (Routledge, 1997), 21–25; quoted in Oast, *Institutional Slavery*, 150; Karen Cook Bell, *Running from Bondage: Enslaved Women and Their Remarkable Fight for Freedom in Revolutionary America* (Cambridge University Press, 2021); Alan Gilbert, *Black Patriots and Loyalists: Fighting for Emancipation in the War for Independence* (University of Chicago Press, 2012); Benjamin Quarles, *The Negro in the American Revolution* (University of North Carolina Press, 1961).

36 James Young, "Eight Dollars Reward," *Virginia Gazette and General Advertiser* (Richmond, VA), July 11, 1792.

37 Oast, *Institutional Slavery*, 151–52. While people were enslaved at William and Mary, faculty there held some antislavery views and were simultaneously slaveholders, such as George Wythe and St. George Tucker. Wythe eventually manumitted his slaves and Tucker never did. William Small also taught at the college; several scholars have maintained that he studied the work of Francis Hutcheson and used his antislavery views in his teaching. While antislavery thought was present at William and Mary, the college continued to own slaves. See Terry L. Myers, "Thinking About Slavery at the College of William and Mary," *William and Mary Bill of Rights Journal* 21, no. 4 (2013): 1215–57, esp. 1235, 1238, 1249–57; Alfred L. Brophy, *University, Court, and Slave: Pro-Slavery Thought in Southern Colleges and Courts and the Coming of the Civil War* (Oxford University Press, 2016), 1–10.

38 Craig Steven Wilder, "War and Priests: Catholic Colleges and Slavery in the Age
of Revolution," in *Slavery's Capitalism: A New History of American Economic
Development*, ed. Sven Beckert and Seth Rockman (Philadelphia: University of
Pennsylvania Press, 2016), 228; Elsa Barraza Mendoza, "Catholic Slaveowners and
the Development of Georgetown University's Slave Hiring System, 1792–1862,"
Journal of Jesuit Studies 8 (2021): 56–80.

39 Wilder, "War and Priests," 239; one historian of Georgetown claimed that Neale
was a teacher at the college in the 1790s. The manuscript account book, however,
states that Neale had "entered" the college on March 25, 1800, and subsequently
paid board and tuition fees. Cf. James S. Easby-Smith, *Georgetown University in
the District of Columbia, 1789–1907*, 2 vols. (New York: Lewis Co., 1907), vol. 1, 36,
38, 46; "Stephen and Tempey 'Boath Ran Away' from the College, 1800," *Georgetown Slavery Archive*, Georgetown University Archives, http://slaveryarchive.
georgetown.edu, accessed February 20, 2018.

40 "Stephen and Tempey 'Boath Ran Away' from the College, 1800."

41 "'Spalding Has Runned Away': Leonard Neale to Francis Neale on the Management of the Missions, July 15, 1805," in Robert Molyneux, S.J. (1 of 4),
1805-01-10-1805-12-16, Box: 1, Folder: 1. Archives of the Maryland Province of the
Society of Jesus. Georgetown University Manuscripts, Booth Family Center for
Special Collections, http://slaveryarchive.georgetown.edu, accessed February 10,
2018.

42 "Sale of Henny from Bohemia, April 1796," *Georgetown Slavery Archive* from
Bohemia Plantation Day Book, 1790–1870, Box 49, Folder 3, Maryland Province
Archives, Booth Family Center for Special Collections, Georgetown University,
http://slaveryarchive.georgetown.edu, accessed July 2, 2018.

43 "Nancy Buys Her Daughter Sophia to Set Her Free, September 19, 1803,"
Georgetown Slavery Archive from St. Thomas Manor Account Book, 1793–
1821, Box 46, Folder 6, Maryland Province Archives, Booth Family Center
for Special Collections, Georgetown University, https://slaveryarchive.
georgetown.edu, accessed July 2, 2018. For enslaved people buying freedom, see Julia Wallace Bernier, *Freedom's Currency: Slavery, Capitalism,
and Self-Purchase in the United States* (University of Pennsylvania Press,
2024).

44 "Boarder Sells Isaac to College, 1807," *Georgetown Slavery Archive*, Georgetown
University Archives, http://slaveryarchive.georgetown.edu, accessed February 13,
2018. Jeremiah Neale and his son James were distant relatives of Leonard Neale
and Francis Neale. See Harry Wright Newman, *The Maryland Semmes and Kindred Families* (1956; Heritage Books, 2007), 313–17.

45 "Isaac Runs Away, 1814," *Georgetown Slavery Archive*, Georgetown University
Archives; "The College Pays Runaway Isaac's Fees, 1814," *Georgetown Slavery
Archive*, Georgetown University Archives, http://slaveryarchive.georgetown.edu,
accessed February 13, 2018; John McElroy, "Thirty Dollars Reward," *The Daily
National Intelligencer*, February 1, 1814.

46 Kemp P. Battle, *History of the University of North Carolina, from Its Beginning to the Death of President Swain, 1789–1868*, vol. 1 (Edwards and Broughton, 1907), 61, 83, 252–53, 268, 320, 523, 534, 600–605, 826; *The Third Annual Report of the American Society*, 139, 142; *Fifth Annual Report of the American Society*, 117; *Tenth Annual Report of the American Society*, 93; *Fifteenth Annual Report of the American Society for Colonizing the Free People of Color of the United States* (Dunn, 1832), 55; Erika Lindemann, "True and Candid Compositions: The Lives and Writings of Antebellum Students at the University of North Carolina," Documenting the American South, University of North Carolina, chapter 3, https://docsouth.unc.edu, accessed June 22, 2018.

47 William Simms, "Notice," *The North Carolina Minerva*, January 28, 1805, 3.

48 J. M. Jenks, "Ten Dollars Reward," *The Star and North Carolina Gazette*, February 11, 1820, 3.

49 S. M. Stewart, "Twenty Dollars Reward," *Hillsborough (NC) Recorder*, November 25, 1829, 3.

50 E. Mitchell, "Fifty Dollars Reward," *North Carolina Standard*, March 13, 1835, 3.

51 William Kirkland, "Thirty Dollars Reward," *Raleigh Register and North Carolina Weekly Advertiser*, July 9, 1804; *Sketches of the History of the University of North Carolina, Together with a Catalogue of Officers and Students, 1789–1889* (University of North Carolina, 1889), 79.

52 [Titus Basfield], *An Interesting History of the Life of the Rev. Titus Basfield, a Colored Minister, in the Associate Presbyterian Church . . . by Himself* (1858; J.S. Davidson, 1868), 4–5, 25–32.

53 [Titus Basfield], *An Interesting History*, 1–32; Erving E. Beauregard, *Old Franklin, the Eternal Touch: A History of Franklin College, New Athens, Harrison County, Ohio* (University Press of America, 1983), 1–11, 16, 26–28.

54 During his time at Franklin a classmate of Basfield's was John Bingham. Together they fostered a lifelong friendship. Bingham became a politician during Reconstruction and was the chief author of the Fourteenth Amendment guaranteeing citizenship for all people born in the United States. See Gerard N. Magliocca, *American Founding Son: John Bingham and the Invention of the Fourteenth Amendment* (New York University Press, 2013), 11, 14–16, 197n29; Ervin E. Beauregard, *Bingham of the Hills: Politician and Diplomat Extraordinary* (Peter Lang, 1989).

55 For studies of Pennington's life, see R. J. M. Blackett, *Beating Against the Barriers: Biographical Essays in Nineteenth-Century Afro-American History* (Louisiana State University Press, 1986), 1–87; David E. Swift, *Black Prophets of Protest: Activist Clergy Before the Civil War* (Louisiana State University Press, 1989), 204–44 and passim; Herman E. Thomas, *James W.C. Pennington: African American Churchman and Abolitionist* (Garland, 1995); Christopher L. Webber, *American to the Backbone: The Life of James W.C. Pennington, the Fugitive Slave Who Became One of the First Black Abolitionists* (Pegasus Books, 2011); Manisha Sinha, "James W.C. Pennington and Transatlantic Abolitionism," in *The Pennington Lectures, 2011–2015*, ed. Jan Stieverman (University of Heidelberg, 2016), 19–36.

56 James W. C. Pennington, *The Fugitive Blacksmith; or, Events in the History of James W.C. Pennington . . .* , 3rd ed. (Gilpin, 1850), 1–56; "Rev. Dr. Pennington," *Frederick Douglass' Paper*, August 14, 1851; Swift, *Black Prophets of Justice*, 209–48.

57 James W. C. Pennington, *A Text Book of the Origin and History of the Colored People* (Skinner, 1841), 4, 13, 91–94, 45, 47–48, 58, 14; on Pennington's engagement with scripture see 4–38; Pennington also shows how slavery in the new world began with the enslavement of Indigenous people and subsequently Africans. Ultimately, he observes, "Slavery had its origin simultaneously with the conquests of this continent (North America), and was invented by that same plundering, bloody and murderous spirit which characterized those conquests" (40). On the history of slavery in the Americas, see 39–44. On the crux of the work focusing on refuting scientific racism, see 45–96. On Pennington's work and the broader Black abolitionist refutation of scientific racism, see Sinha, "Of Scientific Racists and Black Abolitionists," 235–57.

58 Significantly, Pennington emphasized the importance of Christianity for African Americans and wrote pejoratively of African religious traditions, referring to them as "heathenism." He wrote that "Ethiopians were ruined by the corrupting influence of their theology" and that "our ancestors had sublime systems of religion; but the basis of it was false," for it was a "mythological system." See Pennington, *A Text Book*, 33, 34, 36. Pennington was a Presbyterian minister, and here he privileged Christianity over other African religious traditions. But Pennington's remarks suggest another view beyond a rigid dichotomy. He wrote of "that God who must ever be the center and the circle of all true systems of religion and of morals" (38). Perhaps here Pennington is expressing a Christianity infused with the notion of circularity in West African cosmology and specifically the Bakongo cosmogram. In other words, Pennington advocated an African American Christianity.

59 Pennington, *The Fugitive Blacksmith*, 42–56; "Rev. Dr. Pennington"; the quotation on the doctoral degree is in C. Peter Ripley et al., *The Black Abolitionist Papers*, 5 vols. (University of North Carolina Press, 1985–1992), vol. 1, 182–83; Swift, *Black Prophets of Justice*, 209–48; Sinha, "James W.C. Pennington," 19–36; Sinha, *The Slave's Cause*, 309–11; Thomas, *James W.C. Pennington*, 53–54, 179–86; Webber, *American to the Backbone*, 95–104.

60 For works on Garnet's life, see Stuckey, *Slave Culture*, 138–92; Joel Schor, *Henry Highland Garnet: A Voice of Black Radicalism in the Nineteenth Century* (Greenwood Press, 1977); Swift, *Black Prophets of Justice*, chapters 6, 7, and passim; Martin B. Pasternak, *Rise Now and Fly to Arms: The Life of Henry Highland Garnet* (Garland, 1995).

61 Sinha, *The Slave's Cause*, 229–31; Russell W. Irvine and Donna Zani Dunkerton, "The Noyes Academy, 1834–1835: The Road to Oberlin Collegiate Institute and the Higher Education of African Americans in the Nineteenth Century," *Western Journal of Black Studies* 22, no. 4 (Winter 1998): 260–73.

62 Oneida Institute offered college-level education, and it had decisive impact on the movement. As Milton Sernett shows, important Black abolitionists began their

life's work as students at Oneida and Garnet was among the most active, especially beyond the campus. See Milton C. Sernett, *Abolition's Axe: Beriah Green, Oneida Institute, and the Black Freedom Struggle* (Syracuse University Press, 1986), chapter 4.

63 "Important Meeting," *Colored American*, September 2, 1837; "Celebration of the Colored Citizens of Utica, on the First of August," *Colored American*, August 25, 1838; "Celebration of the 1st of August in the City of Troy," *Colored American*, September 28, 1839; Schor, *Henry Highland Garnet*, 19–24, Garnet quoted on 21.

64 "Seventh Anniversary," *Emancipator*, May 15, 1840; "Speech of Henry H. Garnet," *National Anti-Slavery Standard*, June 11, 1840.

65 "For the Colored American," *Colored American*, September 28, 1839; Schor, *Henry Highland Garnet*, 23–24. On the work of other Black students at Onedia, see Milton C. Sernett, "First Honor: Oneida Institute's Role in the Fight Against American Racism and Slavery," *New York History* 66, no. 2 (April 1985): 107–8; Sernett, *Abolition's Axe*, 52–53.

66 Stuckey, *Slave Culture*, 144–45, 178, 187.

CHAPTER 4. THE WHITE ABOLITIONIST INSURGENCY

1 June 26, July 3, and July 10, 1833, *Athenian Society Records*, 1831–1846, Box 12, Folder 17, Amherst College Archives and Special Collections (hereafter cited ACASC); "Intelligence," *African Repository and Colonial Journal* 9, no. 7 (September 1833): 216; *Biographical Record of the Alumni of Amherst College During Its First Half-Century, 1821–1871*, ed. W. L. Montague (Amherst, 1883), 104, 121, 129.

2 "Constitution of the Auxiliary Anti-Slavery Society of Amherst College," *Amherst College Anti-Slavery Society*, Anti-Slavery Records, 1833–1842, Clubs and Societies Collection, box 1, folder 18, ACASC; *The Abolitionist* 1, no. 8 (August 1833): 124–25.

3 When I refer to "students" or "student antislavery societies" in this chapter, the terms refer to white men unless otherwise noted. "Anti-Slavery Society," *Observer and Telegraph* (Hudson, Ohio), December 27, 1832; *The Abolitionist* 1, no. 2 (February 1833): 29; "New England Anti-Slavery Society," *Liberator*, January 12, 1833; "Theological Seminary, Andover," *Liberator*, March 16, 1833; "Constitution of the Waterville College Anti-Slavery Society" and "To the Hon. Trustees of Wat. College," July 4, 1833, Anti-Slavery Society, Student Clubs and Organizations, box 20, folder A8, Colbiana Collection, Colby College Special Collections (hereafter CCSC); *The Abolitionist* 1, no. 8 (August 1833): 125; Frederick Clayton Waite, *Western Reserve University, the Hudson Era* (Western Reserve University Press, 1943), 101.

4 Herman M. Muelder, *Fighters for Freedom: The History of Anti-Slavery Activities of Men and Women Associated with Knox College* (Columbia University Press, 1959); Lawrence T. Lesick, *The Lane Rebels: Evangelicalism and Antislavery in Antebellum America* (Scarecrow Press, 1980); Milton C. Sernett, *Abolition's Axe: Beriah Green, Oneida Institute, and the Black Freedom Struggle* (Syracuse University Press, 1986); J. Brent Morris, *Oberlin, Hotbed of Abolitionism: College, Community, and*

the Fight for Freedom and Equality in Antebellum America (University of North Carolina Press, 2014).

5 Benjamin Quarles, *Black Abolitionists* (Oxford University Press, 1969), 3–23; Manisha Sinha, *The Slave's Cause: A History of Abolition* (Yale University Press, 2016); Merton Dillon, *Slavery Attacked: Southern Slaves and Their Allies, 1619–1865* (Louisiana State University Press, 1990); cf. Anne C. Loveland, "Evangelicalism and 'Immediate Emancipation' in American Antislavery Thought," *Journal of Southern History* 32, no. 2 (May 1966): 172–88; David Brion Davis, "The Emergence of Immediatism in British and American Antislavery Thought," *Mississippi Valley Historical Review* 49, no. 2 (September 1962): 209–30; Robert H. Abzug, *Cosmos Crumbling: American Reform and the Religious Imagination* (Oxford University Press, 1994).

6 David F. Allmendinger, *Paupers and Scholars: The Transformation of Student Life in Nineteenth-Century New England* (St. Martin's Press, 1975), 119–22; William S. Tyler, *History of Amherst College During Its First Half-Century, 1821–1871* (Clark, 1873), 162–63, 204–22; Leverett Wilson Spring, *A History of Williams College* (Houghton, 1917), 62–63, 129–35; John King Lord, *A History of Dartmouth College, 1815–1909* (Rumford Press, 1913), 203–4, 217, 248; Louis C. Hatch, *The History of Bowdoin College* (Loring, 1927), 276–80.

7 Thomas S. Harding, *College Literary Societies: Their Contribution to Higher Education in the United States, 1815–1876* (Pageant Press, 1971); Frederick Rudolph, *Curriculum: A History of the American Undergraduate Course of Study Since 1636* (Jossey-Bass, 1977), 95–98.

8 *Tenth Annual Report of the American Society*, 91; *Catalogue of the Officers, Graduates, and Students of Western Reserve College and Adelbert College, 1826–1916* (Western Reserve University Press, 1916), 8; "Contributions," *African Repository and Colonial Journal* (hereafter *ARCJ*) 7, no. 11 (January 1832): 351; "Intelligence," *ARCJ* 9, no. 1 (March 1833): 28–29; the best analysis of the early slavery controversy at Western Reserve College is Lawrence B. Goodheart, "Abolitionists as Academics: The Controversy at Western Reserve College, 1832–1833," *History of Education Quarterly* 22, no. 4 (Winter 1982): 421–33; also see Waite, *Western Reserve University*, 94–110.

9 Goodheart, "Abolitionists as Academics," 423–24.

10 "Expediency," *Observer and Telegraph*, August 30, 1832.

11 Waite, *Western Reserve University*, 96–98; Goodheart, "Abolitionists as Academics," 425.

12 Elizur Wright Jr., *The Sin of Slavery and Its Remedy: Containing Some Reflections on the Moral Influence of African Colonization* (New York, 1833); "Interesting Correspondence," *Liberator*, January 5, 1833.

13 "Western Reserve College," *Liberator*, November 3, 1832; Beriah Green, *Four Sermons, Preached in the Chapel of the Western Reserve College, on Lord's Days November 18th and 25th, and December 2nd and 9th, 1832* (Cleveland, 1833), quotation from 3, emphasis in the original; Waite, *Western Reserve University*, 98, 101.

14 The letter is dated November 2, 1832, in *Liberator*, January 5, 1833.

15 On proslavery scholars see Alfred L. Brophy, *University, Court, and Slave: Pro-Slavery Thought in Southern Colleges and Courts and the Coming of Civil War* (Oxford University Press, 2016).

16 Green, *Four Sermons*, 9–19, quotations from 10, 13, 15, 19.

17 Green, *Four Sermons*, 20–24, 27.

18 Green, *Four Sermons*, 28–29.

19 Green, *Four Sermons*, 33–52, quotations from 38, 45, 46, 51. ·

20 "Abolition," *Observer and Telegraph*, November 8, 1832.

21 Elizur Wright Jr. to Theodore Weld, December 7, 1832, in *Letters of Theodore Dwight Weld, Angelina Grimke Weld, and Sarah Grimke, 1822–1844* (hereafter *Weld-Grimke Letters*), ed. Gilbert H. Barnes and Dwight L. Dumond (Appleton, 1934), vol. 1, 96; quoted in P. J. Staudenraus, *The African Colonization Movement, 1816–1865* (Columbia University Press, 1961), 201; Sernett, *Abolition's Axe*, 25; Waite, *Western Reserve University*, 101; "Anti-Slavery Society," *Observer and Telegraph*, December 27, 1832; "Letters from Ohio," *Liberator*, January 5, 1833; "Anti-Slavery Society," *Liberator*, January 12, 1833.

22 Green, *Four Sermons*, 3, 4; "Communication," *Observer and Telegraph*, February 7, 1833; Goodheart, "Abolitionists as Academics," 426.

23 Goodheart, "Abolitionists as Academics," 427–31; Goodheart, *Abolitionist, Actuary, Atheist: Elizur Wright and the Reform Impulse* (Kent State University Press, 1990), 58–59; "Order of Exercises" and "Communications," *Observer and Telegraph*, September 5, 1833; Sernett, *Abolition's Axe*, 26–29; Waite, *Western Reserve University*, 100–103; "Intelligence," *ARCJ* 9, no. 8 (October 1833): 245–46, quotation from 246.

24 Goodheart, *Abolitionist, Actuary*, 59; Sernett, *Abolition's Axe*, 29; "Good News from the West!," *The Emancipator*, August 3, 1833; Goodheart, "Abolitionists as Academics," 430; Robert Samuel Fletcher, *A History of Oberlin College, from Its Foundation Through the Civil War*, 2 vols. (Arno Press, 1971), vol. 1, 185.

25 Weld to Wright, January 10, 1833, *Weld-Grimke Letters* 1: 99, emphasis in the original; Robert Abzug, *Passionate Liberator: Theodore Dwight Weld and the Dilemma of Reform* (Oxford University Press, 1980), 86–87.

26 Sernett, *Abolition's Axe*, 25, 27–28, 31.

27 Sernett, *Abolition's Axe*, 31–34; Paul Goodman argued that the manual labor system was a critique of bourgeois culture and capitalist social relations, which were tied to white supremacy and patriarchy. Paul Goodman, "The Manual Labor Movement and the Origins of Abolitionism," *Journal of the Early Republic* 13, no. 3 (Autumn 1993): 356–88, esp. 359–61, 388. Although Goodman wrongly locates the origins of abolition in manual labor, it did provide a pathway to abolition for some evangelicals.

28 Abzug, *Passionate Liberator*, 60–70; Sernett, *Abolition's Axe*, 31–34.

29 "Anti-Slavery Society in Oneida Institute," *Liberator*, August 3, 1833. The notable exception is Muelder, *Fighters for Freedom*, 34–35; Goodman, "The Manual Labor

Movement," 378–79, cites Muelder. See Sernett, *Abolition's Axe*, 36; Fletcher, *A History of Oberlin*, 146–47.

30 H. L. Hammond, "The Gravel Debate: An Anti-Slavery Reminiscence," *The Advance* (Chicago), April 28, 1870. I thank Owen Muelder for directing me to this source.

31 "Anti-Slavery Society in Oneida Institute," *The Abolitionist* 1, no. 8 (August 1833): 125; *Emancipator*, August 3, 1833, 54; "Auxiliary Societies," *ARCJ* 9, no. 6 (August 1833): 215; "Colonization at Oneida Institute," *Emancipator*, March 25, 1834; *Third Annual Report of the American Anti-Slavery Society* (New York, 1836), 94–95.

32 Abzug, *Passionate Liberator*, 74–89; Sernett, *Abolition's Axe*, 31–40; Fletcher, *A History of Oberlin College*, 54–55.

33 Fletcher, *A History of Oberlin College*, 55n43; Dumond and Barnes provide short sketches of Oneida students who left for Lane in *Weld-Grimke Letters*, 1: 36, 52, 84, 88; *General Catalogue of Lane Theological Seminary, 1828–1881* (1881), 9–11.

34 Fletcher, *A History of Oberlin*, 242; Muelder, *Fighters for Freedom*, 47–61.

35 November 10, 1832, March 6, 1833, *Records of the Literary Fraternity*, Waterville College, vol. 2, CCSC; May 22, 1833, *Constitution and Proceedings of the First Division of the Literary Fraternity*, 1832–1837, CCSC; Henry Mayer, *All on Fire: William Lloyd Garrison and the Abolition of Slavery* (St. Martin's Press, 1998), 140; "Constitution of the Waterville Anti-Slavery Society," CCSC.

36 Jeremiah Chaplin, "Address to the Waterville College on July 15, 1833," CCSC.

37 "Students Address to Faculty of College," July 17, 1833, CCSC.

38 Calvin Newton and George W. Keely, "To the Honorable Board of Trustees of Waterville College," July 30, 1833; Jeremiah Chaplin and Thomas J. Conant, "To the Trustees of W. College," July 31, 1833; "Report [of] Rev. John Butler Chairman of [the] Committee to Affect a Reconciliation between [the] President and Others and Keely and Others," n.d., 1833; all documents in the CCSC.

39 *First Annual Report of the Board of Managers of the New England Anti-Slavery Society, Presented January 9, 1833* (Garrison and Knapp, 1833), 3, 43; "Theological Seminary, Andover," *Liberator*, March 16, 1833.

40 "Correspondence," *ARCJ* 9, no. 1 (March 1833): 30; "Intelligence," *ARCJ* 9, no. 5 (July 1833): 154.

41 "Letter from Arthur Tappan, Esq.," *Liberator*, April 6, 1833.

42 Quoted in "Letter on Colonization," *Observer and Telegraph*, August 29, 1833; "Dr. Porter on Slavery and African Colonization," *Vermont Chronicle*, August 9, 1833; "The Slavery Question," *Lynchburg Virginian*, August 12, 1833; "From the New York Journal of Commerce," *Columbia (SC) Telescope*, August 20, 1833; "Rev. Doctor Porter's Letter," *Liberator*, August 24, 1833; the rebuke signed "An Abolitionist" is "Dr. Porter's Letter on Slavery," *Liberator*, September 7, 1833.

43 "Theo. Sem. Andover," *Liberator*, August 31, 1833.

44 D[avid] T. Kimball Jr. and L[ewis] F. Laine, *Apology for Anti-Slavery, Theological Seminary, Andover, August 22, 1833* (n.p.), 1–4, quotations from 1, 2, 3, 4. On Crandall's school, see Jennifer Rycenga, *Schooling the Nation: The Success of the Canterbury Academy for Black Women* (University of Illinois Press, 2025).

45 "Apology for Anti-Slavery," *Emancipator*, September 7, 1833; "Apology for Anti-Slavery," *Genius of Temperance*, September 11, 1833; "Apology for Anti-Slavery," *Liberator*, September 28, 1833.

46 "Emancipation and Amalgamation," *United States' Telegraph*, September 11, 1833; "From the *Virginia Times*: Amalgamation of Races," *United States Telegraph*, September 20, 1833.

47 "Literary Notices," *The Shrine* 1, no. 2 (Adams, 1832), Student and Alumni Publications Collections, Box 13, ACASC.

48 "Communications," *Liberator*, September 14, 1833; July 24, December 4, 11, 1833, *Amherst College Anti-Slavery Society*, Anti-Slavery Records, 1833–1842, ACASC.

49 "Anti-Slavery Convention," *Liberator*, December 21, 1833; *Proceedings of the Anti-Slavery Convention, Assembled at Philadelphia, December 4, 5, and 6, 1833* (Dorr, 1833), 4, 9, 21, 23–24; William Lloyd Garrison to George W. Benson, November 25, 1833, in *William Lloyd Garrison, 1805–1879: The Story of His Life Told by His Children*, ed. Wendell Phillips Garrison and Francis Jackson Garrison (Century, 1885), vol. 1, 394.

50 See Henry B. Stanton's account in the *Emancipator*, March 24, 1834, and printed in the pamphlet *Debate at the Lane Seminary, Cincinnati, Speech of James A. Thome . . .* (Garrison and Knapp, 1834), 3–7; also see "Lane Seminary, March 6, 1834," *Emancipator*, April 22, 1834. Lawrence T. Lesick, *The Lane Rebels: Evangelicalism and Antislavery in Antebellum America* (Scarecrow Press, 1980); Nikki M. Taylor, *Frontiers of Freedom: Cincinnati's Black Community, 1802–1868* (Ohio University Press, 2005); Gilbert H. Barnes, *The Anti-Slavery Impulse, 1830–1844* (Harbinger, 1933, 2nd ed., 1964), 64–88; Abzug, *Passionate Liberator*, 74–112

51 *Proceedings of the New England Anti-Slavery Convention: Held in Boston on the 27th, 28th, and 29th of May, 1834* (Garrison and Knapp, 1834), 4, 21–22; *First Annual Report of the American Anti-Slavery Society . . .* (Dorr, 1834), 39; *Biographical Record of the Alumni of Amherst College, During Its First Half-Century, 1821–1871*, ed. W. L. Montague (Amherst, 1883), 107, 108, 109, 119, 131, 140.

52 Asa Mahan, *Autobiography: Intellectual, Moral, and Spiritual, by Rev. Asa Mahan, D.D., L.L.D.* (Woolmer, 1882), 179; "Premature Triumph and Misplaced Merriment," *The Friend of Man*, September 15, 1836; Barnes, *Antislavery Impulse*, 70–71, 228n15.

53 August 11, 1834, *Amherst College Anti-Slavery Society*, Anti-Slavery Records, 1833–1842, ACASC.

54 Letter to the Faculty, October 21, 1834, Antislavery Collection, ACASC.

55 November 24, 1834, *Amherst College Anti-Slavery Society*, Anti-Slavery Records, 1833–1842, ACASC. The students amended article 2 of their constitution, which mirrored the language and outlook of the Lane abolitionists, in "Preamble," *Liberator*, April 12, 1834; *Proceedings of the New England Anti-Slavery Convention . . .* (1834), 4, 20.

56 "To the Committee of the Anti-Slavery Society in Amherst College," November 26, 1834, Anti-Slavery Records, 1833–1842, ACASC; "Amherst College," January

7 (or 17), 1835, Anti-Slavery Records, 1833–1842, ACASC; "From the New York Evangelist," *Emancipator*, January 20, 1835.

57 "Andover Theo. Sem. Feb. 2, 1835," reprinted from the *Boston Recorder* in *Liberator*, February 21, 1835; "To the Rev. Joseph Tracy, Editor of the *Boston Recorder*," dated February 3, 1835, reprinted in *Liberator*, February 21, 1835.

58 "To the Committee of the Anti-Slavery Society in Amherst College," February 19, 1835, Anti-Slavery Records, 1833–1842, ACASC.

59 February 23, 1835, Anti-Slavery Records, 1833–1842, ACASC; "The Treasurer of the Massachusetts Anti-Slavery Society," *Liberator*, June 6, 1835; "Receipts," *The Anti-Slavery Record* 1, no. 6 (June 1835): 72; "Receipts," *The Anti-Slavery Record* 1, no. 7 (July 1835): 84; John Farwell to Stephen Caswell, June 23, 1835, John Farwell Letters, Historical Manuscripts Collection, box 2, folder 53, ACASC; Frederick Augustus Fiske to Amos A. Phelps, June 25, 1835, Amos A. Phelps Papers, Anti-Slavery Collection, Boston Public Library; *Second Annual Report of the American Anti-Slavery Society . . .* (Dorr, 1835), 23.

60 Leonard L. Richards, *"Gentlemen of Property and Standing": Anti-Abolition Mobs in Jacksonian America* (Oxford University Press, 1970); Nye, *Fettered Freedom*.

61 James Hall, "Education and Slavery," *Western Monthly Magazine and Literary Journal*, May 1834, quotations from 267, 268, 269, 270, 271.

62 Hall, "Education and Slavery," quotations from 272, 272–73.

63 Weld to James Hall, Editor of the *Western Monthly Magazine*, May 20, 1834, in *Weld-Grimke Letters*, 1: 136–46, quotations from 138, 139, 140, 141, 142, 143–44, 145.

64 Weld to James Hall, *Weld-Grimke Letters*, 1: 146.

65 "Anti-Slavery Convention," *Liberator*, December 21, 1833; "Waterville," and "Circular," *Liberator*, May 10, 1834; "Waterville," *Liberator*, June 21, 1834; "Maine Anti-Slavery Convention," *Liberator*, November 1, 1834; "Maine Anti-Slavery Convention," *Vermont Chronicle*, October 31, 1834; "The Treasurer of the American Anti-Slavery Society," *Emancipator*, October 21, 1834; *General Catalogue of Officers, Graduates, and Former Students of Colby College, 1820–1920* (Colby College, 1920), 248, 249.

66 George LeRow to William Lloyd Garrison, October 27, 1834, Garrison Papers, Anti-Slavery Collection, Boston Public Library.

67 George LeRow to Amos Phelps, November 21, 1834, Amos Phelps Papers, Anti-Slavery Collection, Boston Public Library.

68 *General Catalogue of Officers, Graduates, and Former Students of Colby College*, 248, 249, 250.

69 "Defence of the Students," *Liberator*, January 10, 1835; "Statement of the Faculty," *Liberator*, January 17, 1835; Lesick, *The Lane Rebels*, 92–95, 116–19, 126; *General Catalogue of the Theological Seminary Andover, Massachusetts, 1808–1908* (Todd, 1908), 149, 161, 164, 166, 168, 169, 170, 175; for graduates and withdrawals see 134–74; E. Fuller Torrey, *The Martyrdom of Abolitionist Charles Torrey* (Louisiana State University Press, 2013), 34–39; Charles Torrey to Amos Phelps, July 2, 1835, Phelps Papers, Anti-Slavery Collection, Boston Public Library; Eric Foner, *Gateway to*

Freedom: The Hidden History of the Underground Railroad (Basic, 2015), 23, 103–5,
162, 210–24 passim; "Anti-Slavery Meetings at Andover," *Liberator*, July 18, 1835;
"Appeal of Abolitionists of the Theological Seminary," *Liberator*, August 25, 1837;
"Letter from Mr. Stanton," *Emancipator*, September 15, 1836.

70 "Hamilton College Anti-Slavery Society," *New York Evangelist*, November 14, 1835;
*First Annual Report of the Union College Anti-Slavery Society, with an Address to
Students, and an Appendix* (Riggs, 1836), 5, 6, 7, 8.

71 Petition from the Citizens of Clinton to the U.S. House of Representatives,
January [n.d.], 1836, Anti-Slavery Folder, Hamilton College Miscellaneous Files,
Hamilton College Archives (hereafter cited HCMF, HCA), emphasis in the origi-
nal; Petitions from the Inhabitants of Kirkland County to the U.S. Congress, [n.d.]
1837, Anti-Slavery Folder, HCMF, HCA; Members of Hamilton College to the U.S.
Congress, September 26, 1837, Anti-Slavery Folder, HCMF, HCA.

72 Arthur Zilversmit, *The First Emancipation: The Abolition of Slavery in the North*
(Chicago: University of Chicago Press, 1967), 213–15, 215n24; Edgar J. McManus, *A
History of Negro Slavery in New York* (Syracuse University Press, 1966), 174–79.

73 "Abolition in Hamilton College," *Friend of Man*, May 24, 1837; "Hamilton College,"
New York Spectator, November 23, 1835; Members of Hamilton College to the
U.S. Congress, September 26, 1837, Anti-Slavery Folder, HCMF, HCA; Hamilton
College Petition to the Honorable Gentlemen of the House of Representatives,
January 14, 1838, Anti-Slavery Folder, HCMF, HCA.

74 *Proceedings of the New England Anti-Slavery Convention . . .* (1834), 4, 20; Novem-
ber 24, 1834, *Amherst College Anti-Slavery Society*, Anti-Slavery Records, 1833–
1842, ACASC; George LeRow to Amos Phelps, November 21, 1834, Phelps Papers,
Antislavery Collection, Boston Public Library; "Petitions," *National Intelligencer*,
September 23, 1837; Sinha, *The Slave's Cause*, 251–52; Leonard L. Richards, *The
Slave Power: The Free North and Southern Domination, 1780–1860* (Louisiana State
University Press, 2000).

75 November 8, 12, 15, 1841, *Records*, 1837–1841, ACASC, emphasis in the original.

76 Michael E. Jirik, "'We Are and Will Be Forever Anti-Slavery Men!': Student Abolitionists and Subversive Politics at Amherst College, 1833–1841," in *Amherst in the
World*, ed. Martha Saxton (Amherst College, 2020), 298–300; on the Liberty Party
see Richard Sewell, *Ballots for Freedom: Antislavery Politics in the United States,
1837–1860* (Oxford University Press, 1976); Reinhard O. Johnson, *The Liberty
Party, 1840–1848: Antislavery Third Party Politics in the United States* (Louisiana
State University Press, 2009); Bruce Laurie, *Beyond Garrison: Antislavery and Social Reform* (Cambridge University Press, 2005); Corey M. Brooks, *Liberty Power:
Antislavery Third Parties and the Transformation of American Politics* (University
of Chicago Press, 2015).

77 "New Haven Young Men's Anti-Slavery Society," *Emancipator*, December 3, 1840.

78 "Freeman's State Convention, at Syracuse," *Emancipator*, August 20, 1840; *The
Hamilton College Bulletin, Complete Alumni Register 1812–1922* 6, no. 1 (November
1922): 45, 48.

79 "Indiana," *Emancipator*, February 11, 1842.

80 "Editorial Correspondence," *Emancipator*, September 8, 1842; Alvan Stewart, "Editor of the Abolitionist," *Emancipator*, October 13, 1842.

81 Many white student abolitionist men broke with the Garrisonian wing of the movement, siding against women's rights, and favored using institutions like the church for abolition. See for example "Appeal of Abolitionists, of the Theological Seminary," *Liberator*, August 25, 1837.

CHAPTER 5. DEVELOPING BLACK HIGHER LEARNING

1 David Walker, *Walker's Appeal, in Four Articles, Together with a Preamble, to the Colored Citizens of the World, but in Particular, and Very Expressly, to Those of the United States of America*, 2nd ed. (1830), printed in Henry Highland Garnet, *Walker's Appeal, with a Brief Sketch of His Life and Also Garnet's Address to the Slaves of the United States of America* (Tobitt, 1848), 38–44, quotation from 42; Cedric J. Robinson, "David Walker and the Precepts of Black Studies," in *Cedric J. Robinson: On Racial Capitalism, Black Internationalism, and Cultures of Resistance*, ed. H. L. T. Quan (Pluto Press, 2019), 340–53, esp. 345–52; Manisha Sinha, *The Slave's Cause: A History of Abolition* (Yale University Press, 2016), 205–6.

2 Robinson, "David Walker," 340–53; Chuck Morse, "Capitalism, Marxism, and the Black Radical Tradition: An Interview with Cedric Robinson," *Perspectives on Anarchist Theory* 3, no. 1 (Spring 1999): 8; Vincent Harding, *There Is a River: The Black Struggle for Freedom in America* (Harcourt Brace, 1981), 86, on Walker generally, see 81–94. On the notion of Black communities accepting or rejecting leaders of their institutions, see for example Sterling Stuckey, *Slave Culture: Nationalist Theory and the Foundations of Black America* (Oxford University Press, 1987), 92–94.

3 On the idea of "knowledge accumulated through struggle," see Cedric J. Robinson, *Black Marxism: The Making of the Black Radical Tradition* (1983; University of North Carolina Press, 2000), xxx.

4 Frederick Cooper, "Elevating the Race: The Social Thought of Black Leaders, 1827–50," *American Quarterly* 24, no. 5 (December 1972): 604–25; George A. Levesque, "Boston's Black Brahmin: Dr. John S. Rock," *Civil War History* 26, no. 4 (December 1980): 326–46; David W. Blight, "In Search of Learning, Liberty, and Self-Definition: James McCune Smith and the Ordeal of the Antebellum Black Intellectual," *Afro-Americans in New York Life and History* 9, no. 2 (July 1985): 7–25. Of the three cited, Blight takes seriously the strategy of self-elevation.

5 Black abolitionists' early lives as college students have not been studied as formative moments in their life trajectories. Some scholars have included this component of their lives in their broader works on abolition. An important exception is Kabria Baumgartner, *In Pursuit of Knowledge: Black Women and Educational Activism in Antebellum America* (New York University Press, 2019). Other works include Carter G. Woodson, *The Education of the Negro Prior to 1861* (1919; Arno Press, 1968), 256–83; Benjamin Quarles, *Black Abolitionists* (Oxford University

Press, 1969), 34, 106–15. Also see Russell W. Irvine, *The African American Quest for Institutions of Higher Education before the Civil War: The Forgotten Histories of Ashmun Institute, Liberia College, and Avery College* (Edwin Mellen Press, 2010), as well as William B. Hart and Diane Windham Shaw's respective essays in Leslie M. Harris et al., *Slavery and the University: Histories and Legacies* (University of Georgia Press, 2019).

6 "Proposals for Publishing Freedom's Journal," *Freedom's Journal*, March 23, 1827; "Education in Greece," *The Rights of All*, May 29, 1829; "Education," *The Rights of All*, September 18, 1829; Hilary J. Moss, *Schooling Citizens: The Struggle for African American Education in Antebellum America* (University of Chicago Press, 2009), 29–30; Michael Hines, "Learning Freedom: Education, Elevation, and New York City's African American Community, 1827–1829," *History of Education Quarterly* 56, no. 4 (October 2016): 618–45. On Cornish's life, see David E. Swift, *Black Prophets of Justice: Activist Clergy Before the Civil War* (Louisiana State University Press, 1989), chapters 3 and 4, and passim.

7 Moss, *Schooling Citizens*, chapter 2, especially 50.

8 *College for Colored Youth. An Account of the New Haven City Meeting and Resolutions . . .* (New York, 1831), 2–6, quotation from 3; *Minutes and Proceedings of the First Annual Convention of the People of Colour* (1831), 5–7, in *Minutes and Proceedings of the National Negro Conventions, 1830–1864*, ed. Howard Holman Bell (Arno Press, 1969); Sinha, *The Slave's Cause*, 229.

9 *College for Colored Youth*, 5; abolitionists followed the news about the college closely. See for example, "College for the People of Color," *Liberator*, July 9, 1831; "Extraordinary Conduct," *Liberator*, September 17, 1831; several articles in *Liberator*, September 24, 1831; "The African College," *Liberator*, November 26, 1831.

10 Moss, *Schooling Citizens*, 44–45, 62.

11 Cf. Moss, *Schooling Citizens*, 61–62.

12 Colonizationists would later advocate higher learning, particularly medical training, for African Americans with the mandate of leaving the country for Liberia. Woodson, *The Education of the Negro*, 262–63; Russell Irvine, *African American Quests for Higher Education*; William B. Hart, "'To see the diseases . . . of the country': The American Colonization Society's Efforts to Educate Black Physicians for Liberia," Organization of American Historians annual conference, Philadelphia, PA, April 5, 2019, unpublished paper in the author's possession. I would like to thank Professor Hart for sharing his work with me.

13 Baumgartner, *In Pursuit of Knowledge*, 13–46; Sinha, *The Slave's Cause*, 229–31; Irvine and Dunkerton, "The Noyes Academy, 1834–1835," 260–73.

14 M. N. Work, "The Life of Charles B. Ray," *The Journal of Negro History* 4, no. 4 (October 1919): 361–71; Swift, *Black Prophets of Justice*, 78–80; David B. Potts, *Wesleyan University, 1831–1910: Collegiate Enterprise in New England* (Yale University Press, 1992), 7–15, 53–54.

15 "Scandalous Affair," *Liberator*, January 12, 1833; "Colonization Society of the Wesleyan University, Middletown, Connecticut," *African Repository and Colonial*

Journal, April 1833, 60; Craig Steven Wilder, "'Driven . . . from the School of the Prophets': The Colonizationist Ascendance at General Theological Seminary," *New York History*, Summer 2012, 170–71.

16 Many white student abolitionists advocated educational equality in their support for immediatism and Black rights, and some included college education as part of their agenda.

17 Quoted in Swift, *Black Prophets of Justice*, 81, also on Fisk see 96–97; *Liberator*, February 28, 1835; *Zion's Herald*, April 1, 1835; Potts, *Wesleyan University*, 53–55.

18 "Another Specimen!!," *Liberator*, November 2, 1833; "The Reign of Prejudice," *The Abolitionist* 1, no. 9 (November 1833): 175; "Trip to Middletown," *Emancipator*, January 4, 1834; "From Our New Haven Correspondent," *Frederick Douglass' Paper*, October 13, 1854; Swift, *Black Prophets of Justice*, 174–76; Potts, *Wesleyan University*, 54.

19 "Meeting of the United Anti-Slavery Society of New York," *Emancipator*, December 15, 1836.

20 The racist experience propelled Ray, and, as discussed below, Beman as well, to further work in the movement for Black freedom. This is not to portray such an incident in a romantic fashion. Being motivated by a wrong to do something right does not make the wrong right.

21 Work, "The Life of Charles B. Ray," 363–71; Swift, *Black Prophets of Justice*, 81–82, 85, 90–93, 156–62, and passim; Sinha, *The Slave's Cause*, 319–21; Eric Foner, *Gateway to Freedom: The Hidden History of the Underground Railroad* (Norton, 2015), 8, 65–73, 85, 128.

22 Swift, *Black Prophets of Justice*, 178, 183, 184–85, and 186–203; Robert A. Warner, "Amos Gerry Beman—1812–1874, a Memoir on a Forgotten Leader," *The Journal of Negro History* 22, no. 2 (April 1937): 200–221.

23 "From Our New Haven Correspondent," *Frederick Douglass' Paper*, October 13, 1854.

24 *Proceedings of the New England Anti-Slavery Convention, Held in Boston on the 27th, 28th, and 29th of May, 1834* (Garrison and Knapp, 1834), 13–14; "Address of Rev. Peter Williams," reprinted from the *New York Spectator* in *African Repository and Colonial Journal* 10, no. 6 (August 1834): 187; C. Peter Ripley et al., *The Black Abolitionist Papers*, 5 vols. (University of North Carolina Press, 1985–1992), 3:224n10; Sinha, *The Slave's Cause*, 314; Wilder, "Driven," 164, 171; John Stauffer, *The Black Hearts of Men: Radical Abolitionists and the Transformation of Race* (Harvard University Press, 2001), 88; the Centre College story is recounted in "Dartmouth College—A Noble Example," *Colored American*, April 29, 1837; "Facts Respecting Pro-Slavery Colleges and Theological Seminaries," *Colored American*, October 13, 1838.

25 Entries from DeGrasse's diary were printed in William Jay, *Caste and Slavery in the American Church* (Wiley and Putnam, 1843), 14n–17n; "From the Churchman," *Colored American*, April 3, 1841; Wilder, "Driven," 172–76.

26 "Philomathean Lectures," *Colored American*, April 19, 1838; "Ordination," *Colored American*, July 21, 1838; "For the Colored American," *Colored American*, August 11,

1838; "Colored Schools," *Colored American*, January 26, 1839; "Episcopal School," *Colored American*, July 20, 1839; "From the Churchman," *Colored American*, April 3, 1841; Wilder, "Driven," 173.

27 It is important to note that the same qualification applies here as it does for this entire project. African Americans did not have to be officially accepted into colleges to be students or intellectuals. Many more Black activists, men and women, who were not official college students educated themselves by participating in literary societies and other autonomous Black organizations dedicated to learning. At the same time, it has been the aim of this work to study the lives of early formal Black students in the movement and highlight their work while also examining their impact on Black higher learning. For Black women and girls at female seminaries, see Kabria Baumgartner's important work *In Pursuit of Knowledge*; Baumgartner, "'Cruel and Wicked Prejudice': Racial Exclusion and the Female Seminary Movement in the Antebellum North," in *Women's Higher Education in the United States: New Historical Perspectives*, ed. Margaret A. Nash (Palgrave, 2018), 45–68.

28 Maria W. Stewart, "An Address, Delivered at the African Masonic Hall in Boston, Feb. 27, 1833," *Liberator*, April 27, 1833; Maria W. Stewart, "An Address, Delivered at the African Masonic Hall in Boston, Feb. 27, 1833, Concluded," *Liberator*, May 4, 1833.

29 Maria W. Stewart, "Religion and the Pure Principles of Morality, the Sure Foundation on Which We Must Build," *Liberator*, October 8, 1831, printed in *Maria W. Stewart, America's First Black Woman Political Writer: Essays and Speeches*, ed. Marilyn Richardson (Indiana University Press, 1987), 28–42, quotations from 28, 30, 37, 38.

30 Maria W. Stewart, "Farewell Address to Her Friends in the City of Boston," *Liberator*, September 28, 1833, printed in Marilyn Richardson, ed., *Maria W. Stewart, America's First Black Woman Political Writer: Essays and Speeches* (Indiana University Press, 1987), 65–74, quotations from 68, 69, 70, and also Richardson's introductory essay, 20–24.

31 See for example the work of Oyèrónkẹ́ Oyěwùmí, who demonstrates that the unequal power relations between men and women in Western societies are categorically distinct from traditional human relationships among women and men in African contexts. Stewart was a public intellectual, teacher, and activist among her people, notions that were derided in the dominant culture of the United States but were traditionally commonplace among African people. See Oyěwùmí, *The Invention of Women: Making an African Sense of Western Gender Discourses* (University of Minnesota Press, 1997).

32 "Our Friends Hinder Our Improvement," *Colored American*, August 12, 1837; W., "For the Colored American," *Colored American*, June 24, 1837; A Colored Baltimorean, "For the Colored American," *Colored American*, June 17, 1837; see also several articles in *Colored American*, September 2, 1837; Swift, *Black Prophets of Justice*, 99–100.

33 *Proceedings of the New England Anti-Slavery Convention: Held in Boston, May 24, 25, 26, 1836* (Knapp, 1836), 48.

34 *Proceedings of the New England Anti-Slavery Convention . . . 1836*, 54; "Oneida Institute," *Liberator*, April 23, 1836.

35 *Proceedings of the New England Anti-Slavery Convention . . . 1836*, 56–59; Sernett, *Abolition's Axe*, 50–51; Angela M. Leonard, ed., *Antislavery Materials at Bowdoin College* (Bowdoin College, 1992), 12–13, 31, 36; *Biographical Record of the Alumni of Amherst College, During Its First Half-Century, 1821–1871*, ed. W. L. Montague (Amherst, 1883), 34; after 1830 no other Black students were admitted to the regular college course or graduated at either Bowdoin or Amherst until after the Civil War. In 1847–1849 four Black students enrolled in Bowdoin's medical school but not the regular college course. Charles C. Calhoun, *A Small College in Maine: Two Hundred Years of Bowdoin* (Bowdoin College, 1993), 163–64; Harold Wade Jr., *Black Men of Amherst* (Amherst College Press, 1974), 14.

36 *Proceedings of the New England Anti-Slavery Convention . . . 1836*, quotations from 57, 57–58, 58, 59; *Proceedings of the New England Anti-Slavery Convention . . . 1834*, 13. On the Oneida Institute, see Milton C. Sernett, *Abolition's Axe: Beriah Green, Oneida Institute, and the Black Freedom Struggle* (Syracuse University Press, 1986).

37 Stephen Mullen and Simon Newman, *Slavery, Abolition, and the University of Glasgow: Report and Recommendations of the University of Glasgow History of Slavery Steering Committee* (University of Glasgow, September 2018); Stephen Mullen, "British Universities and Transatlantic Slavery: The University of Glasgow Case," *History Workshop Journal* 91, no. 1 (Spring 2021): 210–33; Nicholas Draper, "British Universities and Caribbean Slavery," in *Dethroning Historical Reputations: Universities, Museums, and the Commemoration of Benefactors*, ed. Jill Pellew and Lawrence Goldman (Institute for Historical Research, 2018), 93–107.

38 "Return of Dr. Smith," *Colored American*, September 9, 1837; "Reception of Dr. Smith," *Colored American*, October 28, 1837; "Reception of Dr. Smith by the Colored Citizens of New York," *Colored American*, October 28, 1837; *First Annual Report of the Glasgow Emancipation Society* (Young, 1835), 1–6, 46; *Second Annual Report of the Glasgow Emancipation Society* (Aird and Russell, 1836), 3–4, 8; *Britain and America United in the Cause of Universal Freedom: Being the Third Annual Report of the Glasgow Emancipation Society* (Aird and Russell, 1837), 6, 8, 124–25, 142; "Annual Meeting of the Glasgow Emancipation Society," *Liberator*, June 27, 1835; "Glasgow Emancipation Society," *Liberator*, May 5, 1837; Sinha, *The Slave's Cause*, 339–42; R. J. M. Blackett, *Building an Antislavery Wall: Black Americans in the Atlantic Abolitionist Movement, 1830–1860* (Louisiana State University Press, 1983), 4, 8, 45–46, 196; Blight, "In Search of Learning," 7–8; John Stauffer, ed., *The Works of James McCune Smith: Black Intellectual and Abolitionist* (Oxford University Press, 2006), xxi–xxii; Anna Mae Duane, *Educated for Freedom: The Incredible Story of Two Fugitive Schoolboys Who Grew Up to Change the Nation* (New York University Press, 2020); Christopher L. Webber, *Black Doctor: A Biography of James McCune Smith, MD, the First*

Fully Trained and Credentialed Black Doctor in America (Western New Mexico University, 2024).

39 Sarah Parker Remond to Maria Weston Chapman, October 6, 1859, Anti-Slavery Collection, Boston Public Library; "Personal," *National Anti-Slavery Standard*, November 17, 1860; "Miss Remond in Edinburgh," *National Anti-Slavery Standard*, January 26, 1861; Sirpa Salenius, *An Abolitionist Abroad: Sarah Parker Remond in Cosmopolitan Europe* (University of Massachusetts Press, 2016), 2, 111–14, 165–71; Sibyl Ventress Brownlee, "Out of an Abundance of the Heart: Sarah Ann Parker Remond's Quest for Freedom" (PhD dissertation, University of Massachusetts–Amherst, 1997), 143, 154–57; Dorothy B. Porter, "Sarah Parker Remond, Abolitionist and Physician," *Journal of Negro History* 20, no. 3 (July 1935): 287–93; Sinha, *The Slave's Cause*, 346–47.

40 "The General Theological Seminary of the Protestant Episcopal Church in the U.S.," *Colored American*, September 7, 1839; "Case of Bishop Onderdonk and Mr. Crummell," *Colored American*, December 7, 1839; Wilder, "Driven," 176–83; Alexander Crummell to John Jay, August 9, 1848, Ripley et al., *Black Abolitionist Papers*, 1:143; Wilson J. Moses, *Alexander Crummell: A Study of Civilization and Discontent* (Oxford University Press, 1989), 22–33, 43, 50–51, 55–64, 70–78; Carl R. Stockton, "The Integration of Cambridge: Alexander Crummell as Undergraduate, 1849–1853," *Integrated Education* 15 (March–April 1977): 15–19. Also see Gregory Rigsby, *Alexander Crummell: Pioneer in Nineteenth-Century Pan African Thought* (Greenwood Press, 1987).

41 "British and Foreign Anti-Slavery Society," *Anti-Slavery Reporter*, June 2, 1851, 87–89, quotation from 88; Moses, *Alexander Crummell*, 64–66.

42 Moses, *Alexander Crummell*, chapter 6; Sinha, *The Slave's Cause*, 336.

CHAPTER 6. THE MAKING OF A TRADITION

1 Frederick Douglass, *The Claims of the Negro, Ethnologically Considered: An Address, Before the Literary Societies of Western Reserve College, at Commencement, July 12, 1854* (Lee, 1854), 3–37, quotations from 3, 4, 5, 6, 10; further rebutting Nott et. al., Douglass also showed that the physical characteristics used to explain the supposed inferiority of Black people were common characteristics of other human beings and asserted the environmentalist argument for explaining differences in human complexions around the world. For the culmination of the address and his argument, see especially 34–37. On the idea of the "deep well" of Africana, see Jacob H. Carruthers, *Intellectual Warfare* (Third World Press, 1999), xv and passim.

2 W. E. B. Du Bois, "A Negro Student at Harvard at the End of the 19th Century," *Massachusetts Review* 1, no. 3 (Spring 1960): 443. For the enduring influence of Du Bois's formulation, see Robin D. G. Kelley, "Black Study, Black Struggle," *Boston Review*, March 7, 2016.

3 While Oberlin had a reputation for fostering abolition, at the institutional level it did not promote Black women's rights. Black women like Lucy Stanton and others, however, crafted critiques of racism and sexism and created an environment

of Black feminist thought that defied the gendered provisions and expectations set by white faculty. For that reason Lucy Stanton, even though attending an abolitionist college, was in but not of it. See n42 below.

4 See below as well as Kabria Baumgartner, "Gender Politics and the Manual Labor College Initiative at the National Colored Conventions in Antebellum America," in *The Colored Conventions Movement: Black Organizing in the Nineteenth Century*, ed. P. Gabrielle Foreman, Jim Casey, and Sarah L. Patterson (University of North Carolina Press, 2021), 232–34.

5 Before the Civil War, no more than 4 percent of Oberlin's student population were students of African descent. Oneida Institute was forced to close in 1844 due to lack of financial resources. Historians have also questioned the degree to which social equality was prevalent among the students at Oberlin, as well as the abolitionist colleges of New York Central and Berea. See John Frederick Bell, *Degrees of Equality: Abolitionist Colleges and the Politics of Race* (Louisiana State University Press, 2022).

6 For an excellent biographical sketch of Harris, see Kevin Pierce Thornton, "Andrew Harris, Vermont's Forgotten Abolitionist," *Vermont History* 83, no. 2 (Summer/Fall 2015): 119–56, here 120. Thornton, however, incorrectly asserts that Harris was "very likely" the first Black American college graduate to become active in abolition.

7 "Speeches at the Anniversary," *Emancipator*, May 16, 1839; "Died," *Rochester Daily Democrat*, December 17, 1841 (Harris's obituary); Thornton, "Andrew Harris," 121; On Nott and colonization at Middlebury, respectively, see chapter 2; also see Codman Hislop, *Eliphalet Nott* (Wesleyan University Press, 1971), 403–6.

8 Thornton, "Andrew Harris," 122.

9 Cf. Thornton, "Andrew Harris," 130.

10 "Progress of the Anti-Slavery Cause in Literary Institutions," *American and Foreign Anti-Slavery Reporter*, January 1, 1845; "Colored Students in American Colleges," *Frederick Douglass' Paper*, September 22, 1854; "Colleges and Colored People," *National Anti-Slavery Standard*, November 23, 1843.

11 "Died," *Rochester Democrat*, December 17, 1841; when Wheeler died in 1862, he left three hundred dollars to the colonization society, Thornton, "Harris," 122–23, 151n15, 151n16.

12 "Colored People of Troy" and "General Meeting of the Colored People of Troy," both in *Emancipator*, December 1, 1836.

13 John J. Miter, "Anniversary of the Female Benevolent Society," and Miter, "Colored People of Troy," both in *Colored American*, April 1, 1837.

14 "Union Meeting of the Colored People of Albany, Troy, and Vicinity," *Colored American*, April 15, 1837.

15 "Circular" and "Union Meeting," both in *Colored American*, April 15, 1837, emphasis in the original; it was during this time that Harris likely met Daniel Payne, who later introduced Harris to other leaders in the movement. Thornton, "Andrew Harris," 129–30.

16 The way Harris went about his life resembles Erica Ball's notion of Black abolitionists living an antislavery life. See Erica Ball, *To Live an Antislavery Life: Personal Politics and the Antebellum Black Middle Class* (University of Georgia Press, 2012).

17 "New Agents," *Colored American*, September 30, 1837; "Agents for the American," *Colored American*, October 7, 1837; Harris remained listed as an agent in Vermont through August 1838. See "Agents for the American," *Colored American*, August 25, 1838.

18 "What Has the North to Do with Slavery?," *Liberator*, October 25, 1839; on antislavery in Burlington during Harris's time there, see Thornton, "Harris," 131–32.

19 "To the Church and Congregation at T.," *Colored American*, September 5, 1838; "To the Church and Congregation at T.," *Colored American*, September 15, 1838; Thornton, "Andrew Harris," 132–35.

20 "To the Church and Congregation at T.," *Colored American*, September 15, 1838; Thornton, "Andrew Harris," 135.

21 "Sixth Anniversary," *Emancipator*, May 9, 1839; "Speeches at the Anniversary," *Emancipator*, May 16, 1839; *Sixth Annual Report of the Executive Committee of the American Anti-Slavery Society, with the Speeches, Delivered at the Anniversary Meeting . . .* (Dorr, 1839), 10–12; "The 6th Anniversary of the American Antislavery Society," *Colored American*, May 11, 1839; resolutions listed under "Power of the Free States," *Colored American*, May 18, 1839; Ripley et al., *Black Abolitionist Papers*, 3:294–97; Benjamin Quarles, *Black Abolitionists* (Oxford University Press, 1969), 34.

22 "Sixth Anniversary"; "Speeches at the Anniversary"; "Anniversary of the American A.S. Society," *Liberator*, May 10, 1839; also see the favorable review of Harris's speech from *The New York Observer* reprinted in "Abstract of Speeches," *Liberator*, May 17, 1839.

23 "American Anti-Slavery Society, Meeting for Business," *Liberator*, May 24, 1839; "American Anti-Slavery Society," *Liberator*, May 29, 1840; "American and Foreign Anti-Slavery Society" and "The States," both in *Emancipator*, May 29, 1840; "Business Meeting" and "National Nominating Convention," both in *Emancipator*, May 20, 1841; Quarles, *Black Abolitionists*, 68–69.

24 "New York Vigilance Committee," *Colored American*, May 22, 1841; "Proceedings of the New York State Convention" and "Public Meeting," both in *Colored American*, September 11, 1841; Thornton, "Andrew Harris," 143. For a study of Black ideas on birthright citizenship, see Martha S. Jones, *Birthright Citizens: A History of Race and Rights in Antebellum America* (Cambridge University Press, 2018).

25 Harris's work was tragically cut short. He developed an illness in November 1841 and never recovered. The *Colored American* recorded that Harris had been ill and appended the notice that Harris had died just as the issue was going to print. The obituary in the *Liberator* opined respectfully that Harris "was probably the best educated colored man in our country. As a minister, he was very highly esteemed." As Thornton writes, his life's work is best summarized in a resolution

Harris proposed at the New York Convention: "That we consider it criminal in the sight of God and man, longer silently to submit to our indignities, or suffer them to be transmitted to posterity." See "Afflicting," *Colored American*, December 4, 1841; "Deaths," *Liberator*, December 24, 1841; "Proceedings of the New York State Convention," *Colored American*, September 11, 1841; Thornton, "Andrew Harris," 144, 149–50.

26 Susan Paul, *Memoir of James Jackson, the Attentive and Obedient Scholar, Who Died in Boston, October 31, 1833, Aged Six Years and Eleven Months*, ed. Lois Brown (Harvard University Press, 2000), 1–13, 138–39n17; "Communications," *Liberator*, May 2, 1835; Sinha, *The Slave's Cause*, 218, 254–55, 269, 272, 283; Moss, *Schooling Citizens*, 138.

27 "Practical Anti-Slavery," *Liberator*, July 25, 1835; "Letters from Mr. Thompson," *Liberator*, March 12, 1836; Quarles, *Black Abolitionists*, 90–91.

28 "Letter from President Lord," *Liberator*, January 25, 1834; "A Journey to New Hampshire," *Liberator*, February 1, 1834.

29 After attending George Thompson's lecture in Andover, students at the academy attempted to establish an antislavery society, but the trustees prohibited such activity. As a result, the group of students traveled to Dartmouth because of Lord's and another faculty member, Ebenezer Adams's, positions against slavery and eventually matriculated. See John King Lord, *A History of Dartmouth College, 1815–1909* (Rumford Press, 1913), 251–52.

30 "Trust in God in Public Commotion," *Liberator*, December 12, 1835; "College Anti-Slavery Societies," *Liberator*, April 23, 1836.

31 "Dartmouth College Anti-Slavery Society to Weld," August 1, 1836, *Letters of Theodore Dwight Weld, Angelina Grimke Weld, and Sarah Grimke, 1822–1844*, 2 vols., ed. Gilbert H. Barnes and Dwight L. Dumond (Appleton, 1934), 1:321–22; "Dartmouth College," *Emancipator*, December 8, 1836. Another call went out to Weld and Henry Stanton to visit Dartmouth in April 1837. "That fortress of proslavery Greek and Latin and mathematics must be stormed and taken, and her guns pointed *south*. There are friends now, many and tried hearts already in the garrison there. But the anti-slavery flag is not hoisted . . . Win Dartmouth College." See "Lane Seminary 'Boys,'" *Liberator*, April 28, 1837.

32 "Dartmouth College" and "Progress of the Good Cause in Dartmouth College," both in *Colored American*, April 22, 1837; "Dartmouth College—A Noble Example," *Colored American*, April 29, 1837; "Items," *Emancipator*, June 1, 1837; Forester A. Lee and James S. Pringle, *A Noble and Independent Course: The Life of the Reverend Edward Mitchell* (Dartmouth College Press, 2018), 71–74.

33 "Dartmouth College," *Liberator*, October 26, 1838; "The Chivalry of the Patriarchs," *Emancipator*, June 22, 1837; the news about admissions came in comparison to Harvard, see "Harvard University," *Emancipator*, September 21, 1837; *Third Annual Report of the American Anti-Slavery Society . . .* (Dorr, 1836), 21, 90; *Fourth Annual Report of the American Anti-Slavery Society . . .* (Dorr, 1837), 17, 124; *Fifth Annual Report of the Executive Committee of the American*

Anti-Slavery Society . . . (Dorr, 1838), 3, 130; "Wednesday June 13," *The Farmer's Cabinet*, June 22, 1838; "New Hampshire Convention," *Liberator*, August 31, 1838; "First Annual Meeting of the New Hampshire Young Men's Antislavery Society," *Liberator*, August 30, 1839.

34 "New Hampshire," *Emancipator*, August 6, 1840; "President Lord," *Massachusetts Abolitionist*, August 13, 1840.

35 "Notice," *Liberator*, December 15, 1837; "Notice," *Liberator*, November 30, 1838; "Receipts into the Treasury," *Liberator*, April 5, 1839; "Treasurer's Account," *Liberator*, March 6, 1840; "Festival," *Liberator*, August 14, 1840.

36 Thomas Paul Jr., "Speech of Thomas Paul, a Colored Student of Dartmouth College, Delivered Before the Massachusetts Anti-Slavery Society, January 27, 1841, in the Representatives' Hall, Boston," *Liberator*, February 19, 1841.

37 "Ninth Annual Meeting of the Massachusetts Anti-Slavery Society" and "The State Meeting," both in *Liberator*, February 5, 1841.

38 "Thomas Paul," *Liberator*, September 17, 1841.

39 After graduation, Paul posted notices for starting a school by and for Black people of Boston. He proposed a school where all the branches of learning would be taught. While this particular school did not last, Paul went on to teach successively in Albany, New York; Providence, Rhode Island; and Boston. Including his work as a teacher at Black schools, Paul remained active in the movement. During the late 1840s in Boston, school integrationists opposed Paul's appointment at the all-Black Smith School as they feared he would attract Black students and divert attention from integrationist efforts. The episode illustrated the broader debate over integration versus separate institutions for self-determination. "To the Public," *Liberator*, October 1, 1841; "Great Public Meeting," *Liberator*, October 28, 1842; Moss, *Schooling Citizens*, 172–78.

40 Kabria Baumgartner, "'Cruel and Wicked Prejudice': Racial Exclusion and the Female Seminary Movement in the Antebellum North," in *Women's Higher Education in the United States: New Historical Perspectives*, ed. Margaret A. Nash (Palgrave MacMillan, 2018), 45–67; Kabria Baumgartner, *In Pursuit of Knowledge: Black Women and Educational Activism in Antebellum America* (New York University Press, 2019), chapters 1 and 2.

41 Robert Samuel Fletcher, *A History of Oberlin College: From Its Foundations Through the Civil War*, 2 vols. (Oberlin College Press, 1943); J. Brent Morris, *Oberlin, a Hotbed of Abolitionism: College, Community, and the Fight for Freedom and Equality in Antebellum America* (University of North Carolina Press, 2014); Gary J. Kornblith and Carol Lasser, *Elusive Utopia: The Struggle for Racial Equality in Oberlin, Ohio* (Louisiana State University Press, 2018); John Frederick Bell, "Confronting Colorism: Interracial Abolition and the Consequences of Complexion," *Journal of the Early Republic* 39, no. 2 (Summer 2019): 239–65; John Frederick Bell, *Degrees of Equality*, 15–50, 139–70.

42 Ellen N. Lawson and Marlene Merrill, "The Antebellum 'Talented Thousandth': Black College Students at Oberlin Before the Civil War," *Journal of Negro Educa-*

tion 52, no. 2 (Spring 1983): 142–55; Ellen NicKenzie Lawson with Marlene D. Merrill, *The Three Sarahs: Documents of Antebellum Black College Women* (Edwin Mellen Press, 1984); Carol Lasser, "Enacting Emancipation: African American Women Abolitionists at Oberlin College and the Quest for Empowerment, Equality, and Respectability," in *Women's Rights and Transatlantic Antislavery in the Era of Emancipation*, ed. Kathryn Kish Sklar and James Brewer Stewart (Yale University Press, 2007), 319–45. Lasser's work is significant for showing the distinct way Black women students fashioned their own course of learning and agitation at Oberlin in defiance of white male faculty. Lasser, however, wrongly asserts that Oberlin was "the only institution of higher education in the United States to offer collegiate-level training to African American women in the antebellum years" (321). As Mary Kelley has shown, female seminaries were functionally colleges for women, as they offered the same curriculum. Combined with Kelley's argument of women's seminaries as functional equivalents to colleges, Baumgartner's work shows how Black women gained access to female seminaries and studied there, and as a result of their protests received collegiate learning as well. On Baumgartner's work see n40 above; for Kelley, see *Learning to Stand and Speak: Women, Education, and Public Life in America's Republic* (University of North Carolina Press, 2006), 71–92.

43 Lawson and Merrill, "The Antebellum 'Talented Thousandth,'" 142, 142–43n2, 151, 154; Lasser, "Enacting Emancipation," 325, 327; Morris, *Oberlin, a Hotbed of Abolitionism*, 67.

44 Lawson and Merrill, *The Three Sarahs*, 189–91.

45 Lasser, "Enacting Emancipation," 328.

46 Lawson and Merrill, *The Three Sarahs*, 193.

47 Stanton's commencement address is printed in Lawson and Merrill, *The Three Sarahs*, 203–8, quotations from 203, 204, 205, 207, 208.

48 On the notion of freedom dreams, see Robin D. G. Kelley, *Freedom Dreams: The Black Radical Imagination* (Beacon Press, 2002).

49 "Commencement Exercises," *Oberlin Evangelist*, November 6, 1850; "A Plea for the Oppressed: By Miss Lucy A. Stanton," *Oberlin Evangelist*, December 17, 1850; Martin Robison Delany, *The Condition, Elevation, Emigration, and Destiny of the Colored People of the United States, Politically Considered* (Delany, 1852), 132–33. Lawson and Merrill, *The Three Sarahs*, 193–94.

50 Lawson and Merrill, *The Three Sarahs*, 194–202.

51 These documents are printed in Lawson and Merrill, *The Three Sarahs*, 284, 256–57; *Proceedings of the Black State Conventions, 1840–1865*, vol. 1, ed. Philip S. Foner and George E. Walker (Temple University Press, 1979), 313–14, 340, 341; Lasser, "Enacting Emancipation," 334. On the growing militancy of Black abolitionism in the 1850s, see Vincent Harding, *There Is a River: The Black Struggle for Freedom in America* (Harcourt, 1981), 154–219; Kellie Carter Jackson, *Force and Freedom: Black Abolitionists and the Politics of Violence* (University of Pennsylvania Press, 2019); Sinha, *The Slave's Cause*, 500–586.

52 Lawson and Merrill, *The Three Sarahs*, passim; Lasser, "Enacting Emancipation," 334–39.

53 *Fifth Annual Report of the Executive Committee of the American Anti-Slavery Society . . .* (Dorr, 1838), 24–30; *Sixth Annual Report*, 10–11; "Speech of Henry H. Garnet," *National Anti-Slavery Standard*, June 11, 1840; "Speech of Thomas Paul, a Colored Student of Dartmouth College," *Liberator*, February 19, 1841; Quarles, *Black Abolitionists*, 34.

54 "Vermont," *Emancipator*, June 18, 1845; "Middlebury College and Its Abusers," *Northern Galaxy* (Middlebury, VT), September 23, 1845; "Middlebury College and Governor Slade," *Emancipator*, October 1, 1845; "To the Editor" and "Our Readers Will Notice," both in *Northern Galaxy*, October 7, 1845; David M. Stameshkin, *The Town's College: Middlebury College, 1800–1915* (Middlebury College Press, 1985), 318n37; Hart, "'I Am a Man,'" 162–63.

55 "From the Morning Chronicle," *Liberator*, October 3, 1845.

56 "The Colored Convention," *North Star*, December 3, 1847; Baumgartner, "Gender Politics," 230–45, esp. 236–37; Howard Holman Bell, *A Survey of the Negro Convention Movement, 1830–1861* (1953; Arno Press, 1969), 166–80; on the Black college proposal also see Moses, *Alexander Crummell*, 45; Jane H. Pease and William H. Pease, *They Who Would Be Free: Blacks' Search for Freedom, 1830–1861*, 2nd ed. (University of Illinois Press, 1990), 138–42.

57 Crummell's formulation of Black higher learning can be connected to W. E. B. Du Bois's conceptualization of the purpose of HBCUs in his commencement address at Fisk University in 1933. See W. E. B. Du Bois, "The Field and Function of the Negro College," in W. E. B. Du Bois, *The Education of Black People: Ten Critiques, 1906–1960*, new edition, ed. Herbert Aptheker (Monthly Press, 2001); Joshua Maurice Myers, "Reconceptualizing Intellectual Histories of Africana Studies: A Review of the Literature" (PhD dissertation, Temple University, 2013), 339 and n39. Emphasis added.

58 "The Colored Convention, Report of the Committee on Education," *North Star*, January 21, 1848.

59 "The Colored Convention," *North Star*, December 3, 1847; *Proceedings of the National Convention of Colored People, and Their Friends, Held in Troy, N.Y.* (Kneeland, 1847) in *Minutes of the Proceedings of the National Negro Conventions, 1830–1864*, ed. Howard Holman Bell (Arno Press, 1969), 9–10.

60 "Report of the Committee on Manual Labor School," *Proceedings of the Colored National Convention, Held in Rochester* (Frederick Douglass' Paper, 1853) in Howard Holman Bell, ed., *Minutes of the Proceedings of the National Negro Conventions, 1830–1864* (Arno Press, 1969), 30–33, quotations from 31, 32, 33.

61 See for example, Richard Sewell, *Ballots for Freedom: Antislavery Politics in the United States, 1837–1860* (Oxford University Press, 1976); and Eric Foner, *Free Soil, Free Labor, Free Men: The Ideology of the Republican Party Before the Civil War* (Oxford University Press, 1970).

62 *Proceedings of the Colored Convention, Held in Rochester . . .* , in Bell, *Minutes of the Proceedings*, 33–40, quotations from 34, 35, 37, 38, and 40.

63 *Frederick Douglass' Paper*, March 24, 1854; *Frederick Douglass' Paper*, March 23, 1855; *Proceedings of the Colored National Convention, Held in Franklin Hall, Sixth Street, Philadelphia, October 1855* (National Standard Office, 1856), in Bell, *Minutes of the Proceedings*, 10–13, 25–27.

64 Jelani M. Favors, *Shelter in a Time of Storm: How Black Colleges Fostered Generations of Leadership and Activism* (University of North Carolina Press, 2019), 5–7. The second curriculum coincides with the Black abolitionist vision for higher learning.

65 Russell W, Irvine, *The African American Quest for Higher Education Before the Civil War: The Forgotten Histories of the Ashmun Institute, Liberia College, and Avery College* (Edwin Mellen Press, 2010), 213–28, quotation from 226.

66 Horace Mann Bond, *Education for Freedom: A History of Lincoln University, Pennsylvania* (Princeton University Press, 1976), 247.

67 Favors, *Shelter*, 18–49; also see Bobby L. Lovett, *America's Historically Black Colleges and Universities: A Narrative History, 1837–2009* (Mercer University Press, 2015), 11–12.

68 Federick A. McGinnis, *A History and an Interpretation of Wilberforce University* (Brown Publishing, 1941), 17.

69 On the origins of Wilberforce see McGinnis, *A History*, 17–39; B. W. Arnett and Samuel T. Mitchell, *The Wilberforce Alumnal: A Comprehensive Review of the Origin, Development, and Present Status of Wilberforce University* (Gazette Office, 1885).

70 McGinnis, *A History*, 31–34.

71 Floyd J. Miller, *The Search for a Black Nationality: Black Emigration and Colonization, 1787–1863* (University of Illinois Press, 1975), 93–170.

72 Quoted in Irvine, *The African American*, 248; Bond, *Education*, 250.

73 Bond, *Education*, 254; David McBride, "Africa's Elevation and Changing Racial Thought at Lincoln University, 1854–1886," *Journal of Negro History* 62, no. 4 (October 1977): 364–65. John H. Jackson's commencement address in 1869 revealed his ideological affinity with Crummell's vision of Black students being a part of their communities. McBride writes of Jackson's sentiments, "He admonished his classmates of '. . . the danger arising out of their educational advantages of separating themselves from the masses of their people.'" McBride, "Africa's Elevation," 365.

74 Favors, *Shelter*, 27–29, 30, 31–32, 35–36, 37–47, quotation from 34.

75 McGinnis, *A History*, 37–46; Arnett and Mitchell, *The Wilberforce Alumnal*, 17–18.

76 Hallie Q. Brown, *Homespun Heroines and Other Women of Distinction* (Aldine, 1926), 71–80, quotation from 78.

77 On Brown's life, see Deborah B. Goodwin, "'A Torch in the Valley': The Life and Work of Miss Hallie Quinn Brown" (PhD dissertation, University of Georgia, 2014); Annjennette Sophie McFarlin, "Hallie Quinn Brown—Black Woman Elocutionist: 1845(?)–1949" (PhD dissertation, Washington State University, 1975).

EPILOGUE

1 While the specificities of slavery's ties to universities came to light over the course of the last two decades, Black students and intellectuals have been contesting that connection and its legacies for generations.

2 The ideas in this epilogue have been shaped in important ways by the works of Josh Myers. In addition to his published work, see his "The Form and Function of HBCUs in the 21st Century," lecture, Winston-Salem State University, February 10, 2020; and "The Black Legacy at Universities: Do We Still Need Africana Studies?," lecture, Virginia Tech University, February 24, 2020.

3 W. E. B. Du Bois, *Black Reconstruction in America, 1860–1880* (1935; Free Press, 1998), 637–40, on the General Strike, see 55–127; James D. Anderson, *The Education of Blacks in the South, 1860–1935* (University of North Carolina Press, 1988), 4–32; Heather Andrea Williams, *Self-Taught: African American Education in Slavery and Freedom* (University of North Carolina Press, 2007); Hilary Green, *Educational Reconstruction: African American Schools in the Urban South* (Fordham University Press, 2016).

4 Anderson, *The Education of Blacks*, 4–32, 238–78, 279–85; for histories of HBCUs, see inter alia Bobby L. Lovett, *America's Historically Black Colleges and Universities: A Narrative History, 1837–2009* (Mercer University Press, 2015); and Jelani M. Favors, *Shelter in a Time of Storm: How Black Colleges Fostered Generations of Leadership and Activism* (University of North Carolina Press, 2019).

5 W. E. B. Du Bois, *The Souls of Black Folk: Essays and Sketches* (McClurg, 1904); the full story of Du Bois's experience teaching as a Fisk student among Black people is 66–80; quoted here from 68; also see Anderson, *The Education of Blacks*, 282–83.

6 Du Bois, *Souls*, quotations from 69, 70, 70–71, 73, 73–74, 71. For an important work on Du Bois and Black Studies, see James B. Stewart, "The Legacy of W. E. B. Du Bois for Contemporary Black Studies," *Journal of Negro Education* 53, no. 3 (Summer 1984): 296–311.

7 A similarity can be drawn to how Black people adopted Christianity. They did so on their own terms and to fit their needs and in the process, it blended with African religious traditions; it did not extinguish them. See Michael Gomez, *Exchanging Our Country Marks: The Transformation of African Identities in the Colonial and Antebellum South* (University of North Carolina Press, 1998), 244–90, esp. 267–68.

8 The foregoing is based on Raymond Wolters, *The New Negro on Campus: Black College Rebellions of the 1920s* (Princeton University Press, 1975), 29–69, esp. 36–37, 45, 47, 51, 56–57, quotations from 45, 49, 57. On the context of Black people opposing McKenzie for calling the police due to white violence against Black people in Nashville, see Wolters, 48–49.

9 Wolters, *The New Negro on Campus*; on the history of the 1920s protests at Howard as part of a longer tradition of Black student protest there, see Joshua M. Myers, *We Are Worth Fighting For: A History of the Howard University Student Protest of 1989* (New York University Press, 2019), 11–22.

10 Derrick P. Alridge, *The Educational Thought of W.E.B. Du Bois: An Intellectual History* (Teachers College Press, 2008).

11 As Greg Carr has argued, Black professors at HBCUs, including Du Bois, Charles Johnson, and Oliver Cox, among others such as Carter Woodson, and Black women such as Dorothy Porter, were practicing a form of academic Black Studies. And when we include the Black student protests of the 1920s and 1930s, together Black thinkers and students were applying a Black lens to analyze their social and historical experiences, a notion of academic Black Studies. See Greg Carr, "What Black Studies Is Not: Moving from Crisis to Liberation in Africana Intellectual Work," *Socialism and Democracy* 25, no. 1 (March 2011): 181–82n6.

12 W. E. B. Du Bois, "The Field and Function of the Negro College," in *The Education of Black People: Ten Critiques, 1906–1960*, new edition, ed. Herbert Aptheker (Monthly Press, 2001), 111–33, quotations from 123, 125, 126, 127.

13 Du Bois goes on: "And if it does that, and insofar as it does it, it becomes the perfect expression of the life and the center of the intellectual and cultural expression of its age." Du Bois, "Field and Function," 112, 117.

14 Myers, *We Are Worth Fighting For*, 20; on the tension between HBCUs as institutions versus Du Bois's vision see 11–12, 11n3, 12–22.

15 Quoted in Martha Biondi, *The Black Revolution on Campus* (University of California Press, 2012), 16, 18, 19, 22; on Claudia Thomas and the movement at Vassar, see Claudia Lynn Thomas, *God Spare Life: An Autobiography* (Windsor Media, 2007); on Lenneal Henderson's quotation, see Nan Robertson, "The Student Scene: A Feeling of Powerlessness Provokes Anger Among Militants," *New York Times*, November 20, 1967, 30.

16 Myers, *We Are Worth Fighting For*, 19–20; Josh Myers, Twitter post, November 17, 2019, 9:05 a.m., https://twitter.com/ddhewty/status/1196066894685655044.

17 Vincent Harding, "Toward the Black University," *Ebony*, August 1970, 156–60, quoted on 156, 157, 158. Harding outlined a plan of teaching, research, and learning that centered Black experiences in the United States situated within the context of the experiences and thought of Africans throughout the world, the understanding of which meant a break from the "deadly Western disciplines." In their stead, he proposed an alternative: "the proper understanding, affirmation, and adoption of those complex systems of internal community life and organization which have made it possible for our people to survive in the midst of unspeakable oppression, from the homeland to the diaspora." One area of knowledge Harding specifically highlighted that would inform such work was African spiritual traditions, "recognizing [their] central role in our survival and development" as a way to create an understanding "of a universal black way of life that has traditionally refused to separate the sacred and the secular, a way of life to which many persons now look for hope beyond the fragmented dying of the West" (158). He also had a critique of HBCUs as institutions for institutionally emulating white universities, which further bolstered the call for the creation of the Black university. He also identified Du Bois, among others, as an important thinker on Black education, 157, 158.

18 Toni Cade Bambara, "Realizing the Dream of a Black University (1969)," in *Lost and Found: The CUNY Poetics Document Initiative*, ed. Makeba Lavan and Conor Tomas Reed, Series 7, Number 2, Part 1 (Fall 2017), 13–27, quotations from 19, 19–20, 20, 21, 22, 23, 24, 25, 26; Conor Tomas Reed, *New York Liberation School: Study and Movement for the People's University* (Common Notions, 2023).

19 Robin D. G. Kelley, "Black Study, Black Struggle," *Boston Review*, March 1, 2016; Janelle Jolley, "Dr. Joshua Myers: Dialectically Dismantling the University," parts 1 and 2, *What's Left to Do*, podcast audio, August 4, 2021, www.patreon.com; Greg Carr, "Introduction to Africana Studies: Towards a Freedom Course Design." *Freedom: A Journal of Research in Africana Studies* 1 (2024): 53–73.

INDEX

AASS. *See* American Antislavery Society

ABCFM. *See* American Board of Commissioners for Foreign Missions

abolition, 6, 16; Beman's work for, 162; colonization contrasted with, 130; Hoftstader and Nye on, 237n21; manual labor pathway to, 272n27; Oneida Institute promoting, 103, 118, 269n62; Peckard promoting, 24–25, 108, 115; Pennington advocating for, 100–101; Ray's work for, 161–62; student abolitionist petitions for, 132, 143–46; Templeton supporting, 35; Weld's conversion to, 118; Wheatley's poems on, 23–24, 141; white ministers on, 239n26. *See also* anti-abolition; emancipation; evangelical abolitionists; gradualism; immediatism

abolition, political: of New Haven Young Men's Anti-Slavery Society, 146–47; Stanton, Lucy, agitating for, 193–94

abolitionist dissent, 9–10, 11, 19, 109; of college slavery resistance, 15, 78–79; Lane Controversy influencing, 148; at Western Reserve College, 115–18

abolitionists, 233n5; Black freedom promoted by, 11; *Gentlemen of Property and Standing* on, 238n24; Quaker, 98. *See also* evangelical abolitionists; Russwurm, John Brown; Wright, Theodore S.

abolition movement: Black abolitionists preceding, 110; evangelical abolitionists relationship with, 239n27; Sinha on,

240n30, 240n32; state emancipation distinguished from, 240n32; student abolitionist movement relationship with, 1, 148

ACS. *See* American Colonization Society

AFASS. *See* American and Foreign Anti-Slavery Society

"Africa" (Clark), 68–69

African achievements, Templeton lauding, 34

Africana Studies, 235n9

African College: Bacon's plan for, 63, 256n36; Black abolitionists for, 157; establishment of, 152, 155, 177, 178; slavery threatened by, 156; white people opposing, 156–57

African culture, 86; Black intellectuals influenced by, 105; College of William and Mary enslaved people's African cultural artifacts representing, 81, 82, 83–85, 263n16, 265n27; college slavery resistance of, 73; Colonoware artifacts representing, 81, 82, 263n17, 265n27; cowrie shells representing, 82–84, 264n23, 264nn19–20; *tendwa nza Kongo* representing, 84–85, 265n27

African Free Schools, 23, 38, 41

African history: Douglass on, 175–76; Pennington on, 100, 101, 105; Templeton on, 20, 33

African intellectual traditions, Black community in, 80

African Masonic Hall, Stewart's oration at, 165–66

ABOUT THE AUTHOR

MICHAEL E. JIRIK is Assistant Professor of Black Studies at the University of Missouri in Columbia.